EXAMKRACKERS

1001

MCAT
BIOLOGY
QUESTIONS

OSOTE
PUBLISHING

Published in the United States of America by Osote Publishing, Lexington, KY

ISBN 1-893858-21-9

2006 Edition

Edited by Dr. Jerry Johnson Ph.D.
Design and production by Saucy Enterprizes, LLC [www.saucyenterprizes.com]

To purchase additional copies of this book, call 1-(888)-572-2536 or fax orders to 1-(895)-255-0933

Examkrackers.com

Osote.com

Audioosmosis.com

Printed and bound in the U.S.A.

Acknowledgements

Susan Kim
David Lee
Vitaly Merkulov
Jonathan Orsay

DEDICATION

*To my parents, Leonid and Lyudmila Merkulov, who,
for better or for worse, never set any boundaries.*

TABLE OF CONTENTS

BIOLOGICAL SCIENCES

DIRECTIONS. Most questions in the Biological Sciences test are organized into groups, each preceded by a descriptive passage. After studying the passage, select the one best answer to each question in the group. Some questions are not based on a descriptive passage and are also independent of each other. You must also select the one best answer to these questions. If you are not certain of an answer, eliminate the alternatives that you know to be incorrect and then select an answer from the remaining alternatives. Indicate your selection by blackening the corresponding oval on your answer document. A periodic table is provided for your use.

PERIODIC TABLE OF THE ELEMENTS

1 H 1.0																	2 He 4.0
3 Li 6.9	4 Be 9.0											5 B 10.8	6 C 12.0	7 N 14.0	8 O 16.0	9 F 19.0	10 Ne 20.2
11 Na 23.0	12 Mg 24.3											13 Al 27.0	14 Si 28.1	15 P 31.0	16 S 32.1	17 Cl 35.5	18 Ar 39.9
19 K 39.1	20 Ca 40.1	21 Sc 45.0	22 Ti 47.9	23 V 50.9	24 Cr 52.0	25 Mn 54.9	26 Fe 55.8	27 Co 58.9	28 Ni 58.7	29 Cu 63.5	30 Zn 65.4	31 Ga 69.7	32 Ge 72.6	33 As 74.9	34 Se 79.0	35 Br 79.9	36 Kr 83.8
37 Rb 85.5	38 Sr 87.6	39 Y 88.9	40 Zr 91.2	41 Nb 92.9	42 Mo 95.9	43 Tc (98)	44 Ru 101.1	45 Rh 102.9	46 Pd 106.4	47 Ag 107.9	48 Cd 112.4	49 In 114.8	50 Sn 118.7	51 Sb 121.8	52 Te 127.6	53 I 126.9	54 Xe 131.3
55 Cs 132.9	56 Ba 137.3	57 La* 138.9	72 Hf 178.5	73 Ta 180.9	74 W 183.9	75 Re 186.2	76 Os 190.2	77 Ir 192.2	78 Pt 195.1	79 Au 197.0	80 Hg 200.6	81 Tl 204.4	82 Pb 207.2	83 Bi 209.0	84 Po (209)	85 At (210)	86 Rn (222)
87 Fr (223)	88 Ra 226.0	89 Ac† 227.0	104 Unq (261)	105 Unp (262)	106 Unh (263)	107 Uns (262)	108 Uno (265)	109 Une (267)									

*	58 Ce 140.1	59 Pr 140.9	60 Nd 144.2	61 Pm (145)	62 Sm 150.4	63 Eu 152.0	64 Gd 157.3	65 Tb 158.9	66 Dy 162.5	67 Ho 164.9	68 Er 167.3	69 Tm 168.9	70 Yb 173.0	71 Lu 175.0
†	90 Th 232.0	91 Pa (231)	92 U 238.0	93 Np (237)	94 Pu (244)	95 Am (243)	96 Cm (247)	97 Bk (247)	98 Cf (251)	99 Es (252)	100 Fm (257)	101 Md (258)	102 No (259)	103 Lr (260)

LECTURE 1

100

Biology Passages
Questions 1–113

Passage 101 (Questions 1-7)

Water is the most abundant compound in the human body, accounting for 45 to 75% of total body weight. However, the contribution of water to total body weight varies with gender and decreases with age.

Total body water (TBW) can be measured with *isotope dilution*. After ingestion of a trace dose of a known marker, saliva samples are collected on cotton rolls over a period of several hours. During and post-experimental data is compared to the baseline data. Body mass measured before and after the experiment gives a TBW to total body mass ratio. Data is analyzed according to the mixed model analysis of variance: Volume = Amount (g) / Concentration.

Total body water is distributed between two fluid compartments in the body. These are known as the intracellular fluid (ICF) and extracellular fluid (ECF) compartments. The sum of ICF and ECF volumes is equal to TBW:

$$TBW\ volume = ECFvol + ICFvol$$

There are approximately 70 trillion cells in the human body. Intracellular fluid is contained within the membrane of each cell. ICF accounts for about 55% of TBW and 2/3 of body weight. Extracellular fluid is the fluid in which body cells are bathed. It is present outside body cells and can be further divided into 2 different subcompartments: interstitial fluid (IF) and lymph. Interstitial fluid and lymph comprises 20% of the TBW. Blood plasma adds another 8%.

Together, the interstitial fluid and the plasma make up about 27.5% or roughly 1/3 of TBW. Other extracellular fluids are found in specialized subcompartments such as the digestive tract, urinary tract, bone and lubricating fluids around organs and joints.

1. A dye marker that can penetrate all fluids of the body is injected to measure concentration. According to the passage, which of the following body fluids would have the lowest concentration of this marker?

   A. intracellular fluid
   B. blood plasma
   C. lymph
   D. urinary track subcompartment

2. Isotope dilution technique dose of approximately 6 milligrams of O^{18} labeled water was used as a tracer. Particle concentration estimate was 18.23 M/L. What is the estimate of TBW?

   A. $3.33 \times 10^{e-3}$
   B. $33.3 \times 10^{e-5}$
   C. 0.33
   D. 3.33

3. Edema is characterized by the presence of excess fluid being forced out of circulation into the extracellular space, usually due to circulatory or renal difficulty. Which of the following could be a direct cause of edema?

   A. decreased permeability of capillary walls
   B. increased osmotic pressure within a capillary
   C. increased hydrostatic pressure within a capillary
   D. decreased hydrostatic pressure within a capillary

4. Total body sodium content determines extracellular fluid volume, and is regulated by the balance between sodium intake and sodium loss. Oubain is a poison that causes blockage of the Na^+/K^+ ATPase. Which of the following would occur after administration of oubain?

   A. increased extracellular sodium concentration
   B. increased intracellular potassium concentration
   C. increased cellular water concentration
   D. increased intracellular chlorine concentration

5. In periods of low water intake, the renin-angiotensin feedback mechanism is used to minimize the amount of water lost by the system. The kidney works in conjunction with which of the following organs to excrete acidic metabolites and regulate acid-base buffer stores?

   A. liver
   B. heart
   C. lungs
   D. brain

6. Which of the following characteristics of water make it the most important solvent on earth?

   I.   It is a Bronsted Acid.
   II. It is a Bronsted Base.
   III. It is non-polar.
   IV. It has the ability to form hydrogen bonds.

   A. I only
   B. I, and II only
   C. II, III, and IV only
   D. I, II, and IV only

7. Researchers conducting an experiment needed to estimate total body water. According to the passage, which of the following must be true?

   A. ECF makes up 45% of TBW and is estimated as 2/3 of body weight.
   B. ECF makes up 45% of TBW and is estimated as 1/3 of body weight.
   C. ICF makes up 45% of TBW and is estimated as 1/3 of body weight.
   D. ICF makes up 45% of TBW and is estimated as 2/3 of body weight.

GO ON TO THE NEXT PAGE.

Passage 102 (Questions 8-14)

Free fatty acids are stored as triglycerides in adipose tissue. A three-carbon glycerol molecule contains three hydroxyl groups (one on each of the three carbons), each of which serves as a point of attachment for a free fatty acid. The carboxylic acid group of a free fatty acid reacts with one of the glycerol hydroxyl groups to form a bond.

In response to higher energy demands, triglycerides are mobilized for use by peripheral muscle tissue. The release of metabolic energy in the form of free fatty acids is controlled by a complex series of reactions that are kept under tight control by *hormone-sensitive lipase*. Lipase activators bind receptors that are coupled to adenylate cyclase. The resultant increase in cAMP leads to the activation of an appropriate *kinase* (PKA), which in turn activates *hormone-sensitive lipase*.

Free fatty acids destined for breakdown are transported through circulation while bound to *albumin*. In contrast, fatty acids being transported to storage sites are moved in large lipid-protein particles called *lipoproteins* (i.e., LDL). During high rates of mitochondrial fatty acid oxidation, large amounts of acetyl CoA are generated. If the amount of acetyl CoA generated exceeds the capacity of the Krebs cycle, ketone body synthesis will be used as an alternate pathway. In the early stages of starvation, heart and skeletal muscle will primarily consume ketone bodies to preserve glucose for the brain.

8. Phosphorylated *hormone-sensitive lipase* hydrolyzes the bond between free fatty acids and glycerol. Which of the following bonds is being broken by the lipase?

    A.   ionic by addition of water
    B.   disulfide by addition of water
    C.   hydrogen by loss of water
    D.   ester by addition of water

9. Lipolysis is the main regulation point for fatty acid breakdown. According to the passage, which of the following is NOT a direct product of adipose tissue breakdown?

    I.   glycerol
   II.   acetyl CoA
  III.   ketone bodies

    A.   I only
    B.   I and II only
    C.   III only
    D.   I, II, and III

10. An untreated diabetic who is unable to synthesize insulin experiences ketoacidosis, due to a reduced supply of glucose. Which of the flowing properly correlates with diabetic ketoacidosis?

    A.   Circulating blood insulin levels must be high.
    B.   Ketone body blood acidification is not considered clinically dangerous.
    C.   Concomitant increase in fatty acid oxidation will occur.
    D.   Decreased production of acetyl CoA leads to ketone body production.

11. Albumin makes up 55% of plasma proteins. Fatty acids bind albumin for which of the following reasons?

    A.   Covalent bonding with albumin stabilizes free fatty acid structure.
    B.   Non-covalent binding with albumin increases overall lipid solubility.
    C.   Ionic bonding with albumin increases solubility.
    D.   Binding to albumin stabilizes fatty acid stereospecific configuration.

12. Which of the following serves as the breakdown site for beta-oxidation?

    A.   cytosol
    B.   extramembrane space of mitochondria
    C.   matrix of mitochondria
    D.   smooth endoplasmic reticulum

13. Which of the following organs CANNOT use ketone bodies as an energy source?

    A.   brain
    B.   heart
    C.   muscle
    D.   liver

14. Energy yield is dependent on the availability of a carbon source. The passage suggests that the highest energy yield would occur from the catabolism of:

    A.   long-chain free fatty acids
    B.   short-chain free fatty acids
    C.   unsaturated free fatty acids
    D.   desaturated free fatty acids

Passage 103 (Questions 15-21)

Chylomicrons are synthesized by the small intestine. They contain large quantities of triglycerides with some cholesterol, phospholipids, and apoprotein. Chylomicrons are identified by a surface marker called apoprotein B-48 upon their secretion into the lymphatic circulation.

Plasma lipoprotein lipase hydrolyzes chylomicron triglycerides to release free fatty acids that are then taken up by cells, oxidized for energy, and/or stored. As triglycerides are removed, chylomicrons shrink in size and become chylomicron remnants. Chylomicron remnants are rich in dietary cholesterol. They are taken up by the liver and degraded by lysosomes.

The liver synthesizes very low-density lipoproteins (VLDL) in order to transport triglycerides and cholesterol from the liver to adipose tissue. In the periphery, lipoprotein lipase releases VLDL free fatty acids for tissue uptake; this decreases the triglyceride to cholesterol ester ratio. This converts VLDLs to intermediate density lipoproteins (IDL). A further decrease in the triglyceride content of IDL leads to the formation of very cholesterol rich low-density lipoprotein (LDL).

Many peripheral cells contain LDL receptors on their plasma membranes. Following LDL binding, the receptor/LDL complex is internalized by endocytosis. These vesicles fuse with lysosomes where LDL proteins are hydrolyzed. Cholesterol esters are also hydrolyzed to liberate free cholesterol. The LDL receptor, after delivering LDL, is returned back to the cell membrane.

15. *Lipoprotein lipase* deficiency will lead to serum chylomicron accumulation. This will mostly result in high blood levels of:

    A.   cholesterol
    B.   vitamin B$_{12}$
    C.   triglycerides
    D.   glucose

16. Cholesterol released from cholesterol esters can be used for the synthesis of all of the following EXCEPT:

    A.   cell membranes
    B.   aldosterone
    C.   vitamin D
    D.   cell walls

17. The blood of a person who consumed an increased amount of fat two hours ago would most likely contain:

    A.   an increased level of HDL
    B.   an increased level of chylomicrons
    C.   an increased level of VLDL
    D.   an increased level of LDL

18. Which of the following components make chylomicron particles water-soluble?

    I.   phospholipid head groups
    II.   surface protein
    III.   triglycerides
    IV.   cholesterol

    A.   I and II
    B.   II and III
    C.   I, III, and IV
    D.   I, II, III, and IV

19. Which of the following is true regarding blood lipoproteins?

    A.   Lipoproteins serve to transport water-soluble triglycerides.
    B.   Chylomicron remnants are taken up by peripheral adipose tissue and degraded.
    C.   IDL is converted to VLDL following triglyceride digestion.
    D.   In comparison to VLDL, LDL has a higher cholesterol concentration.

20. Hypercholesterolemia is a genetic condition where functional LDL receptors are low or absent. This will result in:

    A.   increased plasma levels of LDL and decreased serum cholesterol
    B.   decreased plasma levels of LDL and increased serum cholesterol
    C.   increased cytoplasmic LDL levels and decreased cytoplasmic cholesterol
    D.   decreased cytoplasmic LDL levels and increased serum cholesterol

21. Stored triglycerides serve as essentially the only source of fuel for which of the following species?

    I.   hibernating animals
    II.   migrating birds and insects
    III.   animals that eat monthly

    A.   I only
    B.   I and II only
    C.   II and III only
    D.   I, II, and III

4

GO ON TO THE NEXT PAGE.

22. Oxidative phosphorylation traps energy in a high-energy phosphate group and occurs in which of the following locations?

    A. outer mitochondrial membrane
    B. inner mitochondrial membrane
    C. mitochondrial matrix
    D. nucleus

23. Glycolysis is an example of a metabolic pathway. Which of the following is a product of glycolysis?

    A. NADPH
    B. H_2O
    C. glucose
    D. NADH

24. The pyruvate dehydrogenase complex catalyzes the conversion of pyruvate to acetyl CoA. Which of the following changes will increase the metabolic consumption of pyruvate?

    A. high levels of ATP
    B. high levels of NADH
    C. low levels of glucose
    D. low levels of Acetyl CoA

25. Enzyme control is very important. Which of the following is an example of a zymogen?

    A. trypsin
    B. chymotrypsinogen
    C. pepsinase
    D. hexokinase

26. The crystal structure of a mutant mitochondrial enzyme *aconitase* has been determined. Which of the following can directly affect aconitase enzyme activity?

    I. pH
    II. temperature
    III. [S] concentration

    A. I only
    B. I and II only
    C. II and III only
    D. I, II, and III

27. What is the total number of $FADH_2$ molecules produced by glycolysis and the citric acid cycle (two turns of the cycle)?

    A. 1 mole at Succinate to Fumarate conversion
    B. 2 moles at Succinate to Fumarate conversion
    C. 3 moles at Malate to Oxaloacetate conversion
    D. 4 moles at Malate to Oxaloacetate conversion

28. Lipids are less dense than protein; the lower the density of a lipoprotein the less protein it carries. Which of the following molecules has the highest lipid density?

    A. a low-density lipoprotein (LDL)
    B. a very low-density lipoprotein (VLDL)
    C. a chylomicron
    D. a high-density lipoprotein (HDL)

29. Shape is important for binding of the relevant peptide to the receptor protein on the cell surface. Which of the following amino acids should be used to bind to a sterically hindered receptor site?

    A. phenylalanine
    B. glycine
    C. histidine
    D. isoleucine

30. Which of the following components determines the globular conformation of a protein?

    A. number of amino acids
    B. concentration of amino acids
    C. peptide optical activity
    D. sequence of amino acids

_____

Peptides and sizeable proteins exhibit the greatest structural and functional variation of all biologically active macromolecules. All amino acids possess amino and carboxylic functional groups. In addition, there may be extra ionizable groups found on side chains. Because more than one ionizable group may be present, even when the net charge on the molecule is zero, an amino acid molecule may be multi-ionized; this type of arrangement is called the zwitterion.

Enkephalins have morphine-like activity and act as neurotransmitters at nerve junctions to block the transmission of pain. Oxytocin and vasopressin (ADH) are neuropeptides stored in the pituitary gland. Their structures are almost identical, but actions are markedly different. In comparing the 3-D structures, a tyrosine residue forms a hydrogen bond with asparagine in oxytocin, while in ADH this is prevented by hydrophobic bonding between two aromatic rings of tyrosine and phenylalanine. This difference results in a gross difference in 3-D shape of the peptides.

Glutathione (GSH) is vital in protecting red blood cell hemoglobin. High oxygen concentrations can permanently oxidize hemoglobin and prevent effective O_2 binding. Glutathione, with its free -SH group, provides reducing conditions that protect hemoglobin molecules. Two GSH form a disulfide bridge and transfer protons and electrons for reduction

$$G\text{-}SH + G\text{-}SH + \frac{1}{2}O_2 \rightarrow G\text{-}S\text{-}S\text{-}G + H_2O$$

The body maintains a ratio of 500 GSH to 1 GSSG via a key enzyme called *glutathione reductase*. Deficiency of this enzyme leads to irreversible hemoglobin damage, which, if extensive, can be fatal.

Amino Acid	pKa
Lysine	10
Arginine	12
Histidine	6
Tyrosine	10.5

Table 1 Unique AA Side pKa

Protecting Group	Mass Index
Propyl	33.013
Formyl	28.456
Ethyl	28.078
Acetyl	42.056
Butyl	56.108
Anisyl	90.126
Benzyl	90.126
Tricloriacetyl	96.078

Table 2 Protecting groups

31. Which of the following is the only amino acid whose side chain can form covalent bonds?

    A. glycine
    B. cysteine
    C. leucine
    D. proline

32. According to Table 1, arginine can be classified as which of the following?

    A. a basic amino acid
    B. an acidic amino acid
    C. a neutral amino acid
    D. an imino acid

33. When enkephalins fail to pass the signal across the synaptic cleft, pain stimulus is not transmitted. Which of the following will result after imipramine (an enkephalin-degrading peptidase) is injected into a brain synaptic cleft?

    A. An increase in pain neurotransmitter synthesis results and post-synaptic receptor flooding by the pain neurotransmitter occurs.
    B. Brain enkephalin concentration decreases but its secretion is not inhibited.
    C. *Imipramine* acts as a ribosome deactivator that inhibits enkephalin-related peptide synthesis and Golgi modification.
    D. An increase in pain transmission will result because of an increase in receptor synthesis by the post-synaptic sensory neuron.

GO ON TO THE NEXT PAGE.

34. Glutathione counteracts the oxidizing effects of chemicals and pesticides. A drug overdose often depletes body GSH levels. According to the passage, which of the following statements is most likely to be true?

    A. Reduced glutathione functions to protect cellular proteins from thiol oxidation.

    B. $K_{equilibrium}$ constant for glutathione reductase is considered to be very large.

    C. Oxidized GSH protects cellular proteins from oxidation and serves as an intracellular redox buffer.

    D. Mice experiments indicate a $K_{equilibrium}$ estimate of 1 in reference to a normal GSH/GSSG ratio.

35. The masses of commonly occurring protecting groups used in solid phase synthesis are available in Table 2. What would be the predicted mass index for a pentane carbon backbone undergoing a decarboxylation reaction resulting in the release of one mole of carbon dioxide?

    A. 91.343
    B. 38.830
    C. 38.348
    D. 55.981

36. Which of the following properties is unique to oxytocin?

    A. It has a quaternary structure.
    B. It has a tertiary structure.
    C. It has a secondary structure.
    D. It has a primary structure.

37. During carbohydrate metabolism, NADH is produced in which of the following location(s)?

    I. cytosol
   II. mitochondrial matrix
  III. nucleus

    A. I only
    B. II only
    C. I and II only
    D. I, II, and III

Passage 105 (Questions 38-43)

In addition to the common amino acids, a few modified amino acids are found in mature proteins. Examples of these modified proteins are O-Phosphoserine, 3-Hydroxyproline, thyroxine, and carboxyglutamic acid. Hydroxylysine and hydroxyproline are found in significant quantities in collagen.

Collagen is a structural protein that holds cells together and allows for the formation of solid tissue. Hydroxylysine and hydroxyproline form suitable sites for the cross-linking of different collagen fibers, which increases the overall mechanical strength of the collagen assembly.

Hydroxyproline and hydroxylysine are not incorporated into proteins. Rather, the protein is first synthesized with normal proline and lysine. After protein synthesis is complete, some of the proline and lysine residues are modified to hydroxyproline and hydroxylysine. This is an example of post-translational modification.

Collagen types II, III, and I make up the main fibers of animal extracellular structures. Type I collagen makes up roughly 90% of all body collagen. It is the primary component of bone, skin, and tendons. Type II collagen is found in cartilage. Collagen fibers are arranged into rigid plates in bone, in parallel bundles in tendons, and in dense meshes in cartilage.

38. Peptide GG1 is found as a supercoiled right-handed alpha helix. Which of the following is a characteristic of the supercoiled helix?

    A. It is an example of primary peptide structure.
    B. It is an example of secondary peptide structure.
    C. It is an example of tertiary peptide structure.
    D. It is an example of quaternary peptide structure.

39. Prolyl-hydroxylase regulates export of collagen and Lysyl-hydroxylase facilitates its extracellular cross-linking. Which of the following will occur if a mutation increases the cellular concentration of Prolyl-hydroxylase?

    A. There will be a decreased rate of ATP consumption for exocytosis.

    B. Abnormal collagen synthesis would lead to multiple fractures.

    C. Negative feedback inhibition would decrease extracellular levels Lysyl-hydroxylase.

    D. Scar tissue formation would be a result of increased synthesis and activity of Lysyl-hydroxylase.

40. An experiment was conducted to determine the changes that would occur in human protein metabolism with long duration space walking. Which of the following would be LEAST important in achieving this objective?

A. a measure of whole body protein synthesis
B. an evaluation of protein breakdown and plasma protein synthesis rates
C. continuous monitoring of nitrogen intake and excretion
D. tight regulation of fat soluble vitamins intake during the experiment

41. The collagen triple helix interior requires an amino acid with a small side chain. Which of the following amino acids would most likely be found in the interior of a collagen molecule?

A. methionine
B. aspartate
C. tryptophan
D. glycine

42. Scurvy is caused by severe vitamin C deficiency, resulting in a collagen synthesis defect. Which of the following would NOT be a possible symptom of scurvy?

A. defective wound healing
B. bleeding gums
C. vision difficulty
D. ruptured surface capillaries

43. Which of the following is an example of a post-transcriptional modification?

A. amino acid substitution
B. increased amino acid concentration
C. addition of a poly-A tail
D. phosphorylation of amino acid

Passage 106 (Questions 44-49)

Most biochemical reactions occur at an immeasurably slow rate under normal physiological conditions. Reaction rates are increased by the use of biological enzymes. By determining the amount and nature of the enzyme present, reaction rates can be precisely controlled. A completely functional enzyme (an apoenzyme and its cofactor) is called holoenzyme. Organic cofactors (coenzymes) are vitamin derived and directly participate in the reaction being catalyzed.

Enzymes are found in all cellular compartments and may be soluble or membrane-bound. Different soluble enzymes are found in the cytosol, the nucleus, lysosomes, mitochondria, and in the extracellular fluid.

Enterokinase is a key enzyme for the intestinal digestion of protein. Enterokinase deficiency causes severe protein malabsorption with poor growth and development. The enzyme catalyzes the conversion of trypsinogen into trypsin. Trypsin, in turn, activates the other pancreatic proteolytic zymogens (i.e., chymotrypsinogen, procarboxypeptidase, proelastase). Enterokinase is synthesized by enterocytes of the proximal small intestine and can be found both in the brush border membrane and, as a soluble form, in intestinal fluid.

44. Which of the following forces are involved in peptide stability, organization, and enzyme function?

I. Hydrogen bonds
II. Hydrophobic interactions
III. Electrostatic interactions
IV. Disulfide bonds

A. I and II only
B. I, II, and IV only
C. II, III, and IV only
D. I, II, III, and IV

45. A patient is taken to the ER with extensive liver damage. Upon examination, it is discovered that the patient is suffering from hepatitis B. Which of the following is a possible effect of this disease?

A. increased levels of hepatocyte cytoplasmic enzymes in the blood
B. decreased levels of hepatocyte cytoplasmic enzymes in the blood
C. increased liver blood flow and proliferation
D. decreased levels of calcitonin production and release

46. An enzyme may posses more than one ligand-binding site. The binding of a ligand at one site may facilitate binding of another ligand at another site on the same enzyme. This is an example of:

A. heterotrophic allostery
B. positive cooperativity
C. reversible binding
D. negative cooperativity

47. Trypsin is a serine protease with substrate specificity based upon positively charged lysine and arginine side chains. According to the passage, trypsin will affect the reaction by:

A. lowering activation energy and increasing the rate of the forward reaction only
B. not being consumed and increasing the rate of the backwards reaction only
C. increasing the rate of the forwards and backwards reactions
D. altering the equilibrium constant by rapid establishment

48. Enterokinase is composed of 80,000 residues and is derived from a single chain precursor. Disulfide bond disruption and liquid chromatography reveal two different effusion rates. Which of the following must be true regarding enterokinase?

A. It is composed of a heavy chain unimonomer with intra disulfide bonds.
B. It is composed of a heavy chain and light chain homodimer.
C. It is composed of a heavy chain and a 235-amino acid light chain heterodimer.
D. It is composed of a heavy chain dimonomer with inter disulfide bonds.

49. Which of the following is the main function of most soluble vitamins in the human body?

A. serve to maintain concentration gradients
B. function as coenzymes
C. control reaction rates
D. act to enhance the immune system

Questions 50 through 57 are **NOT** based on a descriptive passage.

50. Poor electrolytes are molecular compounds that do not dissociate well in water. Which of the following is an example of a poor electrolyte?

A. Sucrose
B. NaCl
C. H_2SO_4
D. KCl

51. Which of the following molecules is capable of generating the greatest osmotic pressure?

A. 300 mM glucose
B. 300 mM urea
C. 300 mM NaCl
D. 300 mM $CaCl_2$

52. Covalent bonds are the strongest chemical bonds contributing to the protein structure. A peptide bond is formed between which of the following?

A. carboxylic group and amino group
B. two carboxylic groups
C. two amino groups
D. ester group and ammonium group

53. Which of the following serves as the site for collagen polypeptide synthesis?

A. mitochondria
B. smooth endoplasmic reticulum
C. rough endoplasmic reticulum
D. lysosome

54. Parallel and non-parallel beta-pleated sheets are stabilized by which of the following interactions?

A. covalent bonds
B. electrostatic interactions
C. hydrogen bonds
D. hydrophilic interactions

55. Glycolysis is regulated by allosteric enzyme inhibition. Which of the following would be expected to decrease the rate of glycolysis?

  A. high levels of ATP
  B. high levels of AMP
  C. increased blood glucose
  D. a high-fructose meal

56. Isozymes catalyze the same reaction but with different kinetic parameters and possess different subunit composition. Which of the following would you expect to differ between isozymes?

   I. Denaturation profile
  II. Catalytic rate
 III. Substrate specificity

  A. I only
  B. III only
  C. I and II only
  D. I, II, and III

57. *Hormone-sensitive lipase* is activated via a cAMP-dependent protein phosphorylation. Which of the following is a correct classification of cAMP?

  A. enzyme
  B. RNA nucleosome
  C. second messenger
  D. carbohydrate

Passage 107 (Questions 58-63)

Glycolysis is essential for ATP production in order to meet tissue energy needs. During the pathway, one molecule of glucose is converted into two molecules of pyruvate. For each molecule of glucose processed, there is a net gain of two ATP molecules and two reduced NAD^+ molecules per glycolysis.

Cellular supply of NAD^+ is limited. To continue glycolysis and ATP production, NADH must be reoxidized and recycled. Aerobic organisms use molecular oxygen for NADH oxidation, while anaerobic organisms regenerate NAD^+ by fermentation. Because red blood cells do not have an electron transport chain, they must rely solely on glycolytic reactions for ATP production. During periods of heavy exercise, large muscles operate under oxygen debt. During these periods, they, like red blood cells, depend solely on glycolysis to supply ATP.

Hepatic glycogen storage diseases (GSD) are a group of rare genetic disorders in which glycogen cannot be metabolized to glucose in the liver because of a specific enzyme deficiency along the glycogenolytic pathway. Most patients experience muscle symptoms, such as weakness and cramps, as well as individual GSD-specific symptoms.

Pompe's disease, Cori's disease, McArdle disease, and Tarui's disease all cause clinically significant muscle weakness. These inherited enzyme defects usually present in childhood, although some, such as McArdle's disease and Pompe's disease, have separate adult-onset forms. In general, GSDs are autosomal recessive, with specific mutations reported for each disorder.

Deficient Enzyme	Type	Name
glucose-6-phosphatase	I	Von Gierke's disease
alpha 1,4-glucosidase (acid maltase)	II	Pompe's disease
debrancher (amylo-1,6 glucosidase)	III	Cori's disease
brancher	IV	Andersen's disease
muscle phosphorylase	V	McArdle's disease
liver phosphorylase	VI	Hers' disease
phosphofructokinase	VII	Tarui's disease

Table 1 Glycogen Storage Diseases

58. In order to maximize ATP production, which of the following can serve as the initial reactant(s) for glycolysis?

   I. Glucose
   II. Fructose
   III. Galactose
   IV. Hexose Sugar

   A. I and IV
   B. I, II, and IV
   C. I and III only
   D. I, II, and III

59. A patient enters the emergency room suffering from hypoxia (lack of oxygen) caused by hemorrhage and shock. Which of the following is the expected metabolic outcome for this patient under these conditions?

   A. increased ATP production
   B. decreased lactic acid production
   C. increase glycolytic ATP production
   D. decreased rate of pyruvate formation

60. Erythrocytes (red blood cells) lack organelles and have a 120-day life span, after which lymph organs remove them. All of the following processes do not occur in the red blood cells, EXCEPT:

   A. electron transport chain
   B. Na^+/K^+ pump activity
   C. citric acid cycle
   D. lipid synthesis

61. Patients with a GSD are usually diagnosed in infancy or early childhood with high insulin levels, poor physical growth, and a deranged biochemical profile. According to Table 1, which diseases are closely related based on their enzyme etiology?

   A. Andersen's disease and Hers's disease
   B. Von Gierke's disease McArdle's disease
   C. McArdle's disease and Hers's disease
   D. Pompe's disease and Tarui's disease

62. Based on the information provided in the passage, linking 3 pyruvate molecules with a molecule of glucose will produce a carbon backbone of this length:

   A. 12
   B. 13
   C. 14
   D. 15

63. The introduction of continuous nocturnal glucose feeds and uncooked cornstarch has improved the prognosis for patients with hepatic glycogen storage diseases. In these patients, where does glucose get converted into pyruvate?

   A. nucleus
   B. mitochondria
   C. smooth endoplasmic reticulum
   D. cytosol

Passage 108 (Questions 64-70)

The citric acid cycle is the central point for several catabolic pathways. It accepts carbohydrate, fatty acid, and protein entry. Acetyl CoA is the breakdown product of glucose and fatty acids. Amino acids enter the citric acid cycle at one of several points, depending on their structure.

The cycle can be divided into two parts. The first part produces reduced NAD^+ by oxidative decarboxylation, using the reactions between citrate and succinyl CoA. The second part of the cycle contains reactions from succinyl CoA to oxaloacetate (OAA) and functions through an oxidative mode to reform OAA. These reactions produce reduced NAD^+ and FAD^+.

The cycle starts with a two-carbon acetyl group from acetyl CoA attaching to a four-carbon oxaloacetate molecule to produce a six-carbon citrate. During the oxidative decarboxylation reactions, two carbons are lost as CO_2. Thus, two carbons enter the citric acid cycle as acetyl groups, and two carbons are lost as CO_2.

The product of the second decarboxylation reaction is a four-carbon succinyl group attached to CoA. The bond between the succinyl group and CoA is a high-energy thioester bond that is broken in the next reaction. The products of the reaction are succinate and GTP. This is the only reaction in the cycle that directly produces a high-energy phosphodiester bond. Succinate is oxidatively modified in the remaining reactions to reform oxaloacetate. In regard to anabolic pathways, the citric acid cycle provides the starting material for the formation of many "building block compounds" used in biosynthesis reactions.

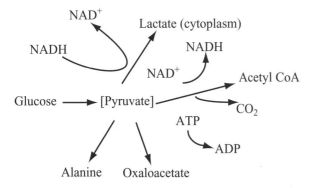
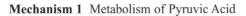

Mechanism 1 Metabolism of Pyruvic Acid

64. According to the passage, the citric acid cycle will result in a net gain of how many carbons?

   A. 0 carbons
   B. 1 carbon
   C. 2 carbons
   D. 4 carbons

65. A sudden excessive glucose intake will cause all of the following to occur EXCEPT:

   A. an increase in citric acid cycle intermediates
   B. possible blood acidosis associated with lactic acid production
   C. a decrease in venous carbon dioxide concentration
   D. synthesis of nonessential amino acids like alanine

66. Extensive research has shown that dandelion root enhances the flow of bile out of the liver. With high consumption of dandelion roots, which of the following is least likely to occur?

   A. There will be an improvement in symptoms associated with liver congestion.
   B. There may be distention of bile duct.
   C. There will be an increase in the concentration of bile and gallstones may appear.
   D. Liver disease may become more manageable because of increased liver fluid flow.

67. When examining the TCA cycle, alpha ketoglutarate dehydrogenase complex requires the set of cofactors as which of the following?

   A. citrate synthase
   B. cis-aconitate
   C. pyruvate dehydrogenase
   D. fumarate

68. According to the passage, which of the following is (are) directly produced by the citric acid cycle?

   I. ATP
   II. NADPH
   III. GTP

   A. I only
   B. III only
   C. I and II
   D. I and III

GO ON TO THE NEXT PAGE.

69. Which of the following is NOT an intermediate of the citric acid cycle?

   A. oxaloacetate
   B. citrate
   C. succinyl CoA
   D. acetyl CoA

70. In the citric acid cycle, citrate (a symmetrical intermediate) is converted to isocitrate (an asymmetrical intermediate). Which of the following best describes the effect the conversion will have on optical activity?

   A. The transition results in an optically inactive compound gaining the ability to rotate the plane of polarized light +24°.
   B. Conversion causes an optically active compound to lose its ability to rotate a plane of polarized light.
   C. This translocation will have no effect on either compound because both are optically active.
   D. The conversion will have no effect because both compounds are optically inactive.

Passage 109 (Questions 71-77)

Gluconeogenesis is the synthesis of glucose from non-carbohydrate precursors. It is essentially a reversal of glycolysis. Any gluconeogenic precursor must contain at least a three-carbon backbone. Free fatty acids are not used as precursors because they are broken down to a 2-carbon Acetyl CoA instead. Non-carbohydrate precursors are converted to pyruvate, dihydroxyacetone phosphate (DHAP), or oxaloacetate, which enter at three entry points in gluconeogenesis. Oxaloacetate requires a malate shuttle to cross the inner mitochondrial membrane. Oxaloacetate is converted to malate, a TCA cycle intermediate, via reversal of the malate dehydrogenase reaction. A cytosolic isozyme of malate dehydrogenase is used to reform oxaloacetate in the cytoplasm.

Three glycolysis reactions display large negative free energy changes and must be bypassed during gluconeogenesis with the use of different enzymes. Therefore, glycolysis and gluconeogenesis are reciprocal in function: when one is on, the other is off.

In the liver, kidney cortex, and in some cases skeletal muscle, glucose-6-phosphate (G-6-P) produced by gluconeogenesis can be stored as glycogen. However, without *glucose-6-phosphatase*, glucose cannot be released from glycogen storage. This causes low blood sugar levels. Because skeletal muscle lacks glucose-6-phosphatase, it cannot deliver glucose to the bloodstream. Therefore, skeletal muscle cells undergo gluconeogenesis exclusively as a mechanism to generate glucose for itself. In fact, most body organs cannot produce glucose for their own use. For this reason, the liver (for the most part) and kidneys are the main sites of gluconeogenesis because of their ability to put glucose into circulation.

Blood Glucose	Protein Phosphate	Pathway Function
HIGH (i.e. after meal)	LOW (Phosphatase is Active)	Glycolysis
LOW (i.e. during sleep)	HIGH (Kinase is Active)	Gluconeogenesis

Table 1 Overall Pathway Regulation

71. According to the passage, which of the following enzymes is found in both the cytoplasm and mitochondrial matrix?

   A. RNA polymerase
   B. malate dehydrogenase
   C. substance P
   D. gyrase

72. Humans consume 160 g of glucose/day, but only about 20g are available in the blood. The essential role of gluconeogenesis is:

A. to remove glucose from the blood plasma and stimulate its storage
B. to coordinate glycolysis enzyme regulation
C. to supply the brain with newly synthesized amino acids
D. to maintain a constant blood glucose level during exercise

73. Some Acetyl CoA is converted to ketone bodies. Which of the following explains why free fatty acids are NOT used as precursors for gluconeogenesis?

A. Free fatty acids are energy poor and are of no use in ATP synthesis.
B. Acetyl CoA is a compound that condenses with oxaloacetate.
C. The body conserves free fatty acids to use for padding and insulation.
D. Ketone bodies are transported to the brain to serve as energy sources during starvation.

74. Ciliated pseudostratified epithelial cells line the small intestinal villi and increase the surface area available for nutrient absorption. Where in these active cells does formation of pyruvate take place?

A. the cell membrane
B. the mitochondrial matrix
C. the smooth ER
D. the cytosol

75. ATP demands are met by metabolizing two energy sources: fatty acids and glucose molecules. Which of the following organs lacks the ability to produce glycogen?

A. cortex of the kidney
B. muscle lining the small intestine
C. right lobe of the liver
D. fascicle of skeletal muscle

76. Which of the following organs is expected to have the largest production of glucose from non-carbohydrate sources?

A. skeletal muscle
B. liver
C. cardiac tissue
D. kidney

77. According to the information in the passage, which of the following statements concerning the malate shuttle is true?

A. It is a peripheral mitochondrial membrane protein.
B. It requires hydrolysis of ATP.
C. It is an integral mitochondrial membrane protein.
D. Oxaloacetate binds to the receptor on the shuttle and gets transported across.

_____

GO ON TO THE NEXT PAGE.

78. Dithiothreitol (Cleland's Reagent) will reduce and break disulfide bonds. This reagent will directly affect which amino acid?

   A. glutamate
   B. cysteine
   C. arginine
   D. selenocysteine

79. Transketolase is an enzyme that catalyzes a reaction in the non-oxidative branch of the pentose phosphate pathway. Transketolase activity is dependent on a prosthetic group, which will attach to its target with which type of bond?

   A. hydrogen bond
   B. ionic bond
   C. covalent bond
   D. dipole/dipole interaction

80. Inorganic cofactors (Zn^{2+} and Ca^{2+}) function as enzymatic structural components, holding enzymes in specific, active forms. Which of the following can serve as a non-organic cofactor?

   A. helium
   B. Fe^{3+}
   C. Fr^{1+}
   D. NADPH

81. Enterokinase is a protease that cleaves after lysine residues (site Asp-Asp-Asp-Lys). It will sometimes cleave at other basic residues. Which of the following amino acids can also serve as a target for enterokinase?

   A. proline
   B. arginine
   C. tryptophan
   D. alanine

82. Citric acid cycle (also known as the Krebs cycle, after its primary discoverer, Sir Hans Krebs), when over-stimulated, produces which of the following?

   A. glucose
   B. amino acids
   C. pyruvate
   D. carbon dioxide

83. In contrast to prokaryotic cells, eukaryotes house the TCA cycle in which of the following locations?

   A. cytosol
   B. nucleus
   C. mitochondria
   D. smooth endoplasmic reticulum

84. Oligomycin is known to bind channels in the mitochondrial FoF_1 ATPase to prevent proton translocation. Oligomycin overdose would lead to which of the following?

   A. decrease in the proton gradient
   B. decrease in ATP production
   C. increase in ATP production
   D. increase in protein synthesis

85. In contrast to hemoglobin iron containing heme, cytochrome heme alternates between oxidized (Fe^{3+}) and reduced (Fe^{2+}) forms. Which of the following must be true regarding hemoglobin molecules?

   A. Fetal hemoglobin has lower O_2 affinity than adult hemoglobin.
   B. Hemoglobin alternates between the oxidized and reduced iron in non diseased state.
   C. Hemoglobin displays positive cooperative oxygen binding.
   D. Carbon monoxide cannot bind hemoglobin.

GO ON TO THE NEXT PAGE.

Passage 110 (Questions 86-91)

Acetyl CoA, the starting material for fatty acid synthesis, is produced in the mitochondrial matrix by the action of the pyruvate dehydrogenase complex. However, fatty acid synthesis occurs in the cytoplasm. Because the inner mitochondrial membrane is impermeable to acetyl CoA, it cannot be directly transferred to the cytoplasm. To get around this, the inner membrane has a carrier for citrate. Acetyl CoA is reacted with oxaloacetate (OAA) to form citrate, which is than transported to the cytoplasm.

Once in the cytoplasm, OAA is converted into pyruvate through a series of reactions that also produce NADPH. Pyruvate is transported back into the mitochondria and the reduced NADPH is used as a reactant for fatty acid synthesis.

The fatty acid synthesis requires 8 molecules of acetyl CoA to produce a 16-carbon lipid molecule called *palmitate*. In the first reaction of the synthesis pathway, 2 acetyl groups are joined to form a 4-carbon ketone intermediate. Energy is provided by malonyl decarboxylation. The remaining reactions reduce the ketone to a methylene (CH_2) group.

The pathway is an example of NADPH dependent reductive biosynthesis. In the subsequent cycles, the intermediate is elongated 2 carbons at a time by adding acetyl groups. Each 2-carbon addition is followed by reduction reactions that reduce the keto (carbonyl) group to another methylene group. The process stops when the intermediate reaches a length of 16 carbons.

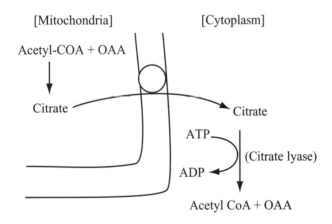

Mechanism 1 Acetyl CoA production

86. A genetic defect in any of the mitochondrial shuttle proteins can lead to weakness and muscle wasting. What is the most likely inheritance pattern of this type of a mitochondrial defect?

    A. spontaneous mitochondrial mutation
    B. a condition inherited from the mother
    C. result of a severe viral infection
    D. the paternal side of the genome is responsible for the condition

87. Which of the following metabolic processes have/has a direct effect on acetyl CoA levels needed for fatty acid synthesis?

    I.   glycolysis
    II. pyruvate dehydrogenase complex
    III. Krebs cycle

    A. I and II only
    B. III only
    C. II and III only
    D. I, II, and III

88. Membrane transport is often ATP-expensive. Citrate shuttle inhibition will cause the accumulation of which of the following and in which location?

    A. glucose in the cytoplasm
    B. oxaloacetate in the mitochondria
    C. Acetyl CoA in the cytoplasm
    D. pyruvate in the cytoplasm

89. *Acetyl CoA carboxylase,* with a covalently attached biotin, catalyzes the first reaction of fatty acid synthesis. Biotin must be which of the following?

    A. an inorganic factor
    B. a prosthetic group
    C. an enzyme
    D. a ribozyme

90. In can be deduced from the passage that another important product of fatty acid synthesis is:

    A. NADPH
    B. acetyl CoA
    C. oxaloacetate
    D. water

91. Palmitate can be altered to form longer fatty acids and/or fatty acids with double bonds. These reactions are expected to occur on the surface of which organelle?

    A. Golgi apparatus
    B. smooth ER
    C. lysosome
    D. rough ER

GO ON TO THE NEXT PAGE.

Passage 111 (Questions 92-98)

The pentose phosphate pathway (PPP) occurs in the cytoplasm. It is extremely important for cells involved in active synthesis (i.e., tumor cells). The function of the PPP is to produce NADPH and ribose-5'-phosphate. NADPH is used for reductive biosynthesis and protection against oxidative damage. Ribose-5'-phosphate is necessary for DNA synthesis.

$NADP^+$ is very similar to NAD^+ except for the additional phosphate group attached to the ribose carbon 2'. The extra phosphate is a signal that prevents $NADP^+$ from being used by the Krebs cycle and other cellular respiration cascades.

The PPP is divided into oxidative and non-oxidative branches. All oxidative branch reactions are irreversible. Glucose-6-phosphate (G-6-P) serves as the starting point. In reactions that follow, intermediates are oxidatively modified to produce NADPH. The first reaction converts G-6-P to a lactone ring, which is later hydrolyzed into a carboxylic acid. When ribose-5-phosphate is needed, ribulose-5-phosphate will be directly converted to ribose-5-phosphate, and all other non-oxidative branch reactions will not occur.

When ribose-5-phosphate is not needed for synthesis it must be converted to glycolysis-necessary compounds (fructose 6-phosphate and glyceraldehyde-3-phosphate) in order to prevent buildup.

92. According to the passage, which of the following is/are products of the pentose phosphate pathway?

 I. $NADP^+$
 II. NADPH
 III. ATP

 A. II only
 B. III only
 C. I and III
 D. II and III

93. Which of the following metabolic pathways occur in the same region of the cell as the PPP?

 A. electron transport chain
 B. citric acid cycle
 C. glycolysis
 D. transcription

94. It can be inferred from the passage that which of the following is the correct reaction order for pentose phosphate pathway?

 A. G-6-P → Ribose-5-P → Ribulose-5-P → Seduheptulose-7-P
 B. G-6-P → Ribulose-5-P → Seduheptulose-7-P → Ribose-5-P
 C. G-6-P → Ribulose-5-P → Ribose-5-P → Seduheptulose-7-P
 D. Seduheptulose-7-P → Ribulose-5-P → Ribose-5-P → G-6-P

95. The extra phosphate is a signal that prevents $NADP^+$ from being used by which of the following organelles?

 A. nucleus
 B. smooth ER
 C. mitochondria
 D. lysosome

96. Not all capillaries are perfused with blood at all times. Selective perfusion of capillary beds is controlled by degree of dilation of which of the following vessels?

 A. veins
 B. arteries
 C. arterioles
 D. aorta

97. NADPH is a specialized coenzyme that is used to supply reducing equivalents to which type of metabolism?

 A. catabolic
 B. anabolic
 C. phosphorylation
 D. hydrolysis

98. Metabolic synthesis is often vast and tightly controlled. Which of the following is a reactant of the pentose phosphate pathway?

 A. glucose-5-phosphate
 B. fructose-6-phosphate
 C. ribose-5-phosphate
 D. glucose-6-phosphate

GO ON TO THE NEXT PAGE.

Kinins are important mediators of the inflammatory response to infection. They are peptides generated from *kininogen* by the actions of a protease known as *kallikrein*. Following activation *kinins* act on the vascular system. The ultimate kinin is known as *bradykinin*, which is a potent agent that increases vascular permeability. *Bradykinin* also causes the contraction of smooth muscle, dilatation of blood vessels, and pain when injected into the skin; in this regard it mimics the actions of histamine. Bradykinin has a short half-life and is rapidly inactivated.

The generation of kinins appears to be triggered by the activation of the Hageman factor (Factor XII). Factor XII is converted into Factor XIIa when it comes in contact with damaged collagen, the basement membrane, and/or activated platelets. Kallikrein is also involved in the fibrinolytic system that relies on plasmin. Plasmin functions to break down formed clots. In addition, plasmin can activate the Hageman factor.

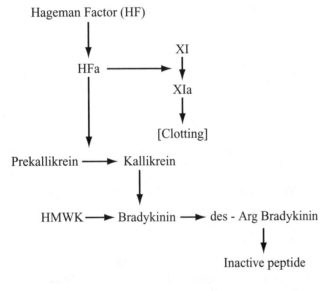

Diagram 1 Kinin Pathway

99. Anti-hypertension drugs (ACE inhibitors) inhibit bradykinase, which breaks down bradykinin. What vascular changes are expected in an individual who overdoses on ACE inhibitors?

   I. severe vascular edema
   II. painful lower limbs
   III. inhibition of the inflammatory response

   A. I only
   B. III only
   C. I and II only
   D. I, II, and III

100. Activated Hageman factor will stimulate the initiation of all of the following responses EXCEPT:

   A. the clotting cascade
   B. kallikrein cascade
   C. renin-angiotensin cascade
   D. inflammatory cascade

101. Kallikrein can serve to further activate more Hageman factor compounds or activate high molecular weight kininogen to bradykinin. This is an example of:

   A. decrease in activation energy
   B. negative reaction feedback
   C. kallikrein self-inhibition
   D. positive reaction feedback

102. An intrinsic biological pathway has been initiated that involves fibrin, plasmin, and platelets. What process is taking place?

   A. repair
   B. digestion
   C. absorption
   D. secretion

103. Which of the listed compounds is NOT considered a protease?

   A. kallikrein
   B. trypsin
   C. chymotrypsin
   D. lipase

104. Which of following is the most important component needed for blood clotting?

   A. plasminogen
   B. plasmin
   C. fibrin
   D. red blood cells

18 **GO ON TO THE NEXT PAGE.**

105. There are four designated levels of protein structure. Hemoglobin, with two alpha and two beta peptide chains, is an example of what type of protein structure?

   A. primary
   B. secondary
   C. tertiary
   D. quaternary

106. Hexokinase and glucokinase (glucokinase displays a higher K_m) both catalyze the first reaction of glycolysis. Based on the fact that K_m is equal to the [Substrate] = $^1/_2 V_{max}$, which of the following must be true?

   A. Glucokinase will be active when there is a high level of the reactant fructose.
   B. Glucokinase is not a zymogen.
   C. Hexokinase and glucokinase are not isozymes.
   D. Hexokinase is always functional and not controlled by negative feedback.

107. All of the following are examples of post-translational modification of a protein EXCEPT:

   A. phosphorylation
   B. methylation
   C. acetylation
   D. addition of a poly-A tail

108. Penicillin binds covalently with a serine residue at the transpeptidase active site and prevents the formation of the bacterial cell wall. Which of the following is true regarding the action of penicillin?

   A. Penicillin acts as a reversible competitive inhibitor.
   B. Penicillin activates transpeptidase, which digests the bacterial cell wall.
   C. Penicillin acts as a irreversible competitive inhibitor.
   D. Penicillin performs the function of a non-competitive inhibitor.

109. Krebs cycle takes place in the mitochondrial matrix and produces NADH and $FADH_2$. Which of the following is a list of Krebs cycle intermediates?

   A. pyruvate, glucose, oxaloacetate
   B. NADH, acetyl CoA, malate
   C. acetyl CoA, $FADH_2$, succinyl CoA
   D. acetyl CoA, malate, oxaloacetate

110. In regard to catabolic reactions, all of the following statements describe the purpose and significance of the citric acid cycle EXCEPT:

   A. The cycle produces reducing equivalents in the form of NADH and $FADH_2$ for use by the electron transport chain.
   B. Citric acid cycle operates in a reductive mode to accomplish NADPH production to supply tissue.
   C. Oxidation of citric acid cycle intermediates requires the presence of oxygen.
   D. The cycle is the main metabolic producer of CO_2.

111. Lipid production and deposition is under hormonal as well as genetic control. Which of the following organs is the major site of fatty acid synthesis?

   A. liver
   B. kidney
   C. brain
   D. muscle

112. A patient presents to the emergency room with type I diabetes and low blood insulin concentration. Which of the following is correct regarding this individual's condition?

   A. His levels of circulating red blood cells are decreased.
   B. Glucose can be found in his urine sample.
   C. His blood glucose level is decreased.
   D. His insulin levels will increase with proper stimulation of the thyroid.

113. Once lipids have been acquired from diet they must be distributed to the peripheral tissue. What organ system is responsible for this task in larger organisms?

   A. excretory system
   B. lymphatic system
   C. muscular system
   D. digestive system

STOP. IF YOU FINISH BEFORE TIME IS CALLED, CHECK YOUR WORK. YOU MAY GO BACK TO ANY QUESTION IN THIS TEST BOOKLET.

LECTURE 2

200

Biology Passages
Questions 114–221

Passage 201 (Questions 114-119)

Chargaff's rules and Franklin/Wilkins x-ray diffraction studies of DNA led Watson and Crick to propose the structure of DNA, for which they were awarded the Nobel Prize.

Watson and Crick's double-helical DNA model consists of two polynucleotide chains that wind into a right-handed double helix. The two strands are arranged in an anti-parallel orientation. The twisting of the double helix results in the formation of two grooves of unequal width on the surface of the helix: the major and smaller grooves, which alternate in the helix. Watson and Crick's model describes the dynamic structure of b-DNA.

In cells, DNA conformation constantly changes as the helix bends in solution and is complexed to proteins. Under physiologic conditions, most DNA occupies the b-DNA state. The a-DNA state is a crystal structural variant that is favored in reduced water solutions. It is most commonly seen base-paired with helical RNA, forming a right-handed helix that is shorter and wider than b-DNA. The z-DNA form is found in synthetic oligodeoxynucleotides as a left-handed helix that is slimmer than the b-form. The z-DNA form has no obvious grooves and is named because of the zigzag appearance of its backbone, which has a role in gene expression.

DNA palindromes are inverted repeats of base sequences occurring on two strands of DNA. Palindromes read the same backwards and forwards and in duplex DNA, the sequences read the same on each strand 5′ to 3′. Hairpins and cruciforms are areas of DNA on one and two-strands, respectively. They are single or double loop(s) formed by complementary base pairing.

114. According to the passage, DNA will occupy which state while mRNA production of the CFTR gene on chromosome 7 is taking place?

    A. b-DNA
    B. a-DNA
    C. z-DNA
    D. all three are equally likely

115. Which of the following nucleotide triplets is the initiation codon coding for methionine?

    A. UGA
    B. AUG
    C. UAA
    D. UAG

116. A dinucleotide is formed when a 5′-phosphomononucleotide is joined to the 3′-OH group of another mononucleotide. Which of the following bonds holds this linkage together?

    A. amide
    B. phosphodiester
    C. glycosidic linkage
    D. hydrogen bonds

117. Which of the following statements correctly describes b-DNA?

    A. b-DNA is usually found in solutions of reduced water.
    B. b-DNA displays a wider helix in comparison to the z-form.
    C. b-DNA forms a grooved left-handed helix.
    D. b-DNA has a helix is shorter and wider than a-DNA.

118. During the period between cell divisions, a nucleolus can be clearly identified within the nucleus. This dark circular structure is responsible for the production of which of the following molecules?

    A. DNA polymerase III
    B. rRNA
    C. peptides
    D. nuclear envelope

119. In the study of human genetics, an individual with an AB blood type is an example of which of the following?

    A. Mendel's inheritance
    B. expressed phenotype
    C. maternal and paternal effect
    D. codominance

The cell is the functional unit of the mammalian body and can be divided into two general compartments: the nucleus and the cytoplasm. A membrane, called the nuclear envelope, surrounds the nucleus. This is only present in eukaryotic cells. The nuclear envelope actually has two membranes, each with the typical membrane structure. The outermost membrane, studded with embedded ribosomes, is continuous with the endoplasmic reticulum.

About 3000-4000 nuclear pores perforate the nuclear envelope. These pores permit chemical traffic to move through in and out of the nucleus. Nuclear pores form where the inner and outer membranes of the nuclear envelope connect.

Heterochromatin is condensed nuclear chromatin that is seen as dense nuclear patches. Abundant heterochromatin is seen in stable cells such as those of the liver or the pancreas. Heterochromatin is considered transcriptionally inactive.

Euchromatin is threadlike and delicate. It is most abundant in active, transcribing cells. The presence of euchromatin is significant because the regions of DNA to be transcribed or duplicated must uncoil before the genetic code can be read.

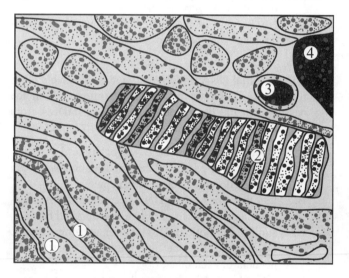

Figure 1

120. Based on the passage, it can be inferred that the rough ER lumen is similar in ionic concentration and overall environment to which of the following?

A. extracellular environment
B. cytoplasmic environment
C. mitochondrial environment
D. inter-nuclear membrane environment

121. Endoplasmic reticulum is a network of tubules, vesicles, and sacs that are interconnected. Which of the following structures are involved in protein synthesis?

   I. smooth ER
  II. rough ER
 III. outer nuclear membrane

A. I only
B. II only
C. II and III only
D. I, II, and III

122. All of the following eukaryotic cells display a unique nucleus EXCEPT:

A. white blood cells
B. macrophages
C. liver cells
D. red blood cells

123. The presence of euchromatin suggests:

A. A viral particle that is actively dividing.
B. A cell with numerous origins of replication.
C. The nucleus of a cerebral cortex neuron.
D. A heart muscle cell in the Go phase of the cell cycle.

124. Mitochondria come in a variety of shapes and sizes and are accurately described by all of the following statements EXCEPT:

A. It is an organelle with a double membrane.
B. Mitochondria do not rely on the nuclear mRNA for protein synthesis.
C. Mitochondria posses infoldings known as cristae.
D. Usually mitochondria are shaped like rods.

125. Which of the following organelles are NOT demonstrated in Figure 1?

A. mitochondrion
B. rough ER
C. nucleus
D. storage vacuole

Passage 203 (Questions 126-131)

Mitochondria have their own genetic material (mtDNA), and there are often numerous copies of the genome present in each organelle. Mitochondrial genes include alleles for rRNA, tRNA, and parts of the respiratory enzyme complexes of the inner mitochondrial membrane. mtDNA has a high mutation rate. In addition, mtDNA is almost always inherited from the maternal cell line, because the mitochondria from the sperm that enters the egg during fertilization is actively degraded upon entering the egg.

As a result of mtDNA mutation, there may exist more than one population of mtDNA in one cell, normal and abnormal. This is known as *heterogeneity*. When all mitochondria in a cell have identical DNA, the cell is homoplasmic; but if the mitochondria vary, they are said to be heteroplasmic. Expression of an inherited mitochondrial disorder depends on the proportion of mutated mtDNA in the cells.

Mutations and deletions in mitochondria are very often limited to a single tissue, and this also contributes to the considerable variability of mitochondrial diseases. Most mitochondrial diseases are expressed in organs rich in mitochondria and high in energy requirements. Two major mitochondrial diseases are Leber's hereditary optical neuropathy (LHON), which is characterized by a rapid loss of central field vision, and mitochondrial encephalomyopathy (MELAS), which is characterized by brain and muscle abnormalities.

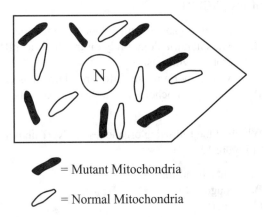

 = Mutant Mitochondria

 = Normal Mitochondria

Figure 1 Mitochondrial Heteroplasmy

126. The mitochondrial heteroplasmy demonstrated in Figure 1 would probably present as pathology of which of the following organs?

   A. brain
   B. spinal cord
   C. vascular spleen
   D. excretory kidney

127. It is suggested in the passage that which of the following enzymes is most likely produced by mtDNA?

   A. glycolysis hexokinase
   B. primase
   C. cytochrome oxidase C
   D. cell membrane ATP synthase

128. Mitochondrial DNA analysis begins with mtDNA extraction from the cell. Which of the following methods can be used in order to "amplify" hypervariable portions of mtDNA molecule?

   A. southern blotting
   B. distillation
   C. ELISA
   D. PCR

129. Based on the information in the passage, can mtDNA be considered a unique identifier in forensic sciences?

   A. Yes, because mitochondria are usually derived exclusively from the ovum.
   B. Yes, because each individual is expected to have a unique pattern of mtDNA.
   C. No, because the maternal mitochondrial cell line is passed on to every offspring.
   D. No, because of the unpredictable nature of maternal/paternal genetic crossover.

130. Mitochondrial DNA (mtDNA) provides a valuable locus for forensic DNA typing. It can be inferred from the passage that the likelihood of recovering mtDNA from degraded and digested eukaryotic cellular samples is:

   A. greater than for nuclear DNA because mtDNA molecules can be present in thousands of copies per cell compared to the nuclear complement
   B. less than for nuclear DNA because mtDNA molecules are composed of only a few hundred bases
   C. similar for both mtDNA and nuclear eukaryotic DNA because at one time both cells existed independent of each other
   D. difficult to predict because the genome size depends on the state of cellular and organelle function

131. Which of the following is an example of a homoplasmic cell line?

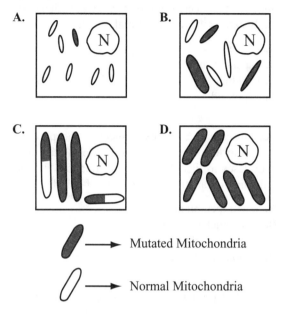

A.
B.
C.
D.

Mutated Mitochondria

Normal Mitochondria

Questions 132 through 142 are **NOT** based on a descriptive passage.

132. During the addition of the incoming dNTP nucleotide, a linkage is formed and a pyrophosphate is released. Which of the following describes a type of bond that occurs between two dNTP molecules?

   A. a coordinate ionic bond
   B. a glycosidic bond
   C. london dispersion interaction
   D. a phosphodiester bond

133. Helicase is the enzyme that "unzips" the helix. In order to maintain the "unzipping," SSBP (single stranded binding protein) is expected to attach to which nucleotide element during replication?

   A. dsDNA
   B. ssDNA
   C. dsRNA
   D. ssRNA

Organism	Genome Size (bp)	# of Haploid Chromosomes	Chromosome Size (bp)	Chromosome Shape
E. coli	5×10^6	1	5.0×10^6	Circular
S. cerevisiae	1.4×10^7	16	8.8×10^5	Linear
Homo sapien	3×10^9	23	1.3×10^8	Linear

134. Humans have so much more DNA to replicate than *E. coli.* According to the above data, how many chromosomes are present in a *Homo sapien* somatic cell after the S phase of the cell cycle?

   A. 16 chromosomes
   B. 23 chromosomes
   C. 46 chromosomes
   D. 92 chromosomes

135. A *photolyase reaction* causes the formation of free radicals, which cause $FADH_2$ to donate electrons to thymine dimmers. Which of the following metabolic processes produces $FADH_2$?

   A. glycolysis
   B. citric acid cycle
   C. nucleotide synthesis
   D. electron transport chain

136. DNA polymerase cannot fully replicate the 3′ DNA end and with every division the DNA gets shorter and shorter. The bubble mechanism prevents the loss of the DNA coding region.

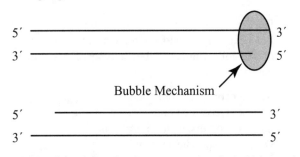

Bubble Mechanism

Which of the following is an example of a bubble mechanism?

A. centromere
B. telomere
C. kinetochore
D. centriole

137. Which of the following RNA molecules is relatively small, with a common secondary structure known as a cloverleaf?

A. rRNA
B. tRNA
C. mRNA
D. hnRNA

138. Under normal circumstances DNA is tightly supercoiled. Which family of enzymes maintains and regulates DNA coiling?

A. the helicase family
B. the topoisomerase family
C. the ligase family
D. the polymerase family

139. The genetic code is composed of three nucleotides coding for each amino acid. How many possible codons exits in nature that code for the 20 amino acids found in polypeptides?

A. 4
B. 20
C. 64
D. 1,000,000

140. Mitochondrial mutations are often limited to a single tissue. In an individual who fails to produce calcitonin, a hormone that decreases blood calcium, which tissue most likely carries the mitochondrial mutation?

A. liver
B. parathyroid
C. kidney
D. thyroid

141. I-cell disease is caused by a defective phosphotransferase needed to form the mannose-6-phosphate tag that targets hydrolases to their lysosomal destination. Which of the following organelles is defective in I-cell disease?

A. cell membrane
B. the nucleus
C. smooth ER
D. Golgi apparatus

142. Fidelity of protein synthesis is determined on the ribosome by the codon-anticodon reaction that occurs between:

A. DNA and DNA polymerase
B. tRNA and rRNA
C. mRNA and rRNA
D. mRNA and tRNA

When more than one gene resides in a transcription unit, it leads to the formation of a *polycistronic* message. In prokaryotes, genes of similar function are often arranged adjacent to each other on the chromosome and are transcribed as a single polycistronic mRNA. This type of an arrangement is called an *operon,* which ensures that proteins serving related functions are synthesized coordinately. Eukaryotes, in general, do not have operons.

There are two RNA polymerases in prokaryotic cells. Transcription begins with the template being recognized by the main RNA polymerase, which requires magnesium to function properly. This is the most important regulatory point of transcription. Different regulatory factors function to recruit the polymerase (activators) or prevent the polymerase from binding (repressors). After DNA unwinding, the RNA polymerase begins synthesis of the first few bases of the nascent RNA strand, which is a relatively slow process.

The second prokaryote polymerase is *primase*, which synthesizes an RNA primer for DNA replication. Eukaryotes have three different RNA polymerases to do the job that the one enzyme does in bacteria.

143. According to the passage, which of the following proteins would be coded by a polycistronic mRNA?

- **A.** heart muscle, lung surfactant, tracheal cartilage
- **B.** Krebs cycle enzyme, NAD^+ synthase, mitochondrial inner membrane channel
- **C.** cell membrane ATPase, ribosome, histone
- **D.** HMG-CoA reductase, ATP synthase, tUMP decarboxylase

144. Transcription is the synthesis of RNA based on a DNA template. RNA polymerase binds to DNA at which of the following sites and unwinds the DNA?

- **A.** operon
- **B.** promoter
- **C.** operator
- **D.** inhibitor

145. Early work on prokaryotic transcription turned out to be easy because the RNA polymerase only required which of the following in order to function in a test tube?

- **I.** an RNA template
- **II.** all the necessary nucleotides
- **III.** magnesium

- **A.** I only
- **B.** II only
- **C.** II and III only
- **D.** I, II, and III

146. Ribonucleotides and deoxyribonucleotides (collectively known as nucleotides) are the building blocks of the nucleic acids. Ribonucleotides *differ* from deoxyribonucleotides in which of the following ways?

- **A.** At the 2′ carbon position, ribonucleotides have a hydroxyl group.
- **B.** At the 2′ carbon position, deoxyribonucleotides have a hydroxyl group.
- **C.** At the 3′ carbon position, ribonucleotides have a hydroxyl group.
- **D.** At the 3′ carbon position, deoxyribonucleotides have a hydroxyl group.

147. A chemist is given two DNA strands of equal length. Each has a different base composition, with strand M having a higher guanine/cytosine fraction than strand A. Which of the following would be expected?

- **A.** Strand M should denature at a lower temperature.
- **B.** Strand A should denature at a lower temperature.
- **C.** Strand A is almost impossible to denature.
- **D.** Both strands should denature at the same temperature.

148. Deamination of cytosine forms uracil. If the deamination enzyme is mutated, which of the following compounds will pair up with the deamination reaction reactant?

- **A.** adenine
- **B.** thymine
- **C.** guanine
- **D.** uracil

Ribosomes have many roles in protein synthesis, including the alignment of the mRNA during initiation of protein synthesis, selection of the proper codon for initiation, peptide bond formation, and termination of translation. Ribosomes have two tRNA-binding sites: the P (peptidyl) site and the A (aminoacyl) site.

The tRNA molecule is a cloverleaf structure with three unpaired loops. The sk-loop contains the anticodon sequence. Every tRNA has the same CCA-3′-OH terminus to which the amino acid is attached via an ester linkage. Each tRNA contains two specific sites: the anticodon site and a site that is recognized by an aminoacyl-tRNA synthetase.

Before being incorporated into a protein, amino acids must first be activated; this is known as *aminoacylation*. *Aminoacylation* is catalyzed by a specific aminoacyl-tRNA synthetase and requires ATP.

amino acid + ATP → aminoacyl-AMP + PP
aminoacyl-AMP + tRNA → aminoacyl-tRNA + AMP

Aminoacylation Reactions

In translation, codon-anticodon interactions determine which tRNA will bind, and this determines the amino acid to be incorporated into protein. The identity of the amino acid is not checked on the ribosome. Some aminoacyl-tRNA synthetases are capable of a type of rechecking certain tRNA sequences involved in translation.

149. The sk-loop will bind with the greatest affinity to which of the following?

A. rRNA
B. amino acids
C. mRNA
D. Golgi apparatus

150. Ribosomal subunits are usually identified by sedimentation coefficients called Svedberg units. Which of the following is a ribosomal subunit found in a prokaryotic cell like *E. coli?*

A. 30 S
B. 40 S
C. 60 S
D. 80 S

151. According to the passage, which of the following components is responsible for translation proofreading activity?

A. the A (aminoacyl) site
B. aminoacyl-tRNA synthetase
C. codon-anticodon interactions
D. ribosomes

152. Isoacceptors are tRNAs that accept the same amino acid but that differ in their specificity. When amino acids undergo *aminoacylation* with isoacceptors, which of the following apply?

   I. an intermediate must form between an amino acid and AMP
  II. an activated amino acid is transferred to tRNA
 III. it is an adenosine triphosphate-independent step

A. I only
B. III only
C. I and II only
D. I, II, and III

153. Ribosomes are huge molecular complexes once they are physically assembled. Which of the following components are necessary for the proper ribosome assembly?

A. mRNA and rough ER
B. rRNA and protein
C. tRNA and cytoplasm
D. polypeptide and DNA

GO ON TO THE NEXT PAGE.

Passage 206 (Questions 154-159)

DNA polymerases have synthesis activity that catalyzes the addition of 5′-deoxynucleotide triphosphates (5′-dNTPs) to the free 3′ end of the primer. The parental strand is the template that directs the addition of complementary 5′-dNTPs.

The DNA polymerase III holoenzyme has high processivity and fidelity. Processivity refers to the number of nucleotides added before the enzyme dissociates from the template. Fidelity refers to the accuracy of DNA synthesis. DNA polymerase III polymerizes the leading strand and the majority of the lagging strand. ATP is needed only initially by the holoenzyme in order to clamp onto a primed template, but afterwards, the holoenzyme is rapid and progresses without additional ATP.

DNA polymerase I has moderate synthesis capability and is utilized to fill in the gaps on the lagging strand after removal of RNA primers. Despite the differences in synthesis, both the leading and lagging strand finish synthesizing DNA at the same time.

DNA polymerase I and III have separate proofreading activities, both of which maintain accuracy in the new DNA chain. The 3′,5′ exonuclease activity removes improperly matched nucleotides from the 3′ end. When DNA polymerase III recognizes an incorrectly paired base, the 3′,5′ exonuclease catalyzes the removal of the improper nucleotide.

154. Which of the following describes DNA replication in chronological order?

   A. SSBP stabilizes the replication fork → unwinding by a helicase → DNA polymerase binds to DNA → primase synthesizes a primer → DNA ligase links Okazaki fragments
   B. DNA polymerase binds to one strand of the DNA → unwinding by a helicase → primase synthesizes a primer → DNA ligase links Okazaki fragments → SSBP stabilizes the replication fork
   C. primase synthesizes a primer → unwinding by a helicase → DNA polymerase binds to DNA → SSBP stabilizes the replication fork → DNA ligase links Okazaki fragments
   D. unwinding by a helicase → SSBP stabilizes the replication fork → primase synthesizes a primer → DNA polymerase binds to DNA → DNA ligase links Okazaki fragments

155. Specific base pairing is required only in the first 2 codon nucleotides of an mRNA. This codon/anticodon interaction is known as "wobble" and is directly associated with which molecule?

   A. ATP
   B. tRNA
   C. RNA polymerase
   D. promoter

156. It can be inferred from the passage that the replication of the chromosome involves what type of DNA polymerase synthesis?

   A. continuous
   B. semi-discontinuous
   C. discontinuous
   D. conservative

157. During DNA synthesis, both strands require an RNA primer to start elongation because it is an:

   A. RNA polymerase that synthesizes short stretches of RNA
   B. RNA ATPase that synthesizes short stretches of complementary DNA
   C. DNA polymerase that synthesizes short stretches of DNA
   D. DNA ATPase that synthesizes short stretches of complementary RNA

158. DNA polymerase III is a very complex holoenzyme, having 10 different subunits. Which of the following is the rate-limiting step in the function of DNA polymerase?

   A. time required to attach to the primed template
   B. slow activity of the proofreader
   C. function at the lagging strand
   D. Okazaki fragment ligation

159. All of the following are true of replication/transcription when polymerases are active EXCEPT:

   A. direction of DNA synthesis is from 5′ to 3′
   B. replication is an energetically expensive process
   C. the end product of translation is RNA
   D. transcription and replication both occur in the nucleus

160. Which of the following components is required for the proper function of DNA-dependent-DNA polymerase?

    I. 4 different nucleotides
    II. DNA template
    III. an RNA primer

    A. I only
    B. II and III only
    C. I and III only
    D. I, II, and III

161. A mature mRNA that is about to be released into the cytoplasm has undergone which of the following post-transcriptional modifications?

    A. RNA intron/exon splicing only
    B. RNA exon splicing and 3′ RNA capping
    C. 3′ RNA poly-A-tail addition and 5′ capping only
    D. 5′ capping, 3′ RNA poly-A-tail addition, and intron/ exon splicing

162. Which of the following macromolecules is repaired rather than degraded?

    A. polysaccharide
    B. polypeptide
    C. polynucleotide
    D. triglyceride

163. All of the following amino acids are optically active EXCEPT:

    A. valine
    B. cysteine
    C. glycine
    D. proline

164. Pepsin, trypsin, and chymotrypsin cleave polypeptides into fragments at a specific point in the middle of the chain. These enzymes are properly characterized as:

    A. endopeptidases
    B. zymogens
    C. ligases
    D. exopeptidases

165. Which of the following DNA lesions will NOT result in a frame shift mutation?

    A. 1 missing base pair
    B. 2 altered base pairs
    C. 3 deleted base pairs
    D. 2 inserted base pairs

166. Which of the following blotting methods involves the transferring of proteins from a gel to membranes, then probing them using antibodies to specific proteins?

    A. northern blotting
    B. southern blotting
    C. western blotting
    D. eastern blotting

167. Antibodies are produced and secreted by plasma cells. Which of the following organelles must be well developed for effective antibody synthesis?

    A. smooth ER
    B. mitochondria
    C. storage vacuole
    D. rough ER

168. In paper chromatography, a sheet of absorbent paper is hung with just the tip immersed in a non-polar solvent. The solvent rises through the paper through capillary action. Which of the following compounds will demonstrate the greatest displacement when placed on the paper near the bottom?

    A. CH_3Cl
    B. Carboxylic acid
    C. Ammonia
    D. $CH_3CH_2CH_3$

169. Which of the following cellular organelles are identified by sedimentation coefficients called S units or Svedberg units?

    A. mitochondria
    B. lysosomes
    C. peroxisomes
    D. ribosomes

170.

Primer (Free 3′ OH) + 5′ PPP $\longrightarrow$ Primer 3′O-P-5′ + PPi

Mg^{+2}, all 4 nucleotides

DNA Polymerase

In the above polymerization reaction carried out by the DNA polymerase, magnesium serves as which of the following?

    A. vitamin
    B. peptide
    C. monovalent metal ion
    D. catalyst

GO ON TO THE NEXT PAGE.

Passage 207 (Questions 171-176)

Protein synthesis starts at the amino end of the peptide and progresses by the addition of amino acids to the carboxylic end. In prokaryotes, the synthesis of a polypeptide chain begins with *N-formylmethionine* (fMet).

The Shine-Delgarno sequence -$^A/_G^A/_G^A/_G^A/_G$CC$^A/_G^A/_G^A/_G^A/_G$C-CCAUG - is a short purine-rich sequence that is positioned 10 base pairs upstream of the 5′ end of the start codon on the mRNA. The pairing between the Shine-Delgarno sequence and the complementary area on the ribosome determines where protein synthesis will begin. A tRNA-anticodon recognizes the start codon on the mRNA and occupies the P-site on the ribosome. Numerous initiation factors (IF-1, IF-2, and IF-3) assist in these events by supplying energy in the form of GTP.

The formation of the peptide bond is catalyzed by the 23S ribosomal RNA, called *peptidyl transferase*. Peptide bond formation does not require an additional energy source. Elongation has 3 phases: binding of the aminoacyl-tRNA, peptide bond formation, and translocation.

171. In a polycistronic prokaryotic RNA, the AUG codon is located adjacent to this Shine-Delgarno element:

- **A.** CCAAACCGGGCCCAUG
- **B.** CCAGGACCCCCCAUG
- **C.** UUUGAGAGAGAGAUUUUUUAUG
- **D.** CCGGGGACCCAAAAGCCAUG

172. Which of the following metabolic pathways is capable of supplying high-energy GTP molecules needed for protein synthesis?

- **A.** glycolysis
- **B.** fermentation
- **C.** citric acid cycle
- **D.** electron transport chain

173. Prokaryotes require which of the following parameters in order to synthesize protein?

- **I.** proper concentration of methionine
- **II.** an amino acid *formylase* to carry out formylation reactions
- **III.** an AUG start/stop codon

- **A.** I only
- **B.** II and III only
- **C.** I and II only
- **D.** I, II, and III

174. Protein translation proceeds as an ordered process and involves all of the following steps EXCEPT:

- **A.** ribosomes "process/read" the mRNA in the 5′ to 3′ direction
- **B.** peptide synthesis proceeds from the amino-terminus to the carboxyl-terminus
- **C.** translation is always carried out by a uni-ribosome per peptide synthesized
- **D.** chain elongation requires the activity of multiple tRNA molecules

175. What is the maximum number of amino acids in a peptide coded by a $(GCAU)^4$ nucleotide chain?

- **A.** one
- **B.** four
- **C.** five
- **D.** seven

176. Many antibiotics inhibit prokaryotic translation without disrupting protein synthesis of the host cell. These antibiotics work via all of the following mechanisms EXCEPT:

- **A.** antibiotics bind to the ribosomal 50S subunit to prevent translation
- **B.** antibiotics bind to the ribosomal 40S subunit to prevent translation
- **C.** antibiotics bind 70S ribosomes at similar sites and with similar efficacies
- **D.** antibiotics bind free ribosomes in the cytoplasm

GO ON TO THE NEXT PAGE.

Passage 208 (Questions 177-182)

The goal of cancer chemotherapy is the removal and/or destruction of every malignant cell. By the time a solid tumor is found, the tumor cell burden is very high. The first step is usually surgery in order to "debulk" the tumor. This is then followed by chemotherapy or immunotherapy. Chemotherapy has its main place in those cancers which are not solid or which are disseminating and not amenable to surgery or radiation.

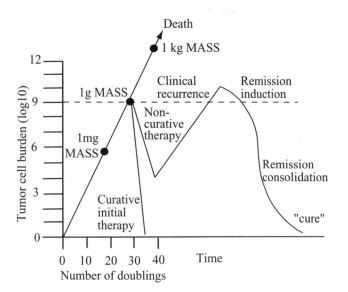

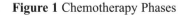

Figure 1 Chemotherapy Phases

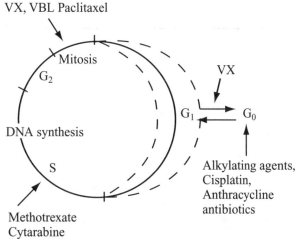

Figure 2 Interphase Mechanism 1

Usually, diagnosis is made when the tumor has a mass of 1 gram or when there are about 1×10^9 cancer cells present. Without intervention this would proceed to death. On the other hand, with curative initial therapy the cancer cell number would drop down to 0. However, therapy is normally non-curative and only kills 99.999% of the cells. Therefore, there will still be 10,000 cancerous cells present when treatment is complete. Non-curative therapy does not cure cancer. It only leads to remission. With non-curative therapy you may have a reappearance of the neoplasm, which will require another round of chemotherapy that may eventually lead to a period of remission or consolidation. Currently, prednisone and oncovin (vincristine) are used to initiate remission, while methotrexate and 6-mercaptopurine are used for maintenance of the remission.

177. According to the information in the passage, which of the following tumors will most likely respond to chemotherapy that relies on anti-cancer (cytotoxic) drugs?

A. white blood cell secreting lymphoma
B. rock-hard breast mass
C. an encapsulated brain tumor
D. a non-metastatic slow-growing skin cancer

178. A slow-growing malignant cell remains in interphase for an extended period of time. Which of the following drug regimens will work best against this neoplasm?

A. methotrexate
B. paclitaxel
C. cisplatin
D. 6-mercaptopurine

179. It can be inferred from the passage that "debulking" a cancer may have which of the following benefits?

A. Debulking is used to accurately assess the nature and extent of the cancer.
B. It may make radiation and chemotherapy more effective.
C. Debulking usually involves the removal of a large section of the surrounding normal tissue.
D. Debulking removes the tumor vascular supply and causes the neoplasm to swell and burst.

180. When non-curative treatments are applied, remission is induced when the tumor burden decreases to:

A. 0 grams
B. below 1 gram
C. below 1 milligram
D. below 1 microgram

GO ON TO THE NEXT PAGE.

181. Methotrexate is a known inhibitor of pyrimidine synthesis. Tissue concentration of which of the following compounds will NOT be decreased in an individual on methotrexate?

   A. guanine
   B. uracil
   C. thymine
   D. cytosine

182. According to Figure 1, death from cancer directly depends on which of the following?

   A. delay in the initiation of treatment
   B. tumor cell mass
   C. rapid cancer cell division
   D. number of cancer cell doublings

Passage 209 (Questions 183-188)

All somatic cells reproduce by mitosis. Prior to mitosis, a cell will spend 95 percent of its time in a resting interval between divisions. The resting interval has a G_1 phase, which displays the most variability; for example, G_1 phase is incredibly short in rapidly dividing dermal cells. Quiescent cells are classified as being in G_0 phase, which is a subdivision of the G_1 phase. The S phase represents nuclear chromosomal replication. Mitochondrial DNA replication occurs during the G_2 phase of the cell cycle. The M phase follows G_2 and includes the events of spindle formation, chromosomal segregation, and cytokinesis.

Cellular classification according to the ability to divide is necessary for clinical treatment. *Labile cells* represent a renewing cellular population. These cells, such as the epithelial lining the GI tract, multiply throughout life. Labile cells are constantly in the mitotic cycle undergoing division. *Stable cells* show a post-adolescent decrease in their ability to divide but retain their ability to undergo mitosis if properly stimulated. *Permanent cells* lose their ability to divide at birth and cannot be stimulated to divide again.

Mammalian cells display limited tolerance to the interstitial environment, tolerating only a limited range of variation in pH, salt concentration, oxygen, and temperature. Cells usually function in groups; each group is specialized to perform a limited number of functions. The framework of tissues is composed of collagen connective tissue, which gives rise to the basement membrane and ground substance or proteoglycans. The location of the cell in the tissue determines cell structure and behavior.

183. Cell division is tightly regulated. Which of the following is TRUE regarding mitosis OR meiosis?

   I. Mitosis shows no homologue pairing.
   II. There is no S phase between meiosis I and II.
   III. Meiosis centromeres do not divide at anaphase I.

   A. I and III only
   B. I and II only
   C. II only
   D. I, II, and III

184. A culture containing one thousand cells is expected to display what percentage of labile interphase cells?

   A. 5 percent of cells will be in interphase.
   B. 847 cells will be in interphase.
   C. Between 93 and 97 percent of cells will be in interphase.
   D. Almost every cell will be in interphase.

GO ON TO THE NEXT PAGE.

185. According to the passage, mammalian cells are expected to display the greatest degree of variability during which of the following phases?

    A.   organelle division phase that follows an appropriate stimulus
    B.   DNA polymerase ATP activity
    C.   rate of nuclear degradation
    D.   quiescent phase nutrient requirement

186. Which one of the following most appropriately fits the description of a *permanent cell?*

    A.   liver hepatocyte
    B.   vessel mesothelium cell
    C.   peripheral axonal sensory cell
    D.   hair follicle cell

187. *Stable cells* in the G_2 phase require stimuli to proliferate. According to the passage, which one of the following could serve as the appropriate proliferation activator?

    A.   liver damage because of chronic alcohol abuse
    B.   growth factor activity in a newborn
    C.   lack of interphase division checkpoints
    D.   high levels of follicle stimulating hormone

188. "Helix-breakers" are amino acids that are often used as biological markers in research. Which of the following amino acids can serve as a marker?

    A.   alanine
    B.   valine
    C.   proline
    D.   isoleucine

Questions 189 through 199 are **NOT** based on a descriptive passage.

189. Myoglobin is an 18 kilo Dalton peptide composed of 153 amino acid residues in a single chain. Which protein structure does a myoglobin molecule occupy?

    A.   primary
    B.   secondary
    C.   tertiary
    D.   quaternary

190. Acid hydrolysis, used to determine protein amino acid sequence, causes a partial destruction of tryptophan and the conversion of asparagine to aspartic acid and glutamine to glutamic acid. All of the following statements are true regarding acid hydrolysis EXCEPT:

    A.   Tryptophan is not estimated properly.
    B.   Asparagine cannot be measured directly.
    C.   Glutamine concentration correlates to the measured level of aspartic acid.
    D.   Measure of glutamic acid is an indirect indicator of the glutamine concentration.

191. The N-glycosidic bond of a guanine molecule is somewhat unstable and can be hydrolyzed by a process known as *depurination.* Which of the following macromolecules is most likely to undergo *depurination?*

    A.   RNA
    B.   protein
    C.   carbohydrate
    D.   lipid

192. Proteins can recover significant activity after being gently denatured and then the denaturants removed. Recovery of activity implies recovery of structure, which depends on which of the following?

    A.   peptide primary structure
    B.   peptide secondary structure
    C.   peptide tertiary structure
    D.   peptide quaternary structure

193. A genetic disease that displays an earlier age of onset with an increase in severity of symptoms with every generation is an example of which of the following?

   A. heterozygous advantage
   B. anticipation
   C. penetrance
   D. codominance

194. Post-translational modifications include attachment of glycoprotein side chains, amino acid hydroxylation, etc. Protein glycosylation most likely occurs in which of the following organelles?

   I. lysosomes
   II. Golgi apparatus
   III. rough endoplasmic reticulum

   A. I only
   B. II only
   C. II and III only
   D. I, II, and III

195. Which of the following compounds is necessary for ribosomal function and is synthesized by the nucleolus?

   A. rRNA
   B. vitamin C
   C. rough ER
   D. ribo-enzyme

196. A *transversion* is a mutation that causes a conversion of a purine to a pyrimidine or vice versa. Which of the following is an example of a *transversion?*

   A. cytosine → guanine
   B. thymine → uracil
   C. adenine → guanine
   D. cytosine → thymine

197. Alanine, valine, leucine, isoleucine, and methionine are non-polar amino acids with aliphatic side chains. Leucine side chain groups can interact with other nonpolar amino acids through:

   A. ionic bonding
   B. hydrophobic interaction
   C. hydrogen bonding
   D. covalent bonding

198. Class II Major Histocompatibility Complex (MHC) proteins are found on cells such as macrophages and histocytes. MHC II stimulates cell-mediated immunity, which depends on which cell type?

   A. macrophages
   B. red blood cells
   C. antibody-producing cells
   D. T-helper cells

199. Cooperativity is measured by the *Hill coefficient* (HC): HC greater than 1 is for positive cooperativity, less than 1 for negative cooperativity, and 1 for non-cooperative systems. What is the HC for hemoglobin?

   A. 3
   B. 1
   C. 0
   D. −1

GO ON TO THE NEXT PAGE.

It is common practice to perform a standard genetic and congenital disease screening on newborns. The disorders tested for are ones that are treatable if detected early.

Tandem mass spectrometry has been used to detect diseases such as aminoacidurias and fatty and organic acid disorders. One disorder this is used to test for is medium chain acyl-CoA dehydrogenase (MCAD) deficiency, which causes an accumulation of multiple unsaturated fatty acids and leads to serious brain damage if not detected early.

Deficiency of the enzyme *phenylalanine hydroxylase* causes the development of phenylketonuria (PKU) in newborns. In these children, phenylalanine (an essential amino acid) is not properly processed by the body. Left untreated, phenylalanine accumulates in the blood and urine and can eventually cause brain damage. Treatment for PKU is to minimize phenylalanine in the diet.

The Guthrie screening test is a bacterial inhibition assay for PKU. Newborn blood samples on filter paper are placed on glucose-free agar plates with a growth-inhibited strain of *B. subtilis*. If there is an excess of phenylalanine in the patient's blood, the bacteria can overcome this growth inhibition and grow. Disks with known amounts of phenylalanine are used to standardize the test. Affected children are then are put on phenylalanine-restricted diets.

200. According to the passage, all of the following lipid digestion and absorption mechanisms are normally functioning in MCAD deficiency EXCEPT:

    A. the pancreatic production of lipase
    B. liver production of bile
    C. the mechanism required to form intestinal micelles
    D. mitochondrial membrane lipid transporters

201. It can be inferred from the passage that screening for which of the following conditions would be most beneficial in terms of decreasing morbidity and mortality?

    A. common cold antibodies
    B. colon cancer
    C. hairline fractures
    D. emotional difficulties

202. The digestion of a meal high in protein begins in which of the following organs?

    A. mouth
    B. esophagus
    C. stomach
    D. small intestine

203. Which of the following is the correct genotype of *B. subtilis*.utilized for accurate newborn PKU screening? [Glu = Glucose; Lac = Lactose; Phe = Phenylalanine]

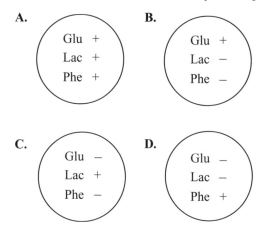

204. *Phenylalanine hydroxylase* converts phenylalanine into another amino acid called tyrosine, which is a precursor of dopamine and norepinephrine. Which of the following statements correctly describes the necessary diet modifications for an individual with PKU?

    A. A carbohydrate-only diet is of little benefit to those with PKU.
    B. Tyrosine becomes an "essential" amino acid to those with PKU.
    C. Lipid consumption must decrease to prevent conversion of fat to phenylalanine.
    D. A decrease in consumption of other amino acids will be beneficial to those with PKU.

Passage 211 (Questions 205-209)

Genomic imprinting is a phenomenon in which the same DNA sequence may have different effects, depending on whether it was inherited from the mother or the father. With the exception of X inactivation in females, it had always been assumed that all genes from both the maternal and paternal chromosomes are fully expressed in the offspring. Genomic imprinting, which is found only in mammals, directly challenges this assumption.

In mammals, all of the genes from one parent are methylated, or imprinted, during gamete formation. Imprinted genes inherited from one parent are transcriptionally inactive in all or most tissues, while the non-imprinted copies from the other parent are active. Imprinting is a random event.

This imprint remains during the mammal's life, but it is erased and regenerated when passed to the next generation. Prader-Willi syndrome and Angelman's syndrome are good examples of genetic imprinting. While each disease exhibits its own distinct phenotype with very different symptoms, both syndromes are due to the same deletions in chromosome 15q11-13. Prader-Willi syndrome is maternally imprinted and Angelman's is paternally imprinted.

205. It is suggested in the passage that the methylated parental genes appear in which of the following forms in the cell nucleus?

  A. holo-DNA
  B. euchromatin
  C. heterochromatin
  D. pseudochromatin

206. According to the Lyon's hypothesis, how many Barr bodies are expected to be present in a cell of an individual with Klinefelter's syndrome (XXY)?

  A. zero
  B. one
  C. two
  D. three

207. Which of the following is a model for Prader-Willi genomic imprinting?

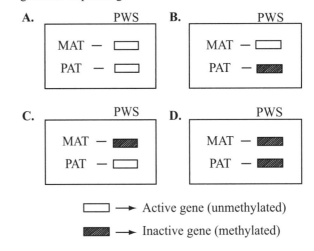

  ☐ ⟶ Active gene (unmethylated)
  ▨ ⟶ Inactive gene (methylated)

208. Which of the following animals is NOT expected to display maternal or paternal influences on the pattern of gene expression?

  A. African elephant
  B. kangaroo
  C. saw whet owl
  D. fin whale

209. Which of the following would most likely be found while examining the primary structure of a DNA-binding protein?

  A. beta-sheet
  B. alpha-helix
  C. globular bonding
  D. covalent bonding

Questions 210 through 221 are **NOT** based on a descriptive passage.

210. Gout is the name for a group of varied disorders caused by a decrease in secretion and excretion of uric acid. Which of the following organs is primarily responsible for elimination of uric acid?

  A. liver
  B. kidney
  C. large intestine
  D. spleen

211. Which of the following statements applies/apply to an autosomal dominant (AD) inheritance?

  I. A person needs a single copy of the mutant gene to inherit the disease.
  II. AD traits do not skip generations.
  III. Father to son transmission is not observed.

  A. I only
  B. I and II only
  C. II and III only
  D. I, II, and III

212. Which of the following is NOT a possible effect that may occur after a mutation?

  A. abnormal protein production
  B. abnormal carbohydrate production
  C. loss of enzyme function
  D. gain of enzyme function

213. In X-linked recessive inheritance, why does the disease gene often appear to skip generations?

  A. X-linked diseases are only expressed in males.
  B. All X-linked diseases display incomplete penetrance.
  C. Disease is primarily transmitted through unaffected carrier females.
  D. Males with an affected gene may transmit but not show the disease.

214. All of the following are true statements about events happening in DNA replication EXCEPT:

  A. RNA primers are necessary to allow polymerase attachment.
  B. DNA polymerase synthesizes and proofreads the DNA during replication.
  C. DNA polymerase adds deoxynucleotides in a 5′ to 3′ direction.
  D. Ligase relaxes positive supercoils that accumulate as the replication fork opens.

215. The following are characteristics of an unknown inheritance pattern:

  I. There is a 25% risk of having a homozygous normal child
  II. There is a 25% risk of having a homozygous affected child
  III. There is a 50% risk of having a heterozygous child

Which of the following Mendel's inheritance patterns most closely fits with the above information?

  A. autosomal dominant
  B. autosomal recessive
  C. X-linked dominant
  D. X-linked recessive

216. Using two six-sided dice, what is the probability (p) of randomly rolling a pair of 2s?

  A. 1/2
  B. 1/6
  C. 1/36
  D. 1/96

217. Adenosine deaminase deficiency is a genetic disease that causes the development of severe combined immunodeficiency (SCID) involving abnormalities in T and B-cells. Which of the following organs are expected to be underdeveloped in a person with SCID?

  A. bone marrow only
  B. thymus only
  C. thymus and bone marrow
  D. neither thymus nor bone marrow

218. Which of the following statements is associated with Okazaki fragments?

  A. They are part of the leading strand.
  B. They are pieces of DNA synthesized to fill in gaps after the removal of primer.
  C. They are covalently linked by DNA polymerase I.
  D. They are synthesized in a 5′-3′ direction by the DNA polymerase.

219. Myoglobin accepts oxygen from hemoglobin and releases it to the cytochrome oxidase system. Which of the following statements most accurately describes the physiological properties of myoglobin?

A. Myoglobin should have higher oxygen affinity than hemoglobin.

B. Myoglobin should have higher oxygen affinity than the cytochrome oxidase system.

C. Hemoglobin should have higher oxygen affinity than myoglobin.

D. Hemoglobin should have higher oxygen affinity than the cytochrome oxidase system.

220. Dialysis relies on a semipermeable membrane with physical pores of a specified size that exactly mimics the cell membrane. Which of the following substances cannot freely diffuse through the semipermeable membrane?

A. neutral gas
B. glucose
C. tiny hydrophobic rods
D. water

221. If a mother and father both have one mutant gene for a disease with an autosomal dominant inheritance, what is their risk of having an affected child?

A. 0
B. 25%
C. 50%
D. 75%

STOP. IF YOU FINISH BEFORE TIME IS CALLED, CHECK YOUR WORK. YOU MAY GO BACK TO ANY QUESTION IN THIS TEST BOOKLET.

LECTURE 3

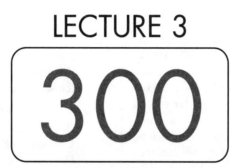

Biology Passages
Questions 222–332

Viruses are broadly grouped as animal, plant, or bacterial. Further classification separates them into DNA versus RNA viruses. Herpes simplex virus type 1 (HSV-1) infection is almost universal. Between recurrent episodes, HSV-1 lies dormant in the nervous system, which it accesses from infected skin via retrograde movement through afferent sensory nerve fibers. During this latency period, the nervous system serves as a viral reservoir from which infection can recur/activate. During viral reactivation, unrecognized shedding is a common way in which herpes simplex is transmitted. Following initial contact, production of herpes virus growth mediators is seen, which are related to tumor necrosis factors. Viral growth factors bind axon terminal receptors.

HSV structural core houses a large DNA genome found around a protein nucleosome. A structurally complex capsid surrounds this core. Outside the capsid are the tegument and a glycoprotein-covered envelope.

Viral infection can be *productive* if the cell is permissive and allows viral replication and virion release. For example, HSV-1 cell infection is often not productive due to a viral genome integration block that occurs upstream. However, stimulation of an infected cell will eliminate this block and allow for virion production. *Abortive infection* results when cells are non-permissive and *restrictive* attacks occur when a few virion particles are produced: viral production then ceases but the genome integration persists.

> HSV-1 Skin Contact → Skin Infection → HSV-1 Transported (Retrograde) Down the Axon → Ganglion Infected → HSV-1 Leaves the Ganglion → Re-infection of the Skin → HSV-1 Released from Skin → Secondary Lesions Heal

Table 1 Steps of Infection

Envelope	Present, with associated glycoproteins
Tegument	Protein-filled area
Capsid	Icosahedral
Core	Toroidal
Genome	Linear dsDNA (ds = double stranded)
Replication	Nuclear machinery
Assembly	Nuclear machinery

Table 2 Properties of Herpes Simplex

222. According to the passage, which infection type results in the integration of the viral genome into the host cell chromosome?

   I. productive infection
  II. abortive infection
 III. restrictive infection

  A. I only
  B. I and III only
  C. II and III only
  D. I, II, and III

223. The infectivity/particle ratio in picornaviruses can be as low as 0.1%. What is the predicted number of infectious particles present in a culture of 10,000 virions?

  A. 1
  B. 10
  C. 100
  D. 1000

224. HSV-1 is shed from the infected area and spread occurs as a result of direct contact with the lesion. From which of the following locations does HSV acquire its glycoprotein-covered envelope?

  A. rough ER during protein synthesis
  B. nuclear membrane after transcription
  C. outer cell wall during lysis
  D. storage vacuoles during lysis

225. Which of the following statements does NOT explain the abortive viral cycle?

  A. Host autoimmune antibodies match the viral antigen and prevent infection.
  B. Hepatitis C (liver infection) infected patient lacks 93% of viral liver cell receptors.
  C. Influenza virus surface antigen displays genetic drift based on random mutation.
  D. Invaded esophagus cells often lack DNA replication machinery.

226. During the latent phase of an HSV infection, viral DNA can be found in neuronal nuclei, in the form of genomic-length circular molecules. Where specifically in the nervous system will the latent virus be localized?

  A. axon hillock near the cell body
  B. afferent nervous system ganglion
  C. neurotransmitter storage vacuoles
  D. lower motor neuron dendrites

227. According to the information presented in the passage, which of the following must be true regarding tumor necrosis factors (TNF)?

    A. TNF function with nerve growth factors to stimulate voltage gated Na+ channels

    B. TNF are actively taken up by dendrites and transported toward neuron cell body

    C. TNF are produced following a malignant cancerous spread through the basement membrane

    D. TNF uptake and transport is inhibited following an injury to the axon terminal

228. According to the passage, radioactive tegument dye will be localized where?

    A. in a protein-filled area between the capsid and the DNA core

    B. in a protein-filled area between the capsid and the envelope

    C. in a protein-filled area between the envelope and extracellular glycoprotein

    D. in a protein-filled area between the DNA core and the nucleosome

---

Passage 302 (Questions 229-235)

Retroviruses, for example HIV-1, possess a lipid envelope, which surrounds a capsid with a dense inner core. The core contains 2 copies of single-stranded RNA, which is complexed with a *reverse transcriptase* and tRNA. Retroviruses also contain *proteases* and *integrases*.

The retroviral life cycle begins with the binding of the viral envelope glycoprotein to a specific receptor on the surface of the target cell. While in the host-cell cytoplasm, the *reverse transcriptase* is used to convert the single-stranded RNA viral genome into double-stranded linear DNA. HIV-1 viral DNA can cross the nuclear membrane and permanently integrate into the host cell genome. Proviral integration usually happens during the S phase of the cell cycle. Therefore, nondividing cells are usually resistant to retroviral infection.

Experiment 1

Nuclear structure of the HIV-1 viral genome was assayed to understand viral DNA stability in the pre-integration state. A "yellow" fluorescent viral protein was utilized to measure the rate of HIV-1 genome decay in the pre-integration state.

Nondividing T-cells were infected with the HIV-1 "yellow" virus. At set times following infection, a percentage of the infected nondividing cells were removed, stimulated to divide (activated), and viral decay was measured over time as a reduction in the fraction of infected T-cells from which virus could be extracted in its entirety following activation.

Results

Data demonstrated that, in HIV-1 infected activated T-cells, reverse transcription proceeded to completion and generated molecules that were suitable for genome integration. In resting inactivated T-cells, reverse transcriptase enzyme kinetics was much slower, with the reaction proceeding to completion in days rather than hours. Pre-integration state stability analysis revealed a viral decay half-life of 1.1 days.

229. Pathogen infectivity and virulence determines the outcome of an infection. Which of the following infection routes is LEAST likely to be used by virions attempting to implant onto living cells?

    A. the respiratory tract through the trachea

    B. the gastrointestinal tract through the esophagus

    C. bone penetration through periosteum

    D. the excretory system through the urethra

230. All of the following statements regarding retroviruses are true EXCEPT:

    A. RNA serves as a template for DNA synthesis
    B. retroviruses alter host cell genetic information by inserting into the chromosome line
    C. eukaryotic cells can produce reverse transcriptase
    D. reverse transcriptase functions in the cytoplasm

231. Which of the following cell types will most likely resist an infection by a retrovirus?

    A. helper T-cells
    B. epithelial cells of the GI tract
    C. epidermal cells
    D. nerve cells

232. Retroviral RNA has a 5´-end cap and a 3´-end polyadenylation site. Which of the following processes is responsible for converting retroviral RNA into the DNA provirus?

    A. translation
    B. transcription
    C. replication
    D. translocation

233. Which of the following conclusions regarding virions is supported by the information provided in the passage?

    A. Retroviruses are diploid.
    B. Virion particles lack enzymes.
    C. Retroviruses actively produce ATP.
    D. Virion reverse transcriptase is found in the envelope.

234. Many laboratories are in the earliest stages of developing anti-integrase compounds. Which of the following is LEAST important in order to produce the most effective medication possible?

    A. compound solubility in body fluids
    B. drug cost
    C. compound half-life
    D. drug toxicity

235. DiGeorge's syndrome (DGS) presents as a severe T-cell deficiency. Which of the following organs failed to develop in an individual diagnosed with DGS?

    A. the bone marrow
    B. the thyroid
    C. the thymus
    D. the spleen

Passage 303 (Questions 236-241)

Glycerol-based phospholipids arrange themselves into micelles under suitable conditions and serve as the basis for biological membranes. These phospholipids are free to: 1) diffuse along the plane of the bilayer—*lateral rotation*, 2) alternate between surfaces (from inner to outer or visa versa)—*flip flop*, and/or 3) spin on their axis—*axis rotation*. Critical micelle concentration (CMC) represents a value above which increasing concentration of that component forces micelle formation. Above CMC, the concentration of surfactant molecules is virtually constant and surfactant is at its optimum level of biological activity.

The membrane interior consists of molten fatty acid chains hydrophobically interacting with each other. At low temperatures cell membrane fluidity decreases; the membrane proceeds to become rigid and fragile. This is the basis for the freeze-fracture technique, which splits any membrane into 2 halves. Once the membrane is split, a p-face (cytoplasmic side) and e-face (extracellular side) result.

Longer fatty acid chains show a mass increase and melt at higher temperature. Unicellular organisms adapt to changing environmental temperatures by changing the fatty acid compositions of their membranes, generating a fluidity/rigidity ratio needed for homeostasis. Higher organisms use fatty acids of about the same length but increase membrane fluidity by elevating the extent of fatty acid unsaturation and/or increasing concentration of cholesterol.

Two experiments were conducted on four unicellular organisms (A-D). Growth index ratio (1= low growth and 10 = high growth) measures the colony number per cm^2.

Organism	% short fatty chains	Temp.	Growth Index
A	31	25° C	2
B	26	25° C	5
C	40	25° C	6
D	11	25° C	4

Table 1 Experiment 1 Results

Organism	% short fatty chains	Temp.	Growth Index
A	17	37° C	8
B	10	37° C	1
C	28	37° C	9
D	7	37° C	4

Table 2 Experiment 2 Results

GO ON TO THE NEXT PAGE.

236. Cellular adaptation involves the packaging of extra material in vacuoles for storage. Which of the following cells would be expected to have a high concentration of storage organelles?

A. adipocyte
B. cardiac cell
C. epithelial cell
D. erythrocyte

237. According to the passage, a decrease in the concentration of cholesterol in the membrane would have which of the following effects on a rigid membrane?

A. increased fluidity
B. decreased fluidity
C. increased electrostatic interaction
D. decreased protein content

238. Which of the following locations would be expected to display the greatest surfactant production?

A. kidney
B. brain
C. lung
D. heart

239. Based on experimental results presented in Tables 1 and 2, which organism prefers to grow at higher temperatures?

A. organism A
B. organism B
C. organism C
D. organism D

240. It can be inferred from the passage that which of the following is a possible movement type associated with *proteins* found in the plasma membrane?

I. Motion along the plane of the membrane
II. Sinking in and out of the membrane
III. Flip-flop in and out of the membrane

A. I only
B. I and II only
C. II and III only
D. I, II, and III

241. At what temperature would you expect the ratio of unsaturated to saturated fatty acids to be the lowest?

A. 10°C
B. 20°C
C. 30°C
D. 40°C

Questions 242 through 251 are **NOT** based on a descriptive passage.

242. The nucleocapsid, an outer portion of the naked capsid virion, protects the virion from the conditions in the gastrointestinal tract. Which of the following is the most likely mode of transmission for the naked capsid virion?

A. aerosol into the lungs
B. fecal oral route into the esophagus
C. through the skin following direct contact
D. through the mouth and into the nervous system

243. It is possible to artificially induce all virally infected cells to simultaneously lyse by exposing them to UV light or X-rays. Which of the following phases did the virus occupy prior to UV exposure?

A. growth lag phase
B. lytic phase
C. initiation phase
D. lysogenic phase

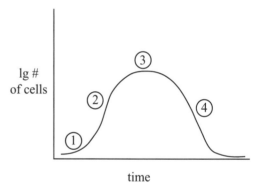

244. When examining a bacterial growth curve, which of the following phases will follow the stationary phase?

A. exponential growth phase
B. lag phase
C. cell death phase
D. constant population phase

245. Blood plasma makes up 5% of total body weight. Which of the following organics will NOT be found in blood plasma after a coagulation cascade?

A. amino acids
B. albumin
C. glucose
D. erythrocytes

---

246. Which of the following is the correct chronological order of events during a viral infection?

   A. attachment → penetration → uncoating → viral synthesis
   B. target cell binding → uncoating → penetration → viral synthesis
   C. attachment → target cell binding → uncoating → viral synthesis
   D. target cell binding → viral synthesis → penetration → uncoating

247. Bacteria can undergo genetic recombination. Which of the following is NOT a mechanism by which bacteria can obtain extra novel DNA?

   A. transformation
   B. conjugation
   C. translocation
   D. transduction

248. It is hypothesized that present-day mitochondria have evolved and adapted through a symbiotic relationship with host cells. Which of the following then must be true?

   A. the outer mitochondrial membrane house cristae and elementary particles
   B. mitochondria are not membrane limited
   C. mitochondria are present in all cells including red blood cells
   D. intercristal space houses low H^+ concentration

249. Which of the following is the most efficient metabolic pathway for producing energy?

   A. lactic acid production and aerobic respiration
   B. anaerobic respiration only
   C. anaerobic respiration and fermentation
   D. glycolysis followed by aerobic respiration

250. Which of the following is a characteristic of a prokaryotic organism?

   A. possesses a nucleus bounded by a nuclear membrane
   B. frequently contains a chitin-derived cell wall
   C. partly relies on glycolysis for ATP synthesis
   D. contains a variety of organelles

251. The nucleus and cytoplasm are bounded by membranes and contain a number of structural components that are classified into 2 categories: organelles or inclusions. Which of the following is properly categorized as an inclusion?

   A. ribosome
   B. lysosome
   C. fat
   D. pigment vacuole

Passage 304 (Questions 252-257)

Singer and Nicolson proposed the classic fluid mosaic model in which the phospholipid membrane is viewed as a two-dimensional bilayer of amphiphilic lipids. The morphology of the lipid system depends not only on the membrane composition, but also on the temperature and other additives such as cholesterol and protein.

Diffusion is the spontaneous mixing of molecules by random thermal motion, driven by the concentration gradient across any membrane. *Mass transfer* is any process in which diffusion plays a role. Fick's first law describes the limitations of membrane diffusion. It states that a solute's [S] rate of diffusion [J] through a membrane depends on the concentration gradient $[S_1] - [S_2]$ multiplied by the membrane surface area [A] and the membrane constant [p].

$$J = pA ([S_1] - [S_2])$$

When active transport is used to transfer necessities across the cell membrane, substrates are moved via a carrier molecule against the concentration gradient. Active transport is one of three types of biological work, the other two being movement and biosynthesis.

Frequently, pinocytosis may be used to transport high molecular weight molecules or large numbers of low molecular weight molecules across the cell membrane. In endocytosis a membrane-bound vesicle is formed to store extracellular molecules. If the vesicle isn't fully digested, an intracellular residual body may form; residual bodies are often seen as a sign of aging.

Molecule	Partition coefficient (*K*)	London Dispersion Forces
A	6.2×10^{-3}	56.4
B	3.7×10^{-4}	86.2
C	5.2×10^{-6}	100.3
D	2.4×10^{-5}	45.5

Table 1 *K* = solubility in oil/solubility in water

252. All molecules possess intrinsic thermal energy, which causes random movement. In solids, random movement may result in which of the following?

   A.   linear movement
   B.   vibrational oscillation
   C.   angular acceleration
   D.   parallel movement

253. Lung alveoli serve to increase the overall surface area available for diffusion. According to the passage, all of the following will increase the rate of diffusion EXCEPT:

   A.   increasing the $([S_1] - [S_2])$ across the cellular membrane
   B.   increasing surfactant production
   C.   the addition of a brush border, which further increases overall surface area
   D.   decreasing the thickness of the basement membrane between the lung and blood vessels

254. According to the passage, which of the following is NOT considered biological work?

   A.   action of the flagella
   B.   albumin production
   C.   osmosis
   D. H^+ ATPase activity

255. Which of the following is true regarding endocytosis?

   I.   a membrane bound vesicle will be digested by primary lysosomes
   II. it requires the use of ATP
   III. it depends on the presence of a cell surface receptor to initiate the recognition sequence

   A.   I
   B.   I and II only
   C.   II and III only
   D.   I, II, and III

256. According to Table 1, which of the following molecules will display the highest diffusion rate constant?

   A.   molecule A
   B.   molecule B
   C.   molecule C
   D.   molecule D

257. Which of the following lipid-soluble compounds can easily cross the *Salmonella* cell membrane?

   A.   prolactin
   B.   insulin
   C.   aldosterone
   D.   glucagon

Nicotinamide adenine dinucleotide (NAD$^+$), nicotinamide adenine dinucleotide phosphate (NADP$^+$), and flavin adenine dinucleotide (FAD$^+$) are three of the most important coenzymes in the cell. NAD$^+$ and FAD$^+$ receive electrons released from substrates during metabolic processes such as glycolysis and the Krebs cycle. Their reactive functionality during electron transfer reactions lies in the nicotinamide, with hydride transfer occurring at the C$_4$ atom. The rest of the molecule, two ribose rings, pyrophosphate (pp), adenine, and adenosine 29-phosphate (in the case of NADP), are responsible for specificity and affinity of enzyme binding.

The cytoplasm houses enzymes that synthesize NADH, which must be transported across the mitochondrial membrane in order to prevent cytoplasmic buildup. This transfer is achieved via one of two shuttles:

Glycerol Phosphate Shuttle (GPS)

Aspartate - Malate Shuttle (AMS)

Electrons flow down the mitochondrial respiratory transport chain, located in the inner mitochondrial membrane, eventually reaching and reducing oxygen. The F$_0$F$_1$ ATPase pump, with an F$_1$ catalytic group, utilizes mitochondrial intermembrane proton gradient for ATP production. ATP is generated from available ADP and inorganic phosphate. Slightly more than 3 protons enter the mitochondria for every molecule of ATP synthesized.

ATP synthesized inside the mitochondria is exported to the cytosol by the ATP/ADP exchanger. This ATP/ADP shuttle completes the oxidative phosphorylation (OXPHOS) process.

REDOX	POTENTIAL
Cytochrome Fe^{+3}/Fe^{+2}	+ 0.06
Pyruvate/Lactate	–0.19
FMN/FMNH$_2$	–0.20
NAD$^+$/NADH	–0.33

Table 1 Reduction Potential (Standard)

OXPHOS respiration is strongly stimulated by high ADP levels and by low intermembrane pH. That is, a high proton gradient is a positive effector of mitochondrial respiration. The higher the proton gradient, the more ATP will be produced.

258. Compounds with large negative standard potentials are strong reducing agents. According to Table 1, which one of the following is a poor oxidizing agent?

    A. FMN/FMNH$_2$
    B. NAD$^+$/NADH
    C. Pyruvate/Lactate
    D. Cytochrome C Fe^{+3}/ Fe^{+2}

259. The ATP/ADP exchanger is responsible for ATP/ADP contra-port from mitochondria. Atractyloside is a competitive inhibitor of this exchanger. High levels of atractyloside will result in:

    A. increased rate of respiration
    B. increased rate of ATP production
    C. increased intermembrane acidity
    D. increased concentration of mitochondrial ADP

260. The nicotinamide product is an important unit of currency in biochemical redox reactions. Genetic damage to which of the following will NOT affect NADH binding properties?

    A. adenine
    B. diphosphate
    C. two ribose rings
    D. pyrophosphate

261. A cardiac muscle cell has 40% more mitochondria than its skeletal counterpart. Which of the following components will most likely be produced in excess during a mitochondrial cardiac cell study?

    A. urea
    B. carbon monoxide
    C. oxygen
    D. water

262.   FMN + NADPH $\rightarrow$ FMNH$_2$ + NADP$^+$

In the above reaction, which of the listed processes is occurring?

    A. flavin luciferase activity
    B. electron transfer and ADP-ribosylation
    C. reduction of a flavin coenzyme
    D. desulfurization of NADP

263. Oxidation of methemoglobin results in the production of six moles of ATP. Roughly how many moles of hydride ion are translocated during the ATP production cycle?

   A.   6 moles
   B.   17 moles
   C.   18 moles
   D.   20 moles

264. The first reaction of the citric acid cycle (CAC) involves acetyl CoA condensing with OAA to form citrate. According to the passage, which of the following will have the maximum effect on CAC activation?

   A.   high ADP, high intermembrane pH, high ATP
   B.   low ADP, high intermembrane pH, high ATP
   C.   low ADP, low intermembrane pH, low ATP
   D.   high ADP, low intermembrane pH, low ATP

Passage 306 (Questions 265-270)

The exterior border of the outer membrane of gram-negative bacteria is composed of *lipopolysaccharides* (LPS). LPS chemical structure has been determined to contain: 1) an *endotoxic lipid A*, which is anchored to the bacterial cell membrane (found under the LPS layer) and 2) a *polysaccharide unit* consisting of an oligosaccharide core and an O-specific chain antigen. O-antigen signifies serotype specificity and is used in epidemiological studies to trace a disease to its source or follow its spread.

Septic shock is the invasion of the bloodstream by bacteria and can pose a major threat to critically ill patients. During septic shock, LPS endotoxin acts as a potent stimulator of the immune response. The presence of LPS often leads to the uncontrolled release of inflammatory cytokines and other inflammation mediators. Release of these pro-inflammatory molecules can lead to shock, multiple organ failure, hemorrhage, and disseminated intravascular coagulation. All of these effects are mediated by the release of tumor necrosis factor, IL-1, and other cytokines.

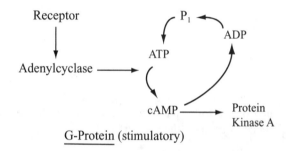

Figure 1

LBP, an acute-phase protein, has a central role in controlling the availability of LPS. A handful of molecules have been identified as antagonists of LBP, preventing its binding to inflammatory cytokine complexes. This may be a future target for drug therapy, resulting in improved plasma clearance of LPS. Phage-displayed peptide libraries are used to probe for specific binding domains on the LBP molecule for LPS.

	Normal	Pre-LPS release	4 Hrs Post-LPS release	10 Hrs Post-LPS release	24 Hrs Post-LPS release
WBC × 10³	70–80	73	24	32	70
RBC × 10³	110–125	118	62	62	67
Hemoglobin	125–150	100	99	97	99
Hematocrit	35–70	62	28	29	20
WBC (%) Differential	41–100	50	25	27	31

Table 1 Pre and Post LPS administration results

GO ON TO THE NEXT PAGE.

265. Which of the following components are necessary for the proper structure and function of lipopolysaccharide layer?

    I.   core molecule
   II. O-antigen
  III. lipid A toxin
  IV. lipo- subunit

    A.   I and IV only
    B.   I, II and IV
    C.   I, II and III
    D.   II and III only

266. *E. coli* exotoxin stimulates a cellular increase in cAMP, which results in a dramatic secretion of water into the lumen of the small intestine. This increased water secretion into the intestinal lumen accounts for the voluminous diarrhea seen in *E. coli* infection. In a patient with an *E. coli* infection, which of the following most likely results?

    A.   a decrease in ATP consumption by the small intestine
    B.   a decrease in overall peristalsis and levels of ADP
    C.   stimulation of the G-protein causes secretory diarrhea
    D.   an increase in normal bacterial flora will occur in two days

267. LPS is held in place by relatively weak cohesive forces. Which of the following attachments must be broken to dissociate LPS from the cell surface?

    A.   hydrophobic interactions
    B.   ionic bonds
    C.   covalent attachments
    D.   amide bonds

268. Which of the following statements correctly describes the outcome of rapid dilation of arteries and arterioles?

    A.   increased peripheral resistance with normal or increased cardiac function
    B.   increased blood pressure even though cardiac function may be decreased
    C.   peripheral resistance will decrease and cardiac function may decrease
    D.   impaired delivery of O_2, and removal of CO_2 by capillary vessels

269. Lipid A (pyrogenic) stimulates the release of interleukin-1 from macrophages, which acts on which of the following to increase basal body temperature?

    A.   cerebral cortex
    B.   hypothalamus
    C.   adrenal medulla
    D.   smooth muscle

270. According to Table 1, which lab value was unaffected by LPS and which lab value displayed fastest to normal rate return, respectively?

    A.   hemoglobin and WBC $\times 10^6$/mm
    B.   WBC (%) differential and hematocrit
    C.   WBC $\times 10^6$/mm and hemoglobin
    D.   hematocrit and RBC $\times 10^6$/mm

271. Chromatin is electron dense and composed of DNA and basic histone proteins, which lie in the grooves of the double helix DNA molecule. In regards to electrostatic interaction, what is the expected charge on a histone?

    A. positive
    B. negative
    C. neutral
    D. depends on the DNA concentration

272. A person with a coenzyme Q deficiency will have a defect in oxidative phosphorylation and an increase in anaerobic respiration. Which of the following would be expected in this person?

    A. accumulation of glucose
    B. accumulation of lactate
    C. high levels of ATP
    D. fructose deficiency

273. All of the following are characteristic of fungi EXCEPT:

    A. fungal diseases are responsive to antibiotic therapy
    B. fungi are usually present in a haploid state
    C. fungi possess chitin cell walls
    D. fungi can reproduce sexually and asexually

274. Thermogenin is a specialized inner membrane protein found in mitochondria. It transports protons back into the matrix bypassing the ATP synthase. What is the expected result post-thermogenin administration?

    A. increased mitochondrial ATP production
    B. accumulation of lactic acid
    C. elevated body temperature
    D. accumulation of glucose in the cytoplasm

275. Lysosomal enzyme extraction is being performed. Which of the following pH readings will inform the researcher that the correct organelle has been biopsied?

    A. 5.1
    B. 7.3
    C. 9.6
    D. 12.1

276. High titer volume enhances the viral transport into the nucleus, inducing GAP_2 cell cycle arrest. Which event occurs during the G_2 phase of the cell cycle?

    A. synthesis of DNA
    B. mitosis
    C. organelle growth and division
    D. cytokinesis

277. Cobra venom (cobra toxin) is a competitive inhibitor of acetylcholine. Which of the following is a likely outcome in an individual bitten by a cobra?

    A. excessive stimulation of most parasympathetic neurons
    B. CNS neuronal degeneration and death
    C. respiratory muscle paralysis
    D. rapid heart rate and dehydration

278. Many local anesthetics such as cocaine, lidocaine, etc. seem to dissolve in the hydrophobic core of the membrane and somehow inhibit some of the membrane-bound proteins. In particular, which of the following channels must be inhibited in order to cause a blockage of nerve conduction?

    A. the sodium channel
    B. the potassium channel
    C. the calcium channel
    D. the chloride channel

279. Vitamin A is lipid soluble. "Night blindness" may be an early sign of vitamin A deficiency and can occur by which of the following mechanisms?

    A. poor lipid absorption by the stomach
    B. incomplete lipid breakdown by mouth enzymes
    C. vitamin is unavailable through diet
    D. lack of amylase production by the pancreas

280. Cone cells are photoreceptors that respond best to which of the following stimuli?

    A. skin response to low-level non-colored light
    B. skin response to colored light
    C. eye response to high-level non-colored light
    D. eye response to colored light

Passage 307 (Questions 281-287)

Lipoteichoic and teichoic acids make up the outer cell membrane and determine the cell shape of gram-positive organisms. These glycerol or ribitol polymers are also involved in signal transduction programs that are responsible for regulating bacterial self-stimulated death or autolysis. Teichoic mutants deficient in the amino acid alanine are unable to control their shape and compartmentation.

The bacterial cell envelope consists of an inner cell membrane, cell wall, and an outer cell membrane. The cell wall is composed of overlapping peptidoglycan lattices that are interconnected by amino acid bridges. The two main cell wall sugars are N-acetyl glucosamine (NAG) and N-acetyl muramic acid (NAM). NAM is only found in bacteria. Muramic acid, D-amino acids, and diaminopimelic acid are not found in fungal cell walls.

Cytoplasm-based peptidoglycan synthesis depends on muramyl penta-peptide attaching to UDP. This muramyl penta-peptide/UDP complex is formed into a disaccharide penta-peptide with an attached *bridge* peptide. *Autolysins* fracture existing cell wall backbones to allow insertion of newly synthesized subunits. If these enzymes are overactive, the cell wall becomes degraded and high osmotic pressure kills the cell. Penicillin-binding proteins function to cross-link the inserted penta-peptide subunits. Teichoic and teichuronic acids are synthesized in the cell membrane before being moved and inserted into the existing cell wall.

281. Peptidoglycan backbone is complex and highly organized. Which of the following bonds will be found during a chemical evaluation of a peptidoglycan bridge?

    A.   phosphodiester
    B.   amide bond
    C.   hydrogen bond
    D.   ionic bond

282. *S. pyogenes* M-protein mediates bacterial attachment to epithelial surfaces of the upper GI tract. A large mutation in the M-protein gene would most likely result in which of the following?

    A.   mucus overproduction by esophageal goblet cells
    B.   bacterial attachment to intestinal CCK-producing cells
    C.   *S. pyogenes* over-attachment and infection of the nasopharynx
    D.   normal bacterial flora migration to the transverse colon

283. According to the passage, which of the following will be obtained by an omnivore that consumes fungus?

    A.   D-amino acids
    B.   muramic acid
    C.   thyroxine
    D.   diaminopimelic acid

284. The pentose phosphate pathway (PPP) occurs at all sites of fatty acid or steroid synthesis. Which of the following sites does NOT carry out PPP activity?

    A.   anterior pituitary gland
    B.   lactating mammary gland
    C.   liver
    D.   adrenal cortex

285. Peptidoglycans are found in all bacteria except *Chlamydia* and *Mycoplasma*. Which of the following then must be true?

    A.   *Mycoplasma* is gram positive.
    B.   *Chlamydia* is an extracellular parasite.
    C.   *Treponema* is identified via light-field microscopy.
    D.   *Mycoplasma* has no cell wall.

286. Which of the following metabolic processes occurs at a site other than the location of peptidoglycan synthesis?

    A.   glycolysis
    B.   Krebs cycle
    C.   fatty acid synthesis
    D.   steroid synthesis

287. It can be deduced from the passage that penicillins prevent bacterial division by inhibiting the synthesis of which of the following components?

    A.   cell membrane
    B.   genetic material
    C.   cell wall
    D.   diaminopimelic acid

Passage 308 (Questions 288-293)

Gram-negative bacteria have an internal cell membrane, a thin proteoglycan layer, and often a polysaccharide-based capsule. Proteoglycans consist of long chains of glycosaminoglycans (GAG) attached to a *core protein*. Each long chain is composed of repeating disaccharide units, which are directly attached to the extracellular matrix. The presence of carboxylic acid and heparan sulfate groups within GAGs gives them a net negative charge at physiologic pH. Na^+ serves as a counter-ion to electrically balance the negative charges on GAGs. In addition, GAG molecules have a polar-compound trapping effect; that is, in the presence of water, they form gels.

Most GAG synthesis occurs within the bacterial cell. The mRNA sequence guides the formation of the *core protein*. Afterwards, tetra-saccharide linking sequences are attached to serine residues on *core proteins* via O_2-glycosidic bonds.

Functions of glycosaminoglycans include:

1. Resist compression due to the gel formation

2. Prevent bulk flow of extracellular fluid during mechanical stress (i.e. change in position)

3. Bind to surface proteins

Bacteriophages have means of breaching the proteoglycan barrier and entering the cell. Lipopolysaccharides, cell wall proteins, teichoic acids, or flagellar proteins are often used as viral receptor sites. During its DNA injection, bacteriophage tail fibers serve as *reversible* attachment sites by individually binding the bacterial cell surface. This reversible binding is Mg^{+2} and Ca^{+2}-dependent and does not occur when these cations are deficient.

288. The reversible bacteriophage-cell binding most likely relies on which of the following adhesion forces?

   A. hydrophobic interactions
   B. electrostatic interactions
   C. covalent interactions
   D. london-dispersion interactions

289. If GAG synthesis were to occur in a eukaryotic cell, the protein core would be modified by the addition of tetra-saccharide residues at this cellular location:

   A. the nucleus
   B. the rough endoplasmic reticulum
   C. the smooth endoplasmic reticulum
   D. the Golgi apparatus

290. *Hyaluron*, the only glycosaminoglycan that is not attached to a *core protein*, is used to link proteoglycans together. Which of the following is a possible function of *hyaluron*?

   A. nerve cell division
   B. heart contraction
   C. peristalsis
   D. wound healing

291. Based on the information presented in the passage, which of the following is NOT found in *all* bacterial cells?

   A. cell membrane
   B. nucleoid
   C. ribosomes
   D. capsule

292. Proteoglycans are a component of animal cell membranes. Which of the following is a possible function of proteoglycans within the membrane?

   A. cell dehydration
   B. attachment point for bacteriophage tail fibers
   C. steroid hormone receptor
   D. cell-to-cell attachment

293. Renal glomerular filtration membrane is composed of several glycosaminoglycans, especially heparan sulfate. According to the passage, what purpose does heparan sulfate serve in the kidney?

   A. It restricts filtration of large negatively charged molecules.
   B. The large negative surface charge acts to stabilize the filtration membrane.
   C. The charge is used to decrease the thickness of the filtration membrane.
   D. It prevents the passage of platelets.

GO ON TO THE NEXT PAGE.

Bacteria possess a number of mechanisms that allow them to transfer genetic material from one cell to another. Fertility factor genes (represented by an F) confer the ability to perform DNA transfers. F^+ male bacterium houses fertility factor genes on a plasmid or on the genome. F^+ bacteria cells can induce pilus formation, which is a bridge used to attach to neighboring bacterial cells. Under normal circumstances, the pilus breaks prior to the entire bacterial genome being transferred to F^- bacteria. F^+ gene also functions as a "tugboat" to pull the genetic information across the pilus into the recipient cell. The process of pilus formation and DNA transfer is known as conjugation.

There are three main fertility factor genes: HFr, F', and F^+. HFr occurs when the F^+ gene becomes integrated into the main bacterial genome. When dealing with HFr, the bacterial genome can be measured in time (min.) from origin of transfer or replication. The amount of time it takes a gene to be transferred indicates its location relative to the origin of replication.

F' is an episome, which is a small circular piece of DNA that contains fertility genes and a few other genes. These other genes are transferred very efficiently from one bacterium to the next. F^+ is a small circular piece of DNA carrying only fertility genes.

294. What is the predicted shape of a *Streptococcus pneumoniae*?

- **A.** long rod with pointed ends
- **B.** small sphere
- **C.** loose spiral
- **D.** thin vibrio

295. Which of the following statements is most effective at disproving concepts of bacterial conjugation, transformation, or transduction?

- **A.** bacterial genomic sequences suggest that genes in the past have moved from one species to another
- **B.** the F^+ gene can be initially found in all cells and then is selectively degraded
- **C.** the spread of antibiotic resistance may have been aided by the transfer of resistance genes within a bacterial population
- **D.** many bacteria possess enzymes that enable them to destroy foreign DNA that gets into their cells

296. Which of the following structures frequently serves as densely packed reserve for material and energy in a bacterial cell?

- **A.** flagella
- **B.** plasmid
- **C.** inclusion
- **D.** fimbriae

297. According to the passage, which of the following is NOT a feature of the F^+ factor or conjugation?

- **A.** DNA transfer requires cell-to-cell contact
- **B.** DNA transfer occurs in one direction only
- **C.** conjugation requires plasmid DNA to recombine with recipient DNA
- **D.** can be used to establish helicase activity at the origin of replication

298. Which of the following is correct regarding conjugation and DNA replication, respectively?

- **A.** both processes are conservative
- **B.** conservative, semi-conservative
- **C.** semi-conservative, conservative
- **D.** neither process is semi-conservative

299. Episomes are known to carry genes that make bacteria resistant to the inhibitory action of antibiotics. Which of the following allows these genes to be transferred so effectively?

- **A.** episomes are genome integrated, which allows for rapid replication
- **B.** F' genes can conjugate across before the pilus breaks
- **C.** the genome has multiple origins of replication
- **D.** F^+ DNA is full of fertility gene repeats and unresponsive to mutation

300. For categorical purposes, F^- bacterium can be properly described as a:

- **A.** male
- **B.** wild-type
- **C.** beneficial mutation
- **D.** female

---

301. Influx of which of the following will cause the release of neurotransmitter-Z into the synaptic cleft?

   A.   influx of Ca^{2+}
   B.   influx of Na^+
   C.   stimulation of gap junctions
   D.   influx of K^+ through myelin

302. Glucose molecules directly rely on a sodium gradient and indirectly on ATP hydrolysis to cross out of the intestinal lumen into epithelial cells. This process is an example of:

   A.   primary active transport mechanism
   B.   secondary active transport mechanism
   C.   facilitated diffusion mechanism
   D.   passive diffusion mechanism

303. An integral membrane glycoprotein tightly interacts with the plasma membrane. Which of the following bonds provides the greatest level of protein/membrane interaction and stability in this case?

   A.   electrostatic interaction
   B.   covalent bond
   C.   hydrophobic interaction
   D.   disulfide linkage

304. Which of the following is NOT true of viruses?

   A.   viruses require a host cell to reproduce
   B.   viruses produce ATP
   C.   viruses contain DNA
   D.   viruses contain RNA

305. Thyroid, aldosterone, and insulin are three major hormonal controls over the sodium/potassium pump. Out of the three listed, in which of the following locations is the cholesterol-derived one produced?

   A.   pancreas
   B.   adrenal cortex
   C.   liver
   D.   thyroid gland

306. Surfactant is a soluble compound that reduces interfacial tension between liquids and will be found in:

   A.   the esophagus
   B.   the trachea
   C.   the alveoli
   D.   the pharynx

307. Viral affinity for specific body tissue is determined by all of the following factors EXCEPT:

   A.   cell's ability to support viral replication
   B.   physical barriers that prevent or assist viral entry
   C.   local temperature, pH, and non-specific body secretions
   D.   lack of digestive enzymes and bile in the GI tract that may inactivate some viruses

308. Which of the following metabolic processes occurs in both the mitochondria and cytosol?

   A.   glycolysis
   B.   gluconeogenesis
   C.   electron transport chain
   D.   Krebs cycle

309. Fluoroacetate, a potent toxin extracted from plants, is converted to fluorocitrate, which is a strong inhibitor of the TCA cycle. Which of the following would be expected in a person exposed to fluoroacetate?

   A.   an increase in intracellular levels of ATP
   B.   an increase in intracellular levels of glucose
   C.   a decrease in levels of ethanol
   D.   a decrease in the function of the electron transport chain

310. All of the following statements apply to microtubules EXCEPT:

   A.   They are able to move vesicles and other storage inclusions.
   B.   They serve a cytoskeletal role.
   C.   They are linear polymers of tubulin.
   D.   They make up the thin myofilament (actin) in skeletal muscle.

Passage 310 (Questions 311-317)

The Fungi Kingdom consists of organisms that continue the ecosystem nutrient cycle. Members of this kingdom decompose wood, paper, cloth, and other products. Although fungi are a large and diverse group of eukaryotes, there are three major fungal divisions of practical importance: mold, yeast, and mushrooms.

Yeasts are unicellular, grow optimally at 37° C, and divide by budding. They grow in sugar-rich habitats such as fruits, flowers, and trees. Molds are multicellular (filamentous) and grow well at below room temperature. Recent information regarding temperature-dependent fungal growth indicates that the *time (X) vs. temperature (Y)* relationship is steeper than originally thought, and not quite as log-linear. Between 4.44° to 23.8° C, growth rates double for each 4° C temperature increase.

Fungi are chemically and genetically similar to animals, which makes fungal diseases difficult to treat. These diseases often affect the outer body surfaces. Fungal infection can also occur on epithelial surfaces of lumenal structures.

Fungal superinfection is an infection on top of an original bacterial infection. A fungal superinfection usually results after antibiotic therapy. Normal body flora is then interrupted, allowing other pathogens to flourish and divide. Fungal diseases are not responsive to antibiotic therapy and there is a limited number of antifungal agents available.

Temp. F	P. type A	P. type B	Yeast
5	0.019	0.016	0.004
10	0.026	0.022	0.008
15	0.035	0.031	0.013
20	0.047	0.043	0.021
25	0.063	0.018	0.033
30	0.084	0.012	0.052

Table 1 Growth rates of fungi as function of temperature.

311. Which of the following information can be used to distinguish yeast from bacterial cells?

 A. fungi are more significant animal pathogens than bacteria
 B. unlike fungi, bacterial species contain rigid cell walls
 C. yeast are much larger than bacterial cells
 D. fungi species lack internal cell structures

312. According to the passage, which of the following can be predicted when comparing new temperature-dependent measuring techniques to old ones?

 A. mycobacteria is no longer acid fast
 B. yeast growth slope shows a larger value
 C. *H. influenza* grows faster than yeast on chocolate agar
 D. mold log-linear factor is larger than expected

313. Despite its name, *Ringworm* is not a worm at all, but a fungal infection with an irregularly shaped lesion. Which of the following locations will be LEAST likely to develop *Ringworm*?

 A. scalp
 B. esophagus
 C. large intestine
 D. liver

314. Three hundred mold colonies were incubated at 10° C; the temperature was then increased to 21° F. What is the predicted colony number at the higher temperature?

 A. 2,330
 B. 1,190
 C. 4,980
 D. 3,450

315. Which of the following must be true regarding gram-positive spore-forming bacteria?

 A. all gram-positive rods form spores when nutrients are limited
 B. spores are highly resistant to heat and chemicals
 C. spores have high metabolic activity and can be destroyed at 160° C
 D. autoclave is not effective in spore elimination

316. According to Table 1, which of the following species can be assumed to be mold?

   I. P. type A
   II. P. type B
   III. P. type C
   IV. yeast

   A. I only
   B. II only
   C. I and IV only
   D. I, III, and IV

317. Saprophyte is any organism that depends on dead plant or animal tissue for a source of nutrition and metabolic energy. Which of the following is the most appropriate definition of a fungus?

   A. eukaryotic multicellular heterotroph
   B. parasitic, eukaryotic plant
   C. saprophytic plants
   D. saprophytic heterotroph

Passage 311 (Questions 318-323)

The first fungi were multicellular organisms that developed independently of plants from colonial protists. Mycorrhizal fungi were the first fungi to relocate out of the aquatic habitat. These fungi grow in plant roots and help obtain phosphorus and other essential nutrients from the soil. The fungus makes these nutrients available to the plant; in exchange, the plant nourishes the fungus.

Like plants and fungi, animals also developed from colonial protists after establishing a division of labor among cells. Each protist colony became hollow and began cell differentiation, forming somatic cells and gametes. Next came a process that is unique and unifying to all animals. Some of the cells folded inwards to produce a blastopore, which continued to fold inward until it formed the digestive tract.

Sponges, of the phylum Porifera, can be accurately categorized as the first animals. Sponges are very primitive and lack a complete digestive tract, digesting their food inside their cells. Sponges most likely originated from choanoflaggellate protists that are found at the bottom of shallow ponds.

Protists themselves were the first eukaryotes and were produced by monerans after membrane infolding and endosymbiosis. Protists served a key role in producing all other types of multicellular eukaryotes. Each line was produced by a different type of protist and arose independently. They are the ancient ancestors of all eukaryotic life in the world, including our own.

318. According to the passage, which of the following statements accurately describes the evolutionary development of fungi, protist, plants, and animals?

   A. Members of the animal kingdom are the only organisms that have a digestive tract.
   B. Members of the protista and animal kingdoms are the only organisms that have a digestive tract.
   C. Fungi developed from plants independently of colonial protists.
   D. Plants developed from colonial protists independently of fungi.

319. Which of the following descriptions applies/apply to members of the kingdom Protista?

   I. lack a nucleus
   II. contain membrane-bound organelles
   III. contain 80S ribosomes

   A. I only
   B. II only
   C. II and III only
   D. I, II, and III

GO ON TO THE NEXT PAGE.

320. Which of the following ecological terms most appropriately describes the relationship between Mycorrhizal fungi and plants?

A. symbiosis
B. mutualism
C. commensalism
D. parasitism

321. All of the following are functions of the animal cell membrane, EXCEPT:

A. regulation of cell-cell interaction
B. maintain structural integrity
C. synthesis of carbohydrates
D. ligand recognition

322. It can be inferred from the passage that which of the following primitive cellular structures were most likely to be well developed in the sponges of the phylum *Porifera*?

A. nucleus
B. lysosomes
C. endoplasmic reticulum
D. peroxisomes

323. Endoparasites live intracellularly in the digestive tract. Which of the following organs is most likely to be inhabited by endoparasites?

A. gall bladder
B. spleen
C. adrenal gland
D. trachea

Questions 324 through 332 are **NOT** based on a descriptive passage.

324. Which of the following is the main action of angiotensin converting enzyme (ACE), which is produced in the lungs?

A. activation of surfactant
B. increase renin synthesis
C. inhibition of the immune response via angiotensinogen
D. increase concentration of angiotensin II

325. *Giardia lamblia* infection causes a disease known as Giardiasis, which presents with non-bloody diarrhea, abdominal pain, cramps, and weight loss. Which of the following systems is infected in a patient diagnosed with Giardiasis?

A. respiratory system
B. excretory system
C. digestive system
D. musculoskeletal system

326. Based on the organization of their cellular structures, all living cells can be divided into two groups: prokaryotic and eukaryotic. All of the following kingdoms are composed of eukaryotic cells EXCEPT:

A. kingdom Plantae
B. kingdom Monera
C. kingdom Protista
D. kingdom Fungae

327. In resting T-cells, enzyme kinetics of the *reverse transcription* process is much slower than in activated T-cells, with the reaction proceeding to completion in three days rather than hours. What is the expected level of genetic material in an activated T-cell?

A. low DNA to RNA conversion
B. high RNA to DNA conversion
C. low RNA to DNA conversion
D. high protein to RNA conversion

328. Surfactant is produced by pneumocytes and is fully functional when conditions allow it to form *micelles*. Which of the following descriptive properties most likely applies to surfactant?

A. It is a hydrophilic compound.
B. It is a hydrophobic compound.
C. It is an acidic compound.
D. It is an enzyme.

329. The nervous system maintains homeostasis via a rapid response mechanism. The motor pathway of the autonomic nervous system generally contains:

A. a long single neuron
B. two neurons
C. three neurons
D. unpredicted number of neurons

330. The autonomic parasympathetic nervous system is utilized to control all of the following organs EXCEPT

A. the heart via acetylcholine
B. muscles constricting the eye via acetylcholine
C. salivary glands of the mouth via acetylcholine
D. cortisol release by the adrenal gland via acetylcholine

331. Prions are filterable particles that can transmit disease but do not generate an immune response. Which of the following cell lines will most likely be elevated in a person exposed to prions?

A. T-cells
B. macrophages
C. plasma cells
D. red blood cells

332. Insulin is a polypeptide synthesized by the pancreas. Which of the following methods can be used in vitro to degrade insulin?

A. hydrolysis
B. dehydration
C. esterification
D. evaporation

STOP. IF YOU FINISH BEFORE TIME IS CALLED, CHECK YOUR WORK. YOU MAY GO BACK TO ANY QUESTION IN THIS TEST BOOKLET.

60

LECTURE 4

400

Biology Passages
Questions 333–445

Cilia and flagella are organelles of motility or propulsion. The asymmetric axoneme, with a negative depolymerized and a positive polymerized end, is a microtubule bundle that forms the core of all eukaryotic propulsion organelles. Microtubule polarity is a very important feature and is responsible for direction-dependent cellular events such as neuron vesicle transport.

The interaction of microtubules results in movement, which is driven by energy-utilizing proteins such as *kinesin*. The axoneme/microtubule complex glides unidirectionally over *kinesin*, which translocates from the negative to positive end on the microtubule. To move forward, the flagellum is rotated counterclockwise and the organism darts ahead in a direction parallel to the flagellum's long axis. If flagellar rotation is set clockwise, the bacterium remains in place to uptake chemoattractants (i.e., glucose). Cilia are rigid during the power stroke and flexible at rest. When cilia are active, they move the cell in a direction perpendicular to the beating pattern. Ca^{2+} and cAMP are two factors regulating ciliary locomotion.

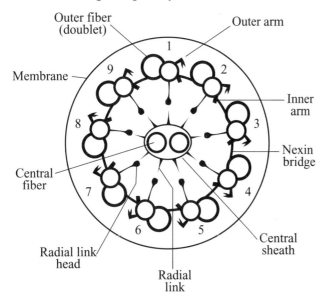

Figure 1

A ciliary cross-section displays a circle of nine peripheral doublets, each of which has one complete microtubule. A core microtubule doublet forms a central sheath, which connects to peripheral doublets by radial spokes. Each peripheral doublet possesses a *nexin* inter-doublet arm, with internal/external arm components, that links and holds peripheral microtubule columns together. Dynein, located on internal/external arms, is a large protein responsible for ATP-dependent beating action. Dynein requires Mg^{2+} and ATP to function properly. Locomotion frequency is higher at increased ATP concentrations. Dynein arms act as swinging cross-bridges to generate force by attaching to neighboring microtubules.

	Cilia Paralysis	Flagella Paralysis	Paralysis of Both
Drug A	1	2	1.5
Drug B	4	4	4
Drug C	2	5	3.5
Drug D	5	3	4

Table 1 Drug Efficiency
(1 = highly efficient, 5 = highly inefficient)

333. According to the passage, which of the following is responsible for peripheral microtubule stability?

    A. dynein
    B. nexin
    C. kinesin
    D. radial spokes

334. *Nocadazol* binds tubulin and inhibits structural microtubule assembly at the positive end. Which of the following would most likely be seen in a patient after a nocadazol injection?

    A. tubule destabilization due to incomplete polymerization
    B. incomplete nexin links
    C. completely inhibited dynein ATPase activity
    D. increased synthesis of rigid cilia

335. According to Table 1, which drug is optimal for esophageal cilia inhibition without causing male sterility?

    A. drug A
    B. drug B
    C. drug C
    D. drug D

336. A bacterium containing both propulsion organelles is chemoattracted north. In which direction do cilia and flagella face, respectively?

    A. east, north
    B. south, east
    C. west, south
    D. north, south

GO ON TO THE NEXT PAGE.

337. According to the passage, which of the following can serve to activate the dynein arm when Mg^{2+} is unavailable?

  A. sodium ion and ATP
  B. calcium ion and ATP
  C. Fe^{3+} and ADP
  D. Be ion and cAMP

338. A cardiac muscle cell is comprised primarily of which of the following?

  A. protein
  B. lipids
  C. water
  D. DNA

339. Charcot-Marie-Tooth disease effects kinesin, a protein similar to dynein. Which of the following is the most likely effect of Charcot-Marie-Tooth disease?

  A. high blood glucose
  B. decreased urinary output
  C. malnutrition
  D. muscle weakness due to axonal dysfunction

Passage 402 (Questions 340-346)

Lysosomes are digestive organelles that store acid hydrolases, which then degrade macromolecules and older organelles. In lysosomal storage diseases, one or more lysosomal hydrolases are non-functional, leading to a buildup of undigested material. They are inherited metabolic disorders. An increase in lysosomal size and number can also be expected in lysosmal storage diseases.

There are 3 steps in lysosomal synthesis:

1. Cellular endocytosis relies on cell surface receptors, which are situated in areas known as coated pits. As extracellular components bind to the cell surface receptors, the coated pits pinch in and off to form *clathrin peptide-coated vesicles*. Once the vesicle is in the cytoplasm, the clathrin coat is lost and homo-vesicles fuse with one another to form an *early endosome*. This fusion relies on snare peptides to allow for vesicle-vesicle interaction.

2. Vesicles from the Golgi apparatus with mannose-6 phosphate surface receptors bud off the trans Golgi complex. These Golgi vesicles contain inactive lysosomal hydrolase enzymes. The Golgi vesicles fuse with the *early endosome*, which contains many H^+ ATPases designed to lower internal lysosomal pH. Out of this fusion, the *late endosome* is born. *Late endosomes* may not be able to digest all vesicular contents.

3. Mature *late endosomes* are known as lysosomes, which are considered the end product of endocytosis.

Peroxisomes are self-replicating bodies within the cell that contain enzymes similar to those found in lysosomes. However, the enzymes in peroxisomes are not obtained from the Golgi apparatus. Peroxisomes detoxify the body of hydrogen peroxide (H_2O_2) and other metabolites via mechanisms that utilize oxygen.

Disease Type	Deficient enzyme	Disease Name	Metabolic Buildup
Mucopoly-sacchari-dosis	L-iduronidase	Hurler's	Heparan and dermatan sulfate
Sphingo-lipidosis	glucocerebrosidase	Gaucher's	Gluco-cerebroside
Sphingo-lipidosis	hexosaminidase A	Tay-Sachs	GM2-ganglioside
MPS II	L-iduronosulfate sulfatase	Hunter	Heparan and dermatan sulfate

Table 1 Lysosomal Storage Disease

340. A late endosome fuses with a phagocytic vacuole forming a phagolysosome. Which of the following cells is responsible for bacterial phagocytosis?

    A. T-cell
    B. macrophage
    C. stomach epithelial cell
    D. liver cell

341. Hydrolases may accidentally leak out of the lysosome but are unlikely to damage any of the internal cellular structures because:

    A. The cytoplasm contains several coenzymes that inhibit hydrolases from functioning.
    B. Hydrolases are only active at an acidic (pH 5.5) pH.
    C. Peroxisomes and other organelles absorb free hydrolases.
    D. Cells rapidly expel all hydrolases via exocytosis.

342. In addition to clathrin-coated vesicles, which of the following enzymes are located in the cytoplasm?

    A. RNA polymerase
    B. Krebs cycle enzymes
    C. enzymes necessary for glycolysis
    D. cell wall synthesis enzymes

343. All of the following regarding lysosomes are true, EXCEPT:

    A. Lysosomes do not degrade old organelles such as the smooth ER.
    B. Lysosomes handle products of receptor-mediated endocytosis.
    C. Phagolysosomes may house digested bacteria parts.
    D. Lysosomes are responsible for cellular waste disposal.

344. Tay-Sachs is a lysosomal storage disease that causes a pathologic accumulation of an undigested substrate. Which of the following is the main cause of the symptoms seen in Tay-Sachs?

    A. absence of lysosomal glucocerebrosidase
    B. defective rough ER
    C. excessive lysosome production to diminish symptoms
    D. stimulation of uncontrolled cell division

345. According to Table 1, which of the following enzymes are active in the same metabolic pathway?

    A. L-iduronidase and hexosaminidase A
    B. glucocerebrosidase and sulfate protease
    C. hexosaminidase A and L-iduronosulfate sulfatase
    D. L-iduronosulfate sulfatase and L-iduronidase

346. Based on the information in the passage, which of the following would be expected to contain the most peroxisomes?

    A. heart
    B. stomach
    C. liver
    D. pancreas

A potential or voltage difference, which can be measured by a voltmeter, exists across membranes of all viable cells The voltmeter electrodes possess a tiny diameter and are inserted into cells to measure some typical values of potential differences, which range from –60 to –90 mV. Regardless of the exact value, the intracellular fluid is always negatively charged.

The resting membrane potential is the result of K^+, Na^+, and Cl^- concentration gradients across the cell membrane and the actions of the sodium/potassium ATPase and other ion pumps. At rest, "leaky" potassium channels display the greatest permeability and consequently determine the resting membrane potential.

In most cells, the resting membrane potential remains relatively constant. However, nerve and muscle cells are exceptions because they are excitable in nature. Excitable cells are those that can be stimulated to create a tiny electrical current that allows the transmission of an action potential.

A depolarization threshold must be overcome in order to fire an action potential. Once the threshold is reached, sodium channels swing open as the ion fills the intracellular environment. During repolarization, sodium channels close and potassium conductivity increases. This recovery phase is also predominated by the sodium/ potassium pump, which resets ionic levels that were altered during the action potential.

Parameter	Intracellular	Extracellular
Na^+	10	140
K^+	120	4
Cl^-	10	110
Ca^{2+}	10^{-4}	2.5
HCO_3^-	10	24
pH	7.1	7.4

Table 1 Average Cellular Concentrations (in mM)

347. Based on information presented in the passage, which of the following will contribute to setting a cell membrane potential?

   I. ion concentration gradient
   II. number of functional channels
   III. open or closed state of channels

   A. I only
   B. III only
   C. I and III only
   D. I, II, and III

348. In a cell with a very negative resting membrane potential (hyperpolarized), which of the following would you expect to occur?

   A. K^+ channels are open, Na^+ and Cl^- channels closed
   B. K^+ and Na^+ channels are closed, Cl^- channels open
   C. Ca^{2+}, Na^+ and K^+ channels are open, Cl^- channels closed
   D. K^+ channels are closed, Na^+ and Cl^- channels open

349. Based on the information presented in the passage, which of the following transport mechanisms is utilized by the "leaky" K^+ channel?

   A. active transport
   B. facilitated diffusion
   C. simple diffusion
   D. endocytosis

350. Hyperkalemia is a condition where the extracellular concentration of K^+ is significantly increased. Which of the following is an effect of hyperkalemia?

   A. resting potential will become more negative
   B. increased difficulty in action potential generation
   C. decreased membrane threshold
   D. decreased urine production

351. According to Table 1, where is the H^+ concentration the greatest?

   A. intracellular compartment
   B. extracellular compartment
   C. both the same
   D. external environment

352. Which of the following ions contributes the most to the resting membrane potential?

   A. Na^+
   B. K^+
   C. Cl^-
   D. H^+

353. According to the passage, which of the following channels is expected to have the greatest cell membrane concentration?

   A. ungated sodium channels
   B. ungated potassium channels
   C. ungated chlorine channels
   D. ungated calcium channels

354. Which of the following neurotransmitters is used by pre-ganglionic neurons of the parasympathetic component of the autonomic nervous system?

    A. acetylcholine
    B. epinephrine
    C. glutamate
    D. gastrin

355. Voltage gated Na^+ channels are involved in bioelectrical activity in which of the following non-excitable cells?

    A. nerve cells
    B. skeletal muscle cells
    C. cardiac cells
    D. epithelial cells

356. A group of cells designed to perform a common function is defined as:

    A. an organ system
    B. a compound
    C. a tissue
    D. a cell

357. All of the following rely on propulsion activity provided by cilia or flagella EXCEPT:

    A. the female reproductive tract
    B. sperm
    C. the urinary tract
    D. the respiratory tract

358. Which of the following somatic sensory receptors are used for pain?

    A. mechanoreceptors
    B. thermoreceptors
    C. nociceptors
    D. chemoreceptors

359. Bacterial metabolism can occur in the presence or absence of oxygen. Organisms that are unable to grow in oxygen are:

    A. obligate anaerobes
    B. facultative anaerobes
    C. microaerophilic
    D. obligate aerobes

360. Purkinje fibers of the cardiac conduction pathway have large diameters and short axons. What can be deduced about their conduction velocity?

    A. slow, Na^+ channel dependent
    B. fast, Na^+ channel dependent
    C. slow, ion channel independent
    D. fast, ion channel independent

361. Neurotransmitters are small molecules that are liberated by a presynaptic neuron into the synaptic cleft and cause a change in the postsynaptic membrane potential. This change can be either:

    I. a direct depolarization
    II. direct hyperpolarization
    III. activation of a second messenger

    A. I and II only
    B. I and III only
    C. II and III only
    D. I, II, and III

362. A capsule is a major virulence factor found in *B. fragilis*. It inhibits phagocytosis and promotes a constant infection by preventing the activity of:

    A. skin cells
    B. T-cells
    C. platelets
    D. macrophages

363. For the purpose of classification, the human spinal cord is defined as part of which of the following?

    A. peripheral nervous system
    B. somatic nervous system
    C. autonomic nervous system
    D. central nervous system

Passage 404 (Questions 364-370)

The neuron is made up of a cell body, axon, dendrites, and axon terminal. An axon extends from the cell body and ends in an axon terminal, from which neurotransmitters are released and cell-to-cell communication takes place. Axons are often wrapped in a whitish lipoprotein layer called *myelin*, which acts as a high-resistance, low-capacitance insulator. The myelin coat is interrupted at intervals by nodes of Ranvier, which are areas where the axon membrane is bare and exposed to the extracellular matrix. Axon terminals are unmyelinated. They are separated from the corresponding effector cell by a synaptic cleft.

Dendrites also arise from the cell body; they are shorter and thinner than axons, and are never myelinated. Dendrites function to increase the cell body receptive area. However, it has been shown that dendrites can also synapse with other dendrites.

Neurons that release acetylcholine (Ach) are called cholinergic neurons. They convey sensory information and control muscular tension/activity. Cholinergic neurons possess inhibitory activity and function as part of the parasympathetic nervous system. (Neurons that release dopamine and norepinephrine, on the other hand, are sympathetic by nature.) There are two types of cholinergic receptors: nicotinic and muscarinic. The nicotinic receptor is a channel protein that opens following ACh binding, allowing for the diffusion of ions. The muscarinic receptor is a membrane protein that, once bound by ACh, causes an indirect ion channel opening through a second messenger cascade. Therefore, the muscarinic synapse is slower than a nicotinic one. Muscarinic receptors predominate at higher levels of the central nervous system, while nicotinic receptors are prevalent in the spinal cord and neuromuscular junctions.

364. The nervous system is divided into *gray* and *white matter*. The *gray matter* is composed of unmyelinated components. Which nervous system component will most likely be found in the *white matter*?

    A.   nucleus
    B.   dendrite
    C.   axon
    D.   synapse

365. According to the passage, where will a muscarinic receptor be located?

    A.   postganglionic parasympathetic neuron
    B.   enteric nervous system surrounding the GI tract
    C.   superior sympathetic ganglion
    D.   cerebellar motor coordination tract

366. Amino acids can act as inhibitory or excitatory neurotransmitters. For instance, GABA, an amino acid, can cause a major inhibitory effect in the CNS. Which of the following is the most likely action of GABA?

    A.   depolarizes the nerve cell
    B.   hyperpolarizes the nerve cell
    C.   stimulates nerve cells to demyelinate
    D.   increases the amount of acetylcholine release

367. Binding of kainic acid to its receptor causes a sodium influx. Which of the following locations has the greatest concentration of sodium ion channels?

    A.   the axon terminal
    B.   nodes of Ranvier
    C.   neuron cell body
    D.   rough ER

368. "Fight or flight" activation of the autonomic nervous system causes which of the following to occur?

    A.   pupil muscle constriction
    B.   blood flow shifts from digestive to skeletal muscle circulation
    C.   constriction of bronchi results
    D.   blood glucose drastically decreases

369.

$$F = \frac{\Delta P \pi r^4}{8\eta l}$$

where F = flow, P= pressure, r= radius,
η= viscosity, and l = length

Poiseuille's Equation

Poiseuille's equation above is used to describe flow through any tube-like pipe. This equation can also be applied to the axon, which functions as a pipe through which the action potential current flows. The equation describes how the length and radius of an axon or dendrite can alter a neuron's resistance to action potentials. Which of the following will have the slowest conduction rate of an action potential?

A. axons, because of the myelin coating properties
B. axons, because of their larger diameter in comparison to dendrites
C. dendrites, because of they are narrower than axons and unmyelinated
D. dendrites, because there are more of them

370. According to the information presented in the passage, autonomic parasympathetic postganglionic neurons bear these receptors:

A. alpha sympathetic
B. beta adrenergic
C. nicotinic
D. muscarinic

Passage 405 (Questions 371-377)

Mitochondrial oxidative phosphorylation is an aerobic process that produces ATP. It is not the flow of electrons that directly causes the ATP synthesis, but rather the energy stored in the transmembrane hydrogen ion gradient. This is known as the chemiosmotic theory, which was proposed in 1961 by British biochemist Peter Mitchell. Mitchell's Nobel Prize–winning theory explained how electron transfer from low to high potentials, culminating in the reduction of oxygen to water, makes the hydrogen ion gradient possible.

There are a number of toxins that can inhibit oxidative phosphorylation. By blocking Complex IV of the electron transport chain (ETC), cyanide prevents the oxidation of all substrates, including NADH, $FADH_2$, and ascorbate, and will prevent phosphorylation of ADP to ATP. *Cyanide* therefore causes a direct inhibition of ATP synthesis.

Amphipathic weak acids are uncoupling agents that transport protons across the inner mitochondrial membrane, dissipating the energy of the transmembrane proton gradient and preventing the production of ATP. While maximum rates of electron transfer are reached, because the translocated protons do not cycle through the ATP-synthase, no ATP is produced. *2,4-dinitrophenol*, a weight-loss agent, is another uncoupler that pokes holes in the inner mitochondrial membrane and, as a side effect, increases body temperature.

When the ATP-synthase is inhibited, ATP production decreases and the proton gradient accumulates at a high level. The rate of oxidative phosphorylation decreases due to a high proton gradient, exerting a back pressure on the primary proton pumps.

Properties	Hydrogen Cyanide (AC)	Cyanogen Chloride (CK)
Boiling Point	30.5° C	13.9° C
Vapor Pressure	690 mm Hg at 30.5° C	1,050 mm Hg at 30.5° C
Vapor Density	0.89 g/ml at 22° C	2.5 g/ml at 22° C
Liquid Density	0.82 g/ml at 22° C	1.20 g/ml at 22° C
Volatility	1.20×10 at 20° C	2.34×10 at 13.0° C
Complete Solubility at:	18° C	14° C

Table 1 Cyanide Data

371. Which of the following compounds is most likely to be an uncoupling agent?

A. H_2SO_4
B. NaOH
C. H_2CO_3
D. HCl

372. A patient enters the ER with cyanide poisoning. Which of the following will be seen as a side effect of cyanide exposure?

A. increased rate of oxygen consumption
B. decreased rate of oxygen consumption
C. increased ATP production
D. decreased rate of glycolysis

373. Uncouplers specifically increase proton permeability. According to the passage, uncouplers can be grouped into the same category as which of the following:

A. ATP-synthase inhibitors
B. electron transport chain blockers
C. proton transport inhibitors
D. hydrophobic carrier molecules

374. The chemiosmotic hypothesis describes the generation of the proton motive force. Which of the following factors are components of this hypothesis?

I. pH difference in the mitochondrial compartment
II. electrical potential difference in the mitochondrial compartment
III. continuous supply of reduced substrates like NADH

A. I only
B. I and II only
C. II and III only
D. I, II and III

375. Cyanide may be present in food, combustion products of synthetic materials, and various industries. Based on the information presented in Table 1, which of the following is NOT true?

A. cyanogen chloride (CK) displays higher overall properties of solubility
B. (AC) must not be as pure, which explains its lower vapor pressure and higher boiling point
C. cyanogen chloride is more reactive and hazardous in comparison to hydrogen cyanide
D. cyanogen chloride and hydrogen cyanide may not be separated using distillation

376. The retina of the eye has a very high rate of oxidative metabolism and requires a great deal of ATP. According to the passage, which of the following is the most likely explanation why patients on *dinitrophenol* have a high risk of blindness?

A. the increased rate of oxidative phosphorylation provides an overabundance of ATP
B. patients sometimes overdose on *dinitrophenol*
C. high blood levels of *dinitrophenol* decrease aerobic ATP synthesis
D. *dinitrophenol* acts as a citrate agonist and an uncontrolled rate of glycolysis results

377. Aspirin (salicylate) is a minor uncoupler. According to the passage, which of the following must be true for those consuming aspirin tablets?

A. low levels of aspirin consumption cause the formation of duodenal ulcers
B. a toxic salicylate overdose occurs with an accompanying fever
C. fourteen daily aspirin tablets will increase clotting rate
D. aspirin causes an increase in mitochondrial intermembrane acidity

---

69

There are three types of pathogenic bacterial strains that can infect a host.

Strain A

Has the highest rate of reproduction and is the most virulent. It kills the host quickly, curtailing its own spread.

Strain B

Has a moderate reproductive rate and an intermediate virulence. The host becomes ill but remains mobile and continues to spread the bacteria.

Strain C

Has a low reproductive rate and is the least virulent. When infected the host is mildly ill and fully mobile, but there is minimal spread of the strain.

The death of the host is unimportant to a parasite that can easily transmit itself to another host. A highly virulent parasite utilizes several methods to continually spread to new hosts. It employs vectors, like ticks or fleas. It delays the onset of the disease, enabling spread during the pre-illness phase. It establishes disease reservoirs by infecting hosts and making them carriers of the disease without ever developing symptoms.

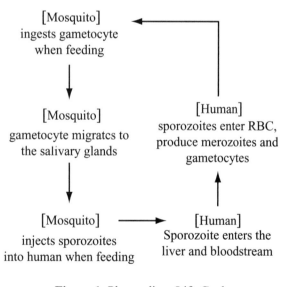

Figure 1 Plasmodium Life Cycle

378. Which of the following statements correctly describe the colonization of the human body?

    I. there are no organisms living on the human body
    II. many non-disease-causing organisms live on the human body
    III. some disease-causing organisms live on the human body

    A. I only
    B. II only
    C. III only
    D. II and III only

379. An anti-mitosis agent would most likely have the greatest inhibitory effect on:

    A. strain A
    B. strain B
    C. strain C
    D. all strains will be equally inhibited

380. Toxoplasmosis is caused by a parasite that establishes a wildlife reservoir and infects humans residing in major U.S. cities. Which of the following animals most likely serves as a toxoplasmosis wildlife reservoir?

    A. elephants
    B. cats
    C. snakes
    D. trees

381. Which of the following methods can be used to prevent the spread of a highly virulent parasite that utilizes a tick to spread the disease?

    A. vaccinate against the parasite only
    B. eliminate the tick and vaccinate against the parasite only
    C. vaccinate against the parasite, eliminate the tick, use an anti-tick repellant
    D. eliminate the host, vaccinate against the parasite, eliminate the tick, use an anti-tick repellant

GO ON TO THE NEXT PAGE.

382. According to the information in the passage, when would strain A be likely to outcompctc the other strains?

    I. when most hosts are immune to the disease
    II. when open sewers, lack of ventilation, and stagnant water serve as reservoirs for the disease
    III. when all hosts are infected with the disease

    A. I only
    B. II only
    C. III only
    D. II and III only

383. Which of the following is the vector for the *Plasmodium spp.*?

    A. human
    B. sporozoite
    C. mosquito
    D. red blood cell

Questions 384 through 393 are **NOT** based on a descriptive passage.

384. Which of the following can serve as a *substrate* for oxidative phosphorylation?

    A. NADH
    B. NAD^+
    C. ATP
    D. glucose

385. The main constituent of microtubules is *tubulin*, a globular heterodimer protein. Which of the following protein structures does tubulin occupy?

    A. primary
    B. secondary
    C. tertiary
    D. quaternary

386. *Superoxide dismutase* catalyses the dismutation of superoxide anion radical to hydrogen peroxide. *Catalase* catalyzes the disproportionation of hydrogen peroxide to water and oxygen. Where in most cells are both of these enzymes found together?

    A. nucleus
    B. peroxisome
    C. lysosome
    D. cytoplasm

387. Depolarization of muscle cell sarcoplasmic reticulum releases Ca^{2+}. Calcium binds to which of the following muscle structures?

    A. troponin C
    B. sarcoplasmic reticulum
    C. actin/myosin complex
    D. muscle ATPase

388. A respiratory tract infection will most likely spare which of the following anatomical locations?

    A. trachea
    B. esophagus
    C. main bronchi
    D. alveoli

GO ON TO THE NEXT PAGE.

389. The nodes of Ranvier serve which of the following functions?

    A.   regenerate the anterograde conduction of the action potential

    B.   stimulate the axon hillock to produce a stronger action potential

    C.   provide a site for acetylcholine to bind to

    D.   provide a space for housing Schwann cells

390. Programmed cell death is called apoptosis. All of the following are examples of programmed cell death EXCEPT:

    A.   Fetus finger formation requires the removal of the tissue between them.

    B.   Synaptic cleft formation between neurons in the brain requires surplus cells to be eliminated.

    C.   Uterus endometrial lining forms to prepare for implantation.

    D.   Tadpole tail is reabsorbed during metamorphosis into a frog.

391. Which of the following cells is responsible for producing myelin in the peripheral nervous system?

    A.   Schwann cell

    B.   lymph

    C.   hepatocyte

    D.   leukocyte

392. Microtubules function alone or form protein complexes to produce complex structures such as:

    I.   muscle cell myosin and actin

    II.   the flagella

    III.   the mitotic spindle apparatus

    A.   I only

    B.   II only

    C.   II and III only

    D.   I, II, and III

393. Acquired immunodeficiency syndrome (AIDS) infects and kills helper (CD_4) T lymphocytes resulting in a loss of:

    A.   humoral immunity

    B.   cell-mediated immunity

    C.   non-specific immunity

    D.   the bone marrow

Passage 407 (Questions 394-399)

Neurons consist of three distinct regions, which include the soma, axon, and dendrites. The soma (cell body) houses the nucleus, perikaryon, and metabolic machinery like the rough and smooth ER. Small vesicles containing newly synthesized proteins can be visualized pinching off the rough ER. The Golgi apparatus, the receptor for synthesized compounds, glycosylates and packages proteins for exocytosis. The smooth ER serves as the site for hormone synthesis.

The axon is a large single process that arises from a specialized region of the soma called the axon hillock. At the hillock an "all or none" signal is initiated once an action potential threshold is reached. A typical neuron also has several dendrites, which serve an input role and establish contact with other neurons.

All living cells use neurons to respond and adapt to their environment. Any given response involves the conversion of stimuli into changes in cellular resting membrane potential (V_m). In nerves, such changes in V_m are transmitted along the axon until being passed on to another neuron or a target cell. The propagation of an action potential is a four-signal mechanism: *input set* consists of a dendrite synaptic action potential. *Integrating set* takes place at the axon hillock. *Conductive set* is the actual action potential. *Secretion set* is the release of a neurotransmitter. With the exception of the *secretion set*, all other components of signal conduction change the electrical properties of the cell membrane.

394. The passage indicates that enzymes synthesized in the rough ER will immediately undergo:

    A.   transportation out of the cell

    B.   transportation into the cell nucleus

    C.   transportation to the Golgi apparatus

    D.   transportation to the smooth endoplasmic reticulum

395. A change in resting membrane potential (Vm) would be associated with which of the following?

    I.   influx of energy

    II.   efflux of K^+

    III.   influx of glucose

    A.   I only

    B.   II only

    C.   II and III only

    D.   I, II, and III

396. The Na^+ / K^+ pump contributes to the resting membrane potential. What is the direct electrogenic contribution of this pump?

   A.   1 Na^+ out of cell for 2 K^+ into the cell
   B.   2 Na^+ out of cell for 3 K^+ into the cell
   C.   3 Na^+ out of cell for 1 K^+ into the cell
   D.   3 Na^+ out of cell for 2 K^+ into the cell

397. The axon terminal is an active region associated with neurotransmitter exocytosis. Which of the following organelles would be expected to be present at a greater than normal concentration at the axon terminal?

   A.   rough ER
   B.   smooth ER
   C.   mitochondria
   D.   lysosome

398. Which of the following will be expected to occur during the *secretion set* of action potential?

   A.   depolarization to decrease the membrane potential
   B. Na^+ current flow into the cell
   C.   entry of Ca^+ at the axon terminal
   D.   bidirectional axon action potential conduction

399. Which of the following is an effect of sympathetic stimulation?

   A.   increased blood flow to the GI tract
   B.   dilation of pupils
   C.   increased blood flow to the kidneys
   D.   decreased activity of skeletal muscles

Passage 408 (Questions 400-405)

The human ear is anatomically divided into external, middle, and internal compartments. Sound enters the external compartment and travels through the ear canal that leads to the eardrum, known as the tympanic membrane, a structure that marks the beginning of the middle ear compartment. The external ear functions to collect sound waves, which exert pressure changes against the eardrum, forcing it to oscillate.

Three ossicles (the smallest bones in the body) of the middle ear, malleus, incus, and stapes, function to multiply the tympanic membrane vibrational force by twenty-fold. The long process of the malleus is attached to the tympanic membrane. When the membrane vibrates in response to sound, the malleus oscillates in concert. The stapes inserts into the oval window, which delivers sound vibrations to the fluid-filled inner ear. The twenty-fold increase in force is important because ossicles must transfer energy from sound waves to liquid ones.

The two smallest human muscles, tensor tympani and the stapedius insert onto the ossicles. The tensor tympani is attached to the malleus and tenses the tympanic membrane by contracting: contraction reduces the transmission of sound and serves to protect the nervous system from loud sounds.

The inner ear contains sensory organs for vestibular and auditory information. Both sensory organs are contained within the bony shell known as the labyrinth. The cochlea senses auditory stimuli. The spaces on either side of the cochlear duct are called the scala vestibula and scala tympani. The cochlear duct is filled with endolymph while the scala vestibula and scala tympani are filled with perilymph. The difference in ionic concentrations between these two fluids is crucial for generating electrical signals in the hair cells when they are mechanically affected by the fluid sound waves.

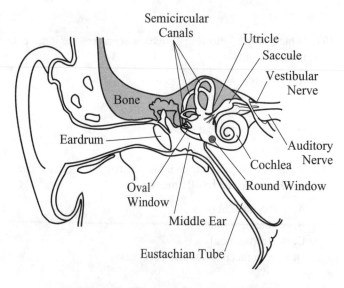

Figure 1 The Inner Ear or Labyrinth

GO ON TO THE NEXT PAGE.

400. The tympanic membrane is a continually growing structure. In this regard, tympanic cells are most similar to which of the following?

    A. nerve cells
    B. skin cells
    C. pancreatic cells
    D. stem cells

401. According to the passage, which of the following is only expected to function during a loud explosion?

    A. the tympanic membrane
    B. the external ear canal
    C. malleus, incus, stapes
    D. stapedius, tensor tympani

402. The bony labyrinth is filled with *perilymph*, which is the stimulus for depolarization and causes an action potential. Which of the following ions is present in high concentration in *perilymph*?

    A. sodium
    B. potassium
    C. chloride
    D. calcium

403. It can be inferred from the passage that ossicles intensify sound by:

    A. decreasing the surface area and increasing the pressure on the inner ear
    B. increasing the overall surface area and decreasing pressure on the inner ear
    C. inhibiting the oscillation frequency of the tympanic membrane
    D. increasing the oscillation frequency of the tympanic membrane

404. Which of the following structures separates the inner ear from the middle ear?

    A. the tympanic membrane
    B. the oval window
    C. the basilar membrane
    D. the external ear canal

405. What type of energy transfer is occurring through the oval window onto the basilar membrane?

    A. mechanical only
    B. chemical only
    C. electrical only
    D. both mechanical and chemical

Passage 409 (Questions 406-412)

Stimulation of the neuromuscular junction releases acetylcholine (ACh) in discrete packages called quanta. These neurotransmitter quanta diffuse across the synaptic cleft, bind nicotinic receptors, and depolarize the muscle end-plate region (sodium ion mediated) and later the entire muscle membrane (sarcolemma). An action potential travels down the length of the sarcolemma-reaching numerous membrane invaginations, known as T-tubules. These tubules plunge into the interior of the muscle fiber, delivering stimulus to the calcium-filled endoplasmic (sarcoplasmic) reticulum. Calcium release allows muscle power stroke to occur.

Myasthenia gravis (MG) is a chronic neuromuscular transmission disorder that displays its symptoms at the motor end plate. An action potential threshold is reached but after much delay, producing weakness and abnormally rapid fatigue of voluntary muscles. Ocular motor disturbances serve as an initial sign of disease onset. Those suffering then follow up with difficulty chewing, swallowing, and talking, and overall limb weakness (rarely limited to local muscle groups such as the neck).

MG usually appears in combination with other autoimmune diseases and patients also present with thymic abnormalities. The thymus contains all the necessary elements for the pathogenesis of myasthenia gravis. However, according to nerve conduction tests, axon terminal acetylcholine vesicles appear normal and neurotransmitter release remains adequate. The increase in conduction time or decrease in action potential stimulus is due to the improper functioning of the postsynaptic nicotinic acetylcholine receptors. This results in postsynaptic insensitivity to the neurotransmitter. Acetylcholine receptors are attacked and destroyed by autoimmune antibodies.

Muscle Cell	Properties:
Resting membrane potential:	–90 mV
Depolarization ion:	Sodium
Duration of the action potential:	5 milliseconds
Type of thin filament:	actin G
Action potential spread:	T-tubules

Table 1 Experimental Muscle Cell FXC-5

406. *Cholinesterase* is essential for acetylcholine hydrolysis in the synaptic cleft. All of the following serve as possible treatment options for myasthenia gravis EXCEPT:

    A. stimulate increase of acetylcholine production and release into the cleft
    B. administer anti-cholinesterase drugs
    C. allow endocytosis of acetylcholine receptors
    D. lower autoantibody production by B-cells

407. Which of the following muscle cells possess membrane invaginations known as T-tubules?

    A. skeletal muscle cells only
    B. cardiac and smooth muscle cells
    C. skeletal and cardiac muscle cells
    D. skeletal, cardiac, and smooth muscle cells

408. Which of the following statements regarding the autonomic nervous system is true?

    A. Acetylcholine causes sympathetic stimulation and muscular vasoconstriction
    B. Acetylcholine causes parasympathetic stimulation and muscular vasodilatation
    C. Norepinephrine causes parasympathetic stimulation and muscular vasoconstriction
    D. Norepinephrine causes sympathetic stimulation and muscular vasodilatation

409. The effects of myasthenia gravis can be most effectively mimicked in laboratory animals by:

    A. injecting acetylcholine receptor antagonist
    B. decreasing neurotransmitter production at the axon terminal
    C. decreasing motor end plate myelination
    D. administering a short-acting drug that blocks the degradation of acetylcholine

410. Which of the following is the cell responsible for autoantibody production?

    A. a bone marrow cell
    B. a B-cell
    C. a T-cell
    D. a macrophage

411. The severity of MG-associated weakness fluctuates during the day and worsens as the day progresses. Which of the following statements can explain this?

    A. MG symptoms increase after prolonged use of affected muscles
    B. treatment with anticholinesterase causes patient exhaustion
    C. antibody levels in the blood increase as the day progresses
    D. smooth muscle fatigue is a result of temporary loss of innervation

412. Which of the following must be true regarding the experimental muscle cell FXC-5?

    A. FXC-5 is a smooth muscle cell that is controlled by the autonomic nervous system.
    B. FXC-5 is hyperpolarized at -110 mV.
    C. FXC-5 is a voluntary controlled cell.
    D. FXC-5 is identical to the muscle that makes up the wall of the heart.

GO ON TO THE NEXT PAGE.

413. Which of the following statements is consistent with smooth muscle architecture?

- **A.** the presence of deep, invaginating T-tubules
- **B.** actin and myosin organized into visible striations
- **C.** multicellular units of muscle tissue that function voluntarily
- **D.** multiunit muscle cells that are active during GI peristalsis

414. Which of the following organs can detoxify the body as peroxisomes detoxify the cell?

- **A.** stomach
- **B.** kidneys
- **C.** liver
- **D.** brain

415. Centrioles are organizational sites for microtubules. During which phase of mitotic division do spindle fibers align chromosomes along the cellular equator?

- **A.** prophase
- **B.** metaphase
- **C.** anaphase
- **D.** telophase

416. Treatment with corticosteroids is used to suppress autoimmune diseases. Under normal circumstances where is cortisol produced?

- **A.** the pituitary gland
- **B.** the adrenal gland
- **B.** the endocrine pancreas
- **D.** the GI tract

417. Thymectomy, the removal of the thymus, has become the standard treatment for myasthenia gravis. Which of the following is the dominating function of the thymus gland?

- **A.** production of cells involved in humoral immunity
- **B.** only important for immunity of adults
- **C.** guides lymphoid cell (T-cell) maturation and self-tolerance
- **D.** responsible for removal and replacement of red blood cells

418. A technique similar to phagocytosis by which a living cell engulfs a minute droplet of liquid is known as:

- **A.** endocytosis
- **B.** exocytosis
- **C.** pinocytosis
- **D.** phago-engulfing

419. Excess *glutamate* activates NMDA receptors, which stimulate cell death. Which of the following is a possible method(s) to prevent NMDA activation?

- **I.** inhibition of *glutamate* synthesis
- **II.** synthesis of an NMDA receptor inhibitor
- **III.** degradation of NMDA regulatory molecule

- **A.** I only
- **B.** I and II only
- **C.** II and III only
- **D.** I, II, and III

420. Substance P is a neuropeptide that is not produced in the presynaptic terminal. Which of the following is the most likely site for substance P synthesis?

- **A.** nucleus
- **B.** peroxisomes
- **C.** rough ER
- **D.** mitochondria

421. An electric current will cause all the following to occur in a nerve cell EXCEPT:

- **A.** degrade excess neurotransmitter in the synaptic cleft
- **B.** cause a unidirectional change in the membrane potential
- **C.** initiate the release of a neurotransmitter
- **D.** cause the opening of sodium channels

422. A neuron soma contains a significant cytoskeleton that is designed to:

- **A.** allow intracellular transport and provide structural integrity
- **B.** allow mitosis but not meiosis to take place
- **C.** be used for nerve cell division
- **D.** synthesize enzymes for protein synthesis

The brain and the spinal cord make up the central nervous system, which is protected by bone. The spinal cord is eighteen inches in length and extends from the brain stem to the first lumbar vertebrae in adults. All input sensory information (afferent) enters the spinal cord by posterior nerve roots and is carried up to the brain. Spinal cord motor outputs (efferent) leave the spinal cord by anterior roots. These nerves carry motor commands from the brain to individual muscles (effectors).

Between the posterior and anterior roots, the denticulate ligament suspends the spinal cord. The ligament has a serrated tooth-like appearance, 21 attachment sites, and is a surgical landmark: it demarcates the exact midpoint between posterior and anterior roots.

The spine is divided into 5 anatomical regions: cervical, thoracic, lumbar, sacral, and coxygeal. Associated with the spine are eight pairs of cervical nerve roots (C1-C8), twelve pairs of thoracic nerve roots (T1-T12), five pairs of lumbar nerve roots (L1-L5), and five pairs of sacral nerve roots (S1-S5). Cervical nerve roots are named for the vertebrae directly below the root as they exit the spinal cord. An exception to the rule is the C8 nerve root, which passes between C7 and T1. The thoracic and lumbar nerve roots derive their names from the vertebrae above exit points.

Nerves lying within the spinal cord are classified as upper motor neurons (UMNs) and function to carry messages back and forth between the brain and the peripheral nervous system. Peripheral nervous system nerves, which branch out away from the spinal cord, are known as lower motor neurons (LMNs).

423. Which of the following nervous system neurons carries a signal to an *effector*?

    A. sensory neuron
    B. interneuron
    C. motor neuron
    D. afferent neuron

424. According to the information presented in the passage, where does C7 nerve root exit the spinal cord?

    A. above C6 vertebrae
    B. above C7 vertebrae
    C. below C7 vertebrae
    D. below C8 vertebrae

425. The knee-jerk reflex is an example of the simplest type of reflex response. All of the following are true regarding the knee-jerk reflex, EXCEPT:

    A. Striking the muscle tendon with a reflex hammer stimulates a specific sensor within the muscle.
    B. A sensory nerve connects with a motor nerve, which then stimulates the muscle to contract.
    C. Sensory information is sent via afferent nerves to the spinal cord.
    D. The brain must be involved for a reflex sequence to occur.

426. If lesioned, which of the following structures would cause the greatest sensory functional deficit?

    A. posterior nerve root
    B. denticulate ligament
    C. efferent nerve root
    D. lumbar vertebrae

427. The spinal cord is considerably shorter in adults in comparison to newborns. An MRI of a newborn may reveal a spinal cord tumor at which of the following levels?

    A. L1
    B. T12
    C. L3
    D. T1

428. According to the information presented in the passage, *effector organs* of the autonomic nervous system include all of the following EXCEPT:

    A. medulla oblongata
    B. smooth muscle
    C. cardiac tissue
    D. blood vessels

429. Which part of the nervous system is responsible for memory and higher mental function?

    A. cerebellum
    B. medulla
    C. hypothalamus
    D. cerebrum

GO ON TO THE NEXT PAGE.

Neurotransmitters can be inhibitory or excitatory and are divided into three principal subsets: 1) acetylcholine, 2) biogenic amines (i.e., dopamine), and 3) bioactive peptides (i.e., substance P).

Biogenic amines form when an amino acid loses a hydroxyl and/or carboxyl functional group. The amino acid phenylalanine initiates the production of dopamine. Phenylalanine is obtained from the diet and is converted into tyrosine by the liver via *phenylalanine hydroxylase*. After being transported to the adrenal medulla, tyrosine undergoes a series of reactions, which convert it to dopamine.

Dopamine plays a major role in addiction (seen in cocaine abusers) and directs nervous system processes that control movement, emotional response, and experience of pleasure and pain. Dopamine is also associated with hallucinations and other symptoms of schizophrenia.

A dopamine-dependent communication pathway degenerates in Parkinson's disease and causes a loss of dopamine in the substantia nigra, an area involved in the coordination of motor function. The blood-brain barrier (BBB) is a collection of capillaries wrapped tightly by endothelial cells. It prevents hydrophilic substances like dopamine from entering the brain and complicates the treatment of Parkinson's disease. L-dopa is hydrophobic; it enters the brain and is converted to dopamine. To improve where L-dopa fails, dopamine agonists are used to communicate with dopamine receptors in the brain. Low dose dopamine agonist/L-dopa combination causes fewer side effects and works longer than either treatment alone.

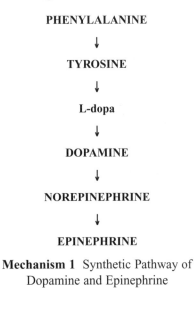

PHENYLALANINE

↓

TYROSINE

↓

L-dopa

↓

DOPAMINE

↓

NOREPINEPHRINE

↓

EPINEPHRINE

Mechanism 1 Synthetic Pathway of Dopamine and Epinephrine

Neurotransmitter (NT)	Enzyme	Status	Location
Acetylcholine	Choline acetyltrans-ferase	excitatory	not localized
Bioactive amines			
Dopamine	Tyrosine hydroxylase	excitatory/ inhibitory	CNS
Serotonin	Tryptophan hydroxylase	excitatory	not localized
Bioactive peptides			
Glycine	amino acid	inhibitory	CNS
Glutamate	amino acid	excitatory	CNS

Table 2 NT Information

430. A dopamine tract from the hypothalamus plays an important role in regulating the release of prolactin. All of the following are true regarding prolactin EXCEPT:

  A. It is produced by the anterior pituitary gland.
  B. It stimulates milk production.
  C. Secretion is inhibited by dopamine.
  D. It is produced in the same area as oxytocin.

431. *Dopa decarboxylase* catalyzes the conversion of L-dopa into dopamine. If *dopa decarboxylase* is denatured, which of the following reactants will accumulate and which product will not form, respectively?

  A. dopamine and tyrosine
  B. phenylalanine and epinephrine
  C. tyrosine and L-dopa
  D. dopamine and norepinephrine

432. Phenylketonuria (PKU) is an autosomal recessive disorder caused by a mutation on chromosome 12. What percentage of children will be carriers of the disease if both parents are heterozygous?

  A. 100%
  B. 75%
  C. 50%
  D. 25%

433. According to the passage, which of the following is true regarding the formation of biogenic amines?

   A. Biogenic amines are more hydrophobic, with higher acidity than the amino acid precursors.
   B. Biogenic amines are less hydrophobic, with lower acidity than the amino acid precursors.
   C. Biogenic amines show decreased hydrogen bond formation and polarity than the precursors.
   D. Biogenic amines show increased hydrogen bond formation and polarity than the precursors.

434. Succinylcholine is used in surgery as a muscle relaxant. Which of the following is the most likely mode of action for succinylcholine?

   A. destroys acetylcholine receptors
   B. increases the release of acetylcholine
   C. increases ADH production
   D. inhibits acetylcholine receptors

435. The adrenal medulla is a mass of neurons with all of the following characteristics EXCEPT:

   A. Its products are tyrosine derived.
   B. It releases epinephrine.
   C. It is responsible for the production of cortisol and aldosterone.
   D. It is located above the kidney.

436. Carbidopa prevents the decarboxylation of L-dopa in the bloodstream. Which of the following statements is true concerning L-dopa and the treatment of Parkinson's disease?

   A. Decarboxylase inhibitors (carbidopa) decrease the blood circulating levels of L-dopa.
   B. Hydrophilic compounds cross the blood brain barrier more readily than hydrophobic ones.
   C. Dopamine antagonists bind receptors in place of dopamine and stimulate those receptors.
   D. Dopamine displays a larger overall dipole moment than L-dopa.

Questions 437 through 445 are **NOT** based on a descriptive passage.

437. All of the following are true regarding the anatomy and properties of the sympathetic nervous system EXCEPT:

   A. It responds to involuntary sympathetic stimulation.
   B. The "fight or flight" response causes pupillary dilation.
   C. Acetylcholine is the main neurotransmitter.
   D. It is part of the autonomic nervous system.

438. Glycosides have been shown to block the activity of the Na^+/K^+ ATPase. Which of the following would you expect to occur in a cell exposed to glycosides?

   A. extracellular Na^+ concentration would increase
   B. intracellular K^+ concentration would increase
   C. ATP consumption would increase
   D. the cell will spontaneously depolarize

439. Peroxisomes and which other cellular organelle are self-replicating?

   A. nucleus
   B. mitochondria
   C. ribosomes
   D. DNA

440. The dominant phase expected for most fungi is:

   A. haploid
   B. diploid
   C. equally haploid and diploid
   D. triploid

441. Which of the following is NOT affected by digestive lysosomal hydrolases?

   A. nucleotides
   B. lipids
   C. proteins
   D. minerals

442. Proteins are marked and delivered to various cellular locations based on:

   A.   the compartmentalization in the rough ER following protein synthesis

   B.   the post-translational modification by the Golgi apparatus

   C.   the regulation signals released by the cytoskeleton

   D.   the specificity of protein transport channels

443. Which of the following is NOT true of *both* cilia and flagella?

   A.   responsible for movement of fluid over cellular surface

   B.   involved in single cell locomotion

   C.   provide sperm with motility

   D.   microtubule-derived structures

444. Monoamine oxidase inhibitors prevent the breakdown of catecholamines (i.e., epinephrine). A person exposed to monoamine oxidase inhibitors would exhibit which of the following?

   A.   constricted pupils

   B.   increased heart rate

   C.   excessive digestive activity

   D.   decreased blood flow to skeletal muscles

445. Sound waves that strike the tympanic membrane or the eardrum have the ability to transfer:

   A.   matter only

   B.   energy only

   C.   matter and energy

   D.   neither matter nor energ

STOP. IF YOU FINISH BEFORE TIME IS CALLED, CHECK YOUR WORK. YOU MAY GO BACK TO ANY QUESTION IN THIS TEST BOOKLET.

LECTURE 5

Biology Passages
Questions 446–556

Passage 501 (Questions 446-451)

Cholesterol-derived hormones are carried by the circulatory system to their specific target organs. Hormones are *always* present in minute concentrations and are capable of both stimulatory and inhibitory effects.

One of the main effects of hormones is the stimulation of other endocrine glands to secrete their product. These types of stimulators are known as trophic hormones. Such endocrine cascading allows for tight control of overall hormone production, which may be affecting several distinct organs.

In some cases, chemicals are secreted into the extracellular space, affecting cells that are in close proximity to the secretory cell. The metabolic effects of such *paracrine* regulators are local, compared to the distal or global effects of hormones. Insulin and prostaglandins can also be released locally in order to perform their designated functions.

Hormones travel through the blood either in free solution or in association with carrier proteins such as albumin. Target cells contain receptors for their specific hormones, which then trigger the metabolic changes necessary by complex mechanisms.

446. The body houses a number of controlled hormone-releasing cascades. According to the passage, an example of a trophic hormone is:

    A.   insulin
    B.   glucagon
    C.   epinephrine
    D.   TSH (thyroid stimulating hormone)

447. ACTH stimulates the release of cortisol from the adrenal cortex. It can be inferred from the passage that the average blood cortisol concentration at 4 pm on a given day would most likely be:

    A.   713 mol/L
    B.   997 mmol/L
    C.   101 nmol/L
    D. 4.7×10^{-4} mol/L

448. Digitalis is a Na^+/K^+ ATPase inhibitor. Which of the following cellular changes will result upon the administration of digitalis?

    A.   There will be an increase in sodium reabsorption by unaffected cells.
    B.   There will be a decrease in the intracellular sodium concentration.
    C.   There will be a decrease in the intracellular potassium.
    D.   There will be an increase in the amount of ATP consumed by the cell.

449. In males seminiferous tubules require high levels of testosterone, which is secreted by nearby interstitial cells of the testes. In this specific situation testosterone is exerting which effect?

    A.   autocrine effect
    B.   exocrine effect
    C.   paracrine effect
    D.   endocrine effect

450. Which of the following is both an endocrine and exocrine gland?

    A.   the pancreas
    B.   the anterior pituitary
    C.   the liver
    D.   the testes

451. Albumin is a critical factor in determining colloid osmotic pressure. Which other plasma protein can be utilized as a transporter of lipid hormones?

    A.   fibrinogen
    B.   myosin
    C.   C peptide
    D.   F-actin

Passage 502 (Questions 452-458)

Growth hormone (GH) is a single-chain polypeptide secreted in a pulsatile pattern throughout life. Its levels reach a physiological maximum, during sleep, puberty, starvation, and stress, to help manage the metabolism of protein, carbohydrates, and fat. Growth hormone receptors are found on most cells in the human body and when stimulated cause cellular hypertrophy (swelling) and hyperplasia (increase in number). *Growth hormone releasing hormone* (GHRH) activates the transcription of the growth hormone gene while *somatostatin* inhibits the release of growth hormone. (The growth hormone gene is similar to that of *prolactin* and *human placental lactogen.*)

Growth hormone has a striking effect on the epiphyseal cartilage of long bones and chondrocyte (cartilage-forming cells) metabolism. It stimulates bone development, which continues throughout childhood and into adulthood. Osteoblasts, osteocytes, and osteoclasts are all stimulated to develop and grow to remodel bones.

Acromegaly and gigantism are two rare syndromes caused by a chronic exposure to growth hormone. Gigantism occurs in youths prior to the fusion of the epiphyseal plate. Acromegaly is seen in adults. Early diagnosis of these diseases may prevent irreversible changes associated with hormone overproduction and may normalize life expectancy.

GH Conc.	mRNA prod.	Blood Glucose	Insulin level	GHRH	Somato-statin
0.10	5	5	5	5	5
0.30	7	4	20	5	8
0.50	10	4	28	4	13
1.50	11	2	28	2	13
3.00	11	1	37	1	13

Table 1 5 = Baseline;
GH conc. of 3.00 = maximum physiological level

452. *Prolactin* and *human placental lactogen* are structurally similar to growth hormone. *Prolactin* is a 198 amino acid peptide with three disulfide bonds. Which of the following is LEAST likely to be the structure of the *human placental lactogen*?

   A. 191 amino acid tertiary structure peptide containing two disulfide bonds
   B. 179 amino acid polypeptide with two disulfide bonds and six beta sheets
   C. 194 amino acid quaternary structure dipeptide with three disulfide bonds
   D. 202 amino acid polypeptide with one disulfide bond and no alpha-helixes

453. Growth hormone is normally involved in tissue repair and has been known to follow a diurnal cycle. At what point during the daily cycle is growth hormone level at its peak?

   A. 9 am
   B. noon
   C. 5 pm
   D. midnight

454. According to Table 1, abnormally high levels of growth hormone directly affect parameters most associated with which of the following diseases?

   A. Down's syndrome
   B. muscular dystrophy
   C. osteoporosis
   D. diabetes

455. The endocrine system functions in conjunction with which of the following systems to maintain homeostasis by coordinating various activities of the body?

   A. digestive system
   B. nervous system
   C. muscular system
   D. circulatory system

456. Growth hormone inhibits the breakdown of protein. When the blood concentration of growth hormone is elevated, which of the following is expected to occur?

   A. a decrease in the consumption of glucose
   B. an increase in the consumption of protein
   C. an increase in the consumption of fat
   D. a decrease in the rate of transcription

457. Blood chemistry panel reveals a calcium level of 13.8 mg/dl with phosphorus of 2.2 mg/dl. (Normal values: 10.0 mg/dl and 6.8 mg/dl, respectively.) What is the most likely source of the problem?

   A. overstimulated parathyroid gland
   B. testosterone deficiency
   C. thyroid cancer
   D. loss of adrenal function

458. Kwashiorkor syndrome is a malnutrition disorder that occurs in those who do not consume enough protein. A patient with this condition would be expected to have which of the following?

   A. normal levels of GH
   B. decreased levels of GH
   C. elevated levels of GH
   D. increased muscle mass

Passage 503 (Questions 459-464)

A typical diet consists of a 1000 mg daily calcium intake. Calcium is poorly absorbed by the small intestine. Consequently about 90% of calcium remains in the intestines and is excreted in feces. The portion that is absorbed into the body will ultimately be excreted in urine.

On any one trip through the kidneys, two-thirds of the calcium that is filtered at the glomerulus is reabsorbed in the proximal convoluted tubule. The remaining one-third is reabsorbed to a variable but tightly regulated extent in the distal convoluted tubule, and the extent depends on the plasma calcium level. The most important factor controlling calcium reabsorption in the distal convoluted tubule, and consequently controlling urinary calcium excretion, is the parathyroid hormone.

The parathyroid gland is composed mainly of chief and oxyphil cells. Chief cells secrete parathyroid hormone (PTH). Parathyroid hormone is a single 84-amino acid polypeptide that is synthesized as a larger preprohormone. PTH increases the plasma calcium ion concentration and decreases plasma phosphate levels.

State	Conc. / Liter	% of Total
Ca^{2+} ion	1.1	50
Salts	0.3	10
Protein bound	1.0	40

Table 1 Possible States of Calcium in Plasma

459. Which calcium states would be capable of crossing the cell membrane and entering the intracellular space?

I. Ca^{2+} salts by simple diffusion
II. Ca^{2+} ion by active transport
III. Ca^{2+} bound to albumin

A. I only
B. II only
C. II and III only
D. I, II, and III

460. A decrease in the plasma calcium level has been shown to increase the neuronal permeability to sodium. Which of the following is a possible symptom associated with decreased plasma calcium concentration?

A. muscle tetany
B. hyperpolarization of neurons
C. decreased action potential formation
D. decreased levels of PTH secretion

461. According to the passage, parathyroid hormone is expected to increase the activity of which of the following cells?

A. osteoblasts
B. osteoclasts
C. red blood cells
D. adipocytes

462. Which of the following terms most accurately classifies parathyroid hormone?

A. exocrine peptide
B. neurocrine hormone
C. paracrine hormone
D. endocrine peptide

463. According to the passage, which of the following best describes the actions of the parathyroid hormone?

A. increased renal calcium reabsorption, increased renal phosphate excretion
B. decreased intestinal calcium absorption, increased renal phosphate excretion
C. decreased renal calcium reabsorption, increased intestinal phosphate absorption
D. increased intestinal calcium absorption, decreased renal phosphate excretion

464. Which of the following compounds needs to be stimulated by PTH in order to function?

A. thyroid hormone
B. vitamin D
C. bone marrow
D. anterior pituitary

465. Solubilization or emulsification of dietary lipids is accomplished by bile salts that are synthesized in and secreted from which of the following organs, respectively?

A. pancreas and liver
B. liver and gall bladder
C. duodenum and pancreas
D. gall bladder and liver

466. The phenylethylamine structure of amphetamines is similar to that of catecholamines, which may explain their actions. Which of the following compounds is a catecholamine?

A. epinephrine
B. thyroxine
C. cortisol
D. substance P

467. A patient suffering from Type I diabetes has extensive destruction of insulin-producing beta-cells. This patient would be expected to have:

A. low levels of blood glucose
B. increased rate of glycolysis
C. decreased rate of glycolysis
D. decreased levels of ketone bodies

468. Patients with pituitary diabetes complain of being always thirsty and passing very dilute urine. This condition most likely results from the deficiency of which of the following compounds?

A. growth hormone
B. prolactin
C. oxytocin
D. ADH

469. Ovaries secrete PGE2, which causes an increase in fluid of a particular follicle, eventually causing ovulation. Which of the following hormones is responsible for ovulation?

A. LH
B. FSH
C. progesterone
D. estrogen

470. There are two major types of synapses. The least common ones are electrical, involving the actual passage of ions between cells. Which of the following tissues is most likely to contain an electrical synapse?

A. nervous system
B. heart muscle
C. spleen mesenchyme
D. cells of the epidermis

471. Which of the following muscle fibers will be most severely affected by a demyelinating disease like multiple sclerosis?

A. alpha-somatic motor and proprioception—velocity 70-120 m/sec
B. beta-touch, pressure—velocity 30-70 m/sec
C. gamma-motor to muscle spindle—velocity 15-30 m/sec
D. C-pain, temperature, mechanoreception—velocity 0.5-2.5 m/sec

472. A male with serum auto-antibodies that bind to the thyroid gland TSH receptors should be considered as:

A. healthy, because negative feedback will regulate the level of thyroid hormone
B. having low levels of thyroid hormone because auto-antibodies block TSH from binding to its receptor
C. having high levels of thyroid hormone because autoantibodies are overstimulating the thyroid gland
D. having low levels of thyroid hormone because auto-antibodies are destroying the thyroid gland

473. Growth hormone releasing hormone (GHRH) stimulates the transcription of the growth hormone gene and is released from which of the following locations?

    A. the kidneys
    B. the hypothalamus
    C. the anterior pituitary
    D. the parathyroid

474. Once released, glucagon induces the phosphorylation of intracellular enzymes through a second-messenger cascade. Which of the following effects will be seen after a mouse receives a high dose injection of glucagon?

    A. an increase in the basal metabolic rate
    B. a decrease in the metabolic rate
    C. an increase in the blood glucose level
    D. a decrease in the blood glucose level

475. Atrial natiuretic peptide is released by the right atrium when the blood pressure is elevated to decrease blood volume. It is designed to counteract the effects of what hormone?

    A. antidiuretic hormone only
    B. aldosterone only
    C. both antidiuretic hormone and aldosterone
    D. neither antidiuretic hormone nor aldosterone

Passage 504 (Questions 476-482)

Calcitonin is synthesized in parafollicular cells of the thyroid gland. It lowers blood calcium and regulates phosphorus metabolism by reducing the *activity* of cells that reabsorb bone. Long-term calcitonin exposure also reduces the *number* of cells that reabsorb bone.

Vitamin D (also known as cholecalciferol), in conjunction with parathyroid hormone, is also a major regulator of body fluid calcium. Cholecalciferol is either obtained from diet or synthesized by the skin in the presence of UV light and promotes bone mineralization.

Mineralization requires adequate calcium. Vitamin D increases the activity of Ca^{2+}-transporting ATPases situated in epithelial cells of the small intestine. Vitamin D also increases the synthesis of calcium-binding proteins, called calbindins (closely related to calmodulin). Calbindins bind Ca^{2+} ions at the small intestine lumen/brush border junction to ferry them into the bloodstream.

Certain drugs that are structurally different from calcitonin can produce a calcitonin-like effect on blood calcium levels. A study was conducted to determine whether the length of the carbon chain on calcitonin-like drug-X has an effect on drug efficacy. The study consisted of injecting compounds (labeled a-f) into four patients (A-D). Compound "a" was synthetic calcitonin. Compounds "b-f" were drug-X with carbon side chains.

7-dehydrocalciferol

↓

25-dihydroxycholecalciferol

↓

1, 25-dihydroxycholecalciferol (cholecalciferol)

Mechanism 1 Vitamin D (Cholecalciferol) Synthesis

PATIENT	a) Calcitonin	b) Methyl	c) Propyl	d) Butyl	e) Octyl	f) Methyl/Octyl
A	−60	−48	−32	−25	0	−14
B	−34	−43	−29	−27	+1	−13
C	−47	−51	−31	−18	−1	−9
D	−17	−40	−16	−22	0	−11

Table 2 All data correlate to changes in blood calcium level.
(−) = a decrease in calcium;
(0) = no change; (+) an increase in blood calcium.

476. Medullary thyroid carcinoma is a type of thyroid cancer that occurs in the parafollicular cells. Which of the following can be used as a tumor marker in order to identify medullary carcinoma?

    A. thyroid hormone
    B. cell membrane receptors
    C. abnormal rate of cellular division
    D. calcitonin

477. According to the passage, calcitonin directly affects and thus indirectly increases the activity of which of the following cells, respectively?

    A. osteoblasts, osteoclasts
    B. osteoclasts, osteoblasts
    C. parafollicular cells, osteocytes
    D. calcium, phosphorus

478. According to the data presented in the passage, methyl carbon chains produce the maximum effect on calcium levels. Which carbon chain length can be properly defined as a competitive inhibitor?

    A. methyl
    B. octyl
    C. methyl/octyl
    D. calcitonin

479. A vitamin D deficiency can lead to a condition called osteomalacia. Which of the following is the most likely symptom of osteomalacia?

    A. soft bones
    B. long bones
    C. excessive calcium deposition
    D. excessive calcitonin deposition

480. Calcium homeostasis is controlled by the interplay of bone, kidney, and intestine. Which of the following compounds is the active form of vitamin D?

    A. 25-dihydroxycholecalciferol
    B. 24, 25-dihydroxycholecalciferol
    C. 1, 25-calbindin complex
    D. 1, 25-dihydroxycholecalciferol

481. Lanthanum is a trivalent ion that blocks calcium channels. Which of the following would most likely increase in concentration if lanthanum is present in the body?

    A. calcitonin
    B. vitamin D
    C. thyroid hormone
    D. calmodulin

482. Which of the following could be used to treat hypercalcemia (too much calcium)?

    A. vitamin D
    B. growth hormone
    C. parathyroid hormone
    D. calcitonin

Amphetamine is still a drug that is abused. It is a sympath-omimetic because it mimics the actions of the sympathetic nervous system. The drug, however, does not directly bind to sympathetic nervous system receptors. This means it acts indirectly by inhibiting the norepinephrine reuptake carrier, known as an alpha2-receptor.

The alpha2-receptor is located on the presynaptic nerve terminal and under normal circumstances removes norepinephrine from the synaptic cleft, transporting it back into the presynaptic neuron where it is either degraded or repackaged into synaptic vesicles.

Amphetamine has a benzene ring that allows it to enter the presynaptic neuron using the alpha2-receptor. It then enters the storage vesicle and displaces norepinephrine from its storage site and can affect its postsynaptic receptors. With time amphetamine concentration reaches equilibrium and the net neurotransmitter release becomes zero. This is knows as the ceiling effect because there will be no more net nervous system stimulation.

Other drugs, like tricyclic antidepressants and cocaine, work on alpha2-receptors by blocking them.

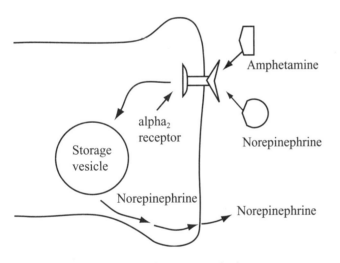

Figure 1 Axon terminal

483. Receptor endocytosis is one method cells use to control hormone stimulation. Which cellular structure must be isolated in order to obtain a cortisol receptor?

    A. plasma membrane
    B. nuclear envelope
    C. ribosomes
    D. smooth endoplasmic reticulum

484. According to the passage, which of the following locations should be analyzed to obtain an accurate estimate of norepinephrine receptors present around a synaptic cleft?

    A. dendrites of the postsynaptic neuron only
    B. axon terminal of the presynaptic neuron only
    C. dendrites of the postsynaptic neuron and the axon terminal of the presynaptic neuron
    D. the entire parasympathetic nervous system needs to be analyzed

485. When discussing the structure of amphetamine it is safe to assume it binds to alpha2-receptor as a:

    A. reversible competitive inhibitor
    B. reversible noncompetitive inhibitor
    C. irreversible noncompetitive inhibitor
    D. irreversible allosteric inhibitor

486. Amphetamine users shortly build tolerance and dependence to the compound, which exerts which of the following short-term effects?

    A. constricts pupils
    B. causes rapid breathing rate
    C. causes diarrhea
    D. decreases heart rate

487. All of the following statements regarding the autonomic nervous system are accurate EXCEPT:

    A. The sympathetic nervous system responds to stressful situations.
    B. The parasympathetic nervous system is essential for life.
    C. The autonomic nervous system is composed entirely of motor neurons.
    D. The parasympathetic system is stimulated by the release of acetylcholine.

488. According to the passage, under normal circumstances the alpha2-presynaptic carrier functions to:

    A. stimulate the parasympathetic nervous system
    B. terminate the action of epinephrine
    C. stimulate the action of norepinephrine
    D. terminate the action of norepinephrine

Passage 506 (Questions 489-494)

Adrenal diabetes is a condition characterized by a high blood glucose level secondary to abnormally high levels of cortisol. This condition has been proven to be moderately responsive to insulin. It is more responsive to insulin than pituitary diabetes but less so than pancreatic diabetes. Pancreatic diabetes is caused by an insufficient insulin output from pancreatic beta cells. Consequently, pituitary diabetes is considered to be weakly insulin-sensitive, adrenal diabetes moderately insulin-sensitive, and pancreatic diabetes strongly insulin-sensitive.

Cortisol secretion is controlled by the adrenocorticotropic hormone (ACTH) secreted from the anterior pituitary gland. ACTH release in turn is controlled by corticotropin-releasing hormone (CRH) secreted by the hypothalamus.

Cortisol causes a reduction in cellular protein by decreasing protein synthesis and increasing protein catabolism in all body tissues except the liver and blood. When cortisol is extremely elevated, muscle wasting may occur to the point that an individual may be unable to rise from a sitting position. The result of protein catabolism is the elevation of amino acids in the blood. The liver utilizes these amino acids to synthesize liver enzymes, blood proteins, and glucose. Constant glucose synthesis causes an elevation in blood sugar.

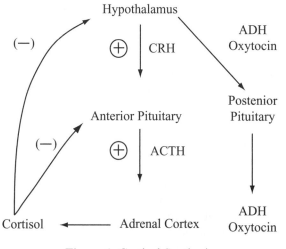

Figure 1 Cortisol Synthesis

489. Selective destruction of the adrenal cortex would produce a deficiency of which of the following cholesterol-derived hormones?

A. aldosterone
B. thyroid hormone
C. estrogen
D. testosterone

490. According to the passage, in order to completely inhibit cortisol synthesis and release which of the following sites should be stimulated via negative feedback?

  I. the hypothalamus
  II. the anterior pituitary
III. the posterior pituitary

A. I only
B. I and II only
C. II and III only
D. I, II, and III

491. A woman has a high blood sugar level, muscle wasting, and decreased levels of ACTH. The *direct* reason for her symptoms is most likely due to:

A. a hormone production insufficiency by the adrenal cortex
B. primary overproduction of ACTH by the anterior pituitary
C. self injections of an exogenous cortisol
D. the destruction of the posterior pituitary gland

492. According to the passage, diabetes may be associated with:

  I. endocrine organs
  II. exocrine organs
III. nervous system organs

A. I only
B. II only
C. III only
D. I and II only

493. Which of the following can serve as a short-term treatment option for someone with extremely elevated cortisol levels?

A. removal of the posterior pituitary in order to inhibit further cortisol release
B. placing the diseased individual on a high-protein diet
C. daily injections of ACTH
D. the removal of the adrenal cortex

494. It is implied in the passage that high amino acid levels in the cytoplasm stimulate which organelle to increase product synthesis?

A. peroxisomes
B. rough ER
C. lysosomes
D. mitochondria

495. Long-standing hypoglycemia (low blood sugar level) results in chronic, excessive levels of counter-regulatory (stress) hormones designed to increase blood glucose. These include all of the following EXCEPT:

A. glucagon
B. cortisol
C. growth hormone
D. prolactin

496. Radioactive iodine is often used as a treatment for tumors of this gland:

A. the parathyroid
B. the pituitary
C. the thyroid
D. the ovary

497. Which of the following enzymes digests protein to allow absorption by the intestine?

A. pancreatic amylase
B. lipase
C. bile
D. chymotrypsin

498. Negative feedback mechanisms regulate cellular homeostasis. A unique network of interconnected cellular chemical reactions can be referred to as:

A. chemistry
B. metabolism
C. allosterism
D. homeo-division

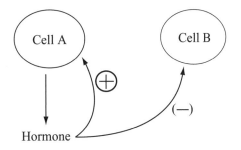

Schematic 1

499. The above schematic represents cell-to-cell hormone signaling. What specific type of signaling is being demonstrated?

A. endocrine
B. autocrine
C. paracrine
D. autocrine and paracrine

500. Selective destruction of which location will greatly reduce the concentration of growth hormone receptors?

A. the plasma membrane
B. the cytosol
C. the nucleus
D. the nucleolus

501. Women with numerous sexual partners are at high risk for abdominal infections, which can cause scars to form in the reproductive system and lead to:

A. increased fertility
B. infertility
C. decreased ovulation
D. decreased levels of estrogen

502. Which of the following endocrine organs secrete insulin and aldosterone, respectively?

A. liver and adrenal gland
B. kidney and pancreas
C. spleen and bone marrow
D. pancreas and adrenal gland

503. The parathyroid is one of two human glands that function to control blood calcium level. What is the anatomic location of the parathyroid gland?

A. The parathyroid is located in the neck behind the larynx.
B. The parathyroid is located near the abdomen.
C. The parathyroid is located above the kidney.
D. The parathyroid is located in the lower brain stem.

504. The movement of material through a membrane by means of specific membrane proteins toward a region of lower concentration is called:

A. active transport
B. simple diffusion
C. facilitated diffusion
D. endocytosis

505. The *intrinsic factor* is essential for the absorption of vitamin B_{12} in the ileum. Which of the following stomach cells secretes intrinsic factor?

A. chief cell
B. mucous cell
C. parietal cell
D. G cell

GO ON TO THE NEXT PAGE.

Passage 507 (Questions 506-511)

Hormones secreted by endocrine glands are of three chemical types: peptide, steroid, and amino acid tyrosine-derived amines. Peptide hormones are synthesized, as any other protein destined for secretion, in the rough endoplasmic reticulum followed by processing in the Golgi apparatus.

Tyrosine-derived *epinephrine* and *norepinephrine* are synthesized in the cytoplasm of glandular cells that make up the adrenal medulla. Once pre-formed, they are stored in vesicles and are released when the body is experiencing physical stress. An experiment was conducted to determine the effect of *epinephrine* on overall mood and mental performance during exposure to physical stress.

Pre-experiment

100 commercial pilots were equally divided into 4 groups.

Groups	Received... (for 1 hour prior to experiment)
Alpha	5 grams of tyrosine and 95 grams of 19 other amino acids
Beta	100 total grams of amino acid tyrosine
Gamma	Intravenous epinephrine injections equal to 100 total grams of tyrosine
Delta	Pill form of epinephrine equal to 100 total grams of tyrosine

Table 1 Group Specifics

Experiment

The 4 groups (alpha–delta) were placed in a controlled environment for 60 minutes. The environment was then rapidly changed to simulate an elevation of 20,000 feet for 30 minutes.

Results

Groups	Mood	Mental Performance	Stress-Related Complaints
Alpha	2	2	3
Beta	4	5	2
Gamma	4	4	1
Delta	1	2	3

Table 2 2 = expected or normal; <2 = less than expected or normal; >2 = more than expected or normal

Steroid hormones are never pre-synthesized. Instead, large amounts of cholesterol and other precursors are present to initiate synthesis when appropriately stimulated. Once synthesized, steroids are immediately released into the blood.

Some endocrine hormones are tightly bound to specific carrier proteins or more loosely bound to plasma albumin while being transported through the blood. Other hormones exist in the blood essentially unbound, free in solution.

506. Which of the following is most likely true regarding the *average* concentration of any endocrine hormones in the blood and their storage?

- **A.** high serum concentration, low storage concentration
- **B.** high serum concentration, high storage concentration
- **C.** low serum concentration, low storage concentration
- **D.** low serum concentration, high storage concentration

507. What is the most likely explanation for group delta not performing as well as group gamma despite receiving the identical concentration of epinephrine?

- **A.** The intravenous injection takes longer to reach the blood.
- **B.** The administered pill dose of epinephrine was digested prior to being absorbed.
- **C.** Delta group subjects were not compliant with their epinephrine regimen.
- **D.** Delta group served as the control for the experiment.

508. The endocrine system is a network of glands that secrete hormones that have proven to be of profound importance in coordinating whole-body function and includes all of the following structures EXCEPT:

- **A.** the posterior pituitary of the brain
- **B.** pancreatic islets of Langerhans
- **C.** the pineal gland of the brain
- **D.** salivary gland of the mouth

509. It can be inferred from the passage that a peptide hormone is not functionally active until it leaves which of the following organelles?

- **A.** the nucleus
- **B.** the rough endoplasmic reticulum
- **C.** the Golgi apparatus
- **D.** the secretory vesicle

GO ON TO THE NEXT PAGE.

510. Which of the following chemical interactions is utilized in order to bind testosterone to albumin?

 A. disulfide bond
 B. hydrogen bond
 C. covalent bond
 D. ionic bond

511. The three categories of hormones differ from one another in how they are synthesized and stored. Which of the following hormones is properly identified as a derivative of the amino acid tyrosine?

 A. thyroid hormone
 B. acetylcholine
 C. aldosterone
 D. oxytocin

Passage 508 (Question 512-517)

In 1935, Sir Henry Dale stated that a neurotransmitter released at one axon terminal could be presumed to be released at other axon terminals of the same neuron. This became known as Dale's principle. (Dale's principle referred only to the presynaptic neuron, because responses of different postsynaptic receptors to a single neurotransmitter varied depending on circumstances.)

The first compound to be classified as a neurotransmitter was acetylcholine (ACh). There were two main categories of acetylcholine (cholinergic) receptors: nicotinic and muscarinic. In the beginning of the twentieth century, they were differentiated by their responses to alkaloids, nicotine and muscarine, but advanced biochemical techniques have shown a more fundamental difference.

The nicotinic receptor is a channel protein that opens to allow diffusion of cations. The muscarinic receptor, on the other hand, is a cell membrane protein that utilizes a second messenger system. As a result, the action of a muscarinic synapse is relatively slow. Muscarinic receptors predominate at the higher levels of the central nervous system, while nicotinic receptors are more prevalent at neurons of the spinal cord and at neuromuscular junctions.

Intravenous infusion of acetylcholine has a complicated effect on the cardiovascular system, which is full of muscarinic receptors. It is believed that acetylcholine mediates the release of the endothelium derived relaxation factor (EDRF) from endothelium cells that line blood vessels.

Infusion Dose of ACh	Vascular Dilation	Blood Pressure	Heart Rate	EDRF Concentration
20-40 mg/minute	↑↑↑	↓↓↓	↑↑	↑↑↑
50-70 mg/minute	↑↑↑↑	↓↓↓	↑↑↑	↑↑↑↑
80-90 mg/minute	↑↑↑↑↑	↓↓↓↓	↓↓	↑↑↑↑↑
100-150 mg/minute	↑↑↑↑↑↑	↓↓↓↓	↓↓↓	↑↑↑↑↑↑

Table 1 Acetylcholine Dosing

GO ON TO THE NEXT PAGE.

512. Which of the following hormones operates utilizing a similar system used by acetylcholine when binding to a muscarinic receptor?

- A. prolactin
- B. cortisol
- C. aldosterone
- D. progesterone

513. According to the passage, which of the following is the appropriate vascular response to the infusion of acetylcholine?

- A. A low dose infusion produces a fall in blood pressure and a reflex decrease in the heart rate.
- B. A low dose infusion produces an increase in blood pressure and a reflex increase in the heart rate.
- C. A large dose infusion produces a decrease in heart rate and a decrease in blood pressure.
- D. A large dose infusion produces an increase in heart rate and a decrease in blood pressure.

514. Which of the following general principles regarding neurotransmitters is *least* likely to be true?

- A. The presynaptic neuron should contain enzymes for the synthesis of the specific neurotransmitter.
- B. Administration of the neurotransmitter under experimental conditions must reproduce the specific event seen during normal synaptic transmission.
- C. Postsynapse receptor blockage should have no effect on neurotransmitter signal transfer.
- D. Enzymes that destroy the neurotransmitter may be present in the synaptic cleft and when active inhibit signal transfer.

515. What dose of acetylcholine is appropriate for a hypertensive individual who cannot tolerate added stress on the heart?

- A. 30 mg/minute
- B. 60 mg/minute
- C. 80 mg/minute
- D. 170 mg/minute

516. Acetylcholine functions to decrease the heart rate. In which of the following locations can one expect to find the least-oxygenated blood?

- A. entering the left ventricle
- B. in the systemic arterioles
- C. leaving the pulmonary artery
- D. in large veins

517. When experiments were conducted using *nicotine* and *muscarine*, which of the following nervous system components were being stimulated?

- I. neuromuscular junctions
- II. parasympathetic nervous system
- III. sympathetic stimulation of target organs

- A. I only
- B. III only
- C. I and II only
- D. I, II, and III

GO ON TO THE NEXT PAGE.

Passage 509 (Questions 518-523)

The female reproductive cycle begins with a complex interaction between the hypothalamus, the anterior pituitary, and the ovaries. The cycle begins with menstruation, which lasts 4-5 days. The follicular (proliferative) phase follows menstruation and lasts 10-16 days. Ovulation occurs right before the luteal (secretory) phase, which is always a constant 14 days in duration. Taken as a whole, the average menstrual cycle is 28-30 days.

Administration of synthetic estrogen with progesterone is used to prevent ovulation. These exogenous hormones interfere with the endocrine signaling necessary to stimulate the release of the luteinizing hormone (LH). Although ovulation is prevented, the uterine lining, known as the endometrium, continues to proliferate and shed monthly.

Birth control pills are taken early in the menstrual cycle: they must be started during the follicular phase and continued beyond the time when ovulation would be expected. Once the woman has entered the luteal phase, birth control pills are stopped (the woman continues to take the placebo), allowing estrogen and progesterone to drop. When hormone levels are low enough, menstruation will occur and a new cycle will begin.

Permanent birth control implants release mostly progesterone. They are surgically placed below the epidermis and can prevent pregnancy for up to five years. They may cause amenorrhea (ceasing of menstruation) but are effective and otherwise well tolerated.

518. The chance of pregnancy is increased if sperm are deposited into the uterus on the day of ovulation. Urine should be checked for which of the following to accurately predict when ovulation is occurring?

   A. follicle-stimulating hormone
   B. estrogen
   C. luteinizing hormone
   D. growth hormone

519. Oral contraception relies on synthetic versions of estrogen and progesterone instead of natural hormones because:

   A. Synthetics have been devised to have a shorter biological half-life.
   B. Natural hormones are quickly removed from circulation and degraded by the liver.
   C. Synthetic hormones bind LH receptors with greater affinity than natural hormones.
   D. Synthetics cross the blood-brain barrier and therefore have more side effects.

520. Estrogen has been shown to increase the number of FSH and LH receptors in the thecal and granulose cells. Estrogen stimulation is an example of:

   A. negative feedback
   B. positive feedback
   C. neurocrine regulation
   D. desensitization

521. The *proliferative phase* of the menstrual cycle is highly variable in duration. Which of the following is most conclusive in explaining this occurrence?

   A. The follicular phase is prompted by the pituitary and its effect depends on serum hormone concentrations, which often fluctuate.
   B. Hormones stimulate the ovary to always release a follicle on the 14th day of a 28-day cycle.
   C. Secretory and follicular phases are both genetically controlled and as a result function like clockwork.
   D. Proliferative variability depends on signals from the uterus that are released when the endometrial lining has properly thickened.

522. Women with a condition called *endometriosis* have endometrial tissue that grows in areas outside the uterus. This ectopic endometrial tissue is hormone sensitive and may appear in the fallopian tubes, in the abdomen, etc. Which of the following is a possible effect of endometriosis?

   A. No effect, because the tissue is responsive to hormonal regulation.
   B. Infertility, because the extra endometrial tissue may prevent the passage of sperm.
   C. Increased fertility, because the ectopic tissue will facilitate implantation of the zygote.
   D. No effect, because the endometrium is not involved in the menstrual cycle.

523. Which of the following is the correct order of events in the menstrual cycle?

   A. Menstruation → Luteal phase → Ovulation → Secretory phase
   B. Menstruation → Proliferative phase → Ovulation → Luteal phase
   C. Ovulation → Proliferative phase → Ovulation → Secretory phase → Menstruation
   D. Ovulation → Follicular phase → Menstruation → Luteal phase

---

524. Abnormal testicular development can sometimes lead to a condition called cryptochordism in which the testes do not fully descend into the scrotum. The most likely cause of developing cryptochordism is an:

A. excess estrogen
B. excess FSH
C. lack of testosterone
D. lack of cortisol

525. The stimulus to activate *hormone-sensitive lipase* cascade and raise blood glucose levels can be achieved by which of the following hormones?

A. insulin
B. glucagon
C. acetylcholine
D. testosterone

526. Which of the listed processes occurs in the small intestine but NOT in the colon?

A. peristalsis
B. water absorption
C. nutrient absorption
D. potassium secretion

527. Growth hormone is synthesized in which of the following glands?

A. anterior pituitary
B. posterior pituitary
C. hypothalamus
D. hippocampus

528. According to the established chemical classification, hormones fall into which of the following basic categories?

A. proteins, sugars, and steroids
B. peptide, steroid, and tyrosine derived
C. male hormones and female hormones
D. stimulator hormones and receptor hormones

529. All of the following are reabsorbed by secondary active transport in the proximal convoluted tubule EXCEPT:

A. glucose
B. amino acids
C. phosphate
D. urea

530. Which of the following is an important source of new gene combinations for growth factors?

A. cytokinesis
B. chromatin condensation during meiosis or mitosis
C. splitting of sister chromatids during anaphase mitosis
D. crossing over during meiosis

531. Which of the following organelles is responsible for protein modification and carbohydrate synthesis?

A. Golgi apparatus
B. rough ER
C. lysosome
D. peroxisome

532. In order to maintain homeostasis several antagonistic endocrine relationships exist in the human body. An example of one would be:

A. ACTH and TSH
B. oxytocin and prolactin
C. insulin and glucagon
D. vitamin D and parathyroid hormone

533. One cause of infertility in females is the ovulation of immature ova. In most cases this is caused by hyposecretion of:

A. FSH
B. LH
C. oxytocin
D. estrogen

534. Most second messenger systems that have been explored to date are initiated by ligands binding to receptors. Which of the following hormones does NOT depend on a second messenger system?

A. insulin
B. cAMP
C. estrogen
D. thyroid-stimulating hormone

Sodium and water levels are regulated by aldosterone to maintain a normal body fluid volume. Specifically, aldosterone stimulates the activity and abundance of the Na^+/K^+ ATPase. Properly regulated fluid volume maintains the blood pressure in the normal range.

A study was conducted to evaluate whether aldosterone has an effect on the Na^+/K^+ ATPase of rat aorta. Cells under study were pumped full of radioactive ^{86}Rb. The pump function was measured by counting the ^{86}Rb excreted from aortic cells by the ^{86}Rb/K ATPase. Addition of aldosterone induced a rapid activation of the Na^+/K^+ ATPase, followed by a return to control values after 120 minutes. The aldosterone-induced increase in ^{86}Rb/K ATPase was prevented by the new mineralocorticoid receptor antagonist *eplerenone*. The inhibition of aldosterone gene transcription (via actinomycin D) or protein synthesis (via cycloheximide) had no effect on aldosterone action on Na^+/K^+ ATPase. These findings indicate that aldosterone has a nongenomic effect on the Na^+/K^+ ATPase of the vascular system through sodium pump regulation. This effect is mediated through protein kinase C activation.

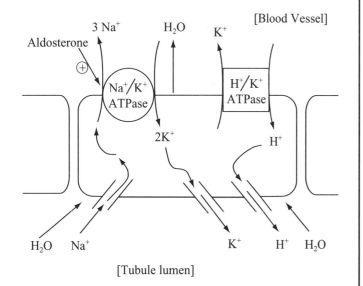

[Tubule lumen]

Figure 1

535. What method was used by ^{86}Rb to leave the rat aortic cell?

    A. simple diffusion
    B. active transport
    C. facilitated diffusion
    D. ATP dependent exocytosis

536. Conn's syndrome is an aldosterone oversecreting tumor of the adrenal gland. Which of the following effects would be expected in a patient suffering from Conn's syndrome?

    A. high blood pressure
    B. no effect on the potassium concentration
    C. an increase in the secretion of renin
    D. acidosis in the blood

537. Actinomycin D is an orange/red powder that is used to inhibit cancer growth. According to the passage, the effectiveness of actinomycin D depends on it entering the:

    A. cytoplasm
    B. cell membrane
    C. smooth endoplasmic reticulum
    D. nucleus

538. Aldosterone acts to decrease water loss by increasing the reabsorption of sodium at the:

    A. Bowman's capsule
    B. distal convoluted tubule
    C. proximal convoluted tubule
    D. loop of Henle

539. The new mineralocorticoid receptor antagonist eplerenone is functioning when a:

    I. decrease in blood volume is noted
    II. decrease in urine potassium is noted
    III. decrease in urine volume is noted

    A. I only
    B. I and II only
    C. III only
    D. I, II, and III

540. What vascular system delivers aldosterone to its target receptors in the kidney?

    A. urine
    B. blood
    C. lymphatics
    D. interstitial hormone fluid

GO ON TO THE NEXT PAGE.

The body has three mechanisms to irreversibly remove hormones from circulation: they include target cell uptake, metabolic degradation, and urinary excretion. The *metabolic clearance rate* (MCR) is a measure of the total hormone removed by all three mechanisms. When a certain amount of hormone is removed from the blood, this can be thought of in terms of the equivalent volume of blood that is *totally* cleared of the hormone. For example, 1 nanogram of hormone is removed from the blood in a certain amount of time. The *metabolic clearance rate* for that hormone is whatever volume of blood has been totally depleted of that 1 nanogram. In equation form the *metabolic clearance rate* is:

$$\text{MCR} = \frac{\text{rate of hormone elimination}}{\text{plasma hormone concentration}}$$

Equation 1

Volume of distribution (VD), depending on the plasma concentration, is the total amount of hormone in the body. The ratio of MCR to the *volume of distribution* is the *fractional turnover rate*, sometimes denoted by the letter K. The plasma *half-life* is the reciprocal of K.

$$\text{Half-life } (t_{1/2}) = 0.7 \times \text{VD} / \text{MCR}$$

Equation 2

The half-life is correlated to the degree a hormone binds to blood proteins. A hormone that travels mostly bound to a protein will have a longer half-life.

The kidney and liver are the two main organs for removing hormones. Peptide hormones are water-soluble and are filtered by the kidney glomerulus but are subsequently reabsorbed by the nephron. So only a small amount of active hormone ends up in the urine.

541. All of the following will decrease the expected hormone half-life EXCEPT:

  A. a decrease in the total hormone in the body
  B. a decrease in the fractional turnover rate
  C. an increase in the metabolic clearance
  D. an increase in the plasma hormone concentration

542. Endocrine hormones vary widely in the pharmacokinetics of their action. Which of the following is an accurate comparison between lipid-soluble progesterone and water-soluble ACTH?

  A. Lipid-soluble hormones have a slow onset but a short duration of action.
  B. Lipid-soluble hormones have a slow onset but a long duration of action.
  C. Water-soluble hormones have a fast onset and a long duration of action.
  D. Water-soluble hormones have a slow onset and a long duration of action.

543. The same concept of *clearance* that is seen in hormone degradation is also an important measure of function for this organ:

  A. the heart
  B. the kidney
  C. the lung
  D. the intestine

544. The kidney protein reabsorption described in the passage occurs where in the nephron?

  A. the glomerulus
  B. the collecting duct
  C. the Bowman's capsule
  D. the proximal convoluted tubule

545. Which of the following functions are performed by a receptor to initiate a proper reaction "cascade"?

  I. allows for a high degree of specificity
  II. amplifies the incoming signal
  III. causes the modification of the binding ligand

  A. I only
  B. I and II only
  C. II and III only
  D. I, II, and III

546. What target cells make up the organ that is expected to uptake oxytocin?

  A. the hypothalamus
  B. the uterus
  C. the posterior pituitary
  D. the liver

547. Up to 20 years of age the male breast can be stimulated to secrete milk. Which of the following hormones would be needed to stimulate the production of breast milk?

    A.   vasopressin, GH, prolactin
    B.   progesterone, LH, oxytocin
    C.   oxytocin, prolactin, estrogen
    D.   testosterone, progesterone, aldosterone

548. Paracrine and autocrine hormones do not depend on blood-borne transport and as a result are not expected to interact with all of the following EXCEPT:

    A.   endothelial cells of the renal artery
    B.   albumin
    C.   sperm
    D.   platelets

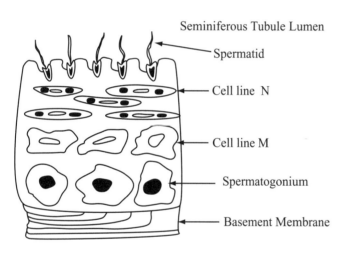

Seminiferous Tubule Lumen
Spermatid
Cell line N
Cell line M
Spermatogonium
Basement Membrane

549. Seminiferous tubules are located in the testes. In the above figure, cell line M is most likely a collection of:

    A.   haploid primary spermatocytes
    B.   diploid primary spermatocytes
    C.   haploid secondary spermatocytes
    D.   diploid secondary spermatocytes

550. Studies have enabled the pharmaceutical industry to modify peptides to produce ADH analogues that do not increase the blood pressure yet have greater antidiuretic activity. What do these analogs do?

    A.   increase sodium reabsorption by the distal convoluted tubule
    B.   stimulate carotid sinus blood pressure baroreceptors
    C.   stimulate water aquaporin channels in the collecting duct
    D.   increase renin production and release

551. Elevated levels of potassium in the blood must be immediately corrected. What would be the expected response by the adrenal gland to the increased potassium?

    A.   block the secretion of aldosterone
    B.   no effect; aldosterone only reabsorbs sodium
    C.   stimulate the secretion of aldosterone
    D.   the adrenal does not secrete aldosterone

552. Which anatomical structure seems to enhance all processes necessary for the synthesis of thyroid hormone, including the production of the iodide transporter, thyroid peroxidase and thyroglobulin?

    A.   anterior pituitary
    B.   posterior pituitary
    C.   thyroid gland
    D.   parathyroid gland

553. IGF-1 is the primary protein synthesized in response to growth hormone. A mouse with a partial deletion of both IGF-1 genes would be expected to have which of the following presentations?

    A.   increased heart rate and no thyroid hormone release
    B.   deafness and a growth deficiency
    C.   brittle bones and decreased calcium levels
    D.   anemia and lack of lipid digestion

554. Mitosis produces two daughter cells from a single parent and serves all of the following purposes EXCEPT:

- **A.** tissue growth
- **B.** organ repair
- **C.** cell transduction
- **D.** scar tissue formation

555. Spermatogenesis is the production of sperm and it begins in which of the following locations?

- **A.** the epididymis
- **B.** the vas deferens
- **C.** seminal vesicles
- **D.** seminiferous tubules

556. Which of the following is/are considered critical components of the menstrual cycle?

- **I.** Progesterone stimulation of the endometrial lining
- **II.** FSH stimulation of ovarian follicle development
- **III.** Epinephrine release by the adrenal medulla

- **A.** I and II only
- **B.** II and III only
- **C.** I and III only
- **D.** I, II, and III

STOP. IF YOU FINISH BEFORE TIME IS CALLED, CHECK YOUR WORK. YOU MAY GO BACK TO ANY QUESTION IN THIS TEST BOOKLET.

LECTURE 6

Biology Passages
Questions 557–667

Passage 601 (Questions 557-563)

Hydrochloric acid (HCl) is the best-known component of gastric juice. When stimulated, by gastrin, acetylcholine, and/or histamine, parietal cells secrete HCl at a concentration of 165 mM, which is equivalent to a pH of 0.9. Each parietal cell has a hydrogen ion concentration that is roughly 3 million fold higher than that in the blood. Hydrogen ions are released into the stomach lumen by the H^+/K^+ ATPase or the "proton pump" in exchange for potassium. Once hydrogen ions are released, chloride is secreted against both concentration and electric gradients via an active transport mechanism.

Histologically, each parietal cell undergoes a drastic change in its morphology prior to releasing HCl. Cytoplasmic tubulo-vesicular membranes, normally abundant in the resting cell, virtually disappear while canalicular membranes enlarge. Intracellularly stored proton pumps, potassium, and chloride channels are fused with canalicular membranes just prior to the secretion of the acid. Once released, HCl travels via deep plasma cell invaginations, known as canaliculi, into the lumen of the stomach.

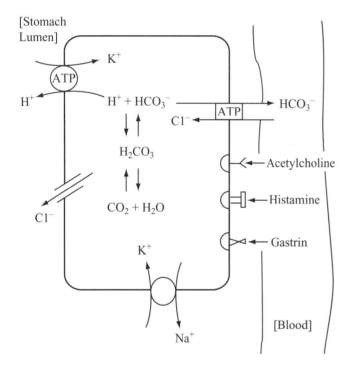

Mechanism 1 HCL Secretion by Parietal Cells

557. Which of the following GI cells secretes pepsinogen?

- **A.** parietal cell
- **B.** P-cell
- **C.** chief cell
- **D.** pancreatic cell

558. The cephalic and oral phases of gastric secretion are abolished by a vagotomy (the cutting of the vagus nerve). Which parietal cell stimulant is non-existent following a vagotomy?

- **A.** histamine
- **B.** acetylcholine
- **C.** gastrin
- **D.** sodium-potassium pump

559. Under normal physiological conditions with a properly functioning Na^+/K^+ pump, which of the following ions has the highest intracellular concentration?

- **A.** Ca^{2+}
- **B.** Cl^-
- **C.** K^+
- **D.** Na^+

560. An ingested poison makes its way through the digestive tract. After passing through the duodenum, it will next be propelled into:

- **A.** the appendix
- **B.** the jejunum
- **C.** the large intestine
- **D.** the ileum

561. The passage suggests that the most effective way to control unwanted acid secretion would be treatment with:

- **A.** surgery to remove the vagus nerve
- **B.** both an antihistamine and an antigastrin
- **C.** an anti-acetylcholine at the GI acetylcholine receptor
- **D.** a proton pump inhibitor

562. Which of the following statements best explains the error present in the parietal cell HCl secretion in Mechanism 1?

- **A.** Parietal cell acid secretion will cease because of the accumulation of intracellular potassium.
- **B.** The sodium-potassium ATPase is pumping its ions in the wrong direction.
- **C.** Histamine is a peptide and should bind a nuclear receptor.
- **D.** HCl secretion is a passive process.

563. The bicarbonate (HCO_3^-) produced in parietal cells is absorbed into the bloodstream in exchange for Cl^-. What is the expected blood pH when the Cl^-—HCO_3^- exchanger is fully functional?

- **A.** The blood is experiencing an "acidic tide."
- **B.** The blood is experiencing an "alkaline tide."
- **C.** The blood remains at the normal physiological pH.
- **D.** The blood becomes neutral with pH of 7.0.

Passage 602 (Questions 564-569)

During early embryological development, no organs have formed yet. All that exists is the *celom*, a wide tubular space in which organs will form. Around the *celom* is a muscular wall of mesodermal origin. As development progresses, the long *celom* cavity divides into four smaller celoms: one for the heart, two for the lungs, and one for the abdomen. They become known as the pericardial, pleural, and peritoneal cavities, respectively. A pericardial, pleural, or peritoneal membrane lines each celom. Specifically, pleura cover the lungs, pericardium surrounds the heart, and peritoneum and mesenteries line the abdomen.

Organs growing into the *celom* use their volume to fill up the cavity. As they grow, they drag with them a membrane, which lined the celom. A membrane always surrounds each organ. Organs are either suspended within the celomic cavity or they are attached to the inner body wall. The lungs and the small intestine are 2 examples of suspended organs, which are more or less free-floating. Attached organs include the liver or the kidney. Both are tightly wrapped and pressed against the posterior abdominal wall.

Each celomic membrane has two layers: the parietal layer lines the outer surface of the celom, while the visceral layer lies directly on the organ. Both visceral and parietal linings are one and the same, a continuous surface.

564. Which of the following structures is an example of a "blind tube" entering the celom?

   I. digestive system
   II. respiratory system
  III. vascular system

   A. I only
   B. II only
   C. III only
   D. I and III only

565. The intraembryonic celom forms as a split in the mesoderm. What other structure is derived from mesoderm?

   A. epithelial lining of the trachea and bronchi
   B. muscles of the tongue
   C. retina, iris, and optic nerve
   D. epidermis, hair, and nails

566. Organs that have the least amount of free movement within the body can be difficult to repair if injured. One would suspect that damage to which organ would require the most expertise to repair?

   A. the heart
   B. the liver
   C. the lung
   D. the intestine

567. Which anatomical structure is located external to the celom?

   I. the liver
   II. head and neck
  III. an upper limb

   A. I only
   B. II only
   C. II and III only
   D. I, II, and III

568. According to the passage, the organ that houses glomeruli is associated with:

   A. peritoneal cavity
   B. pericardial cavity
   C. the pleural cavity
   D. the adrenal cavity

569. Blood coming through the umbilical vein is shunted around the liver through the:

   A. aorta
   B. foramen ovale
   C. ligamentum venosum
   D. ductus venosus

Passage 603 (Questions 570-576)

While there is no absolute "cure" for obesity, its management requires a calorie-restricted diet in proportion to the current nutritional recommendations.

Stomach stapling was the first attempt to control obesity via surgical means. Most anti-obesity efforts, however, have centered on drugs that treat obesity by modifying food intake. These drugs increase satiety by changing the rate of gastric emptying, decreasing intestinal absorption, etc. Over-the-counter weak adrenergic agents, such as phenopropylolamine and dexatrim, are not as effective at achieving weight loss. They temporarily decrease appetite while depleting the hypothalamus of norepinephrine, which leads to withdrawal symptoms of food obsession and depression.

Two other anti-obesity drugs should be mentioned. *Orlistat* is a streptomyces derivative that inhibits lipase, an enzyme involved with fat metabolism. *Orlistat* use can lead to modest weight loss when combined with nutritional counseling. When taking the drug, because ingested fat is neither metabolized nor absorbed, it shows up in the stool. (About 0.5% of patients have diarrhea.) *Sibutramine* is another anti-obesity drug, which inhibits the reuptake of both norepinephrine and serotonin. Its side effects are dry mouth and constipation.

There are about 100 deaths each year due to people taking over-the-counter adrenergic agents such as Metabolite® or the "Slim Tea®." "Slim Tea" is made in Arizona from the chaparral herb. Unfortunately, it can cause hepato-renal failure in some people.

570. According to the passage, levels of which of the following hormones may also be altered in those persons taking phenopropylolamine?

    A. testosterone
    B. oxytocin
    C. prolactin
    D. epinephrine

571. Concentration of which of the following cells will NOT be affected by stomach surgery?

    A. chief cells
    B. beta-cells
    C. parietal cells
    D. mucous neck cells

572. Currently marketed anti-obesity medications induce the feeling of satiety by modifying signals to which structure?

    A. the hypothalamus
    B. the medulla oblongata
    C. the cerebellum
    D. the spinal cord

573. Which of the following is a possible side effect of long-term *orlistat* use?

    A. decreased absorption of proteins and carbohydrates
    B. constipation
    C. severe appetite inhibition
    D. depleted body stores of lipid-soluble vitamins

574. According to the passage, "Slim Tea" damages which of the following digestive accessory organs?

    A. kidneys
    B. liver
    C. pancreas
    D. stomach

575. Brain, liver, and red blood cells are known to absorb glucose independently of insulin. What is the predicted effect of high cortisol level on the cell glucose shuttle pump?

    A. decreased rate of glycolysis
    B. increased level of insulin
    C. increased rate of glycolysis
    D. decreased level of insulin

576. According to the passage, stomach stapling is a surgical method used to control obesity by:

    A. forcing more digestion to occur in the esophagus
    B. decreasing the release of lipase
    C. causing early satiety by decreasing the gastric space
    D. decreasing the intestinal absorption

GO ON TO THE NEXT PAGE.

577. What is found at the esophagus-stomach, stomach-duodenum, and ileum-colon junction sites?

A. high density of villi
B. sphincters
C. specific sites for peristalsis
D. enzyme release points

578. The nephron sodium-hydrogen exchange carrier, which is an anti-port carrier, is the main mechanism used to remove Na^+ ions from urine. When the carrier is functioning, what is the approximate pH of the urine?

A. 12.2
B. 7.4
C. 7.0
D. 6.0

579. All pancreatic enzymes are synthesized and secreted by the acinar cells. Which of the following enzymes is secreted as an inactive precursor that is converted to its active form in the lumen of the small intestine?

A. lipase
B. chymotrypsinogen
C. amylase
D. colipase

580. Saliva is a complex mixture with lubricating and pH buffering properties. What enzyme found in saliva is also secreted by the pancreas?

A. trypsin
B. amylase
C. pepsin
D. chymotrypsin

581. Dextrans are glucose polymers that are neutral but can be made either positive or negative by chemical attachment of cationic or anionic groups. Assuming normal renal function, what type of dextran is more likely to be filtered from blood?

A. positively charged dextran
B. negatively charged dextran
C. neutral charged dextran
D. all dextrans will be equally filtered

582. What part of the digestive tract is commonly divided into three segments based on anatomy and function: duodenum, jejunum, and ileum?

A. the large intestine
B. the stomach
C. the small intestine
D. the esophagus

583. The kidneys and the respiratory system work together to maintain the pH of the body fluids at a constant value. The respiratory system performs this duty by controlling the concentration of which of the following?

A. HCl
B. carbon dioxide
C. bicarbonate
D. oxygen

584. The pancreatic islets of Langerhans contain both the insulin-secreting and glucagon-secreting cells. The islets also secrete which paracrine hormone that inhibits the release of both insulin and glucagon?

A. pepsin
B. somatostatin
C. trypsin
D. cortisol

GO ON TO THE NEXT PAGE.

585. The nephron is a hollow, convoluted tube of cells. It is engineered to concentrate urine by removing water at which of the following sites?

 I. proximal convoluted tubule
 II. descending limb of the loop of Henle
 III. ascending limb of the loop of Henle

 A. I only
 B. II only
 C. I and II only
 D. I, II, and III

586. All of the following are derived from the embryonic ectoderm layer, EXCEPT:

 A. the blood vessel
 B. the skin
 C. the eye
 D. the nervous system

587. Fixed acids, such as lactic, pyruvic, and acetoacetic acids, are produced by cellular metabolism and expelled into the blood. Which of the following metabolic processes produces lactic acid?

 A. glycolysis
 B. fermentation
 C. electron transport chain
 D. amino acid synthesis

Passage 604 (Questions 588-593)

Diabetes Mellitus (DM) is the 6th leading cause of death in the U.S. (about 70,000 deaths in 2000). Diabetes is also the #1 cause of non-traumatic amputations, along with blindness and kidney failure. DM Type 1 (IDDM) is an insulin-dependent autoimmune condition that results from the complete destruction of pancreatic β-cells, which results in little to no insulin production. DM Type 2 [NIDDM] is a non-insulin dependent or insulin-resistant condition. People diagnosed with NIDDM do have a basal level of insulin, but it is too low to effectively control blood glucose levels. Insulin resistance due to faulty or down-regulated receptors seems to be the prevailing theory explaining the epidemic number of DM Type 2 seen. (DM Type 2 is also associated with obesity in both adults and children.)

Insulin is stored in acidified granules as a zinc hexomer. When it is released, the neutral external pH dissolves the zinc complex, and insulin is released into the bloodstream. Insulin receptors have two α and two β subunits. Insulin reacts with the α portion of the receptor, resulting in a phosphorylation cascade involving a tyrosine kinase. Downstream of this are the intracellular effects of insulin on glucose uptake and regulation.

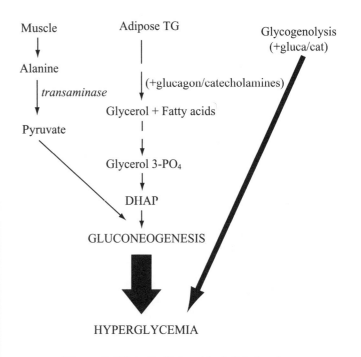

Figure 1 Diabetic Ketoacidosis Mechanism

588. The metabolism of glucose is regulated by a complex orchestration of hormones. All of the following endocrine products increase blood glucose concentration EXCEPT:

 A. epinephrine
 B. glucagon
 C. calcitonin
 D. cortisol

589. After glucose is transported into the cytoplasm, it can be directed toward which of the following metabolic pathways?

I. deposition as glycogen
II. synthesis of pyruvate and/or lactate
III. production of adipose tissue

A. I only
B. I and III only
C. II and III only
D. I, II, and III

590. Based on the passage, which of the following methods can be used to obtain a definitive diagnosis of type I insulin-dependent diabetes?

A. detecting the presence of islet cell antibodies
B. performing an insulin receptor count
C. testing for elevated blood sugar concentration
D. screening individuals for obesity

591. The digestive system is a series of hollow organs joined in a long, twisting tube. Which of the following are two solid organs associated with the GI tract?

A. spleen and liver
B. pancreas and gall bladder
C. lymph nodes and jejunum
D. liver and the pancreas

592. If the production of glycerol-3-phospahate is inhibited, can hyperglycemia still occur?

A. Yes, but the hyperglycemic individual will experience muscle wasting.
B. Yes, but DHAP accumulation will be observed.
C. No, pyruvate and glycogenolysis are incapable of stimulating hyperglycemia.
D. No, because the inhibition of transaminase will also occur.

593. The passage suggests that all of the following structures might be damaged in a diabetic individual EXCEPT:

A. the villi of the small intestine
B. the Bowman's capsule
C. the retina
D. peripheral lower limb vessels

Passage 605 (Questions 594-599)

Numerous lifestyle factors play a role in various cancers. Smoking, diet, consumer products, and medical procedures are among many on the list. It is estimated that 3% of cancers may be attributed to excessive alcohol consumption. Different countries have different risks for different cancers. Why does Africa have such a high incidence of liver cancer? It may be because of a high prevalence of hepatitis B or the high residential distribution of selenium.

Cancer screening is used to detect cancer or risk of cancer in a patient who has no signs or symptoms of the disease. A person who already exhibits signs and symptoms of the disease needs a diagnosis, not a screening. Cancer screening can involve either primary or secondary prevention or both.

Primary prevention involves the prevention of a cancerous growth by removing a precancerous lesion. Such prevention might include a Pap smear, colonoscopy, and sigmoidoscopy. A Pap may indicate dysplasia, a lesion several steps away from a full-blown cancer.

Secondary prevention is the early detection and treatment of a cancer. Slowly progressing cancers are more likely to be identified by this type of screening. Cervical cancer, which needs many years to grow, is likely to be picked up by a Pap smear. On the other hand, screening is not good for pancreatic cancer because it progresses so quickly.

Type of Cancer	Percent due to alcohol (males)	Percent due to alcohol (females)
Oral cavity	50%	40%
Larynx	50%	40%
Esophagus	30%	30%
Liver	30%	30%

Table 1 Cancers Associated with Alcohol Consumption

Cancer	High Incidence	Low Incidence	Risk Ratio
Colon	Scotland	Japan	4:1
Stomach	Japan	U.S.	8:1
Esophageal	Iran	Israel	10:1
Liver	Africa	England	100:1

Table 2 International Differences in Cancer Rates

594. It can be inferred from the passage that excess alcohol consumption is most likely to result in a cancer of which organ system?

A. digestive system
B. cardiovascular system
C. integumentary system
D. renal system

595. Which of the following is diagnostic for a well-advanced cancerous lesion?

I. an abnormal result on a primary prevention screening
II. tissue biopsy with malignant cells present
III. exposure to a known carcinogen

A. I only
B. II only
C. I and II only
D. I, II, and III

596. Which of the following statements correctly describe the association between hepatitis B and liver cancer?

A. Hepatitis releases a toxin after being metabolized by the liver.
B. Hepatitis prevents the liver from storing bile.
C. Hepatitis causes a liver infection that may mutate some cells.
D. Hepatitis destroys every accessory organ of the circulatory system.

597. Japan has a high incidence of stomach cancer. If someone from Japan moves to the United States, his or her risk of developing stomach cancer is expected to:

A. remain about the same
B. decrease
C. increase
D. depends on his or her alcohol consumption

598. Radon occurs naturally from the breakdown of uranium in the soil and is associated with cancer of the alveoli. This carcinogen enters the body as a:

A. solid particle
B. gas
C. liquid
D. pseudo substance

Category	Death Rate	Mortality Ratio
Nonsmoker, no asbestos	11.3	1.0
Nonsmoker, asbestos	58.4	5.2
Smoker, no asbestos	122.6	10.9
Smoker, asbestos	601.6	53.2

Data for cancer mortality ratios for multiple risk groups

599. Based on the above data, what is the association between exposure to multiple carcinogens and mortality?

A. effects of multiple risk factors are synergistic
B. effects of multiple risk factors are additive
C. effects of multiple risk factors are preventive
D. effects of multiple risk factors cannot be determined accurately from the data presented

Passage 606 (Questions 600-605)

The large intestine is functionally divided by the transverse colon into two parts, the right and left colon. The right colon—made up of the cecum and ascending colon—plays a major role in water and electrolyte absorption and the fermentation of undigested sugars. Its left counterpart—made up of the descending colon, sigmoid colon, and rectum—is predominantly involved in the storage and evacuation of stool.

Under normal physiological conditions, approximately 1.6 liters of fluid enters the colon each day, but only 100-200 milliliters are excreted in the stool. On average, the maximum absorptive capacity of the colon is about 4.5 L per day. The fundamental feature of colonic electrolyte transport is the ability of the colon mucosa to generate a large osmotic ion gradient between the lumen and the intracellular space. The Na^+/K^+ ATPase creates this osmotic gradient by pumping sodium out of the cell. As sodium re-enters the cell, down its concentration gradient, water is passively drawn with it out of the colonic lumen. The potassium pumped into the cell by the Na^+/K^+ ATPase can also be secreted into the lumen.

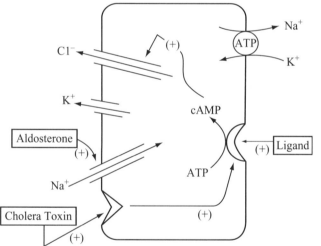

Figure 1 Colon Electrolyte Transport

600. Under normal physiological conditions, the colon secretes which of the following compounds?

   A.   sodium ions
   B.   230 mL of water
   C.   aldosterone
   D.   potassium ions

601. To measure the highest concentration of lactic acid a probe should be placed into which compartment of the large intestine?

   A.   the cecum
   B.   the sigmoid colon
   C.   the transverse colon
   D.   the rectum

602. The adrenal cortex hormone, aldosterone, attaches to identical receptors in the colon and the nephron. What is the expected result of aldosterone binding to its colon receptor?

   A.   increased potassium reabsorption
   B.   increased sodium reabsorption
   C.   increased water secretion
   D.   no effect; aldosterone only affects the kidney

603. Vibrio cholera toxin is produced by a gram-negative bacterium with a single polar flagellum. Cholera infection causes copious, painless, watery diarrhea by which of the following mechanisms?

   A.   Immotile cholera causes a drastic decrease in the intracellular concentration of ATP.
   B.   Overstimulation of a second-messenger channel activating system.
   C.   Cholera enterotoxin inactivates the adenylate cyclase enzyme in the intestinal cells.
   D.   Motile cholera inhibits adequate ligand binding necessary to stimulate cAMP production.

604. Angiotensin II and which other hormone act to stimulate the adrenal gland?

   A.   epinephrine
   B.   FSH
   C.   aldosterone
   D.   ACTH

605. Hirschsprung's disease causes a constriction of the colon because of absent innervation. Which of the following symptoms would be expected in a patient with Hirschsprung's disease?

   A.   diarrhea
   B.   colonic shrinkage
   C.   constipation
   D.   increased potassium secretion

GO ON TO THE NEXT PAGE.

606. What organ needs to be isolated in order to specifically study the conversion of vitamin D to its active form, synthesis of renin, and the release of erythropoietin?

A. lung
B. bone marrow
C. intestine
D. kidney

607. A radioactive marker is utilized to detect the location of FSH receptors in a male. The radioactivity would most likely be concentrated in which of the following structures?

A. the ovary
B. the testes
C. the anterior pituitary
D. the adrenal gland

608. Cholecystokinin (CCK) is released by cells in the duodenum and proximal jejunum in response to fat and protein being present in the intestine. All of the following enzymes are expected to be released in response to CCK, EXCEPT:

A. liver's bile
B. salivary amylase
C. pancreatic lipase
D. pancreatic chymotrypsin

609. The energy released by the movement of sodium down its electrochemical gradient is used to move glucose up its gradient. Other compounds are also moved by this mechanism, which is known as:

A. primary active transport
B. secondary active transport
C. facilitated diffusion
D. simple diffusion

610. Which of the following organs are not properly functioning in a mouse with induced hepato-renal failure?

A. liver and spleen
B. pancreas and kidney
C. stomach and intestine
D. liver and kidney

611. Which of the following is the main activating factor of aldosterone secretion during periods of dehydration?

A. ACTH
B. sympathetic nervous system
C. renin
D. spontaneous adrenal release

612. As a protective mechanism, mucous is secreted by the epithelium along the entire GI tract. The mucous usually contains bicarbonate, which serves what purpose?

I. acts as a GI buffer
II. digests proteins
III. prevents the digestive tract from becoming acidic

A. I only
B. I and III only
C. II and III only
D. I, II, and III

613. The most common cause of infertility in women is a failure to ovulate that is most likely caused by:

A. a hypersecretion of FSH
B. a hypersecretion of LH
C. a hyposecretion of LH
D. the dilation of the cervix

614. Bile acids are secreted continuously by the liver and are stored in the:

A. spleen
B. small intestine
C. gall bladder
D. liver

615. A digital probe is placed into the opening of the urethra and guided into the excretory system. Which of the following statements maps out the anatomical structures encountered by the probe as it is maneuvered into the body?

A. urethra → bladder → opening to the ureter → ureter → renal pelvis

B. kidney → ureter → opening to the bladder → bladder → urethra

C. urethra → bladder → opening to the ureter → ureter → prostate → ureter → renal pelvis

D. urethra → opening to the ureter → prostate → vas deferens → epididymis

616. A urethral stone will cause a blockage in the excretory system, which increases the hydrostatic pressure in the Bowman's space. Which of the following will occur as a result of a urethral stone?

A. The filtration of blood toxins will decrease.

B. The filtration of blood toxins will increase.

C. Vasoconstriction of the renal blood vessels will occur.

D. No major effect is expected because the second kidney is fully functional.

Passage 607 (Questions 617-622)

The pancreas is an elongated, tapered organ located behind the stomach. The right side of the organ, called the head, is the widest part and lies in the curvature of the duodenum. The tapered body of the pancreas ends near the spleen. The islets of Langerhans, which are clumps of cells scattered throughout the gland, produce endocrine secretions that include insulin, glucagon, pancreatic peptide, somatostatin, and other hormones.

The exocrine portion of the pancreas takes up roughly 77 percent of the total glandular volume. It consists of acinar cells, which secrete primarily digestive enzymes, and ductal cells, which secrete fluids and electrolytes. Pancreatic secretion is regulated by several peptides released by the gastrointestinal tract. Secretin and cholecystokinin (CCK) stimulate pancreatic secretions, whereas somatostatin and pancreatic polypeptide inhibit pancreatic enzyme release.

The pancreas secretes about 20 digestive enzymes and cofactors. Some enzymes are activated in the duodenum by enterokinases and calcium. These enzymes account for most of the intraluminal digestion of dietary proteins, triglycerides, and carbohydrates. They are also important in the cleavage of certain vitamins (such as A and B_{12}) from their carrier molecules, thereby allowing them to be absorbed efficiently. Because pancreatic enzymes are secreted in great excess, maldigestion and serious nutritional deficiencies occur only when more than 90% of the gland has been destroyed.

617. Which of the following is NOT an acinar cell product?

A. lipid-digesting lipase

B. bond-breaking gyrase

C. peptide-hydrolyzing trypsinogen

D. neutralizing HCl

618. Stimulation of target organs by the parasympathetic vagus nerve would exert which of the following effects?

A. acetylcholine-stimulated increase in pancreatic secretion

B. norepinephrine inhibition of pancreatic secretion

C. norepinephrine-stimulated increase in the heart rate

D. acetylcholine inhibition of the GI tract

619. Pancreatitis is an inflammatory process that causes pancreatic enzymes to autodigest the gland. Which of the following would be expected in a patient suffering pancreatitis?

    A.   excessive pancreatic secretions
    B.   lipid-soluble vitamin deficiency
    C.   increased protein digestion and absorption
    D.   excessive fat absorption

620. Insulinoma is a common tumor of the endocrine pancreas that presents with excessive insulin secretion. Which of the following is an affect of insulinoma on the body?

    A.   hyperglycemia
    B.   low glycogen levels
    C.   decreased protein synthesis
    D.   increased rate of glycolysis

621. All of the following functions are performed by an organ that neighbors the pancreas EXCEPT:

    A.   removal of aged blood cells
    B.   release of insulin
    C.   filtering out bacterial agents
    D.   white blood cell storage

622. Which of the following, when released into the blood, stimulates the pancreas to discharge bicarbonate and neutralize the contents of the intestine?

    A.   somatostatin
    B.   bicarbonate
    C.   pancreatic polypeptide
    D.   secretin

Passage 608 (Questions 623-628)

Reabsorption of water is regulated by antidiuretic hormone (ADH, or vasopressin). It is released when there is a shortage of water in the body. By binding to receptors in the collecting duct of the kidney, ADH increases the permeability of the duct to water by inducing the production of water channels.

On kidney pathology: a bladder infection can cause inflammation (also known as cystitis) and painful urination. Young women are more commonly affected than men. A more serious infection of the urinary tract is called pyelonephritis (infection of the kidneys). This usually results from an infection of the ascending urinary tract. Bacteria travel upward from the external opening of the urethra into the bladder, and from there, through ureters into the kidneys. Urinary tract stones, strictures, and anything that obstructs the flow of urine can lead to pyelonephritis. Recurrent episodes of pyelonephritis can severely impact kidney function. Patients with pyelonephritis feel sick and uneasy, with symptoms such as lower back pain and fever. There will often be both red blood cells and white blood cells found in the urine.

623. The role of the kidney in homeostasis, or the regulation of the internal environment, includes all of the following EXCEPT:

    A.   filtering blood at the glomerulus
    B.   secreting steroid hormones
    C.   maintaining the acid-base balance
    D.   regulating the blood pressure

624. Vasopressin analogs that inhibit the synthesis of ADH would most likely work at which of the following sites?

    A.   collecting duct
    B.   anterior pituitary
    C.   posterior pituitary
    D.   hypothalamus

625. When carbohydrates are consumed, they are broken down into different sugar molecules: sucrose, maltose, lactose, etc. Where in the GI tract does disaccharide digestion take place?

    A.   in the HCl-filled pylorus of the stomach
    B.   in the villi-covered lumen of the colon
    C.   at the brush border enzymes of jejunum and ileum
    D.   via salivary amylase in the mouth

626. The intestine and the proximal convoluted tubule both possess a surface specialization known as the "brush border." Which of the following is the dominant component of the brush border?

    A. cilia
    B. microvilli
    C. stereocilia
    D. zonula occludens

627. Women are especially susceptible to bacteria, which may invade the excretory system and cause an infection. Which of the following statements is the most likely explanation for this phenomenon?

    A. Female anatomy has a very short urethra in comparison to the male anatomy.
    B. Female anatomy has a very short ureter in comparison to the male anatomy.
    C. Male excretory system is lined with special phagocytic cells.
    D. Male's bladder is physically smaller than that of a female bladder.

628. Which of the following structures would most likely be infected in cystitis but *not* in pyelonephritis?

    A. urethra
    B. bladder
    C. ureter
    D. prostate

Passage 609 (Questions 629-634)

Sodium is the major cation of the extracellular compartment, which consists of plasma and interstitial fluids. The kidneys are responsible for the maintenance of body sodium content. Approximately 67% of filtered sodium is reabsorbed in the proximal convoluted tubule. Sodium reabsorption is load dependent; the amount of sodium reabsorbed depends on the amount of sodium filtered. If the amount of sodium filtered increases, so will the reabsorption.

Sodium is reabsorbed by several different mechanisms, depending on the carrier type, in the proximal convoluted tubule. As a general rule, Na^+ is transported down its concentration gradient as it enters the tubular cell cytoplasm.

The nephron sodium-hydrogen pump is an anti-port carrier. It translocates sodium ions from the nephron lumen into the tubular cell cytoplasm as hydrogen ions are propelled in the opposite direction. The exchanger is a secondary active transport carrier because sodium ions are transported down their electrochemical gradient. Sodium is also transported down its concentration gradient to allow reabsorption of solutes (i.e., glucose) needed by the body. Each secondary active transport carrier is specific for a given solute.

629. If the amount of filtered sodium increases from 29 mg/ml to 62 mg/ml, the amount of sodium reabsorbed by the proximal tubule will be:

    A. approximately 31 mg/ml
    B. approximately 40 mg/ml
    C. approximately 58 mg/ml
    D. approximately 110 mg/ml

630. It can be inferred from the passage that the main anion of the intracellular space is:

    A. sodium
    B. potassium
    C. calcium
    D. chloride

631. Which of the following are approximate pH values for the proximal tubule cell and the tubular lumen, respectively?

    A. cellular pH 7.4, lumenal pH 6.1
    B. cellular pH 5.3, lumenal pH 8.2
    C. cellular pH 2.9, lumenal pH 12.9
    D. cellular pH 13.1, lumenal pH 3.1

632. SIADH is a condition characterized by the excessive secretion of ADH. Which of the following will occur in people with this condition?

    A.   increased plasma osmolarity
    B.   dilute urine
    C.   concentrated urine
    D.   increased urine flow rate

633. An uncontrolled diabetic patient may occasionally have glucose appear in the urine. Which of the following statements is the best explanation for this phenomenon?

    A.   High plasma levels of glucose cause glucose to be secreted by the proximal tubule.
    B.   The kidney is a significant site for glucose synthesis, which causes glucose to occasionally appear in urine.
    C.   The high concentration of glucose saturates the reabsorption pumps, causing glucose to appear in the urine.
    D.   The vasa recta transports glucose into urine.

634. Starch is a glucose polymer with an alpha-1, 4 linkage. In which of the following locations does starch digestion begin?

    A.   esophagus
    B.   mouth
    C.   stomach
    D.   small intestine

Questions 635 through 645 are **NOT** based on a descriptive passage.

635. Foods high in triglycerides induce the feeling of satiety after a meal. Which of the following locations serve as sites of triglyceride digestion?

    I.   esophagus
    II.   stomach
    II.   small intestine

    A.   I and II only
    B.   II and III only
    C.   III only
    D.   I, II, and III

636. *Nephrogenic diabetes insipidus* is a condition characterized by a lack of kidney response to antidiuretic hormone. Which of the following is present in a person suffering from nephrogenic diabetes insipidus?

    A.   elevated blood glucose concentration
    B.   glucose present in the urine
    C.   low levels of plasma antidiuretic hormone
    D.   extremely dilute urine

Cortical Nephrons	Juxtamedullary Nephrons
short loop of Henle	long loop of Henle
thin descending limb	thin descending limb
thick ascending limb	thin ascending limb

Table 1 Nephron Specifics

637. Nephrons are classified as cortical or juxtamedullary. The renal concentration of each nephron determines the extent to which an organism can concentrate urine. Which of the following kidneys would produce the maximum urine concentration?

    A.   85% cortical nephrons and 15% juxtamedullary nephrons
    B.   55% cortical nephrons and 45% juxtamedullary nephrons
    C.   50% cortical nephrons and 50% juxtamedullary nephrons
    D.   25% cortical nephrons and 75% juxtamedullary nephrons

GO ON TO THE NEXT PAGE.

638. Which of the following organs secretes enzymes that are absolutely essential for normal digestion and nutrient absorption?

- **A.** pancreas
- **B.** stomach
- **C.** mouth
- **D.** colon

639. To measure the reaction rate of glycolysis the tester should be placed into which intracellular compartment?

- **A.** the cytoplasm
- **B.** the mitochondria
- **C.** the nucleus
- **D.** the cell membrane

640. Pheochromocytoma is an adrenal gland tumor releasing abnormally high levels of epinephrine. Which of the following is a possible side effect of a pheochromocytoma?

- **A.** high blood pressure
- **B.** shock due to low blood pressure
- **C.** low heart rate
- **D.** constricted pupils

641. Cimetidine is a drug that blocks receptors on gastric parietal cells. Which of the following would be expected upon administration of cimetidine?

- **A.** an increase in the stomach pH
- **B.** an increase in the hydrogen ion concentration in the stomach
- **C.** a decrease in the release of pepsin
- **D.** an increase in ATP consumption by the parietal cell

642. From the stomach to the rectum, the digestive tract is organized into 3 layers, the mucosa, the muscularis mucosa, and the submucosa. The muscularis mucosa is most likely composed of what type of muscle?

- **A.** voluntary skeletal muscle
- **B.** involuntary smooth muscle
- **C.** voluntary smooth muscle
- **D.** a combination of voluntary skeletal and involuntary smooth muscle

643. All of the following are end products of digestion, EXCEPT:

- **A.** sucrose
- **B.** amino acids
- **C.** monoglyceride
- **D.** fructose

644. Administration of a bolus dose of aldosterone will have which of the following effects on the blood pressure, blood sodium, and blood potassium?

	Blood Pres.	Blood Na^+	Blood K^+
A.	increase	increase	decrease
B.	increase	decrease	increase
C.	decrease	Increase	decrease
D.	decrease	decrease	increase

645. Proteins that are exported from the cell are synthesized in which of the following locations?

- **A.** free ribosome
- **B.** smooth ER
- **C.** rough ER
- **D.** lysosome

Passage 610 (Questions 646-651)

The renin-angiotensin system is located within the renal *juxtaglomerular apparatus* (JGA). The apparatus sits where the nephron distal convoluted tubule and the glomerulus are in close proximity to each other. The JGA is composed of three main cell types: macula densa, juxtaglomerular, and mesangial cells.

The macula densa is a receptor that responds to low NaCl levels in the fluid entering the distal nephron. When stimulated, the macula densa signals juxtaglomerular, cells to release renin. Renin is a proteolytic enzyme that acts on a plasma protein known as angiotensinogen. A deca-peptide is cleaved from angiotensinogen; the cleaved fragment is angiotensin I. A second important protease is *angiotensin converting enzyme* (ACE), which is found in the lungs. ACE catalyzes a two-amino acid cleavage from angiotensin I to produce angiotensin II (ATII).

Angiotensin II is a potent stimulator of mechanisms that increase blood pressure. ATII directly stimulates the secretion of aldosterone from the adrenal gland, which promotes the reuptake of water from the collecting tubule of the nephron. It also causes vasoconstriction of the vascular system. Vasoconstriction increases the peripheral resistance, which in turn increases systemic blood pressure.

Location	Na^+	H_2O
Proximal tubule	66%	66%
Loop of Henle	25%	15%
Distal tubule	8%	4%
Total	98%	85%

Table 1 Nephron Reabsorption Data

646. Angiotensin II is composed of how many amino acids?

- A. 32 amino acids
- B. 18 amino acids
- C. 10 amino acids
- D. 8 amino acids

647. According to Table 1, the proximal convoluted tubule reabsorbs filtrate with what osmotic concentration?

- A. hyperosmotic in comparison to nephron lumenal contents
- B. isosmotic in comparison to nephron lumenal contents
- C. hypoosmotic in comparison to nephron lumenal contents
- D. osmolarity depends on the hormone stimulation

648. Captopril, an ACE inhibitor, is utilized to treat high blood pressure for all of the following reasons EXCEPT:

- A. It stimulates vasodilation of blood vessels.
- B. It inhibits the endocrine system from releasing aldosterone.
- C. It competitively inhibits angiotensin II receptors.
- D. It decreases angiotensin II, which decreases blood pressure.

649. Decreased sodium flow through which nephron segment is most likely to stimulate the macula densa?

- A. the renal pelvis
- B. the proximal convoluted tubule
- C. the collecting duct
- D. the renal calyx

650. A diuretic is a drug that promotes the excretion of water from the body. Which of the listed diuretics is most likely to exert a particularly powerful effect?

- A. spironolactone action in the collecting duct
- B. thiazide action in the distal convoluted tubule
- C. furosemide action in the loop of Henle
- D. mannitol action in the Bowman's capsule

651. Which of the following organcllcs synthesizes angiotensinogen?

- A. nucleus
- B. lysosome
- C. smooth endoplasmic reticulum
- D. rough endoplasmic reticulum

     GO ON TO THE NEXT PAGE.

Passage 611 (Questions 652-657)

The kidney filtration barrier is a series of structures through which metabolic waste products must pass in order to move out of the blood and into the functional nephron. Specifically, the barrier is made up of the endothelium, basement membrane, and filtration slits.

The characteristics of the filtration barrier, especially the basement membrane, determine which blood constituents can and cannot enter the nephron. As with any other filter, only material small enough to pass through the openings in the filter will do so.

Pores in the capillary wall that allow filtration are called endothelial fenestrae (the Latin term for windows). These fenestrae are large, with diameters of around 70-90 nm, and not very selective. Their main function is to prevent the filtration of blood cells. Beyond the endothelial layer is the basement membrane, which occupies the space between the capillary and podocytes. In general, only the smallest plasma components can pass through the pores in the basement membrane. It is the most selective part of the filtration barrier. At the physiological pH, the basement membrane has numerous anions attached to it.

Podocytes are cells that line the Bowman's capsule. They have processes that extend and wrap around glomerular capillaries, forming filtration slits. Materials small enough to pass through the basement membrane will move through the filtration slits into Bowman's space. The podocytic processes contain contractile elements that can be used to control the filtration rate: contraction decreases the size of filtration slits and filtration as a result.

652. Netrans are glucose polymers that can be either positively or negatively charged. Which of the following would have the lowest concentration in the proximal convoluted tubule?

    A. amino acid lysine
    B. positively charged netrans
    C. negatively charged netrans
    D. glucose molecules

653. A person stranded in the desert faces the risk of severe dehydration. Which of the following will be maximally stimulated to prevent water loss?

    A. anterior and posterior pituitary
    B. adrenal cortex and thyroid gland
    C. hypothalamus and adrenal gland
    D. renal gland and anterior pituitary

654. According to the passage, endothelium is found where?

    A. in the basement membrane
    B. in the capillary walls
    C. in the podocytes
    D. in the nephron cells

655. Hypothyroidism has been shown to cause accelerated arteriosclerosis (clogging of blood vessels with fat), which affects renal function. Which of the following is the best explanation for this finding?

    A. Increased basal metabolism causes damage to most systemic blood vessels.
    B. Hypothyroidism decreases metabolism and increases phospholipid and cholesterol levels.
    C. Decreased metabolism can damage the aortic arch by inhibiting proper receptor stimulation.
    D. Hypothyroidism increases blood pressure by clogging glomerular filtration sites in the kidney.

656. A fluorescent dye is utilized to "tag" antidiuretic hormone receptors. The greatest concentration of dye is expected in which of the following structures?

    A. proximal convoluted tubule
    B. renal capillaries
    C. loop of Henle
    D. collecting duct

657. The ascending loop of Henle is NOT permeable to which of the following?

    A. sodium
    B. potassium
    C. chloride
    D. water

GO ON TO THE NEXT PAGE.

658. Which of the following is the correct sequence for the cardiac conduction pathway?

- A. AV node, SA node, bundle of His, Purkinje fibers
- B. SA node, AV node, bundle of His, Purkinje fibers
- C. SA node, bundle of His, Purkinje fibers, AV node
- D. Purkinje fibers, SA node, AV node, bundle of His

659. What structure originates from the renal pelvis and extends all the way to the urinary bladder?

- A. the vas deferens
- B. the ureter
- C. the major calyx
- D. the urethra

660. The amino acid sequence is useful in determining the origin of a protein. The first amino acid incorporated into every eukaryotic protein is:

- A. cysteine
- B. valine
- C. alanine
- D. methionine

661. For electrical neutrality an anion must follow sodium as it shifts from the extracellular to the intracellular space. Which of the following is the most appropriate anion of choice?

- A. potassium
- B. chlorine
- C. calcium
- D. oxygen

662. Digitalis is a drug that blocks the Na^+/K^+ ATPase and causes which of the following consequences?

- A. decreased intracellular calcium concentration
- B. decreased intracellular sodium concentration
- C. decreased intracellular potassium concentration
- D. increased extracellular sodium concentration

663. Which of the following organs secretes gastrin, intrinsic factor, and pepsin and absorbs alcohol?

- A. the small intestine
- B. the stomach
- C. the liver
- D. the pancreas

664. 180 liters of fluid enters the 2-4 million nephrons that make up the 2 kidneys. Most of that fluid is returned to circulation by reabsorption. As a rough estimate, what percentage of fluid that enters the nephrons is excreted daily?

- A. more than 25 percent
- B. almost 11 percent
- C. almost 5 percent
- D. less than 2 percent

665. The concentration of sodium in pancreatic juice approximately equals its concentration in plasma, and at all rates of pancreatic secretion, potassium concentration is also similar to that found in plasma. It can therefore be assumed that at all rates of secretion, pancreatic juice is essentially:

- A. hypertonic
- B. isotonic
- C. hypotonic
- D. cannot be determined

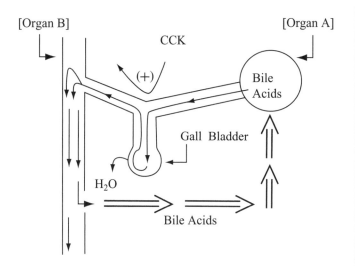

[Organ B] CCK [Organ A]

(+)

Bile Acids

Gall Bladder

H₂O

Bile Acids

666. In the above mechanism, which of the following functions is being performed by Organ A?

   I. bile acid storage
  II. bile acid synthesis
 III. bile acid fat emulsification

  A. I only
  B. II only
  C. II and III only
  D. I, II, and III

667. What is the shortest portion of the small intestine that serves as a "mixing pot" for digestive enzymes and compounds?

  A. ileum
  B. duodenum
  C. cecum
  D. jejunum

STOP. IF YOU FINISH BEFORE TIME IS CALLED, CHECK YOUR WORK. YOU MAY GO BACK TO ANY QUESTION IN THIS TEST BOOKLET.

LECTURE 7

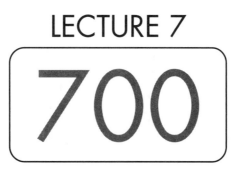

Biology Passages
Questions 668–781

Passage 701 (Questions 668-673)

Starling's laws describe the contractile behavior of the heart.

Law 1: An increase in the venous blood return to the heart increases the amount of blood pumped out by the heart. (The amount of blood pumped out by the heart is known as the *cardiac output*.) An increase in the venous return to the right side of the heart causes an increase in the right atrial volume, which then increases the left ventricle blood volume. (The left ventricle blood volume is known as the *preload*.) An increase in the *preload* increases the total blood volume ejected by the heart.

Starling's laws describe how the heart overcomes an increase in the *afterload*.

Law 2: *Afterload* is the resistance to blood flow created by the aorta. An increase in the *afterload* decreases the amount of blood ejected by the heart and increases the total blood volume in the ventricle for the next cardiac contraction. This extra volume induces a greater stretch of the cardiac tissue, and, under normal circumstances, the ventricle will contract with greater force on the subsequent heartbeat.

Law 3: The heart rate can both extrinsically and intrinsically alter the force of the cardiac contraction. Intrinsic changes occur through the Starling mechanism. An increase in the heart rate increases the amount of blood pumped by the heart. However, as the heart rate increases, the amount of blood entering the heart decreases, decreasing *preload* and lowering the blood volume ejected by the heart. If only the heart rate increases, the blood volume ejected by the heart will remain unchanged.

668. Keeping in accordance with cardiac physiology, which of the following statements outlines the normal blood flow through the heart?

    A. mitral valve → right ventricle → pulmonary artery → lungs
    B. mitral valve → left ventricle → aortic valve → aortic arch
    C. vena cava → right atria → left atria → left ventricle
    D. right ventricle → pulmonary artery → pulmonary vein → lungs

669. According to the passage, the Starling's laws of the heart describe:

    A. how the parasympathetic stimulation in decreasing the heart rate
    B. how a decrease in afterload increases the work load on the heart
    C. the relationship between the preload and the blood volume ejected by the heart
    D. how an increase in the heart rate increases the pre-load

670. The *end-diastolic volume* is the amount of blood found in the left ventricle at the end of diastole. Starling's term that equals the end-diastolic volume is:

    A. afterload
    B. preload
    C. cardiac output
    D. heart rate

671. While deriving his 3rd law, Starling needed to increase the cardiac heart rate and may have used which of the following mechanisms to do so?

    I. acetylcholine
    II. norepinephrine
    III. epinephrine

    A. I only
    B. II only
    C. II and III only
    D. I, II, and III

672. An individual who must deliver more oxygen to tissue will do so most effectively by which of the following mechanisms?

    A. increasing both the preload and the afterload
    B. increasing preload and decreasing afterload
    C. increasing afterload and the heart rate
    D. decreasing blood volume and preload

673. Varicose veins are twisted, superficial, and associated with lower extremity swelling. They are caused by poor venous return of blood to the heart and fall under which Starling's law?

    A. Starling's law 1 only
    B. Starling's law 2 only
    C. Starling's law 3 only
    D. Starling's laws 1 and 2 only

Passage 702 (Questions 674-679)

Blood pressure is the measure of the force imparted on the blood by the contraction of the heart, which propels the blood through the circulatory system. The pressure difference between various parts of the circulatory system drives the blood flow by forcing blood from an area of high pressure to a receptive area of lower pressure.

During ventricular contraction (systole), the blood pressure is highest, resulting in blood vessel distention. During ventricular relaxation (diastole), the blood volume pumped out of the heart drains into the body, making the blood pressure drop and allowing blood vessels to recoil. The pressure difference between systole and diastole is known as the pulse pressure. Pulse pressure measurement can be used to assess cardiovascular fitness and function. A high pulse pressure may be indicative of a reduction in the compliance of an artery, as seen in the elderly, or of very low peripheral resistance, as seen in marathon runners.

Blood pressure is regulated and maintained by the elasticity of major arteries. The chemical energy used by the ventricle during systole is transformed and imparted to the blood as pressure or potential energy. Some of the energy of flow causes elastic arteries to expand. If the arterioles were to close, the energy would remain stored in the elastic elements of the arterial wall. The arterioles, however, are not closed and flow continues, dissipating the pressure wave as blood leaves toward the peripheral blood vessels.

674. Which of the following is the main factor that contributes to a high pulse pressure in a trained athlete?

A. a decrease in artery compliance only
B. low peripheral resistance only
C. a decrease in artery compliance and low peripheral resistance
D. neither a decrease in artery compliance nor low peripheral resistance

675. According to the passage, if blood pressure were considered to be potential energy, then the actual flow of blood would be considered:

A. potential energy
B. kinetic energy
C. electrical energy
D. thermal energy

676. Which of the following compounds can serve as a possible source of "chemical energy" to fuel the heart?

  I. ATP
 II. glucose
III. nucleic acids

A. I only
B. II only
C. I and II
D. I, II, and III

677. It can be inferred from the passage that which of the following locations should have the lowest blood pressure to serve as an ideal receptive area?

A. the lungs
B. the right atrium
C. the pulmonary vein
D. the capillaries

678. Which of the following factors are capable of altering arterial blood pressure?

  I. amount of blood volume entering the arteries
 II. elasticity of the blood vessel
III. resistance to blood flow

A. II only
B. III only
C. I and III only
D. I, II, and III

679. Which of the following conditions will yield the highest possible pulse pressure?

A. high systole and low diastole
B. low systole and low diastole
C. high systole and high diastole
D. low systole and high diastole

GO ON TO THE NEXT PAGE.

Passage 703 (Questions 680-685)

The circulatory system provides oxygen to cells. As a general rule, smaller animals have a higher rate of oxygen consumption per unit body mass in comparison to larger animals. Cardiac output is the volume of blood pumped by the heart per unit time and depends on the 1) *heart rate* (HR) and the 2) *stroke volume*, which is the volume of blood ejected in one ventricular contraction.

$$Cardiac\ Output = (HR) \times (Stroke\ Volume)$$

When comparing a medium-sized fish with a medium-sized mammal, the method each animal uses to increase the cardiac output can be determined and compared to the volume of oxygen consumed. Table 1 data shows that for both animals, an increase in activity causes an increase in the oxygen demand. This type of analysis can be misleading when comparing animals with circulations that allow the mixing of arterial and venous blood. Such animals are reptiles, amphibians, and animals that uptake a considerable amount of oxygen through their skin.

Animal	Parameter	At Rest	Very Active	Change
Medium Fish	Cardiac Ejection Volume	0.59 ml	1.15 ml	+ 2.1
	Heart Rate	35 per minute	61 per minute	+ 1.6
	Blood Flow	19 mL/min	65 mL/min	+ 3.1
Medium Mammal	Cardiac Ejection Volume	1.85 ml	1.67 ml	– 0.1
	Heart Rate	150 per minute	730 per minute	+5.6
	Blood Flow	200 mL/min	1120 mL/min	+ 5.8

Table 1 Medium-size Animal Data

680. To maximize the cardiac output, a large animal would stimulate the heart to:

- A. increase the heart rate and ejection volume
- B. increase the heart rate and red blood cell concentration
- C. increase ejection volume but decrease the heart rate to allow for proper ventricular filling
- D. increase ejection volume and decrease physical exertion

681. The oxygen carrying capacity of blood is similar in small and large animals. According to the passage, in regards to the expected cardiac function:

- A. small and large animals have comparable heart rates and cardiac outputs
- B. large animals must have hearts that can pump blood at a higher rate to supply all that bulk
- C. small animals must have hearts that can pump blood at a higher rate to meet tissue demands
- D. there is little correlation between animal size and the heart rate

682. Your body has approximately 5 liters of blood. With the cardiac muscle contracting 72 times/minute and the average volume of ejection being 70 ml, what timeframe is needed to circulate the entire blood volume through the heart?

- A. approximately 30 seconds
- B. approximately 1 minute
- C. approximately 2 minutes
- D. approximately 5 minutes

683. Inhibition of the kidney product renin would be expected to have which of the following outcomes?

- A. an increase in blood pressure
- B. a decrease in blood pressure
- C. increased contractility
- D. renal failure

684. In comparing various medium-sized animals it can be determined that:

- A. most medium-sized animals respond to increased activity in similar fashion
- B. an active fish increases cardiac output by increasing the heart rate
- C. an active animal usually increases the ejection volume
- D. a swimming fish increases the ejection volume by increasing the cardiac output

685. Invertebrate ancestors of vertebrates did not have mouths, but used their gill slits for filter feeding instead of oxygen uptake. Oxygen was taken up instead through their skin. Which of the following animals is capable of oxygen uptake through the skin?

- A. fish
- B. lampreys
- C. frogs
- D. snakes

686. An increase in the right atrial volume causes an increase in the left ventricular volume. The blood must enter all of the following anatomical chambers to reach the left ventricle from the right atrium, EXCEPT:

    A. right ventricle
    B. vena cava
    C. pulmonary vein
    D. left atrium

687. Which of the following vessels carries blood similar in oxygen and carbon dioxide concentration to blood found in the pulmonary artery?

    A. the pulmonary vein
    B. the aorta
    C. a major branch of the aorta
    D. a major branch of the vena cava

688. Disorders like hypertension, atherosclerosis, and stroke are the leading causes of morbidity and mortality in the developed countries because of damage to which organ system?

    A. musculoskeletal system
    B. vascular system
    C. nervous system
    D. digestive system

689. Which of the following factors would NOT alter the blood pressure within the vascular system?

    A. increasing the smooth muscle tone of the artery
    B. damage and blood vessel scarring
    C. change in the number of blood vessels
    D. decrease in the number of epithelial cells

690. There are certain sites where the cells of the immune system are organized into specific structures. Structures that *do not* replenish the cells of the immune system are classified as peripheral lymphoid tissues and include all of the following, EXCEPT:

    A. lymph nodes
    B. spleen
    C. tonsils
    D. thymus

691. Adenosine triphosphate is what kind of biological molecule?

    A. lipid
    B. peptide
    C. nucleotide
    D. carbohydrate

692. The movement of oxygen from the alveolar sacs into the blood:

    A. is an active process that relies on millions of alveolar sacs
    B. requires transport proteins and an enormous surface area for gas exchange
    C. is a passive spontaneous process that depends on the diffusion distance
    D. is a non-spontaneous event that may or may not depend on a concentration gradient

693. Taking a deep breath of fresh air and delivering it deep into the alveoli requires the use of which of the following conduction pathways?

    A. mouth → esophagus → trachea → main bronchi → secondary bronchi
    B. nose → pharynx → larynx → trachea → main bronchi
    C. mouth → larynx → pharynx → esophagus → secondary bronchi
    D. nose → pharynx → esophagus → lower esophageal sphincter → stomach

694. Self/non-self recognition is achieved by having every cell display a marker based on the major histocompatibility complex (MHC). Any cell not displaying this marker is treated as non-self and attacked. The condition in which the immune system attacks normal pancreatic cells is known as:

    A. infection
    B. autoimmunity
    C. allergy
    D. pancreatitis

695. Which of the following cardiac valves are located on the left side of the heart?

    A. mitral and aortic valves
    B. aortic and pulmonic valves
    C. tricuspid and mitral valves
    D. mitral and pulmonic valves

GO ON TO THE NEXT PAGE.

Passage 704 (Questions 696-701)

The human heart is four-chambered and consists of two atria and two ventricles. The right side of the heart receives CO_2-rich blood from the peripheral vascular system and ejects it into pulmonary circulation where the gas exchange occurs. O_2-rich blood leaves the pulmonary system to enter the left side of the heart, which supplies systemic circulation.

To prevent inappropriate mixing of blood, the four cardiac chambers are separated by *septums*. Communication between the chambers is established through four one-way valves. The blood passes from the atria to the ventricles and then to either the pulmonary circulation or the aorta. Backflow of blood would significantly reduce the effectiveness of the cardiac pump.

To understand the beat to beat cardiac function, the heart rate must be taken into account. Stroke volume is the volume of blood pumped by the left ventricle per heartbeat. The cardiac output is the stroke volume multiplied by the heart rate. Normally, the stroke volume is between 70 and 140 ml. The heart rate can vary from under 50 beats/min. while resting, to over 200 beats/min. during exercise. Therefore, the cardiac output of adults is approximately 3–5 liter/min during rest but can rapidly increase by 4–7 fold or more during exercise.

696. The closed circulatory system contains deoxygenated blood in all of the following locations EXCEPT:

   A. the right atrium
   B. the right ventricle
   C. the pulmonary vein
   D. the vena cava

697. Aortic stenosis is the narrowing of the aortic valve. Which of the following is an expected stroke volume in an individual with aortic stenosis?

   A. 55 ml
   B. 70 ml
   C. 100 ml
   D. 165 ml

698. The right side of the heart receives carbon dioxide-rich blood derived from which metabolic pathway?

   A. glycolysis
   B. the Krebs cycle
   C. the electron transport chain
   D. protein synthesis

699. What is the expected cardiac output for a person running a marathon with a heart rate of 130 and a maximum stroke volume?

   A. 12.20 liters per minute
   B. 18.20 liters per minute
   C. 6.80 liters per minute
   D. 28.50 liters per minute

700. Which of the following is the primary force that drives the flow of blood?

   A. pressure gradient
   B. concentration gradient
   C. electrical gradient
   D. suction

701. Which set of valves are directly associated with the left atria?

   A. mitral valve and aortic valve
   B. tricuspid valve and pulmonic valve
   C. vena cava valve or the tricuspid valve
   D. bicuspid valve or the mitral valve

Passage 705 (Questions 702-708)

Breathing is controlled by involuntary mechanisms that can be temporarily overridden by voluntary effort. These voluntary impulses originate in the cerebral cortex and travel to the respiratory motor neurons.

The involuntary breathing centers are located in the medulla and pons of the brain stem. These breathing centers receive information about the body's oxygen needs from two major sources: the central chemoreceptors in the brain stem and the peripheral chemoreceptors in the walls of the circulatory system.

Central chemoreceptors normally exert the strongest control over breathing movements. They respond to changes in the arterial CO_2 concentration by detecting the level of hydrogen ions in the blood. Peripheral chemoreceptors respond primarily to decreases in arterial O_2 concentration, and to some degree the pH. The control of peripheral chemoreceptors over breathing movements is normally weak, but these receptors become important during severe anoxia (lack of oxygen). The peripheral chemoreceptors sense oxygen and hydrogen ion levels as blood leaves the lungs, and signals are sent to the brain stem. The central and peripheral chemoreceptors provide minute-to-minute control of breathing movements.

$$H_2O + CO_2 \leftrightharpoons H_2CO_3 \leftrightharpoons HCO_3^- + H^+$$

Reaction 1: Dissolution of carbon dioxide

702. External respiration allows the exchange of carbon dioxide for oxygen at any altitude. Which of the following is NOT an adaptation to living high above the sea level?

   A. an increase in 2,3 BPG concentration, which shifts the O_2 dissociation curve to the right
   B. increased production of red blood cells by the bone marrow
   C. decreased synthesis of erythropoietin by the kidney
   D. hyperventilation

703. According to the passage, which of the following would be expected to have the greatest effect on the breathing effort?

   A. slight change in venous carbon dioxide
   B. large decrease in arterial oxygen
   C. large increase in arterial carbon dioxide
   D. no change in hydrogen ion concentration

704. The medulla and the pons fall into which division of the nervous system?

   A. the central nervous system
   B. the peripheral nervous system
   C. the somatic nervous system
   D. the voluntary nervous system

705. According to the information presented in the passage, dissection of this structure will reveal peripheral respiratory chemoreceptors:

   A. cerebral cortex
   B. aortic arch
   C. medulla
   D. lungs

706. Lung stretch receptors are located in the smooth muscle of airways and are stimulated by the distention of the lungs. What is the most probable outcome once the lung stretch receptors have been activated?

   A. There will be a decrease in the breathing frequency.
   B. There will be an increase in breathing depth.
   C. Immediate stimulation of rapid breathing.
   D. Immediate cessation of breathing all together.

707. The central chemoreceptors are *least* likely to respond to changes in blood concentration of which of the following?

   A. carbon dioxide
   B. hydrogen ion concentration
   C. pH
   D. oxygen concentration

708. Central chemoreceptors monitor and control the rate of diaphragmatic contraction. A cardiovascular analog of a central chemoreceptor may be:

   A. the bundle of His
   B. the SA node
   C. the cardiac muscle
   D. the sympathetic nervous system

Passage 706 (Questions 709-715)

The pulmonary circulation starts in the right side of the heart. The venous blood is pumped out of pulmonary arteries into alveolar capillaries, where gas exchange occurs. Once oxygenated, blood is carried by the pulmonary venous circulation into the left side of the heart. The total volume of blood flowing through the lungs is essentially equal to that flowing through the systemic circulation, 5 L/min at rest. During exercise, the blood flow out of the heart can increase considerably and so does the pulmonary blood flow.

Pulmonary arterial vessels are short, thin-walled, and large in diameter compared to their systemic counterparts. This yields a system with significant characteristics. The first is low resistance to blood flow, which serves to minimize the body's expenditure of energy. Low resistance to flow means lower blood pressure in the pulmonary vessels, which in turn poses the least impediment to gas diffusion while adequately controlling fluid loss from the capillaries.

The second aspect is that the large arteries, with thin, distensible walls, give the pulmonary circulation a high compliance (volume change per unit of applied pressure, ml/mm Hg). The significance of high compliance is that the pulmonary arteries can accommodate about 2/3 of the volume pumped in one ventricular contraction by ballooning out as the right ventricle contracts.

Structure	Glands	Cell Type	Support
Trachea	Mucous	Goblet and Ciliated cells	Hyaline cartilage
Bronchioles	No Glands	Ciliated, Clara, Goblet cells	Smooth muscles
Respiratory Bronchioles	No Glands	Clara and Type I and II pneumocytes	Type III collagen
Alveoli	No Glands	Type I and II pneumocytes	Type III collagen

Table 1 Respiratory System Features

709. Based on the per hour blood flow rate, which structure is expected to pump the most blood?

- **A.** right ventricle
- **B.** left ventricle
- **C.** both ventricles pump the same amount of blood
- **D.** left atria

710. Acute pulmonary edema is a condition defined by the accumulation of extra fluid in the lungs. Which of the following factors may account for this condition?

- **A.** a decrease in the pulmonary arterial pressure
- **B.** a decrease in the systemic arterial pressure
- **C.** an increase in the pulmonary resistance
- **D.** an increase in the pulmonary capillary permeability to plasma proteins

711. Bronchial circulation supplies blood to the non-gas-exchanging parts of the lung and arises from the aorta. Which of the following is true regarding bronchial blood flow?

- **A.** Bronchial circulation will have a lower pressure than systemic circulation.
- **B.** Pulmonary circulation will have a higher pressure than bronchial circulation.
- **C.** Blood in the pulmonary artery will have a higher oxygen content than blood in the bronchial circulation.
- **D.** Bronchial circulation receives blood from the left side of the heart.

712. Dilated pulmonary vasculature on X-ray without an underlying pathology is most likely to occur during:

- **A.** systole, accommodating 1.6 liters on average
- **B.** diastole, accommodating 1.6 liters on average
- **C.** systole, accommodating 70 ml on average
- **D.** diastole, accommodating 70 ml on average

713. Which of the following statements apply to the respiratory system anatomy?

- **I.** the 2 lungs are protected by the rib cage
- **II.** the 2 lungs are separated by the heart
- **III.** the lung bases rest on the diaphragm

- **A.** I only
- **B.** II only
- **C.** I and II only
- **D.** I, II, and III

GO ON TO THE NEXT PAGE.

714. Which of the following descriptions apply to *clara cells,* which protect the bronchial epithelium with their secretory products?

- **A.** Clara cells have a wide distribution covering almost every segment of the respiratory tract.
- **B.** Clara cells depend on ciliary cells for nutrients and survival.
- **C.** Clara cells are always present in areas with high concentration of type III collagen.
- **D.** Clara cells are never seen in areas with mucous glands.

715. Which of the following would be expected to decrease pulmonary circulatory resistance?

- **A.** cholesterol induced hardening of major lung arteries
- **B.** an increase in the number of pulmonary capillaries
- **C.** spasmic constriction of major lung arteries
- **D.** narrowing of the mitral valve

Questions 716 through 725 are **NOT** based on a descriptive passage.

716. Which of the following statements correctly describes the respiratory tract?

- **I.** the right lung is larger than the left
- **II.** expiration is predominantly a passive phenomenon
- **III.** air enters the lungs because of created negative pressure

- **A.** I only
- **B.** I and II only
- **C.** II and III only
- **D.** I, II, and III

717. All of the following are zymogens EXCEPT:

- **A.** fibrinogen
- **B.** plasminogen
- **C.** pancreatic pepsinogen
- **D.** trypsin

718. The major focus of oxygen transport in the blood compartment is the hemoglobin contained in red blood cells. In contrast, the carriage of carbon dioxide by the blood is predominantly in the form of:

- **A.** dissolved gas
- **B.** hemoglobin-bound gas
- **C.** albumin-attached gas
- **D.** bicarbonate ion

719. Plasma components that end up in the nephron would most likely be reabsorbed in which of the following structures?

- **A.** the glomerulus
- **B.** the proximal convoluted tubule
- **C.** the loop of Henle
- **D.** the distal convoluted tubule

720. Which of the following statements correctly describes a *secondary* immune response?

- **A.** It is the initial body response to a new invader.
- **B.** It is the only possible response mounted by a healthy body.
- **C.** It is the failure of the body to respond to a new invader.
- **D.** It is a rapid body response to an invader that has been in the body before.

GO ON TO THE NEXT PAGE.

721. After being engulfed by a macrophage, an infective microbe, *listeria*, escapes out of the lysosome into the cytoplasm. In terms of relative size, which of the following categorizes *listeria* on the cellular predator/prey spectrum?

A. on average, *listeria* is much larger than a macrophage

B. several macrophages are needed to destroy *listeria* because *listeria* is the same size as a macrophage

C. a macrophage is much larger than *listeria*

D. because macrophages assemble into an attack unit, no statement regarding size is appropriate

722. Peyer's patches are large aggregates of lymphoid tissue found in the longest section of the small intestine. To dissect out a Peyer's patch, an incision would have to be made in the:

A. colon
B. duodenum
C. jejunum
D. ileum

723. Individuals with a congenital heart defect may have abnormal shunting of blood from the right side of the heart to the left, which usually decreases the pulmonary blood flow. What other signs and symptoms should be expected?

A. increased oxygen content in the venous blood
B. very poor body oxygenation
C. sickle cell anemia
D. no other major signs and symptoms seen

724. Zollinger-Ellison syndrome is a pancreatic gastrin-secreting tumor that stimulates parietal cells. Which of the following would be expected in a patient with Zollinger-Ellison syndrome?

A. increased pepsin secretion
B. increased erosion of the stomach lining
C. abnormally thick mucus protection against ulcers
D. decreased hydrogen ion secretion

725. Which of the following body fluids are responsible for transporting the agents of the immune system?

I. venous blood only
II. arterial blood only
III. lymphatic fluid only

A. I only
B. I and II only
C. II and III only
D. I, II, and III

Passage 707 (Questions 726-731)

The respiratory system begins at the nostrils. Air is then conducted through the larynx and the trachea. The trachea is a cartilaginous tube that divides into two main bronchi, which further subdivide into smaller conducting pathways that ultimately end with terminal alveoli.

The trachea is considered a 1st generation passageway, and the two main bronchi are 2nd generation airways. Each division thereafter is an additional generation. Overall, there are about seventeen generations before the air reaches terminal bronchioles, which mark the end of the airway-conducting zone.

On average, the total lung weight is about 300-400 grams. Upper and middle lobes are anterior, while the lower lobes are posterior. Gas exchange requires 0.25 seconds or 1/3 of the total transit time for a red blood cell to take place. The entire blood volume found in the body passes through the lungs each minute at a rate of 5 liters per minute. The conducting zone does not allow for appreciable blood-gas exchange to take place. Transitional and respiratory zones, on the other hand, do allow gas exchange to occur.

In spite of the cartilage that surrounds the trachea, the tracheo-bronchial system is not a series of rigid pipes. It is surrounded by both longitudinal and circular smooth muscles that constantly change the tube diameter in order to minimize the anatomic dead space without unduly increasing resistance to airflow.

726. Which of the following is the correct number of bifurcations (branching points) that take place prior to reaching the terminal bronchioles?

A. 16
B. 17
C. 18
D. 33

727. Inflammation of the voice box causes hoarseness. If the vocal cords are involved, which of the following structures is infected?

A. pharynx
B. larynx
C. esophagus
D. nasal cavity

728. An hour into his workout, a professional swimmer would be expected to have which of the following data for gas exchange time (in seconds) and red blood cell transit time (in seconds)?

A. 0.25 and .50
B. 0.25 and .75
C. 0.15 and .25
D. 0.15 and .50

729. After a person is stabbed in the back with a piece of glass, which of the following lung lobes would most likely be damaged?

A. upper lobe
B. middle lobe
C. lower lobe
D. cannot be determined from the information provided

730. The narrow portion of the upper airway allows for air humidification upon entry into the respiratory tract. What is the expected difference between environmental and alveolar air?

A. Alveolar air has more oxygen in comparison to the environment.
B. Alveolar air has more carbon monoxide in comparison to the environment.
C. The respiratory tract air has more water vapor in comparison to the environment.
D. The respiratory tract air has a lower carbon dioxide concentration in comparison to the environment.

731. Which of the following is the average weight of the right lung?

A. 130 grams
B. 160 grams
C. 175 grams
D. 215 grams

Passage 708 (Questions 732-737)

Blood is a heterogeneous suspension of differentiated cells. It is considered a "tissue" with nearly the same water content as other body tissues. Blood is easily separated into its constituent components by centrifugation. A blood sample is spun down to reveal three distinct layers based on their relative densities. The uppermost layer, plasma, is a yellow-colored fluid that accounts for 55 percent of the blood volume. The middle layer, the "buffy coat," accounts for less than 1 percent of the total blood volume. The "buffy coat" contains white blood cells and platelets. The bottom layer, accounting for 45 percent of the blood volume, is composed of red blood cells.

Plasma is 90 percent water and 10 percent dry matter. It is full of organic substances like glucose, lipids, proteins, and hormones. Albumin is the major plasma protein and the main contributor to the oncotic pressure of plasma. It is also a carrier for various fat-soluble substances. The majority of plasma proteins are synthesized and released by liver cells (hepatocytes) into the blood.

Buffy Coat Isolation:

Anti-coagulated blood is spun down in a narrow test tube. The plasma layer is carefully removed without disturbing the "buffy coat." 2% glutaraldehyde buffer is gently layered on top and the tube is refrigerated for 2 hours. Once embedded in the solid plasma, the resultant disc is removed from the test tube, trimmed, and processed into a resin.

732. According to the passage, the function of which of the following organ systems should be evaluated in a person demonstrating a severe decrease in plasma proteins?

A. digestive system
B. respiratory system
C. lymphatic system
D. cardiovascular system

733. When examining the blood of a patient with a disseminated bacterial infection, the researcher expects to notice mitotic division being performed by which of the following cells?

I. red blood cells
II. white blood cells
III. infectious bacteria

A. I only
B. III only
C. II and III only
D. I, II, and III

734. According to the passage, which of the following is the most numerous cell type present in the blood?

    A. red blood cell
    B. white blood cell
    C. platelet
    D. plasma

735. If the technique is performed correctly, the 2% glutaraldehyde buffer is expected to seep through which of the following layers first on its way through the tube?

    A. the red blood cells layer
    B. the plasma layer
    C. the buffy coat layer
    D. the dry matter layer

736. What is the expected hematocrit or the red blood cell concentration in an individual diagnosed with anemia?

    A. 65 percent
    B. 55 percent
    C. 45 percent
    D. 35 percent

737. In the bone marrow, platelets are derived from which of the following precursor cells?

    A. phagocytes
    B. megakaryocytes
    C. erythrocytes
    D. monocytes

Passage 709 (Questions 738-743)

The discussion of cancer and its growth leads right into the topic of immunology because a tumor is simply another antigen that the immune system needs to destroy. The overall immune system approach to detecting and destroying a cancerous growth, however, is slightly different in comparison to how the body handles bacteria. Several experiments, utilizing mice as model subjects, were conducted to determine how the immune system deals with a cancerous growth.

Experiment 1:

Day 1:   An alpha-tumor was induced and allowed to grow in the *AM*-mouse.

Day 180:   To reduce the tumor burden, the alpha-tumor was resected from the *AM*-mouse. (*Tumor burden* is the number of cancer cells in an animal.) 0 cancer cells were detected in the *AM*-mouse 4 weeks after the surgery.

Day 264:   Alpha-tumor cells that were resected from the *AM*-mouse were injected back into the *AM*-mouse.

Day 1000:   0 cancer cell burden was detected in the *AM*-mouse.

Experiment 2:

Day 1:   Alpha-tumor cells (resected from the *AM*-mouse used in Experiment 1) were injected into a naïve AM_2-mouse.

Day 264: AM_2-mouse is overwhelmed by the alpha-tumor and dies.

Experiment 3:

Day 1000:   Marker $CD8^+$ T-cells were obtained from the *AM*-mouse used in Experiment 1 and injected into a "new" naïve AM_2-mouse with a 100 day old alpha-tumor.

Day 2000: AM_2-mouse is alive with a 0 cancer cell burden.

738. Based on the evidence presented in Experiment 1, what is the best course of treatment for a large stage III cancerous growth in the abdomen?

    A. reinjection of tumor cells into a cured patient to test if the individual is truly tumor free
    B. performing immediate surgery to remove the tumor
    C. injecting $CD8^+$ T-cells specific for the tumor
    D. relying on the innate immune system and using the wait-and-see approach

739. Cancer is an abnormal growth of once normal body cells. Based on the informration presented in the passage, what is most likely to be true regarding surface receptors expressed by cancerous cells in comparison to those seen on normal tissue?

A. Both normal and cancerous cells express identical receptor types and concentrations if found in the same tissue.
B. Cancer cell receptors are identical to those on normal cells but are expressed uniquely or in significantly higher concentrations.
C. Cancer cell receptors are nothing like the receptors found on normal tissue.
D. Cell receptors lose their importance in end-stage cancer.

740. Based on the passage, which of the following statements would strongly *weaken* the validity of the results obtained from the 3 experiments?

A. Identical cancer cells were utilized to conduct experiments 1 and 3.
B. Allow the tumor burden to increase in Experiment 2.
C. *AM*-mouse and *AM₂*-mouse were not of the same species.
D. Cancer growth is unpredictable and the experiment lacked a control group.

741. In order to produce a specific antibody against a particular antigen, which of the following cell types would need to be stimulated?

A. phagocytic cell
B. granulocyte
C. plasma cell
D. T-helper cell

742. The alpha-tumor being utilized in *experiments 1-3* can be accurately classified as a:

A. slow-growing malignancy
B. benign mass
C. aggressive tumor
D. unresectable tumor

743. According to the passage, the best way to prevent cancer growth and induce remission is by:

I. inducing a cell-mediated immune response
II. inducing a humoral immune response
III. initiating surgery to decrease the cancer cell burden

A. I only
B. II only
C. I and III only
D. I, II, and III

744. Aortic stenosis is defined as a narrowing of the aortic valve. Which of the following is an expected outcome in a patient diagnosed with aortic stenosis?

    A.   increased blood flow into the aorta
    B.   increased ventricular size
    C.   decreased blood volume in the left ventricle after contraction
    D.   decreased work conducted by the heart

745. Multiple cartilage rings keep the trachea from collapsing. Tracheal cartilage is identified as tissue that is:

    A.   full of osteoblasts and osteocytes
    B.   based around a Haversian canal system
    C.   vascular and highly innervated
    D.   receiving nutrients by simple diffusion

746. Circulatory shock is defined as an inadequate blood flow throughout the body. Which of the following is the *least* likely to cause shock?

    A.   insufficient cardiac contraction
    B.   increased blood pressure
    C.   low overall blood volume
    D.   blockage of a blood vessel

Complete Blood Count (CBC)	
CELLS	NORMAL RANGE
WBC	3.9-11.1 thous./cu.mm
RBC	4.2-5.70 mil./cu.mm
Hemoglobin	13.2-16.9 g/dL
Platelets	150-400 thous./cu.mm

747. Based on the complete blood count, which of the following labs correlates with the presence of infection?

    A.
WBC	9.9 thous./cu.mm
RBC	3.1 mil./cu.mm
Hemoglobin	15.0 g/dL
Platelets	270 thous/cu.mm

    B.
WBC	20.1 thous./cu.mm
RBC	4.5 mil./cu.mm
Hemoglobin	14.0 g/dL
Platelets	400 thous./cu.mm

    C.
WBC	5.9 thous./cu.mm
RBC	4.9 mil./cu.mm
Hemoglobin	18.1 l g/dL
Platelets	560 thous./cu.mm

    D.
WBC	7.7 thous./cu.mm
RBC	7.5 mil./cu.mm
Hemoglobin	10.0 g/dL
Platelets	180 thous./cu.mm

748. Long-term homeostasis is under the control of which of the following?

    A.   hormones
    B.   neurotransmitters
    C.   nerves
    D.   medulla

749. The macula densa is located in the wall of the distal convoluted tubule. What adrenal hormone binds in close proximity to the macula densa?

    A. cortisol
    B. aldosterone
    C. ADH
    D. epinephrine

750. An animal cell undergoing anaerobic respiration will be expected to produce which of the following products?

    A. ethanol
    B. ethanol and ATP
    C. lactic acid
    D. lactic acid and ATP

751. A cell with no nucleus, with a limited life span, and derived from the fragmentation of a large bone marrow cell called megakaryocyte is the:

    A. red blood cell
    B. platelet
    C. white blood cell
    D. T-cell

752. Some peripheral nerves that innervate lymph nodes and other immune system components have been discovered to be adrenergic (release norepinephrine). This would suggest that:

    A. The parasympathetic nervous system may influence immune activity.
    B. The sympathetic nervous system does not influence immune activity.
    C. The parasympathetic nervous system releases norepinephrine.
    D. The sympathetic nervous system may influence immune activity.

Passage 710 (Questions 753-759)

Host defenses are composed of two complementary, frequently interacting systems: innate and acquired immunity. The innate immune system is the first line of defense against infectious agents. It attempts to protect the body in a nonspecific manner utilizing: 1) phagocytic cells, such as monocytes, macrophages, neutrophils, eosinophils, and natural killer cells (NK); 2) physical barriers, like skin and mucous membranes; 3) proteins, such as complement, lysosyme, and interferon.

The complement system is a collection of plasma proteins that are synthesized by the liver. These proteins assemble in a specific sequence forming a membrane-attack complex (MAC) that lyses foreign invaders. Complement proteins, C3b, iC3b, and C4b, act as opsonins that enhance phagocytosis by "coating" invaders as they attempt to enter the body. Coated pathogens attract neutrophils and macrophages, which have complement protein receptors that trigger receptor-mediated endocytosis.

Natural killer cells are one of the most important cells involved in the innate immune response. They attack and remove virus-infected and malignant cells. They also bind antibody Fc regions to kill cells coated with antibodies; this is termed as antibody-dependent cell-mediated cytotoxicity. Natural killer cells can also be stimulated to make interferon, which induces the production of macrophages.

Neutrophils	Monocytes
Short-lived (few days); life span may be extended in the presence of infection	Long-lived (months–years)
Origin: Bone marrow myeloid precursors	**Origin:** Bone marrow myeloid precursors
Predominant cell at site of bacterial infection (production increases following bacterial infection)	Develop into tissue macrophages

Table 1 Nonspecific Immune Cells

753. The lymphoid system is responsible for the immunological defense of the body. Which of the following is NOT a component organ of the immune system?

    A. lymph node
    B. thyroid
    C. thymus
    D. spleen

754. Which of the following compounds is also produced by the organ that synthesizes complement?

   A. high density lipoprotein (HDL)
   B. cortisol
   C. erythropoietin
   D. renin

755. According to the passage, complement proteins are capable of which of the following interactions?

   A. hydrophobic only
   B. hydrophilic only
   C. hydrophobic and hydrophilic
   D. ionic bonding

756. Innate immunity relies on major anatomical barriers like the skin to prevent pathogenic activity. Which of the following cell types is not involved in innate immunity?

   A. neutrophils
   B. phagocytic cells
   C. natural killer cells
   D. humoral immune cells

757. The key component of the complement system is protein C3. Deficiency of protein C3 is expected to produce which of the following outcomes?

   A. There will be an increase in the formation of membrane attack complexes to compensate for the deficiency.
   B. The deficiency will completely cripple the immune system and death will occur in early childhood.
   C. A person with pathologically low levels of serum C3 will be predisposed to recurrent bacterial infections.
   D. Interferon will be synthesized to stimulate macrophages to combat infection.

758. According to the passage, which of the following are the expected functions of the complement system?

   I. opsonization and phagocytosis
   II. stimulation of the inflammatory response
   III. complement-mediated cytolysis

   A. I only
   B. III only
   C. II and III only
   D. I, II, and III

759. Red blood cells have a life span of 120 days. The spleen filters blood for aging cells and removes them via ATP-dependent methods. According to the passage, removal of which cell type creates the most drain of the energy stores?

   A. monocytes
   B. neutrophils
   C. red blood cells
   D. all three cell types cause comparable energy consumption

GO ON TO THE NEXT PAGE.

Bacteria, fungi, viruses, and other infectious agents are foreign to the body and are known as *antigens*. *Antigens* are looked for and recognized by the immune system. Once recognized, the acquired immunity may be stimulated to defend against these *antigens* by releasing antibodies.

Antibodies have two very useful characteristics. First, they are extremely specific; each antibody binds to and attacks one particular antigen. Second, some antibodies, once activated for a particular *antigen,* continue to confer resistance against that antigen.

A vaccine is a preparation of killed or weakened bacteria or viruses that, when introduced into the body, stimulates the production of antibodies. The outcome is the resistance to an infectious organism without actually getting sick.

Phagocytosis is the major nonspecific cellular defense mechanism that is induced by antibodies. Certain cell types attach themselves to invading microbes that have been covered with antibodies. The microbes are engulfed by the phagocytic cell lines and digested. At least four cell types are known to be phagocytic. Macrophages are one of them and are usually found in tissue. They are derived from monocytes, which are synthesized in the bone marrow.

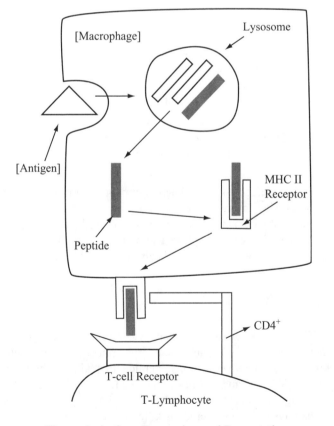

Figure 1 Antigen Processing and Presentation

760. Innate immunity functions to prevent the entry of microorganisms into tissue. Which of the following mechanisms are considered components of innate immunity?

   I. the integumentary system
  II. actively beating cilia
 III. coughing

  A. I only
  B. II only
  C. I and III only
  D. I, II, and III

761. Transferred maternal antibodies protect the infant for the first 9 months of life. Which organelle takes over antibody production once transferred immunity phases out?

  A. bone marrow
  B. ribosome
  C. thymus
  D. liver

762. As demonstrated by the HIV epidemic, the initial immune system response to any antigen absolutely requires that the antigen be recognized by:

  A. macrophages
  B. T lymphocytes
  C. plasma cells
  D. B lymphocytes

763. According to the passage, which of the following is the precursor to a macrophage?

  A. antibody
  B. antigen
  C. monocyte
  D. erythrocyte

764. Thymic hypoplasia is a disease of infancy in which the child is deprived of a thymus. Which of the following is expected to occur in an infant with thymic hypoplasia?

- **A.** onset of respiratory distress and breathing difficulties
- **B.** B-cells fail to mature and are not effective
- **C.** cell-mediated immunity is weak or nonexistent
- **D.** an increase in immunoglobulin (antibody) levels

765. A researcher is considering the possibility of macrophages serving as pathogen reservoirs because not all engulfed bacteria are killed by macrophages. Is this a plausible hypothesis?

- **A.** Yes, intracellular parasites can survive or multiply inside of phagocytes.
- **B.** Yes, unsuccessful pathogens attract phagocytes, and are ingested and killed.
- **C.** No, because pathogen reservoirs can only exist for viral infections.
- **D.** No, because other cells can become phagocytic and assist macrophages in phagocytosis.

766. Antigens are classified as exogenous or endogenous depending on how they are processed. In order to stimulate an immune response, the macrophage, acting as an antigen-presenting cell, must:

- **A.** present an intact antigen to the T-lymphocyte
- **B.** synthesize an MHC I receptor
- **C.** establish a multi-site attachment with the T-lymphocyte
- **D.** synthesize the CD4⁺ peptide arm

Passage 712 (Questions 767-772)

Acute inflammation is an early response to a bacterial infection characterized by the formation of an exudate, which is a whitish cellular fluid full of dead neutrophils. Inflammation involves at least two major defense components: antibodies and lymphocytes. Antibodies are used to "tag" the infecting agent, while lymphocytes are attracted to the marked pathogen and eradicate it via phagocytosis.

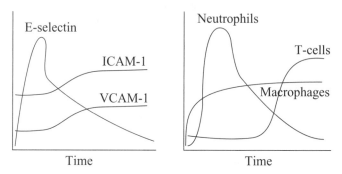

Early Inflammation
Time-dependent receptor interactions

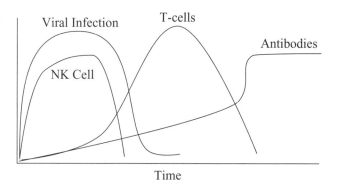

Viral Infection
Time-dependent immune system response
(NK = Natural Killer cell)

Before phagocytosis can begin, lymphocytes must reach the infection site. In order to do so, agents that increase vascular permeability are synthesized and released by the cardiovascular system. This allows plasma proteins and lymphocytes to leave the circulatory system and gain access to the site of infection.

Steps in phagocytosis:

The microbe binds to a phagocyte receptor → phagocyte membrane "zips up" around the microbe (an energy-dependent process that involves actin, a peptide that allows rhythmic contraction-relaxation to re-occur) → microbe is ingested by the phagocyte and stored in a phagosome → phagosome forms a phagolysosome → microbe is killed by lytic enzymes.

767. According to the passage, which of the following is least likely to be considered a characteristic of inflammation?

A. a decrease in blood flow
B. structural changes to the associated vasculature
C. accumulation of leukocytes
D. exudation of fluid

768. During a viral infection, the cell line that is first to respond belongs to the:

A. innate immunity
B. acquired immunity
C. specific immunity
D. cell-mediated immunity

769. It can be inferred from the passage that during a state of non-infection, where are most of the leukocytes located?

A. in the liver
B. being pumped throughout the cardiovascular system
C. stored in the bone marrow
D. guarding entranceways (i.e., mouth, nose) into the human body

770. Which of the following properties is responsible for forcing fluid out of the circulation?

A. capillary hydrostatic pressure
B. capillary oncotic pressure
C. lymphatic hydrostatic pressure
D. cardiac electrostatic force

771. Chédiak-Higashi syndrome is an autosomal recessive condition that is characterized by a defect in phagocytic cell digestion. In finding a cure for this syndrome, efforts should focus on what organelle?

A. the ribosome
B. the Golgi apparatus
C. the mitochondria
D. the lysosome

772. Which of the following conclusions can be reached regarding the mechanics of the inflammatory response?

A. T-cells bind ICAM-1 and are the first to respond to a viral stimulus.
B. Antibodies must be synthesized before an inflammatory reaction can occur.
C. Neutrophils bind E-selectins during an inflammatory response.
D. Macrophages are the third cell type to arrive at the site of inflammation.

GO ON TO THE NEXT PAGE.

773. Which of the following is the site for B-cell and T-cell maturation, respectively?

    A.   kidney, spleen
    B.   lung, thymus
    C.   bone marrow, bone marrow
    D.   bone marrow, thymus

774. Allergic reactions can stimulate the release of histamine and leukotrienes, which are potent broncho-constrictors. Which of the following would occur during an allergic reaction?

    A.   a decrease in the resistance to airflow
    B.   an increase in the reabsorption of sodium
    C.   a decrease in arterial blood oxygen content
    D.   an increase in the frequency of deep breaths

775. Which division of the autonomic nervous system has the most dominant effect on the heart?

    A.   the somatic nervous system
    B.   the sympathetic nervous system
    C.   the enteric nervous system
    D.   the parasympathetic nervous system

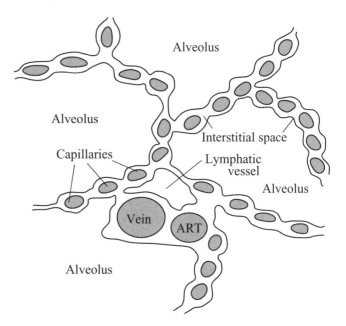

776. A biopsy of an organ revealed the above structure on a histology slide. Which of the following organs was biopsied?

    A.   the liver
    B.   the kidney
    C.   the lung
    D.   the spleen

777. Small bean-shaped structures that lie along the course of the lymphatic system, particularly in the neck, axilla, and groin, are most likely to be:

    A.   valves
    B.   aggregations of macrophages
    C.   lymph nodes
    D.   connection points to the arterial system

778. A pH meter used to determine the blood hydrogen ion concentration is expected to demonstrate that blood is:

    A. more alkaline than the skin
    B. less alkaline than the skin
    C. of similar pH when compared to the skin
    D. just as acidic as the skin

779. Which portion of the upper airway humidifies the air inhaled into the respiratory tract?

    A. the mouth
    B. the trachea
    C. the nose
    D. the alveoli

780. Narrowing of which of the following heart valves would cause blood to accumulate in the left atrium?

    A. tricuspid valve
    B. aortic valve
    C. mitral valve
    D. pulmonic valve

781. The complement system allows for communication between the innate and adaptive branches of the immune system. Which of the following organelles synthesizes protein complement components?

    A. nucleus
    B. endoplasmic reticulum
    C. liver
    D. peroxisome

STOP. IF YOU FINISH BEFORE TIME IS CALLED, CHECK YOUR WORK. YOU MAY GO BACK TO ANY QUESTION IN THIS TEST BOOKLET.

STOP.

LECTURE 8

800

Biology Passages
Questions 782–888

The bicep muscle is covered with 3 connective tissue elements. *Epimysium* is dense irregular connective tissue that surrounds the entire bicep muscle and continues to become a tendon. An incision into the *epimysium* reveals bundles of muscle cell filaments known as fascicles. Each fascicle is surrounded by the *perimysium*. *Endomysium*, composed of reticular fibers and an external lamina, surrounds each individual muscle cell filament. Contractile forces exerted by individual muscle cells are transferred to the connective tissue elements, which harness all contractile forces and exert them on a tendon and/or local aponeuroses.

A muscle filament is a linear array of sarcomeres that formed when hundreds of myoblasts fused into a multinucleated cell known as the syncytium. Myoblasts are precursors to skeletal muscle fibers. When the syncytium is forming, not all cells fuse. Some cells remain under the basement membrane but above the sarcolemma and are known as satellite cells. Local injury stimulates satellite cells to divide and add new nuclei to muscle. However, satellite cells do not have enough proliferative action to actually regenerate damaged muscle. Severe structural damage leads to the death of the muscle myotube. It is replaced by connective tissue cells called fibro-blasts.

Sarcomeres are packed into a filament with their nuclei forced to the periphery of the cell. When examining a profile of a skeletal muscle, be sure that the encountered nuclei are underneath the sarcomere cell membrane. Otherwise it is possible to mistake the sarcomere cell nucleus for a fibroblast or a satellite cell. Fibroblasts have a dense, round nucleus and are found in the extracellular space where they lay down *endomysium*.

Properties	White Fiber	Red Fiber	Intermediate Fiber
Contraction velocity	fast	slow	fast
Glycogen level	high	low	variable
Mitochondria content	low	high	high
Myoglobin content	low	high	high

Table 1 Properties of Muscle Fibers

782. Red muscle fibers are heavily dependent on which of the following in order to function properly?

   I.   oxygen concentration
   II. ATP levels
   III. intracellular glucose storage

   A.   I and II only
   B.   II and III only
   C.   III only
   D.   I, II, and III

783. Which of the following statements correlates with the information in Table 1?

   A.   intermediate fibers are dominant in all muscle tissue
   B.   red fibers are fast but easily fatigued
   C.   white fibers are rich in Krebs cycle enzymes but lack ATPase concentrations seen in red fibers
   D.   slow muscle fibers are rich in Krebs cycle enzymes and are not easily fatigued

784. According to the passage, which of the following locations contains the highest concentration of fibroblasts?

   A.   the muscle cell filament
   B.   the muscle tendon
   C.   the fascicle
   D.   the bone

785. Cells that make up a grouped fascicle are directly surrounded by which of the following structures?

   A.   collagen of the endomysium tube
   B.   connective tissue perimysium
   C.   dense epimysium
   D.   reticular fiber endomysium

786. According to the passage, *epimysium* covers the bicep muscle and continues to that it to:

   A.   cartilage
   B.   bone
   C.   another muscle
   D.   the hip joint

787. It can be deduced from the passage that satellite cells perform which of the following tasks?

   A.   satellite cells regenerate the basement membrane
   B.   satellite cells fill muscle fibers with dense nuclei
   C.   satellite cells are a reserve of myoblasts
   D.   satellite cells are part of the contractile apparatus

788. A well-developed short-distance sprinter would most likely have quadriceps with what muscle fiber makeup?

   A.   mostly white fiber
   B.   mostly red fiber
   C.   mostly intermediate fiber
   D.   some white fiber, some red fiber, some intermediate fiber

---

Passage 802 (Questions 789-795)

A skeletal muscle is made up of thousands of cylindrical muscle fibers running from a point of origin to the point of insertion. These fibers are bound together by connective tissue that also passes blood vessels and nerves. An increase in strength and muscle mass comes about through an increase in the thickness of the individual fibers, as well as an increase in the amount of connective tissue present.

A skeletal muscle cell is composed of an array of myofilaments that are stacked lengthwise and run the entire length of the cell. The myofilaments form light (I-bands) and dark (A-bands) bands. Dark bands are mostly myosin with some actin. Light bands are mainly actin being bisected by the Z-line. The Z-line is a collection of numerous peptides, with α-actinin holding actin myofilaments in register. In a relaxed skeletal muscle cell, myosin does not extend the entire length of the sarcomere and the thin myofilaments do not meet in the middle.

Myosin has a globular head on one end and a tail at the other. It is made of 2 monomers, heavy and light meromyosins. Actin is a polar molecule with a positive and a negative end. It can grow in one direction only.

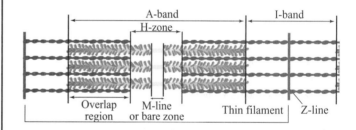

789. According to the passage, where does actin originate in the sarcomere?

   A.   the A-band
   B.   the Z-disk
   C.   myosin
   D.   the M-line

790. The myosin myofilament can be cleaved into a head and a tail piece. All of the following are accurate in describing the position of myosin in a sarcomere EXCEPT:

   I.   A-band is the length of a myosin myofilament
   II.   A-band contains thin and thick myofilaments
   III.   A-band does not include actin-binding sites

   A.   I and II only
   B.   II and III only
   C.   III only
   D.   I, II, and III

791. Which tissue type requires stimulation from the somatic nervous system in order to initiate a contraction?

  A. skeletal muscle
  B. smooth muscle
  C. cardiac muscle
  D. intestinal muscle

792. During muscular contraction, various polarized light bands behave characteristically. Which of the following events occurs during the relaxation of a muscle?

  A. Z-lines are rapidly pulled closer together.
  B. The width of the I-band remains unaltered.
  C. The area occupied by the H-band area will decrease.
  D. No change is observed in the width of the A-band.

793. In resting muscle fibers, calcium accumulates in which of the following structures located in close proximity to A and I-bands?

  A. mitochondria
  B. lysosome
  C. Golgi apparatus
  D. sarcoplasmic reticulum

794. All of the following processes supply muscles with an energy source, like ATP, EXCEPT:

  A. glycolysis
  B. cellular respiration
  C. creatine phosphate
  D. fatty acid synthesis

795. According to the passage myosin occupies which protein structure?

  A. primary
  B. secondary
  C. tertiary
  D. quaternary

Passage 803 (Questions 796-802)

The control of movement requires a continuous flow of sensory information from both receptors and visual stimuli. A receptor that provides information about the movement or position of a body part is called a proprioceptor: two major ones are the Golgi tendon organ and the muscle spindle. The Golgi tendon organ lies in series with the muscle and is sensitive to changes in tension. The muscle spindle lies in parallel with the muscle and is sensitive to changes in length.

Flies were used to pinpoint the necessity of head movement in flight. The focus was placed on the proprioceptors located in the head, which input into the central nervous system. The prosternal organ is the main proprioceptor of the head and neck region. It has 2 hair plates with 100 mechanosensory hairs on each.

Experiment 1:

The fly's head was moved passively while in flight, which caused the fly to follow with its body. A torque meter was used to measure the turn made in flight. When the mechanosensory hairs were shaved on one side the fly could no longer compensate for head movements with body turning movements.

Experiment 2:

The specific hair plates on the fly were shaved and the fly was placed in a white wind tunnel, which eliminated all visual input. When hairs on the right hair plate were shaved, the fly would roll its head to the left compensating for the over-excitation of the right prosternal organ. Eventually, the fly would compensate for the tilt somewhat. When both hair plates were shaved, the head tilt would cease to occur, but the head roll variation was different in flies with intact prosternal organs.

796. A slow, continuous curl of a 20-pound weight toward the chest with the right bicep muscle would most likely stimulate which of the following?

  A. the Golgi tendon organ only
  B. the muscle spindle only
  C. the Golgi tendon organ and the muscle spindle
  D. neither the Golgi tendon organ nor the muscle spindle

797. Which of the following statements explains why at the end of the first experiment the fly could not compensate for the passive head movements?

    A.   The nervous system could not sense that the head was turned.
    B.   The body could not sense that the head was turned.
    C.   The body was experiencing motor paralysis.
    D.   The torque meter was disconnected.

Angle	Head Position
0	straight forward
+	left tilt
−	right tilt

798. A fly in a homogenously white wind tunnel with a shaved left prosternal organ would be expected to initially tilt its head to a:

    A.   angle of 0 degrees
    B.   positive angle
    C.   negative angle
    D.   positive or negative angle

799. According to the passage, the prosternal organ delivers information to which of the following?

    A.   the peripheral nervous system
    B.   the spinal cord
    C.   the notochord
    D.   the autonomic nervous system

800. Which of the following diagrams depicts the location of a Golgi tendon organ in reference to a muscle?

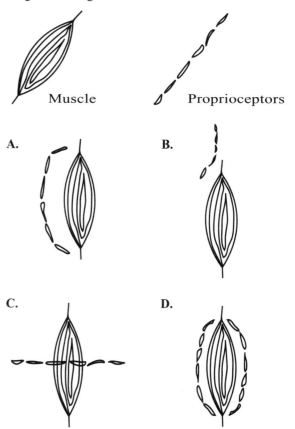

Muscle   Proprioceptors

A.   B.

C.   D.

801. When the fly rolls its head to the right, the higher frequency of action potentials is being delivered from which of the following locations?

    A.   left muscle spindle
    B.   left prosternal organ
    C.   right Golgi tendon organ
    D.   right prosternal organ

802. The muscle spindle contains 3 types of intrafusal fibers: two types are sensory afferent and two types are motor neurons, called gamma. Gamma neurons contain intracellular machinery to synthesize which of the following?

    A.   cortisol
    B.   epinephrine
    C.   acetylcholine
    D.   norepinephrine

Questions 803 through 811 are **NOT** based on a descriptive passage.

803. Calcium released from the sarcoplasmic reticulum will diffuse and bind to which thin myofilament?

- **A.** F-actin
- **B.** myosin
- **C.** tropomyosin
- **D.** troponin C

804. The T-tubule membrane network is integrally involved in excitation-contraction coupling in which of the following muscle types?

- **I.** skeletal muscle
- **II.** cardiac muscle
- **III.** smooth muscle

- **A.** I only
- **B.** I and II only
- **C.** II and III only
- **D.** I, II, and III

805. When a stethoscope is placed on the chest, the "lub-dup, lub-dup…" heart sounds can be auscultated. Which of the following events is occurring during the "dup" heart sound?

- **A.** closing of the atrioventricular valves
- **B.** opening of the atrioventricular valves
- **C.** closing of the aortic/pulmonic valves
- **D.** opening of the aortic/pulmonic valves

806. What compound is often used by muscle tissue to drive thermodynamically unfavored reactions?

- **A.** adenosine diphosphate
- **B.** oxygen
- **C.** adenosine triphosphate
- **D.** glucose

807. Which of the following structures is distal to the wrist?

- **A.** the elbow
- **B.** the fingers
- **C.** the shoulder
- **D.** the forearm

808. Which of the following cells are found in woven (immature) bone?

- **A.** fibroblasts
- **B.** osteocytes
- **C.** keratinocytes
- **D.** chondrocytes

809. In an unstimulated cell, the membrane potential that is negative inside relative to the outside is knows as:

- **A.** an action potential
- **B.** the resting membrane potential
- **C.** the voltage threshold
- **D.** membrane depolarization

810. A baby is born with a congenital cardiac defect that allows right atrial blood to bypass the lungs and enter the left atrium. Which of the following structural defects must be surgically repaired to save this baby's life?

- **A.** ductus venosus
- **B.** foramen ovale
- **C.** ductus arteriosus
- **D.** ductus vena cavas

811. Which component of the nervous system stimulates the contraction of musculature that lines the blood vessels?

- **A.** the central nervous system
- **B.** the somatic nervous system
- **C.** the autonomic nervous system
- **D.** the voluntary nervous system

GO ON TO THE NEXT PAGE.

The heart has two related functions, generating electrical activity and pumping blood. Cardiac mechanical performance (measured by the LV Vol.) is driven and monitored by the electrical activity (measured by the ECG). A small number of cardiac cells are considered "excitable" and are similar to neurons in that regard. A collection of excitable cells can be found in the sinoatrial node, which has ionic currents flowing through voltage-gated and time-dependent channels. (An inward current occurs when positively charged ions cross the cell membrane to enter the cell. Conversely, an outward current is generated when positive ions cross out of the cell.)

Voltage dependence is a property of protein gated channels. The gates are sensitive to the membrane potential (Vm) and a change in the Vm will cause gates to open or close. In nerves and skeletal muscle, only two currents, sodium (I_{Na}^+) and potassium (I_K^+), generate an action potential. However, in cardiac myocytes, the electrical activity is made complicated by the involvement of channels selective for Na^+, Cl^-, Ca^{2+}, and K^+.

Cardiac electrical activity arises from a pacemaker that is myogenic, in that action potentials are initiated by cardiac myocytes themselves. Local currents use gap junctions to cross from cell to cell in order to depolarize the entire atrial muscle.

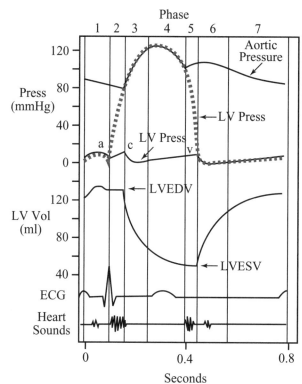

KEY

Phase 1   Atrial contraction
Phase 2   Isovolumetric contraction
Phase 3   Rapid ejection
Phase 4   Reduced ejection
Phase 5   Isovolumetric relaxation
Phase 6   Rapid ventricular filling
Phase 7   Reduced ventricular filling

Abbreviations:

LV Press = left ventricular pressure
LVEDV = volume in the left ventricle before it contracts
LVESV = volume in the left ventricle after it contracts
LV Vol. = left ventricular volume
a = a-wave
c = c-wave
v = v-wave

812. It can be inferred from the passage that a trained cardiologist is expecting to hear how many heart sounds when auscultating the chest of a normal individual?

    A.   one heart sound
    B.   two heart sounds
    C.   three heart sounds
    D.   four heart sounds

813. Which of the following ions is involved in initiating the cardiac action potential but not skeletal muscle action potential?

    A. high concentration of extracellular sodium
    B. high concentration of intracellular potassium
    C. high concentration of extracellular chloride
    D. high concentration of extracellular calcium

814. Phase 5 marks the end of the ventricular contraction and the closing of which of the following valves?

    A. mitral valve
    B. tricuspid valve
    C. aortic valve
    D. capillary valve

815. Which of the following events is the first to occur during a cardiac cycle?

    A. an action potential
    B. the opening of the necessary ion channels
    C. depolarization
    D. cardiac myocyte contraction

816. The cyclic, minute-to-minute function of cardiac myocytes is complicated and involves which of the following outward current generators?

    I. selective channels for Na^+ and K^+
    II. selective channels for Cl^-
    III. selective channels for Ca^{2+}

    A. I only
    B. II only
    C. II and III only
    D. I, II, and III

817. According to the passage, all of the following structures rely on a voltage-dependent mechanism, EXCEPT?

    A. sodium–potassium ATPase
    B. skeletal muscle cells
    C. leaky potassium channels
    D. red blood cells

818. Different phases of the cardiac cycle can be determined by examining the ventricular volume at a given time. Based on the ventricular volume, which of the following phases correlates with the begining of systole?

    A. phase 2
    B. phase 3
    C. phase 5
    D. phase 6

Passage 805 (Questions 819-824)

The cardiovascular system consists of the heart, arteries, elements of microcirculation, and veins. The aorta and the common iliacs are elastic arteries. As blood continues to move distally, elastic arteries gradually transform into muscular ones. So, arteries proximal to the heart are elastic and those more distal are muscular.

The heart has three distinct layers. The most prominent layer is the *myocardium*, which is comprised primarily of muscle fibers. Cardiac muscle cells (myocytes) have a centrally located nucleus, banding to give striations, and numerous mitochondria to generate all the necessary ATP. Atrial myocytes contain secretory granules, which store the atrial natriuretic factor (ANF). The distention of the atrial chamber induces the release of ANF into circulation. ANF is carried to the kidneys, where it stimulates the elimination of sodium and water.

The *myocardium* is in contact with the *endocardium*, the innermost layer of heart. The *endocardium* is lined with simple squamous endothelium, which is extremely important as an anti-thrombogenic agent. Without *endothelium*, the chambers of the heart would plug with coagulated blood. The outermost layer of heart is the *epicardium*, which is filled with unilocular fat. Found in the fat are branches of the coronary circulation and the autonomic nervous system fibers.

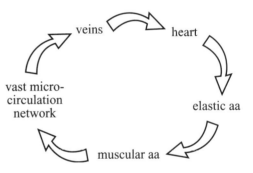

Figure 1 Path of Cardiovascular Circulation

819. Which of the following statements is correct in describing the relative thickness and pressure generated by the ventricular myocardium?

    A. It is the same thickness as the atrium.
    B. The pressure generated by the right ventricle is greater than that of the left.
    C. It is much thicker than the atrium.
    D. Both the atrium and the ventricle generate identical pressures during contraction.

820. While referring to the passage and focusing on the digestive system, which of the following organs is the most proximal to the mouth?

   A. the stomach
   B. the large intestine
   C. the pancreas
   D. the small intestine

821. ANF granules are found exclusively in the atrial myocardium. Which of the following systems directly opposes the actions of the atrial natriuretic factor?

   A. the hypothalamus → anterior pituitary → TSH → thyroid hormone
   B. renin → angiotensin I → angiotensin II → aldosterone
   C. the hypothalamus → posterior pituitary → ADH
   D. Leydig cells → testosterone → estrogen → dihydrotestosterone

822. Papillary muscles and chordae tendinae connect to cardiac valves. It can be assumed that the endocardium, papillary muscles, chordae tendinae, and cardiac valves are all covered by the:

   A. myocardium, the middle layer of cardiac tissue
   B. endocardium, the innermost layer of cardiac tissue
   C. endothelium, the inner layer attached to the endocardium
   D. epicardium, the outermost layer of cardiac tissue

823. Which of the following circumstances causes the release of the atrial natriuretic factor?

   A. high blood pressure
   B. increased heart rate
   C. low blood pressure
   D. decreased heart rate

824. In a newborn, which of the following arteries receives blood directly from the heart?

   A. left and right coronary arteries, pulmonary artery, and aorta
   B. the aorta and pulmonary artery
   C. hepatic artery, aorta, pulmonary trunk
   D. the pulmonary vein, left coronary artery, and aorta

Passage 806 (Questions 825-830)

A heart attack is caused by a sudden occlusion of a coronary artery. Death usually occurs when the occlusion causes an abnormal heartbeat (severe arrhythmia) or death of cardiac muscle (a myocardial infarction). In both situations, the heart can no longer adequately pump blood to supply the brain and other body organs. Almost all heart attacks occur in people who have a history of coronary artery disease.

The wall of a coronary artery has 3 distinct layers: the *intima*, the *media*, and the *adventitia* layers. The *intima* is composed of endothelial cells that cover the artery's lumenal surface, connective tissue, and elastic tissue called the internal elastic lamina. Endothelial cells secrete chemicals that regulate arterial vasodilation/vasoconstriction and the growth rate of the arterial wall. The *media* is primarily smooth muscle, which contracts and relaxes to control the blood pressure and blood flow through the artery. The *adventitia* contains potent factors that promote blood clotting. These clots can limit excessive bleeding following an injury to the arterial wall.

In coronary artery disease, injury to the *intima* leads to the thickening of the arterial inner lining known as intimal proliferation, which is caused by the migration of smooth muscle cells into the intima, where they reproduce to secrete protein elements of connective tissue. With time, cholesterol, other fats, and inflammatory cells enter the thickened intima to form atherosclerotic plaque, which grows to accumulate scar tissue and calcium.

825. A vessel that is resistant to intimal proliferation is most likely deficient in which of the following layers?

   A. the intima
   B. the media
   C. the adventitia
   D. layers have nothing to do with plaque

826. When a heart attack occurs, endothelial cells are expected to secrete chemicals that:

   A. dilate blood vessels to increase blood pressure
   B. dilate blood vessels to decrease blood pressure
   C. constrict blood vessels to increase blood pressure
   D. constrict blood vessels to decrease blood pressure

GO ON TO THE NEXT PAGE.

827. According to the passage, which layer of a coronary artery is closest to the blood that rushes through the cardiovascular system?

    A.   the intima
    B.   the media
    C.   the adventitia
    D.   the serosa

| | | | | | | | | | | | | | | | | | | |

Time Duration: 15 sec.

Figure 1 Non-Arrhythmic Heart Rate

(| - represents a single heart beat)

828. The normal heart rate is between 60 to 100 beats per minute. Any deviation from the normal is considered to be an arrhythmia (i.e., sinus tachycardia). Which of the following diagrams represents a patient who should be treated for arrhythmia? (Each answer choice correlates to time duration of 15 sec.)

    A. | | | | | | | | | | | | | | | | | | |
    B. | | | | | | | | | | | | | | | | | | |
    C. ||| || | ||| | | | | | | | | | || || || ||
    D. | | | | | | | | | | | | | | | |

829. When examining the media layer of the coronary artery, all of the following would be a normal finding, EXCEPT:

    A.   single nucleated cells
    B.   T-tubules
    C.   non-striated cells
    D.   actin and myosin

830. According to the passage, a chronic injection of which of the following hormones should theoretically decrease ion concentration and affect the rate at which plaque develops?

    A.   thyroid hormone
    B.   calcitonin
    C.   glucagon
    D.   testosterone

Questions 831 through 839 are **NOT** based on a descriptive passage.

831. Every muscle cell has a single motor end plate that responds to which of the following neurotransmitters?

    A.   norepinephrine
    B.   epinephrine
    C.   acetylcholine
    D.   acetylcholine esterase

832. A tear of the anterior cruciate ligament requires 1 year of physical therapy and rehab to properly heal. The reason for the lengthy recovery is that the injury severs the attachment between:

    A.   muscle and bone
    B.   bone and bone
    C.   muscle and muscle
    D.   muscle and joint

833. Which of the following is considered to be immature bone that is first synthesized during development and in fracture repair?

    A.   woven
    B.   lamellar
    C.   compact
    D.   spongy

834. At the neuromuscular junction, neurotransmitters cross the synaptic cleft and depolarize the muscle cell, which opens:

    A.   sodium-gated channels
    B.   potassium-gated channels
    C.   calcium-gated channels
    D.   chloride-gated channels

835. Muscle cells contain all of the following high-energy molecules to use as sources for chemical reactions EXCEPT:

    A.   adenosine triphosphate (ATP)
    B.   nicotinamide adenine dinucleotide (NADH)
    C.   creatine phosphate
    D.   flavin adenine dinucleotide (FAD^+)

836. If administered, acetylcholine and norepinephrine would have which of the following effects on the heart rate and force of contraction, respectively?

    A.   no measurable changes, increase
    B.   decrease, no measurable changes
    C.   decrease, increase
    D.   increase, increase

837. What family of molecules can serve as an energy source, act as a coenzyme, and store genetic information?

  A. peptides
  B. lipids
  C. carbohydrates
  D. nucleic acids

838. All of the following statements apply to cells that occupy bone, EXCEPT:

  A. Bone stem cells (osteoprogenitor cells) are precursor, that differentiate into osteoblasts.
  B. Osteoblasts are active in bone deposition.
  C. Osteocytes are trapped within mineralized bone, which they maintain.
  D. Osteoclasts are similar to macrophages and actively deposit bone.

839. Aplastic anemia is a serious disorder that results when the bone marrow fails to produce blood cells. Aplastic anemia may be either acquired or inherited. Which of the following is an example of an inherited aplastic anemia?

  A. A large bone tumor invades the bone marrow and inhibits cellular synthesis.
  B. An anticancer antibiotic inhibits the function of the bone marrow.
  C. A limb amputation decreases the body bone marrow concentration.
  D. A newborn has a diminished bone marrow stem cell population.

Passage 807 (Questions 840-845)

Smooth muscle is responsible for the contractility of hollow organs, for example the uterus. Its structure differs from that of skeletal muscle, although it can develop isometric force per cross-sectional area that is equal to that of skeletal muscle. However, the speed of smooth muscle contraction is only a small fraction of that of skeletal muscle. In general, smooth muscle contains much less protein (100 mg/g muscle) than skeletal muscle (190 mg/g). Notable is the decreased myosin content, 16 mg/g in smooth muscle versus 69 mg/g in skeletal muscle. On the other hand, the amounts of actin and tropomyosin are the same in both types of muscle.

Smooth muscle contains a myosin light chain kinase (MLCK), which is activated by Ca^{2+}-calmodulin. MLCK transfers a terminal phosphate group to a hydroxyl group on a serine and/or threonine. Both amino acids are found on the phosphorylatable myosin light chain. The reaction is as follows:

$$\text{light chain-OH} + \text{Mg-ATP}^{2-} \rightarrow\rightarrow \text{light chain-O-PO}_3^{2-} + \text{Mg-ADP}^- + \text{H}^+$$

Reaction 1

Dephosphorylation is catalyzed by the smooth muscle myosin light chain phosphatase (MLCP). The reaction is as follows:

$$\text{light chain-O-PO}_3^{2-} + \text{H}_2\text{O} \rightarrow\rightarrow \text{light chain-OH} + \text{HPO}_4^{2-}$$

Reaction 2

840. If the myosin light chain kinase is functioning at the V_{max}, which of the following changes is expected in the cytoplasm?

  A. a depletion in the concentration of magnesium
  B. the organelles are exposed to an acidic environment
  C. an increase in the concentration of HPO_4^{2-}
  D. an increase in the concentration of alcohol

841. According to the passage, it is safe to assume which of the following theories regarding the intracellular architecture of muscle cells?

  A. Skeletal muscle cells have a higher concentration of free ribosomes in comparison to smooth muscle cells.
  B. Smooth muscle cells have a higher concentration of free ribosomes in comparison to skeletal muscle cells.
  C. Skeletal muscle cells consume less ATP for protein synthesis in comparison to smooth muscle cells.
  D. Smooth muscle cells consume more ATP for protein synthesis in comparison to skeletal muscle cells.

GO ON TO THE NEXT PAGE.

842. All of the following structures are hollow organs EXCEPT:

- **A.** the bladder
- **B.** the blood vessel
- **C.** the liver
- **D.** the stomach

843. A phasic smooth muscle performs short and transient contractions. Which of the following tasks would most likely be performed by a phasic smooth muscle?

- **A.** rhythmic contraction of the left atrium
- **B.** intestinal peristalsis
- **C.** continual contraction of an arterial wall
- **D.** flexion of the wrist

844. According to the passage, which of the following scenarios requires an endocrine hormone to stimulate the contraction of smooth muscles?

- **A.** the release of acetylcholine into the neuromuscular synapse
- **B.** the release of oxytocin to stimulate the contraction of the uterus
- **C.** the release of glucagon to elevate blood glucose concentration
- **D.** aldosterone induced increase in the reabsorption of sodium by the colon

845. Which of the following compounds is hydrolyzed by the MLCK to alter the hydroxyl group on a serine?

- **A.** glucose
- **B.** adenosine triphosphate
- **C.** AMP
- **D.** calcium-calmodulin

Passage 808 (Questions 846-851)

Bone is formed two ways, either from the condensation of mesenchymal tissue into intramembranous bone, or from the indirect conversion of an intermediate cartilage model into endochondral bone. Intramembranous ossification occurs in the mandible, as well as frontal, parietal, and maxillary bones. It is carried out by osteoblasts, which perform synthesis on highly vascular embryonic connective tissue. The environment of the connective tissue, specifically the availability of vasculature, determines which bone type will develop.

Endochondral bone formation takes place at the vertebral column, the pelvis, and during the synthesis of long bones. New bone forms in primary ossification centers, which are located within the mesenchymal tissue or in the cartilaginous model. Secondary endochondral ossification centers appear later, at the end of the cartilage model within the epiphysis. With time, ossification proceeds toward the end of the bone, where a plate of cellular activity appears. The plate is located between the epiphysis and the diaphysis and later becomes the site for longitudinal bone growth. Ossification centers of the epiphysis and of small wrist bones appear at different ages.

When synthesis is complete, all bones are covered by a thin layer of connective tissue called the periosteum. The deepest layer of the periosteum is full of osteoprogenitor cells, which are reserved for periods of growth and repair.

846. According to the passage, primary endochondral ossification can take place in which of the following locations?

- **A.** in mesenchymal tissue only
- **B.** in a cartilaginous model only
- **C.** in mesenchymal tissue and in the cartilaginous model
- **D.** in neither the mesenchymal tissue nor the cartilaginous model

847. All of the following components play a role in determining the type of bone development to take place, EXCEPT:

- **A.** the presence of low-pressure capillaries
- **B.** local drainage performed by the lymphatics
- **C.** the presence of vessels carrying deoxygenated blood
- **D.** concentration of muscular arteries

GO ON TO THE NEXT PAGE.

848. Osteoprogenitor cells differentiate into osteoblasts and are active during osteogenesis. What can be predicted about the concentration of bone cells in a growing human embryo?

    A. expect a low concentration of osteoclasts
    B. expect a higher than normal concentration of osteoblasts
    C. expect to see no active osteoprogenitor cells
    D. expect a decreased concentration of osteoblasts and osteoclasts

849. Bones found in which of the following locations develop via intramembranous ossification?

    A. bones of the upper extremity
    B. bones of the face and skull
    C. bones of the thigh region in the leg
    D. cartilage of the nose and ears

850. Osteoblasts do not undergo mitosis and respond to which of the following hormones that increases bone resorption:

    A. thyroid hormone
    B. PTH
    C. ACTH
    D. calcitonin

851. All of the following statements apply to the base substance used for endochondrial bone formation EXCEPT:

    A. It is avascular.
    B. It is highly innervated and is incredibly sensitive to pain.
    C. It receives nutrients by means of simple diffusion.
    D. It can be found in the walls of the trachea and the larynx.

Passage 809 (Questions 852-858)

The peak bone mass occurs approximately ten years after the actual physical growth stops. From that point, males and females lose about 1% of their bone mass for each year of life. However, women experience a tremendous drop in bone mass at menopause, which does not occur in men. The established threshold for long bone fractures is 50% of the peak bone mass. Females reach this point a lot sooner than men do because of the drastic bone density changes seen post-menopause.

Individuals diagnosed with osteopenia are chronically losing their bone mass. The disease is caused by overly active osteoclasts that relocate deep into bone tissue, almost reaching the marrow. Once there, osteoclasts begin to chew out holes that get permanently filled with osteoid, which prevents the formation of the Haversian systems, and bones begin to degenerate.

Osteoporosis is a loss in bone mass that occurs when bone resorption exceeds bone formation. With time osteoporosis can cause a compression of the spine cord, a complication known as the Dowager's Hump. Osteoporosis can be distinguished from osteopenia using a dual x-ray system that measures wrist and lumbar spine densities, which are compared to an average bone density seen in healthy adults. To be diagnosed with osteopenia, an individual must demonstrate a bone density of 0 to 2.5 standard deviations away from a healthy adult mean. In osteoporosis the bone density is greater than 2.5 standard deviations away from a healthy adult mean.

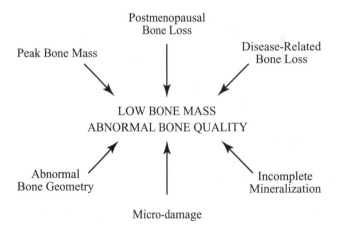

Figure 1 Factors that Contribute to Bone Fragility

852. Which of the following statements explains why in osteopenia the formation of osteoid causes bones to degenerate?

    A. a lack of a blood supply
    B. a local buildup of oxygen
    C. an overactive concentration of osteoblasts
    D. destruction of the bone marrow

GO ON TO THE NEXT PAGE.

853. Which of the following individuals is at the greatest risk for a long bone fracture?

A. male A is 57, growth stopped at 21 years of age
B. male B is 49, growth stopped at 17 years of age
C. male C is 51, growth stopped at 19 years of age
D. female A is 43, premenopausal, growth stopped at 18 years of age

854. It can be inferred that all of the following are contributing factors that lead to bone fractures EXCEPT:

A. average muscle mass
B. being female
C. poor vision
D. decreased calcium intake

855.

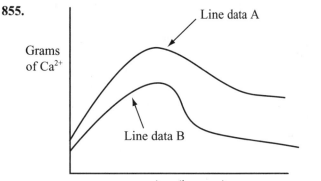

Grams of Ca^{2+}

Line data A

Line data B

Age (in years)

In the above graph, male/female age (in years) is plotted vs. bone mass (in grams of Ca^{2+}). Based on the plotted data, which of the following statements are accurate?

I. line data A represents male bone-density plot
II. using line data B, the average age of menopause can be determined
III. line data B is an example of a bone disease

A. I only
B. I and II only
C. III only
D. I, II, and III

856. According to the information presented in the passage, changes in estrogen concentration, especially following menopause, have which of the following effects on bone?

A. At normal levels estrogen is osteo-protective by inhibiting osteoclast activity.
B. At any level estrogen is osteo-degrading by activating osteoclast activity.
C. Estrogen is a potent inhibitor of PTH and is therefore needed to raise blood calcium.
D. Postmenopausal treatment with estrogen will not cause an increase in bone density.

857. In terms of increasing severity, which of the following is accurate?

A. low blood calcium → peak bone mass level under 84% → osteopenia → osteoporosis
B. low blood calcium → osteopenia → bone mass level under 83% → osteoporosis
C. bone mass level under 83% → low calcium level → osteopenia → osteoporosis
D. bone mass level under 87% → low calcium level → osteoporosis → osteopenia

858. Approximately at what age does a human being reach his or her peak bone mass?

A. 19
B. 26
C. 32
D. 45

GO ON TO THE NEXT PAGE.

859. Which of the following structures is found in smooth muscle?

A. troponin
B. T-tubules
C. myosin light chain kinase
D. striations

860. Two strands of fibrous actin are wound into a helix to make up the thin filament. There are several other proteins also associated, of which the most important are troponin (globular) and tropomyosin (fibrous). In order to bind calcium, troponin must occupy which of the following structures?

A. primary
B. secondary
C. tertiary
D. quaternary

861. Digestion of carbohydrates occurs in which of the following locations?

I. the mouth
II. the stomach
III. the small intestine

A. I and II only
B. I and III only
C. II and III only
D. I, II, and III

862. Which of the following metabolic pathways is believed to be common to virtually every living cell?

A. photosynthesis
B. glycolysis
C. Krebs cycle
D. electron transport chain

863. All of the following contain smooth muscle EXCEPT:

A. aorta
B. uterus
C. bladder
D. tongue

864. Which of the following situations would stimulate the bone marrow to synthesize cells?

I. exposure to an environment with a decreased oxygen concentration
II. chronic internal bleed
III. a prolonged bacterial infection

A. I only
B. II and III only
C. I and III only
D. I, II, and III

865. A histologist can identify which of the following muscle cell types by the presence of gap junctions?

I. skeletal muscle cells
II. cardiac muscle cells
III. smooth muscle cells

A. I only
B. II only
C. II and III only
D. I, II, and III

866. Which muscle type has no T-tubules and no visible striations because of the poorly developed, disorganized myofilaments?

A. smooth muscle
B. skeletal muscle
C. cardiac muscle
D. voluntary muscle

867. If the main cardiac pacemaker is damaged by an ischemic event, the heart rate will be governed by the:

A. SA node
B. AV node
C. bundle of His
D. Purkinje fibers

Passage 810 (Questions 868-874)

There are five permanent cell types found in bone tissue. Osteogenic cells maintain and repair bone by giving rise to bone-forming and bone-destroying cells. Osteoclasts are derived from monocytes, are eosinophilic (pinkish), and multi-nucleated. They have a distinctive ruffled border that allows them to seal onto bone and release hydrolytic enzymes and acids. The holes osteoclasts leave behind are called the Howship's lacunae. Immature bone has a high concentration of osteoclasts to complete postnatal development by remodeling woven bone and replacing it with secondary or mature bone.

Osteoblasts are found in areas of high metabolism within bone. They do not divide but rather convert into another cell population. Osteoblasts secrete unmineralized ground substance around a cartilage model. The ground substance then calcifies around areas termed as primary and secondary centers of ossification. (The primary center of ossification is at the diaphysis, located in the middle of long bones.) Once calcification has occurred, osteoblasts change into cells that maintain bone. These maintenance cells maintain healthy bones by secreting enzymes and regulating proper nutritional support and blood supply.

Once fully matured and calcified, long bones have distinct architecture: the epiphysis is mostly spongy with a thin shell of dense bone, while the diaphysis is mostly dense bone with a spongy lining of the medullary cavity. The thin outer shell houses the bone-lining cell population that regulates the movement of calcium and phosphate into and out of the bone. It is mostly made up of osteoblasts.

868. Which of the following cells are found in woven (immature) bone?

  A. fibroblasts
  B. osteocytes
  C. keratinocytes
  D. chondrocytes

869. Once released form the bone marrow, monocytes can differentiate into macrophages. Based on this information, it can be inferred that:

  A. osteoclasts are related to red blood cells
  B. osteoclasts are related to phagocytes
  C. osteoclasts are related to T-cells
  D. osteoclasts are related to B-cells

870. The inorganic portion of bone is composed of mainly calcium and phosphate. All of the following compounds are involved in bone maintenance by regulating inorganics EXCEPT:

  A. the parathyroid hormone
  B. vitamin D
  C. the thyroid hormone
  D. calcitonin

871. Substance A-90 is a synthetic thyroid gland product that is similar in structure to calcitonin. According to the passage, when A-90 is injected into the bloodstream, which cell population would it most likely bind to?

  A. osteogenic cell population
  B. stem cell population
  C. bone-lining cell population
  D. osteoclast population

872. Osteoblasts are somatic cells with a regular life span. Which of the following processes is utilized to replenish the aging osteoblast population?

  A. mitosis
  B. differentiation of osteoprogenitor cells
  C. meiosis
  D. binary fission

873. A high concentration of which of the following compounds would be sampled in the lacunae after an osteoclast has been peeled off?

  A. ammonia
  B. H_2O
  C. calcitonin
  D. HCl

874. According to the passage, the primary ossification center is protected by which of the following bone types?

  A. mostly immature (woven) bone
  B. thick dense bone surrounding a spongy center
  C. thick dense bone surrounding the epiphysis
  D. mostly spongy bone covered by a thin, dense shell

Passage 811 (Questions 875-880)

Paget's disease of bone is a localized skeletal disorder of unknown cause that is characterized by abnormal bone remodeling brought about by waves of bone resorption and reformation. The bone changes are divisible into three phases: the osteolytic phase, the mixed osteolytic and osteoblastic phase, and a final osteosclerotic phase. Paget's disease begins as a focus of active bone resorption (osteolytic phase), which may affect a single bone (monostotic) or progress to involve extensive areas of nearby cylindrical and flat bones (polyostotic).

The osteolytic phase is followed by the osteoblastic formation of highly vascular woven bone or, more commonly, by the simultaneous occurrence of both osteoclastic and osteoblastic activity ("mixed" phase). Histologically, the mixed phase accounts for the elevated levels of serum alkaline phosphatase activity and osteoid. Microscopically, the mixed phase of Paget's disease resembles the bone changes in hyperparathyroidism.

In the final stage of Paget's disease, the resorptive activity wanes and sclerotic bone forms (sclerotic phase). The bone trabeculae become thick and prominent, particularly along the lines of stress. Although often rocklike because of a lack of remodeling, the sclerotic bone is poorly organized, structurally weak, and predisposed to transverse fractures.

875. Hormone treatment is one method being currently used to treat the early phase of Paget's disease. Some side effects include vomiting, diarrhea, and abdominal pain, but these effects are usually temporary. A three week treatment with which of the following hormones lessens bone pain and forms new bone?

- A. parathyroid hormone
- B. cortisol
- C. calcitonin
- D. glucagon

876. A diagnosis of Paget's disease can be made when higher than normal levels of alkaline phosphatase are found in:

- A. the bone
- B. the blood
- C. the digestive tract
- D. the urine

877. According to the passage, the osteolytic phase of Paget's disease is carried out by which of the following cells?

- A. osteocytes
- B. osteoblasts
- C. osteoclasts
- D. osteoprogenitors

878. Hearing loss is common in advanced stages of Paget's disease. This information implies which of the following?

- I. the disease has the ability to alter hydroxyapatite
- II. hearing is dependent on bones
- III. Paget's disease infects and damages nerves

- A. I only
- B. I and II only
- C. II and III only
- D. I, II, and III

879. A study was conducted on 107 untreated individuals diagnosed with Paget's disease. Out of the 107 participants, how many individuals would be expected to develop the osteoblastic phase of the disease?

- A. 0 individuals
- B. 47 individuals
- C. 79 individuals
- D. 107 individuals

880. What is the state of calcium homeostasis during the mixed phase of Paget's disease?

- A. There is a decrease in blood concentration of calcium.
- B. There is an increase in the calcium reabsorption by the kidneys.
- C. There is an increase in calcium reuptake into bone.
- D. There is an increase in the calcium elimination by the kidneys.

_____

881. Which of the following metabolic processes converts a molecule of glucose into pyruvate, requires energy in the form of two ATPs, and relies on glyceraldehyde phosphate dehydrogenase as an important mid-cycle enzyme?

A. the electron transport chain
B. glycolysis
C. the Krebs cycle
D. fermentation

882. Which of the following structures transports the most oxygenated blood?

A. the pulmonary vein
B. the vena cava
C. the right atrium
D. the umbilical artery

883. When examining hyaline cartilage under a microscope, one expects to find which of the following?

A. canaliculi
B. microscopic blood vessels
C. peptide fibers
D. Volkmann's canals

884. Smooth muscle has an adequate mitochondrial content to supply all of its energy needs through oxidative phosphorylation; however, smooth muscle utilizes a large degree of glycolysis even under well=oxygenated conditions. Which of the following would be expected in large quantities in a smooth muscle cell?

A. pyruvate
B. citrate
C. lactate
D. ATP

885. Which of the following glands secretes a hormone that decreases the blood calcium concentration?

A. the anterior pituitary
B. the parathyroid gland
C. the thyroid gland
D. the pineal gland

886. Continuous production of blood cells is necessary all through life because each cell has a finite life span. Which of the following organs removes aged blood cells and is located on the left side of the body?

A. spleen
B. liver
C. stomach
D. pancreas

887. Which of the following vessels prevents the proper amount of blood flow to the fetal liver?

A. ductus arteriosus
B. ductus venosus
C. ductus ovale
D. hepatic vein

888. Which of the following is a functional cell unit of a muscle filament?

A. sarcolemma
B. sarcomere
C. sarcoplasmic reticulum
D. sarcoidosis

STOP. IF YOU FINISH BEFORE TIME IS CALLED, CHECK YOUR WORK. YOU MAY GO BACK TO ANY QUESTION IN THIS TEST BOOKLET.

LECTURE 9

Biology Passages
Questions 889–1001

Passage 901 (Questions 889-894)

The Hardy-Weinberg equilibrium predicts how gene frequencies are transferred from one generation to the next, given a specific set of assumptions. If gene frequencies remain unchanged over time, the expected frequencies in the next generation would be q^2, p^2, and $2pq$.

The existence of a *genetic drift* prevents the Hardy-Weinberg population from actually existing. However, that does not necessarily negate the predictive properties of the Hardy-Weinberg equilibrium. The *genetic drift* is a change in gene frequency from the expected genotype simply by chance. This is a severe problem in small populations, but is minimal in larger ones.

Population-Y has the following genotypic frequencies:

- homozygous dominant = 0.83
- heterozygous = 0.16
- homozygous recessive = 0.01

In addition to *genetic drift*, random mating requires attention and is checked by examining whether expected genotypic frequencies correlate to actual genotypes in a given population. For instance, in reference to *population-Y*, the expected percentage of randomly mating homozygous dominant individuals is 68.9% (computation: $0.83 \times 0.83 \times 100$).

The following proof demonstrates how the genotypic allele frequency remains stable over time in *population-Y*.

$$p = f(LL) + \tfrac{1}{2}f(Ll)$$
$$p = p^2 + \tfrac{1}{2}(2pq)$$
$$p = p(p + q)$$
$$p = p\,[p + (1 - p)]$$
$$p = p$$

In the absence of any factors that alter the allele frequency, the genotypic and allelic frequencies remain the same from generation to generation. These conclusions have been demonstrated experimentally to be valid and form the basis upon which all population and evolutionary genetic research is based.

889. All of the following belong to a specific set of assumptions applied to the Hardy-Weinberg equilibrium, EXCEPT:

- A. an infinitely large population size
- B. a randomly mating population
- C. a population free from mutation
- D. a population that may have migrated

890. Recently obtained data, on a population of Brazilian white squirrels, demonstrated a significant deviation from the expected data based on mating patterns between Ww × ww mammals. Based on this information it can be assumed that:

- A. Random mating was occurring in Brazilian white squirrels.
- B. Random mating was not occurring in Brazilian white squirrels.
- C. Random mating may be occurring in Brazilian white squirrels but data on a WW × WW cross is needed to confirm.
- D. Random mating patterns in Brazilian white squirrels cannot be predicted based on the information provided.

891. In addition to the equations presented in the proof, which other equation applies to the Hardy-Weinberg equilibrium?

- A. $p = p(p + q)$
- B. $p + q = 100$
- C. $q = 1 - p$
- D. $p = q$

892. In humans, random mating is most likely to occur for which of the following traits?

- A. intelligence
- B. blood type
- C. physical appearance
- D. personality

893. The Hardy-Weinberg equation can be used to determine the number of individuals in a specific population with a homozygous dominant genotype, by specifically focusing on which of the following terms?

- A. q^2
- B. p^2
- C. $2pq$
- D. $\tfrac{1}{2}\,pq$

894. According to the passage, the Hardy-Weinberg equilibrium is useful in predicting which of the following?

- A. the physical appearance of a population
- B. the genetic makeup of a population
- C. the environmental consequences on a population
- D. both the physical appearance and the genetic makeup of a population

Passage 902 (Questions 895-901)

A sex-determination system determines the development of sexual characteristics in an organism. The most common sex-determination systems involve a genetic mechanism. However, some systems involve other variables such as temperature.

In the XY sex-determination system, × and Y chromosomes are distributed unequally to males and females. A male always inherits his Y chromosome from his father and his X chromosome from his mother. A female inherits one X from each parent. In males, every gene present on the X chromosome is expressed. Genes present on an X chromosome in females may or may not be expressed, depending on whether they are dominant or recessive. Hemophilia A, Duchenne's muscular dystrophy, and colorblindness are 3 diseases with an X-linked recessive inheritance pattern. The carrier mother will transmit the disease to half of her sons and daughters.

In the WZz sex-determination system, found in birds and some insects, females have three different kinds of chromosomes, and males have two of the same kind of chromosomes. *Hymenoptera* bees rely on a haploid-diploid system under which males are haploid and females diploid. When the queen bee mates with a drone, her daughters share 75% of their genes with their mother: this is not the case in the XY sex-determination system. This is believed to be significant for the development of eusociality, as it increases the significance of kin selection. In some species of reptiles sex is determined by the temperature at which the egg is incubated. Other species, such as some snails, practice sex change: adults start out male, then become female.

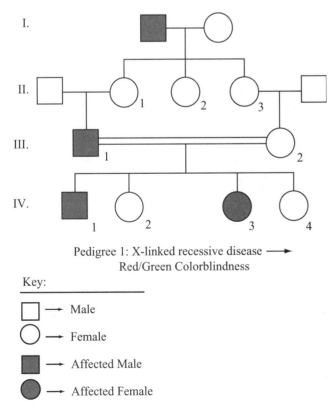

Pedigree 1: X-linked recessive disease ⟶
Red/Green Colorblindness

Key:

☐ ⟶ Male

◯ ⟶ Female

■ ⟶ Affected Male

● ⟶ Affected Female

895. A *hemizygous* genetic condition is having only one set of genes instead of two, as in the case of:

- **A.** loci on the X chromosome in females
- **B.** loci on the Y chromosome in females
- **C.** loci on the X chromosome in males
- **D.** loci on chromosome 7 in males

896. Based on the sex-determination system seen in birds, which of the following genotypes represents a mature female bird?

- **A.** ZZ
- **B.** WWZ
- **C.** WZW
- **D.** WZz

897. According to the passage, which of the following species undergo sex-determination based on the temperature at which the egg is incubated?

- **A.** snails
- **B.** insects
- **C.** alligators
- **D.** bees

898. Daughters from the XY and WZ sex-determination systems are expected to share what percentage of their genes with their mother?

- **A.** 25 percent
- **B.** 50 percent
- **C.** 75 percent
- **D.** 100 percent

899. In pedigree 1, what is the expected genotype of the unmarried female in the second generation?

- **A.** homozygous $X^A X^A$
- **B.** heterozygous
- **C.** homozygous $X^a X^a$
- **D.** cannot be determined from the information provided

900. According to the passage, which of the following is characteristic of an X-linked recessive inheritance?

  A. The incidence of disease is much higher in females.
  B. The disease can often skip generations.
  C. Heterozygous females usually show signs of the disease.
  D. Carrier females do not exist.

901. In pedigree 1, what is the familial relationship between the couple in the third generation?

  A. they are first cousins
  B. they are second cousins
  C. they are in-laws with unique bloodlines
  D. they do not have a familial relationship

Passage 903 (Questions 902-908)

Cystic fibrosis, one of the most common autosomal recessive diseases among Caucasians of Northern European origin, is caused by the cellular misprocessing of the CFTR glycoprotein. The trouble actually begins at the genetic level, with a mutant CFTR gene that codes for a CFTR glycoprotein that is synthesized but fails to mature and cannot proceed beyond the endoplasmic reticulum. This underlying biochemical defect causes a problem with the transport of chloride across epithelial tissue, resulting in salt and ion imbalances.

The major organs affected by the disease are the lungs and the pancreas. Signs and symptoms of the disease include the secretion of thick mucus that closes off the airway and causes recurrent infections and chronic obstructive lung disease: the lungs become highly susceptible to bacterial infection because of the inability to clear the mucus. Most patients are deficient in digestive enzymes and may suffer from chronic malnutrition.

The gut is also affected by cystic fibrosis and 10% of affected neonates are born with *meconium ileus*, a fecal material plug that blocks the junction between the ileum and the cecum. Only 3-10% of patients are fertile, with males almost always infertile. Cystic fibrosis patient usually die from infection and pulmonary failure; however, recently approved therapeutic measures have increased the length and quality of life.

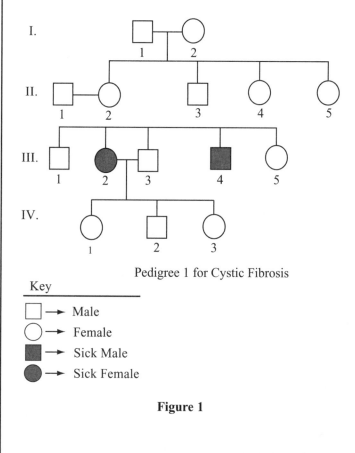

Pedigree 1 for Cystic Fibrosis

Key

☐ → Male
○ → Female
■ → Sick Male
● → Sick Female

Figure 1

902. In conditions that cause nutrient malabsorption, such as pancreatic insufficiency and cystic fibrosis, doctors sometimes prescribe digestive enzymes to improve the absorption of food. Which of the following enzymes would most likely be administered?

- A. pepsin
- B. aldosterone
- C. bile
- D. lipase

903. According to the passage, the obstruction of the ileum by thick meconium secondary to absence of the normal pancreatic enzymes in children with cystic fibrosis will prevent digestive matter from entering:

- A. the stomach
- B. the colon
- C. the small intestine
- D. the kidneys

904. In the past centuries, heterozygotes for cystic fibrosis were postulated to have been more resistant to cholera epidemics. This is an example of:

- A. incomplete penetrance
- B. heterozygote advantage
- C. homozygous recessive inheritance
- D. genetic immunity

905. According to the pedigree, what is the most likely genotype of a couple who had a child born with cystic fibrosis?

- A. The father is heterozygous and the mother is homozygous dominant.
- B. The father is heterozygous and the mother is heterozygous.
- C. The father is homozygous dominant and the mother is homozygous affected.
- D. The father is homozygous normal and the mother is homozygous dominant.

906. In cystic fibrosis, 75% of children appear phenotypically normal but may carry the mutant gene. How many phenotypically normal children are genotypically normal homozygous?

- A. 25 percent
- B. 33 percent
- C. 50 percent
- D. 66 percent

907. According to the passage, which of the following is expected to demonstrate abnormal pathology in a person with cystic fibrosis?

- A. the spleen
- B. the conduction bronchioles
- C. arteries
- D. nerves to the bladder

908. It can be inferred from the passage that the abnormal CFTR gene and glycoprotein undergo all of the following processes EXCEPT:

- A. transcription
- B. translation
- C. post-translational modification
- D. replication

GO ON TO THE NEXT PAGE.

909. Blood type depends on the presence of certain antigens on the surface of red blood cells. Which of the following are important classifications to describe blood types in humans?

   I. the ABO blood typing
  II. hemoglobin concentration
 III. Rh factor

  A. I and II only
  B. I and III only
  C. II and III only
  D. I, II, and III

910. Drifting alleles can disappear all together from the population gene pool. If all but one allele for a given gene disappears, the proportion of individuals who carry it will never stray from 100 percent, unless which of the following events occurs?

  A. genetic drift
  B. spontaneous mutation
  C. Hardy-Weinberg equilibrium is satisfied
  D. forced selection

911. Which of the following nucleotides is found only in DNA?

  A. uracil
  B. adenine
  C. guanine
  D. thymine

912.

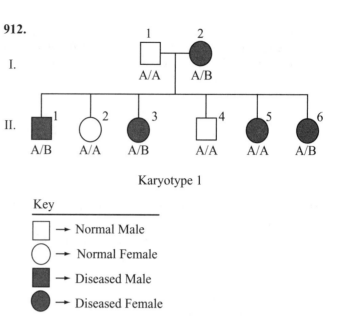

Karyotype 1

Key
□ → Normal Male
○ → Normal Female
■ → Diseased Male
● → Diseased Female

In the above figure, the I-2 individual has been diagnosed with an autosomal dominant disease. Based on this information it can be assumed that some type of a genetic crossover had to occur in which of her offspring?

  A. individual I-1
  B. individual II-2
  C. individual II-5
  D. individual II-6

913. Which of the following is the most likely outcome when a healthy cell suddenly sustains genomic damage following an exposure to ultraviolet light?

  A. The cell would continue with its life cycle.
  B. The cell would undergo immediate self-death.
  C. The cell would stall the cell cycle to repair the damaged DNA.
  D. The cell would become malignant and divide uncontrollably.

914. The gram stain is the most important and universally used staining technique in the bacteriology laboratory. It is used to distinguish between gram-positive and gram-negative bacteria, which have distinct and consistent differences in their:

  A. organelles
  B. cell walls
  C. nutrient requirements
  D. life span

GO ON TO THE NEXT PAGE.

915. NAD$^+$/NADH molecule has a pivotal role in which of the following metabolic processes?

    I. glycolysis
   II. Krebs cycle
  III. electron transport chain

    A. I and II only
    B. I and III only
    C. II and III only
    D. I, II, and III

916. A woman with a 47, XXX karyotype is expected to display how many Barr bodies?

    A. 1
    B. 2
    C. 3
    D. 4

917. Which of the following female structures is most analogous to the male vas deferens?

    A. ovary
    B. fallopian tube
    C. uterus
    D. vagina

918. Which of the following is the expected outcome for a population with a tendency of recessive alleles to disappear?

    A. The population would soon become homozygous recessive.
    B. The population would soon become heterozygous.
    C. The population would soon become homozygous.
    D. The population would soon become extinct.

Passage 904 (Questions 919-924)

Recently, scientists have learned that members of the *Sir2* enzyme family, called sirtuins, play critical roles in metabolism, aging, and gene expression by increasing cellular respiration, which is the process of using oxygen to convert calories into energy. It has been proven that diets restricted in calories increase the average life span, with a concomitant boost in sirtuin activity. In other studies, sirtuin-activating compounds found in red wine increased the life span of ethanol-producing cells.

On the molecular level, sirtuins control *acetyl CoA synthetase*, an enzyme that converts acetate, a source of calories, into acetyl CoA. Acetyl CoA then directly feeds into the Krebs cycle. It is well known that cells can survive using many different sources of energy like fats, sugars, and protein. However, cells missing sirtuin proteins can no longer live on acetate as an energy source. If sirtuins do modify *acetyl CoA synthetase*, turning on the production of acetyl-CoA could explain why restricting the calorie intake would extend the life span.

X-ray crystallography has been used to study sirtuin structure, while the protein was bound to 2 molecules associated with its biological function. One part of the sirtuin was bound to NAD$^+$, a molecule with a pivotal role in metabolism. The other part of the sirtuin was bound to a histone protein. It seems that sirtuins modify histones, which keep DNA tightly coiled, to prevent certain regions from being exposed to DNA replicating machinery.

Sirtuins rely on NAD$^+$ to function but a limited amount of NAD$^+$ is available in the cell at any given time. When NAD$^+$ is being used by a metabolic process, it may not be available for sirtuins to do their job, which is to shut down unnecessary gene expression. The unchecked genetic activity expends energy, promotes genetic abnormalities, and may be associated with aging.

919. According to the passage, the life span of which of the following cells was increased by sirtuin-activating compounds?

    A. plant cells
    B. fungal cells
    C. animal cells
    D. protist cells

920. According to the new research, which of the following methods would most likely slow down the aging process?

    A. increasing the concentration of histones
    B. increasing the concentration of NAD$^+$
    C. decreasing calorie intake of fat but increasing calorie intake of carbohydrates
    D. decreasing the concentration of NAD$^+$

921. It is stated in the passage that sirtuins increase the rate of cellular respiration. Based on the passage, which of the following metabolic processes fall under the heading of cellular respiration?

   I. glycolysis
  II. Krebs cycle
 III. electron transport chain

 A. I and II only
 B. II and III only
 C. III only
 D. I, II, and III

922. According to the information provided in the passage, can animal cells that are missing sirtuin proteins carry out the Krebs cycle?

 A. Yes, because glycolysis produces pyruvate, which is converted into acetyl CoA.
 B. Yes, because the electron transport chain is inactive, not the Krebs cycle.
 C. No, sirtuins are mandatory for the Krebs cycle to function.
 D. No, acetate is the only product that feeds into the Krebs cycle.

923. While bacteria and yeast are both single-celled organisms, yeast cells are preferred by scientists conducting sirtuin research for which of the following reasons?

 A. The eukaryotic yeast cell version of sirtuin would more likely reflect the protein's role in animal cells.
 B. The prokaryotic yeast cell version of sirtuin would more likely reflect the protein's role in animal cells.
 C. The eukaryotic bacterial cell version of sirtuin would more likely reflect the protein's role in animal cells.
 D. The prokaryotic bacterial cell version of sirtuin would more likely reflect the protein's role in animal cells.

924. Sirtuins activate the first step of acetate's conversion by removing an acetyl group from a lysine, which is categorized as:

 A. a lipid
 B. a carbohydrate
 C. an amino acid
 D. a nucleotide

Passage 905 (Questions 925-931)

Population geneticists monitor allele frequencies from generation to generation in search of a genetic drift, a chance event caused by an over or underproduction of alleles when compared to some expected average. Using this perspective, the allele frequency in the offspring population reflects a sampling of the alleles of the preceding generation.

Genetic drift changes the characteristics of a species over time. Unlike natural selection, genetic drift occurs only in small populations that have separated from a larger one. As a result, the post-drift individuals may not be representative of the genotype of the larger population. There are several subtypes of genetic drift. One example, seen in human populations, is called the *founder effect*, which occurs when a small group of original founders start a settlement, and their genes form the basis for an entirely new gene pool. Breeding within this small gene pool will lead to an amplification of alleles they carry.

Gene flow is another factor, in addition to genetic drift, to affect the population gene pool, which is all the genetic information present in a breeding population. Gene flow is caused by migration. New alleles are introduced into a population by immigration with subsequent intermarriage, which causes a change in the relevant allele frequencies seen in a population. Population gene flow can be traced through history by correlating allele frequencies in present-day populations with events documented historically.

925. The *founder effect* is occasionally associated with a reduction in genetic diversity, and overall health and fitness that is most likely caused by the occurance of:

 A. inbreeding only
 B. population bottleneck only
 C. both inbreeding and population bottleneck
 D. neither inbreeding nor population bottleneck

926. According to the passage, the occurrence of a sudden genetic drift, associated with a lengthy isolation of a population of ground finches, is expected to have which of the following outcomes?

 A. genetic disconnect
 B. speciation
 C. regression
 D. mutation

927. Ethnic and religious groups are genetic isolates and have a higher incidence of rare autosomal disorders in comparison to non-isolates. This type of scenario is best explained via which of the following?

  A. founder effect only
  B. caused isolation only
  C. founder effect and caused isolation
  D. coincidental occurrence

928. Which of the following concepts directly apply to natural selection?

  I.   preserved traits provide an advantage to their holders
  II.   always used in reference to an extremely large population
  III. allows the unsuccessful member of a population to leave more offspring

  A. I only
  B. I and II only
  C. II and III only
  D. I, II, and III

929. Which of the following scenarios will make the Hardy-Weinberg equilibrium no longer true?

  A. when dealing with population that randomly mates
  B. when dealing with a population that occasionally migrates
  C. when dealing with a population with no mutations
  D. when dealing with a population that is excessively large

930. Which of the following is the best methodology to use in order to track gene flow?

  A. urine samples
  B. ABO blood types
  C. historical documentation
  D. archeological digs

931. A 37-year-old male had his allele frequency sampled. According to the passage, the obtained data can be used to most accurately assess the allele frequency of which other family member?

  A. his 26 year old brother
  B. his 8 year old daughter
  C. his 47 year old paternal uncle
  D. his 92 year old maternal grandfather

Passage 906 (Questions 932-937)

For spermatogenesis to occur, the right hormonal environment is necessary. GnRH is released by the hypothalamus and transported to the anterior pituitary gland, where it controls the release of two gonadotropins, luteinizing hormone (LH) and the follicle-stimulating hormone (FSH). (The names FSH and LH come from the analogous functioning hormones in females. There are no follicles or anything "luteinizing" in males.) Estrogen is also required for spermatogenesis and is synthesized from testosterone by Sertoli cells. (Estrogen production in males is about 20% of that in females.)

A mature sperm cell consists of a head and a tail. The head has a haploid set of chromosomes and cytoplasmic remnants from the progenitor cell. The anterior surface of the head is covered by the acrosome, which contains proteolytic enzymes, the most notable of which is *hyaluronidase*. These enzymes function to break down the cell wall around the ova, allowing the genetic material to fertilize the egg. The sperm tail has an enlarged section called the body, which is densely packed with mitochondria. The rest of the tail is essentially a single flagellum, full of contractile proteins, actin and myosin.

Fully capacitated sperm (activated and fertile) can travel in the female reproductive tract at 1 to 4 mm/min. In addition, peristaltic waves of muscle contraction by the female reproductive tract can further increase their overall speed. It is common for some sperm to be abnormal in their structure, motility, or number. If a large proportion of sperm is malformed then the male himself is likely to be infertile, even though some of the sperm appear normal.

932. The sperm acrosome comes from a cellular organelle that glycosylates proteins and regulates cellular secretion. Which of the following organelles is the acrosome derived from?

  A. the smooth ER
  B. the lysosome
  C. the nucleus
  D. the Golgi apparatus

933. According to the passage, if a certain sperm organelle that relies on a hydrogen ion gradient were to suddenly rupture, which area of the sperm would be expected to have the lowest pH?

  A. the acrosome
  B. the tail
  C. the body
  D. the flagellum

934. According to the passage, in a woman who presents with symptoms that point to an excess production of testosterone, which other abnormalities should be expected?

A. an increase in the activity of the anterior pituitary
B. an increase in the concentration of estrogen
C. a decrease in the concentration of prolactin
D. a decrease in the concentration of estrogen

935. In females, a surge of luteinizing hormone (LH) causes ovulation to occur. Based on our understanding of the male reproductive system, does luteinizing hormone exist in males?

A. Yes, it acts on the testes to release testosterone.
B. Yes, it acts on the testes to mature sperm.
C. No, because males do not ovulate.
D. No, the detection of LH in a male is a sign of an endocrine problem.

936. *Lophotrichous streptococci* have multiple flagella located on the same spot on the bacterial surface. These organisms are expected to possess which of the following shapes?

A. spherical
B. rod-like
C. comma-shaped
D. spirochete-like

937. Besides in the contractile apparatus of the sperm's flagellum, where else can one expect to note a large concentration of actin?

A. in the nervous system
B. in the cardiac muscle cell
C. in the top layer of the epidermis
D. in the sperm head region

Questions 938 through 947 are **NOT** based on a descriptive passage.

938. Organism-ks30 is fastidious (optimal growth temp. of 32°C and a generation time of 10-12 hours) and requires the Barbour-Stoenner-Kelly (BSK) media to grow. Approximately how much time (measured in days) would be necessary to obtain both offspring and the great-grandparent generation on the same BSK media plate?

A. $1/2$ day
B. 1 day
C. $1\,1/2$ days
D. 2 days

939. All bacteria require carbon for growth and reproduction. Parasitic bacteria that obtain carbon from organic nutrients such as sugar are:

A. autotrophic
B. heterotrophic
C. cyanotrophic
D. nitrate/sulfur-trophic

940. Bumblebees live in colonies, while depending on neighboring plants and each other for survival. The bumblebee hive is a living system that gathers energy to ensure its survival and represents:

A. a population
B. an ecosystem
C. a community
D. a niche

941. In biology, which of the following is a grouping in the classification of living organisms having one or more related or morphologically similar species?

A. kingdom
B. order
C. genus
D. species

942. Which of the following statements describes the relationship between phenotype and genotype?

A. the genotype codes for the phenotype
B. the phenotype codes for the genotype
C. the genotype and phenotype both code for different proteins but are not interrelated
D. the genotype codes for DNA and phenotype codes for protein

943. The origin of life and the relationships between its major lineages are controversial. The gap between prokaryotes and eukaryotes is widely considered as a major missing link in evolutionary history. Which two eukaryotic organelles are generally considered to be derived from endosymbiotic bacteria?

    A. the nucleus and the mitochondria
    B. the Golgi apparatus and the lysosome
    C. the smooth endoplasmic reticulum and the cytoplasm
    D. the mitochondria and the chloroplast

944. What field of science modifies genetic material for some kind of a practical end without much focus on explaining the effect of genes on phenotype?

    A. population genetics
    B. genetic engineering
    C. epigenetics
    D. molecular biology

945. Horizontal gene transfer is any process that transfers genetic material to a non-offspring. Which of the following methods of horizontal gene transfer involes the random uptake and insertion of novel genes into a bacteria?

    A. conjugation
    B. transformation
    C. transinversion
    D. transduction

946. Which of the following serves as the progenitor cell for a mature sperm cell?

    A. primary spermatocyte
    B. spermatogonium
    C. secondary spermatocyte
    D. spermatid

947. In the late 1600s Ariaantje and Gerrit Jansz emigrated from Holland to South Africa, bringing along an allele for a metabolic disease called porphyria. Today more than 30,000 South Africans carry this allele, which can be traced back to this couple. This is a remarkable example of:

    A. genetic drift
    B. population bottleneck
    C. natural selection
    D. the founder effect

Passage 907 (Questions 948-954)

The protein truncation test (PTT) is an in vitro assay that identifies mutated cancer genes by examining the RNA extracted from lymphocytes. Some mutations cause protein truncation or shortening, which yields a smaller product in comparison to the wild-type (normal) protein product. The PTT compares yielded protein lengths and reports any discrepancies, allowing for a relatively rapid analysis of DNA. When a truncated protein is detected, a direct sequence analysis is performed to identify the specific area of DNA with the problem. Currently, the PTT is used as a screening test for mutant BRCA1, APC, and other cancer genes. However, other molecular markers may be needed to assess staging, therapy, and prognosis.

The BRCA1 mutation is responsible for a small percent of breast cancers seen in women. Other factors, such as penetrance and body susceptibility, determine whether a carrier of a BRCA1 mutation develops breast cancer or not. However, the overall risk of breast cancer for women with BRCA1 mutation is considered to be in the seventy-percent region. Women carriers of BRCA1 mutations who develop cancer in one breast have increased risk of developing cancer in the other breast. BRCA1 mutation is also associated with a forty-five percent lifetime risk of ovarian cancer and an increased risk of colon cancer. Men with BRCA1 mutations can also develop breast cancer.

BRCA1 mutations can be scattered throughout the gene, making the technical aspects of mutation analysis extremely challenging. Different types of mutations have been identified: missense, nonsense, frameshift, and some affecting mRNA splicing and regulation. Because of the variability in mutation types, at present the only accurate method to test for the BRCA1 mutation is direct sequencing and comparison of both copies of the gene.

948. Which of the following would most likely cause the most severe mutation of the BRCA1 gene?

    A. regulation mutation of tRNA
    B. a nonsense mutation
    C. a missense mutation
    D. a silent mutation

949. A new alpha-zero-1-neoplasm performs a high level of purine synthesis. Which of the following serum compounds would serve as the best marker for the presence of alpha-zero-1?

    A. guanine
    B. thymine
    C. uracil
    D. cytosine

950. According to the passage, all of the following cells can be assayed by the protein truncation test, EXCEPT:

- **A.** T-cells
- **B.** stem cells
- **C.** plasma cells
- **D.** B-cells

951. A reversion is a back mutation that restores the defect caused by the original mutation. Which mutation type is likely to have the highest probability of reversion?

- **A.** a large base pair addition
- **B.** a base inversion
- **C.** a base substitution
- **D.** a small deletion

952. Critics of the protein truncation test believe that the test is not cost-effective because of which of the following possible limitations?

- **I.** PTT only detects tumor cells that release truncated peptides.
- **II.** PTT is time consuming.
- **III.** PTT is not definitive and requires additional steps.

- **A.** I only
- **B.** II only
- **C.** I and III only
- **D.** I, II, and III

953. Which of the following statements correctly describes members of a homologous chromosome pair?

- **A.** Homologs are always the same size.
- **B.** Homologs are always the same shape.
- **C.** Homologs always carry identical alleles..
- **D.** Homologs always carry alleles for the same genes..

954. A researcher opted to use the protein truncation test specifically on rRNA. Which of the following cellular locations would need to be "tapped" to obtain rRNA?

- **A.** the nucleus
- **B.** the mitochondria
- **C.** the nucleolus
- **D.** the cytoplasm

Passage 908 (Questions 955-962)

Mark is a 7-year-old boy with moderate mental retardation, a long face, and large ears. His younger sister, Nancy, has a low normal intelligence quotient but her appearance is normal. A few years ago Mark was diagnosed with fragile X syndrome. At the time of the discovery, because fragile X often displays atypical X-linked inheritance patterns, the entire family was asked to submit a molecular analysis, which appears below.

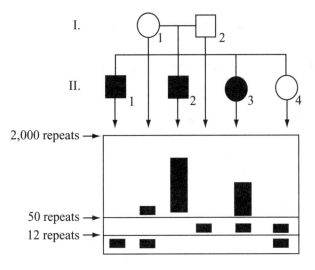

Figure 1 Cytogenetics for Mark's family

It is understood that fragile X syndrome is caused by a large expansion of the CGG triplet repeat, which is then hypermethylated. The hypermethylation represses the expression of the FMR1 gene, which leads to the absence of the FMR1 protein (FMR1P) and subsequent mental retardation. FMR1P is an RNA-binding protein that shuttles between the nucleus and the cytoplasm. Silencing the FMR1 gene is believed to prevent the translation of new proteins.

A normal individual displays 6-50 CGG triple base repeats on the FMR1 gene. A premutation is an intermediate number of repeats, usually between 51 and 230 in number. Normal males are known to carry the premutation without having any signs of the disease. Males born with a full mutation (>231 CGG repeats) are always affected, but females carrying a full mutation can be affected to varying degrees. Among females who have one fragile X chromosome with a full mutation, only 35% are clinically affected.

955. Which of the following organelles "targets" the FMR1P and other proteins with oligosaccharides in order to guide them to specific intracellular compartments?

- **A.** the nucleus
- **B.** the Golgi
- **C.** the storage vesicle
- **D.** the cell membrane

956. According to the passage, which of the following is directly responsible for the mental retardation seen in fragile X syndrome?

    A. overexpression of the FMR1 gene
    B. lack of an RNA-binding protein
    C. a premutation expansion of hypermethylated CGG triplet repeats
    D. a decreased concentration of the FND1-A protein

957. The mutation seen in the fragile X syndrome alters the concentration of which of the following nucleotides?

    A. purines only
    B. pyrimidines only
    C. both purines and pyrimidines
    D. neither purines nor pyrimidines

958. Based on the cytogenetics diagram, which individual in the second generation is Mark?

    A. individual 1
    B. individual 2
    C. individual 3
    D. individual 4

959. As per the passage, the fragile X syndrome inhibits which of the following steps in the central dogma?

    A. the conversion of DNA into "new" DNA
    B. the conversion of DNA into RNA
    C. the conversion of RNA into protein
    D. the conversion of protein into mature protein

960. A few visible breaks called "fragile sites" are seen in individuals with premutations. How many members of Mark's family are expected to display "fragile sites"?

    A. one member
    B. three members
    C. five members
    D. all members

961. How many siblings does Mark's sister, Nancy, have?

    A. 1 male sibling
    B. 2 males siblings
    C. 2 males siblings and 1 female sibling
    D. 2 male siblings and 2 female siblings

962. Based on the inheritance pattern for fragile X, how did Mark obtain the disease?

    A. spontaneous mutation was the cause of his condition
    B. Mark inherited the premutation from his father, who himself is unaffected
    C. Mark's mother has a premutation, which she transmitted to her offspring
    D. both his mother and his father are equal contributors to Mark's mutation

Passage 909 (Questions 963-968)

Lyme disease is caused by a spirochete *Borrelia burgdorferi*. Spirochetes are prokaryotes that move by means of an endoflagella. They are not classified as either gram positive or negative. When *B. burgdorferi* is gram-stained, the cells stain a weak gram-negative by default, as safranin is the last dye used.

B. burgdorferi, deer ticks, and mammals must all exist in one area for Lyme disease to occur. The tick life cycle consists of three distinctive stages: larvae, nymph, and adult. A blood meal is required for ticks to molt from the larvae to the nymph stage. The natural reservoir for the spirochete is the white-footed mouse. Ticks transfer the disease to the white-tailed deer, humans, and other warm-blooded animals after a blood meal on an infected animal.

The indirect immunofluorescent assays (IFAs), enzyme-linked immunosorbent assays (ELISA), and western blotting are 3 commonly used methods to diagnose Lyme disease. Western blot uses an antibody to detect one protein in a mixture of any number of proteins while giving you information about the size of the protein and cellular accumulation. In a protein that is quickly degraded, western blotting will not work but the radioimmune precipitation (RIP) assay is available and can also measure the rate of protein synthesis.

All assays are associated with a high degree of cross-reactivity, because blood from patients with Rocky Mountain spotted fever, mononucleosis, and rheumatoid arthritis often test positive for Lyme disease. A new serodiagnostic test for Lyme disease, known as the Gundersen Lyme Test (GLT), is available on the market. GLT uses flow cytometry to detect bacterial antibodies in the blood of infected individuals. The test is no more sensitive than conventional tests at diagnosing Lyme disease but does eliminate cross-reactivity and has sensitivity near 100%.

963. According to the passage, which of the following assumption must be correct in order for the western blot analysis to work in diagnosing Lyme disease?

  I. *B. burgdorferi* must secrete a unique protein into the blood
  II. T-cells are used to produce antibodies for the western blot
  III. *B. burgdorferi* protein must have a long blood half-life

  A. I only
  B. I and III only
  C. II and III only
  D. I, II, and III

964. Which of the following terms describes a spirochete population in which both the birth and death rates and tissue emigration and immigration rates balance each other?

  A. decreasing in number
  B. increasing in number
  C. stable
  D. unstable

965. In the gram stain, cells are heat fixed and then stained with several dyes. According to the passage, which of the following dyes provides color to gram-negative cells?

  A. crystal violet dye
  B. iodine
  C. alcohol
  D. safranin

966. The principal activity of the rough endoplasmic reticulum is best assayed using which of the following methods?

  A. indirect immunofluorescent assays (IFAs)
  B. western blotting
  C. enzyme-linked immunosorbent assays (ELISA)
  D. radioimmune precipitation (RIP) assay

967. An individual bitten by a tick wishes his blood smear examined to rule out Lyme disease. A red flag should go up if the blood smear shows cells of which morphology?

  A. spherical
  B. rod-like
  C. extra-wide
  D. "S" shaped hair-like

968. According to the passage, antibiotic injections administered to which of the following mammals would most likely completely eradicate the existence of Lyme disease?

  A. white-tailed deer
  B. humans
  C. deer tick
  D. white-footed mouse

GO ON TO THE NEXT PAGE.

969. The wings of insects, birds, and bats all serve the same function, are similar in structure, but evolved independently. This is an example of what evolutionary process?

- **A.** convergent evolution
- **B.** divergent evolution
- **C.** directional evolution
- **D.** stabilizing evolution

970. FMRP protein shuttles between the nucleus and the cytoplasm. Which of the following compounds are expected to shuttle from the cytoplasm into the nucleus?

- **I.** mRNA
- **II.** DNA polymerase III
- **III.** histones

- **A.** I only
- **B.** II and III only
- **C.** III only
- **D.** I, II, and III

971. Smoking is contraindicated for women with a history of breast cancer because carcinogens in cigarette smoke:

- **A.** can make these women resistant to chemotherapy
- **B.** can bring premature menopause and decrease estrogen levels
- **C.** can increase the nondisjunction frequency in their eggs
- **D.** can increase the frequency of "second hit" mutations

972. DF508, a three base pair deletion of the 10th exon on the 508th codon, is the most common cystic fibrosis mutation. DF508 is present in almost 90% of cystic fibrosis patients and is properly classified as:

- **A.** a frameshift mutation
- **B.** a silent mutation
- **C.** an in-frame mutation
- **D.** a missense substitution

973. A density-dependent factor is one where the effect of the factor depends upon the original density and size of the population. Which of the following is most likely to be a density-dependent factor?

- **A.** freezing temperature
- **B.** outbreak of a communicable disease
- **C.** a monthlong drought
- **D.** extremely hot weather

974. The highest concentration of mature sperm would be found in which of the following locations?

- **A.** testosterone-producing Leydig cells
- **B.** seminiferous tubules
- **C.** vas deferens
- **D.** epididymis

975. A homozygous dominant trait can be differentiated from a heterozygous trait by examining:

- **A.** the genotype only
- **B.** the phenotype only
- **C.** both genotype and phenotype
- **D.** neither genotype nor phenotype

976. Nucleic acids are polymers made up of monomers called mononucleotide units. These mononucleotide units themselves are made up of smaller components. Each mononucleotide contains which of the following units?

- **A.** a phosphate unit only
- **B.** a hexose sugar unit only
- **C.** both phosphate and hexose sugar units
- **D.** neither phosphate nor hexose sugar units

977. Atmospheric gases cause the sun's short wavelength radiation to be selectively scattered or reflected away from earth. Which of the following is the most severely scattered form of radiation?

- **A.** infrared light
- **B.** blue light
- **C.** UV light
- **D.** red light

GO ON TO THE NEXT PAGE.

Passage 910 (Questions 978-984)

Hermansky-Pudlak syndrome (HPS) is a rare group of auto-somal recessive diseases whose manifestations include oculocutaneous albinism, bleeding, and lysosomal ceroid storage. Its etiology has been related to defects in the HPS genes.

Albinism is a disorder of amino acid metabolism that results in a congenital hypopigmentation of ocular and systemic tissues. In tyrosinase-negative oculocutaneous albinism, the congenital inactivity of the enzyme *tyrosinase* prevents the cell from using amino acid tyrosine in the formation of the pigment melanin. In tyrosinase-positive oculocutaneous albinism, *tyrosinase* activity is normal, but cells are unable to sequester the synthesized melanin in melanosomes.

Tyrosinase-positive albinism has been associated with HPS. Because patients with HPS can produce some melanin, varying amounts of skin pigmentation may be present. Secondary to the albinism are visual defects, including photophobia (light sensitivity), strabismus (crossed eyes), and nystagmus (involuntary eye movements).

The 16–base pair frameshift duplication on exon 15 is the most common mutation in HPS-1 and is usually seen in Puerto Ricans. HPS-2 is caused by a mutation in the gene encoding the beta-3A subunit of the heterotetrameric AP3 complex (*ADTB3A*), which resides on chromosome 5. The impaired function of specific organelles indicates that the causative genes encode proteins operative in the formation of lysosomes. The affected individuals also report platelet dysfunctions, pulmonary fibrosis, inflammatory bowel, and kidney disease, which may all be linked to ceroid accumulation in cells of various organs. Ceroid is a waxlike substance that causes tissue damage, and, upon kidney involvement, leads to increased excretion of urinary dolichol.

978. All of the following mutations of the HPS-1 gene are associated with a frameshift on the 15th exon, EXCEPT:

- **A.** a 16–base pair deletion
- **B.** a 21–base pair insertion
- **C.** a 7–base pair deletion
- **D.** a 26–base pair insertion followed by a 3-base pair deletion

979. Which of the following problems would be symptomatic for a person with a platelet dysfunction?

- **A.** digestive problems, malnutrition, and constipation
- **B.** chronic infections, poor immune response, and frequent hospitalizations
- **C.** easily bruised skin, nosebleeds, and extended bleeding times
- **D.** fatigue, anemia, and poor tissue oxygenation

980. Albinism is defined as a failure of melanin production in the skin. According to the passage, a person with albinism is at an increased risk of complications with which other body system?

- **A.** the nervous system
- **B.** the cardiovascular system
- **C.** the musculoskeletal system
- **D.** the excretory system

981. For HPS to cause inflammatory bowel disease, the cellular ceroid accumulation would have to occur in which of the following locations?

- **A.** the mouth
- **B.** the kidney
- **C.** the liver
- **D.** the colon

982. A healthy couple, with a family history of Hermansky-Pudlak syndrome (HPS), seeks genetic counseling regarding their risk of having a child HPS. Is there any reason for these two healthy individuals to be concerned?

- **A.** Yes, two healthy parents have a 25% risk of having a child with Hermansky-Pudlak syndrome if they are both carriers of the disease.
- **B.** Yes, two healthy parents have a 50% risk of having a child with Hermansky-Pudlak syndrome if they are both carriers of the disease.
- **C.** No, two healthy parents have a 0% risk of having a child with Hermansky-Pudlak syndrome even if both parents are carriers of the disease.
- **D.** No, two healthy parents will only have a 100% risk of having a child with Hermansky-Pudlak syndrome if they are both carriers of the disease.

983. According to the passage, which of the following diseases are associated with accumulation of the amino acid tyrosine?

- **A.** tyrosinase-positive oculocutaneous albinism only
- **B.** tyrosinase-negative oculocutaneous albinism only
- **C.** both tyrosinase-positive and tyrosinase-negative oculocutaneous albinism
- **D.** neither tyrosinase-positive or tyrosinase-negative oculocutaneous albinism

984. As per the passage, the detection of dolichol in urine that is proven to be in the normal range most likely indicates pathology of:

- **A.** the liver
- **B.** the renal system
- **C.** the digestive system
- **D.** no major organ system

GO ON TO THE NEXT PAGE.

Passage 911 (Questions 985-992)

Galactose, metabolized from a disaccharide milk sugar, enters glycolysis by its conversion to glucose-1-phosphate, which requires three enzymes: *galactokinase, galactose-1-phosphate uridyl transferase*, and *UDP-galactose-4 epimerase*.

There exist two inherited disorders of galactose metabolism. Classic galactosemia is an autosomal recessive disorder caused by enzyme defects in both *galactose-1-phosphate uridyl transferase* and *galactokinase*. Clinical findings with galactosemia include impaired liver function, presence of galactose in urine (known as hypergalactoseuria), urinary excretion of galactitol and hyperaminoaciduria. Galactosemia can also cause blindness unless galactose is completely excluded from the diet. Blindness is caused by the synthesis of galactitol, with the reaction catalyzed by the NADPH-dependent *galactose reductase* present in neural tissue. At high concentrations, galactitol causes osmotic swelling, with resultant formation of cataracts. The second disorder of galactose metabolism is caused by a deficiency of *UDP-galactose-4-epimerase*. In some people this deficiency is mostly benign, affecting only red and white blood cells.

Classical galactosemia is tested for by measuring blood levels of *galactose-1-phosphate uridyl transferase*. Radioactively labeled C^{14}-galactose-1-phosphate is used as a substrate with UDP-glucose. At the end of the incubation period, the unreacted galactose-1-phosphate is degraded to galactose by the addition of alkaline phosphatase. The reaction mixture is then spotted onto small pieces of DEAE chromatography paper. The C^{14}-galactose is washed off with water while the UDP-C^{14}-galactose remains bound to the paper and is then measured by the liquid scintillation counter.

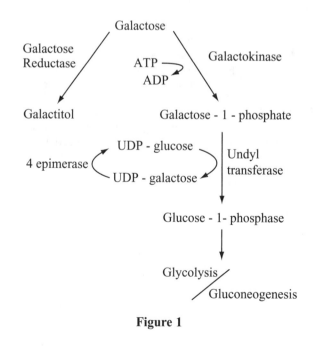

Figure 1

985. An untreated newborn diagnosed with classical galactosemia is expected to have an accumulation of which of the following substances in the blood?

   A. galactose only
   B. galactose-1-phosphate only
   C. both galactose and galactose-1-phosphate
   D. neither galactose nor galactose-1-phosphate

986. Which of the following cells are expected to have the highest concentration of *galactose reductase*, which synthesizes the toxic galactitol?

   A. skin hair cells
   B. lens cells of the eye
   C. epithelial cells of the stomach
   D. thyroid gland cells

987. According to the passage, a diet high in which of the following sugars is most likely to elevate the blood galactose concentration?

   A. fructose
   B. sucrose
   C. lactose
   D. maltose

988. Which of the following compounds is the major reactant in the synthesis of galactitol?

   A. galactose-1-phosphate
   B. glucose-1-phosphate
   C. galactose
   D. UDP-glucose

989. Which of the following genotypes is least likely to cause failure to thrive, vomiting, and diarrhea in a neonate born with galactosemia?

   A. heterozygous recessive
   B. homozygous recessive
   C. heterozygous
   D. X-linked

GO ON TO THE NEXT PAGE.

990. Even on a galactose-restricted diet, some individuals exhibit persistently elevated erythrocyte galactose-1-phosphate levels because:

    A. erythrocytes metabolize galactose in the mitochondria

    B. erythrocytes metabolize galactose in the smooth ER

    C. erythrocytes metabolize galactose in the cytoplasm

    D. erythrocytes metabolize galactose in the Golgi apparatus

991. It can be inferred from the passage that the term *hyperaminoaciduria* describes the presence of:

    A. glucose in the blood

    B. glucose in urine

    C. protein in the blood

    D. protein in urine

992. In testing for galactosemia, C^{14}-galactose-1-phosphate is added as a competitive inhibitor to which of the following compounds?

    A. galactose

    B. galactose-1-phosphate

    C. glucose-1-phosphate

    D. galactitol

Questions 993 through 1001 are **NOT** based on a descriptive passage.

993. The maximum number of individuals a habitat can support as determined by the resources available in the region bounding the population in question is known as:

    A. density dependent factor

    B. population size

    C. carrying capacity

    D. offspring potential

994. A group of interbreeding individuals of the same species that is isolated from similar groups of the same species is an example of a:

    A. realized niche

    B. fundamental niche

    C. population

    D. species

995. Females (XX) can have one of three possible genotypes for any X-linked gene. For any X-linked gene, how many possible genotypes can a male have?

    A. 1

    B. 2

    C. 3

    D. 4

996. Which phase of cell division is characterized by the formation of *chiasmata* between bivalent chromosomes as the nuclear membrane disintegrates?

    A. prometaphase I of meiosis

    B. prophase of mitosis

    C. telophase I of meiosis

    D. interphase of mitosis

997. The legs of vertebrates and the legs of insects serve similar functions but are *not* evolutionarily related. As a result such structures are properly categorized as:

    A. homologous

    B. analogous

    C. divergent

    D. additive

998. The pathways involved in energy production, which break down large compounds into smaller waste products such as carbon dioxide and water, are specifically termed as:

A. catabolic pathways
B. anabolic pathways
C. synthetic pathways
D. anaerobic pathways

999. An individual with type-A blood will have which of the following antibodies in his bloodstream?

A. antibodies directed against red blood cells with type A antigens
B. antibodies directed against red blood cells with type B antigens
C. antibodies directed against red blood cells with type O antigens
D. antibodies directed against red blood cells with type AB antigens

1000. Cystic fibrosis is an autosomal recessive disease that affects Caucasians of European descent. Cystic fibrosis heavily damages the lungs and the pancreas, which belong to which of the following organ systems, respectively?

A. cardiovascular, renal
B. respiratory, paracrine
C. excretory, nervous
D. respiratory, digestive

1001. By 1900 hunting of the northern elephant seal had reduced its population to only 20 survivors. When the hunting ceased, the rebounding elephant seal population would most likely suffer from which of the following?

A. natural selection
B. chronic mutation
C. population bottleneck
D. phenotypic plasticity

STOP. IF YOU FINISH BEFORE TIME IS CALLED, CHECK YOUR WORK. YOU MAY GO BACK TO ANY QUESTION IN THIS TEST BOOKLET.

STOP.

LECTURE 1

100

Answers & Explanations
Questions 1–113

ANSWERS TO LECTURE 1

1.	A	39.	D	77.	C
2.	B	40.	D	78.	B
3.	C	41.	D	79.	C
4.	C	42.	C	80.	B
5.	C	43.	C	81.	B
6.	D	44.	D	82.	D
7.	B	45.	A	83.	C
8.	D	46.	B	84.	B
9.	C	47.	C	85.	C
10.	C	48.	C	86.	B
11.	B	49.	B	87.	C
12.	C	50.	A	88.	B
13.	D	51.	D	89.	B
14.	A	52.	A	90.	D
15.	C	53.	C	91.	B
16.	D	54.	C	92.	A
17.	B	55.	A	93.	C
18.	A	56.	C	94.	C
19.	D	57.	C	95.	C
20.	D	58.	A	96.	C
21.	D	59.	C	97.	B
22.	B	60.	B	98.	D
23.	D	61.	C	99.	C
24.	D	62.	D	100.	C
25.	B	63.	D	101.	D
26.	D	64.	A	102.	A
27.	B	65.	C	103.	D
28.	C	66.	C	104.	C
29.	B	67.	C	105.	D
30.	D	68.	B	106.	B
31.	B	69.	D	107.	D
32.	A	70.	A	108.	C
33.	B	71.	B	109.	D
34.	A	72.	D	110.	B
35.	D	73.	B	111.	A
36.	D	74.	D	112.	B
37.	C	75.	B	113.	B
38.	B	76.	B		

1. **A is correct.** Fluid with a high water percentage will have a low solute concentration—simple dilution. According to the passage, intracellular fluid (ICF) accounts for 2/3 of total body water (TBW) and thus would show the lowest solute (or marker) concentration. Answer choices B, C, and D all represent extracellular fluid (ECF).

2. **B is correct.** According to the equation provided in the passage, Volume = Amt(g) /Concentration. Thus: .006 / 18 = $3.33 \times 10^{e-4}$ or $33.3 \times 10^{e-5}$

3. **C is correct.** An increase in hydrostatic pressure within a capillary would create a stronger force on the fluid inside, increasing the amount of fluid that leaks out of the capillary and into the extracellular space. This would lead to edema. Decreasing hydrostatic pressure within a capillary, on the other hand, would do the opposite: decrease force on the fluid in the capillary, leading to decreased leakage of fluid into the extracellular space. Decreasing capillary permeability would not cause edema because the increased impermeability of the capillary would cause even less leakage of fluid into the extracellular space. If the osmotic pressure were increased within a capillary, this would only increase the reabsorption of fluid back into the capillary and no edema would result.

4. **C is correct. This is a High Yield MCAT fact: the Na^+/K^+ ATPase functions to transport 3 Na^+ ions out of the cell and 2 K^+ ions in.** Disrupting the ATPase pump would degrade the ion concentration gradient normally maintained by the pump, and ions would proceed in the direction of their natural equilibrium. That is, Na^+ would build up in the cell while K^+ would increase in the extracellular environment. Water would then follow the movement of sodium into the cell, causing massive swelling and eventually lysis of the cell.

5. **C is correct.** The kidney works in conjunction with the lungs to excrete acidic metabolites and regulate acid-base buffer stores. CO_2, which contributes to the acidity of blood, is expelled via the lung. The lungs may try to correct an abnormally high acid concentration by increasing expirations (i.e., hyperventilation) and thereby increase CO_2 expiration.

6. **D is correct. This is a High Yield MCAT topic.** Water can act as both an acid ($H_2O \times H^+ + OH^-$) and a base ($H_2O + H^+ \times H_3O^+$). Water is also a *polar compound* that certainly hydrogen bonds (i.e., surface tension). FYI: a Bronsted acid donates hydrogen ions, while a Bronsted base picks up hydrogen ions.

7. **B is correct.** According to the passage, ICF makes up 55% of TBW and about 2/3 of total body weight. Because ICF plus ECF equals TBW, this means that ECF makes up 45% of TBW and is estimated to be 1/3 of total body weight.

8. **D is correct.** The first paragraph gives a detailed description of the type of bond *hormone-sensitive lipase* hydrolyzes by the addition of water (answer choice C can be eliminated)—"The **carboxylic acid group (COOH)** of a free fatty acid reacts with one of the glycerol **hydroxyl groups (OH$^-$)** to form a bond."

Free fatty acids bond to glycerol via an *esterification reaction* (a carboxylic acid group of a fatty acid reacts with one of the glycerol hydroxyl groups to form a bond), which forms **ester bonds**. These are the bonds that must be broken by *hormone-sensitive lipase* during triglyceride hydrolysis. Hydrolysis is the addition of water to a bond.

9. **C is correct.** Adipose tissue functions as the major storage site for fat in the form of triglycerides. According to the passage, triglycerides are broken down by the hormone-sensitive lipase to produce free fatty acids and a glycerol. Therefore, glycerol is a direct product of adipose tissue breakdown. The correct answer must be C. Free fatty acids are converted into acetyl CoA, which is oxidized by the Krebs cycle into ATP or utilized to produce ketone bodies. These latter mechanisms are not considered direct products of lipolysis. FYI: Ketone bodies are only produced when levels of acetyl CoA exceed the capacity of the Krebs cycle.

10. **C is correct.** This is a tricky application question. To start, insulin-dependent diabetes results from a *lack* of insulin production by pancreatic beta cells. Under normal circumstances, insulin would stimulate a cell to take up glucose from circulation. However, this could not occur in a type I diabetic. Although the blood glucose levels of a diabetic would be very high, little of the glucose would actually be getting into the cells since no insulin is being produced to stimulate transport into the cells. As a result, cells function as though they are in starvation mode. Ketone bodies are made, which cause the ketoacidosis seen in type I diabetes. Blood acidosis is very dangerous and will lead to rapid health decline and death. According to the passage, increased acetyl CoA levels lead to ketone body production. Thus, answer choice D is incorrect.

11. **B is correct.** Albumin is the most important plasma protein because it provides the bulk of oncotic pressure in blood vessels, thus maintaining proper vascular osmolarity. Without vascular osmolarity, fluid would leak out of cells and into the interstitium, causing a form of swelling known as edema. Some lipid-soluble molecules also bind to albumin for the purpose of increasing their solubility in blood plasma. All compounds hitching a ride on albumin do so via weak, non-covalent molecular interaction (i.e., hydrogen bonding).

12. **C is correct.** According to the passage, beta-oxidation occurs in the mitochondrial matrix. There is no such

thing as a mitochondrial extra membrane space.

13. **D is correct.** According to the passage, heart and muscle tissue both utilize ketone bodies to save all available glucose for the brain. It is implied that as starvation proceeds, the brain will have no choice but to utilize glucose/ketone body combination in order to upkeep metabolic function. That means that the brain uses ketone bodies as well. By the process of elimination the correct answer must be D.

14. **A is correct.** Acetyl CoA is an important 2-carbon metabolic intermediate in cells. According to the passage, free fatty acids serve as a carbon source for acetyl CoA production. The longer the fatty acid backbone, the greater the energy yield will be. Double bonds cause fatty acid unsaturation and decrease energy storage potential. That is why unsaturated fats are considered more healthful; they are easier to burn off.

Passage 103 (Questions 15-21)

15. **C is correct.** According to the passage, chylomicrons contain *large quantities of triglycerides* with *some cholesterol*, and protein. *Lipoprotein lipase* hydrolyzes chylomicron triglycerides and releases free fatty acids. Therefore, if *lipoprotein lipase* ceases to function, blood triglyceride levels will certainly rise. Vitamin B_{12} is needed for DNA synthesis and unrelated to chylomicrons.

16. **D is correct.** Cholesterol is an important biological molecule that has roles in cell membrane structure as well as the synthesis of the steroid hormones (vitamin D, testosterone, aldosterone, cortisol, estrogen). It is also used to conjugate bile before it is excreted. Human cells do not have cell walls, which eliminates D. Bacterial cell walls are composed of peptidoglycans, which are produced by protein synthesis.

17. **B is correct.** According to the passage, chylomicrons are synthesized by the small intestine and contain dietary fat. These would be the lipoproteins most likely elevated after a high-fat meal. HDL ("good cholesterol") levels are fairly constant and can only be increased by exercise or medication. The liver synthesizes VLDL, a precursor to LDL. According to the question stem, only two hours have elapsed since the meal; it is safe to assume that chylomicron concentration will be higher than VLDL because dietary lipids must first reach the liver for VLDL synthesis to occur.

18. **A is correct.** A chylomicron, a type of micelle, has a polar surface composed of proteins (apoproteins) and phospholipid head groups (similar to those found in the cell membrane), which make it water soluble. Cholesterol and triglycerides are *water insoluble* and require carriers to travel through circulation.

19. **D is correct.** According to the passage, chylomicrons (synthesized in the intestinal mucosa) are hydrolyzed by *lipoprotein lipase* to chylomicron remnants (which are taken up by the liver). Thus, answer choice B is eliminated. VLDL molecules are converted to IDL. IDL leads to the formation of cholesterol-rich LDL. Answer choice A is false because lipoproteins serve to transport *water-insoluble triglycerides*. If triglycerides were soluble, there would be no need for lipoproteins. It is stated in the passage that LDL lipoproteins are very cholesterol rich. The correct answer is D.

20. **D is correct.** According to the question stem, familial hypercholesterolemia is caused by defective cellular LDL receptors. Without LDL receptors, LDLs will not be transported into the cell. Therefore, cytoplasmic LDL must be low. In addition, without LDL receptors, LDLs cannot transport cholesterol into the cells, making cholesterol levels in the plasma high. In fact, cholesterol will continue to build up in the blood without ever entering cells. Individuals suffering from familial hypercholesterolemia may experience heart attacks as early as 20 years of age.

21. **D is correct.** During long periods of fasting, hormone-sensitive lipase supplies the body with nutrients by depleting adipose (fat) tissue stores. Therefore, stored triglycerides are essentially the only source of fuel available to hibernating animals, migrating birds or insects, and creatures that rarely consume meals (i.e., once a month). Glucose obtained from a meal high in carbohydrates will only last for about eight hours. Then hunger results and additional food consumption must occur.

Independent Questions (Questions 22-30)

22. **B is correct.** Oxidative phosphorylation, or the electron transport chain, is located on the inner mitochondrial membrane. The mitochondrial matrix houses the Krebs cycle. The outer mitochondrial membrane does not directly participate in oxidative phosphorylation or the Krebs cycle

23. **D is correct. This is a High Yield MCAT topic.** Glycolysis takes place in the cytoplasm under anaerobic conditions. 1 Glucose and 2 NAD^+ molecules are the two reactants of glycolysis. 2 molecules of pyruvic acid, 2 molecules of NADH, and 2 molecules of ATP are the main products of glycolysis. Activation of glycolysis requires 2 ATP.

24. **D is correct.** Glucose is converted into 2 moles of pyruvate via glycolysis. The combined action (stimulation/inhibition) of glycolysis and the Krebs cycle keeps the concentration ratio of glucose to pyruvate relatively constant. When glucose levels are low, there is diminished pyruvate production and this eliminates answer

choice C. According to the question stem, after glycolysis, pyruvate is converted to acetyl CoA, which enters the Krebs cycle. As a result, when acetyl CoA levels are low, pyruvate consumption increases. The correct answer choice is D. High levels of ATP and NADH are negative inhibitors of glycolysis because they are found on the product side of glucose oxidation. ATP and/or NADH accumulation serves as an inhibitory signal that stops pyruvate synthesis.

25. **B is correct.** All pancreatic peptidases are secreted as zymogens, inactive enzymes ending in –ogen, in order to prevent self-digestion. Trypsinogen and chymotrypsinogen (both ending in –ogen) are the two major pancreatic zymogens. Trypsin is no longer a zymogen. It has been cleaved into its active form.

26. **D is correct. This is a High Yield MCAT topic.** Enzymes increase the rate of chemical reactions and their activity is influenced by the temperature, pH, and [Substrate] concentration.

27. **B is correct. This is a High Yield MCAT topic.** Glycolysis produces two molecules of NADH but does not produce $FADH_2$. Each turn of the Krebs cycle produces one molecule of $FADH_2$; two turns of the cycle would therefore yield 2 molecules of $FADH_2$. It is not necessary to memorize the steps of the Krebs cycle for the MCAT. Know the *overall reaction* and what stimulates and shuts off the pathway.

28. **C is correct.** According to the question stem, lipoproteins with low density transport mostly lipids and very little protein (i.e., on average VLDL transports more lipids than LDL). Chylomicrons are formed by the small intestine and transport post-meal dietary lipids to the rest of the body. As a result, chylomicrons have the lowest density and the highest lipid content out of all the lipoproteins.

29. **B is correct.** The question is asking which of the following is the smallest amino acid. The answer is glycine, with a H^+ serving as the side R-group. **This is a High Yield MCAT fact.**

30. **D is correct.** This is a must know: the primary protein structure (the amino acid sequence) determines the overall 3-D shape of a protein and structure determines function.

Passage 104 (Questions 31-37)

31. **B is correct. This is a High Yield MCAT fact:** cysteine is the only amino acid whose side chain can form a covalent bond with another cysteine; this type of interaction yields a **disulfide bond**. Disulfide bonds are important for the 3-D structure of globular proteins.

32. **A is correct.** There are two ways to answer this question. The first way is to actually be familiar with the three basic amino acids: histidine, lysine, and arginine. The correct answer is A because arginine is one of the three. **Knowledge of the two acidic (aspartic and glutamic acids) and three basic amino acids (histidine, lysine, and arginine) is necessary for the MCAT.**

The second method of obtaining the correct answer is by the information provided in Table 1. Two out of the three basic amino acids have a pKa above 7. Histidine is an exception.

33. **B is correct.** According to the passage, enkephalins *act to block* pain transmission. The question stem informs that *imipramine* will cause the degradation of enkephalins, which will result in greater pain transmission and sensation. There is no information informing the reader of whether imipramine acts to stimulate or inhibit protein or post-synaptic receptor synthesis. Therefore, answer choices A, C, and D are incorrect.

34. **A is correct.** According to the passage, the body has a 500 GSH to 1 GSSG ratio, which functions to protect hemoglobin from oxidation. Glutathione provides *reducing, not oxidizing* conditions (answer choice C is eliminated) to protect hemoglobin from oxidation. A $K_{equilibrium}$ constant is equal to [Products] / [Reactants]. Thus, 1 / 500 will result in a tiny K_{eq}, eliminating answer choices B and D.

35. **D is correct.** The question stem informs that the starting compound—pentane—will undergo a decarboxylation (loss of one mole of CO_2), which would result in a 4-carbon butane. According to Table 2, butane weighs 56.108. Answer choice D is the closest number to 56.108.

36. **D is correct. This is a High Yield MCAT fact**: the primary protein structure is simply the order of its amino acids. By convention, this order is always written from amino end to carboxyl end. Every protein will have its own unique amino acid sequence.

37. **C is correct. This is a High Yield MCAT topic.** Two equivalents of NADH are produced in the cytoplasm by glycolysis. Furthermore, three molar equivalents of NADH are produced per turn of the Krebs cycle, which occurs in the mitochondrial matrix. The nucleus is not involved in NAD^+ reduction.

Passage 105 (Questions 38-43)

38. **B is correct. This is a High Yield MCAT topic.** A protein has a complex three-dimensional structure that is described in terms of a structural hierarchy, from primary to quaternary. The primary structure of a protein

is simply the sequence of amino acids in that protein. Secondary structure describes local conformations such as alpha-helixes and beta-sheets, which are held together by hydrogen bonds. Tertiary structure refers to a higher level of folding in which the helices and sheets of the secondary structure fold upon themselves. Quaternary structure arises when two or more polypeptide chains are bound together, usually by hydrogen bonds (i.e. hemoglobin).

39. **D is correct.** High levels of Prolyl-hydroxylase will result in increased collagen exocytosis and therefore increased ATP consumption. This will cause an increase in lysyl-hydroxylase synthesis as well, to keep up with its cross-linking duties. You do not need to memorize these details for the MCAT. Abnormal collagen formation will not result, only an overproduction of normal collagen. No fractures would be expected to occur, but all of the excess collagen would lead to thick scar tissue formation.

40. **D is correct.** Answer choices A, B, and C directly affect and control protein synthesis and mass. Furthermore, all three could be utilized to measure protein metabolism. Lipid-soluble vitamins have little direct involvement in protein synthesis. Thus, lack of vitamins needed for protein synthesis is not an issue. The correct answer is D.

41. **D is correct. This is a High Yield MCAT fact:** Glycine has an R-group consisting of a hydrogen atom, making it the smallest amino acid. In addition, it is the only amino acid that is not chiral. A chiral compound requires 4 different substituents around the alpha-carbon; glycine has 2 hydrogens around the alpha-carbon.

42. **C is correct.** This is a challenging question. Human vision relies on vitamin A. According to the question stem, a lack in vitamin C will result in problems with collagen synthesis. Collagen is a structural protein, so the answer choices that represent structural defects are the ones that should be eliminated (this is a NOT question, remember). Answer choices A, B, and D all display defects in structural synthesis.

43. **C is correct.** The question is asking for a post-transcriptional modification, a modification that occurs immediately following RNA synthesis. Phosphorylation, carboxylation, and hydroxylation are all examples of *post-translation modification*, a modification that occurs immediately following protein synthesis. You do not need to memorize these examples. Just be aware that these are the type of reactions that take place in the Golgi apparatus to prepare the protein for intended function. The addition of a poly-A-tail is an example of a *post-transcriptional RNA modification*. **This is a High Yield MCAT fact.**

44. **D is correct. This is a High Yield MCAT question**, which asks which forces stabilize an enzyme's 3-D structure. All forces listed are partly responsible for enzyme stability and globular arrangement, which correlates to proper function.

45. **A is correct.** According to the passage, "[d]ifferent soluble enzymes are found in the cytosol…inside mitochondria and the extracellular fluid." Liver damage as caused by Hepatitis B or any other liver disease is actually damage to individual hepatocytes (liver cells). As these cells are injured, they often lyse, resulting in the spillage of their cytosolic contents. These contents include cytosolic enzymes, which are then released into the bloodstream. Blood liver enzyme tests are often conducted to determine the level of liver function and/or damage. Calcitonin, which is produced by the thyroid gland, controls Ca^{+2} blood concentration and has nothing to do with proper liver function.

46. **B is correct.** One ligand increasing the binding of the following ligands is known as *positive cooperativity*. **A High Yield MCAT example would be oxygen binding to hemoglobin, which displays a sigmoidal curve.**

47. **C is correct. This is a High Yield MCAT topic.** Enzymes *lower activation energy* and *increase both the forward and reverse reaction rates*. Furthermore, enzymes are never consumed by the reaction, have no effect on equilibrium constant (K_{eq}), and have no effect on reaction ΔH, ΔS, and/or ΔG.

48. **C is correct.** The question stem informs that disulfide bond disruption and liquid chromatography revealed two different effusion rates—that is, two different times (sec.) required to pass through the chromatography chamber. Two different effusion rates implies that there are two different size peptide chains going through the chamber. Thus, enterokinase must be a heterodimer that is composed of 2 different peptide chains. A homodimer protein would have shown a single effusion rate because both peptides would be identical in size and would move through the chromatography chamber at the same rate.

49. **B is correct.** According to the passage, soluble vitamins function as coenzymes. Enzymes control proper reaction rates.

50. **A is correct.** Dissociating compounds like salts (NaCl and KCl) and acids (H_2SO_4) often appear on the MCAT. These will dissociate, forming ions (electrolytes) like Na^+, Cl^-, H^+, SO_4^{-2}, K^+, and Cl^-. Sucrose, glucose, and fructose are examples of non-dissociating compounds.

51. D is correct. Osmolarity is determined by the total concentration of dissolved particles in solution. So, the compound that when dissolved creates the greatest concentration of ions will have the highest osmolarity. To determine which answer choice has the highest osmolarity, one has to look at the number of ions each answer choice can dissociate into. Glucose and urea do not dissociate and will result in osmolarity of 300mOsmoles each. NaCl will result in an osmolarity of 600mOsmoles because it will dissociate into a mole of Na^+ and a mole of Cl^-, with each adding 300 mOsmoles to the solution. However, $CaCl_2$ is capable of dissolving into one mole of Ca^{+2} and two moles Cl^-. As a result, $CaCl_2$ will generate the greatest osmolarity, which will equal 900 mOsmoles.

52. A is correct. A peptide bond is formed between two amino acids, with one amino acid contributing a -COOH group and the other a NH_2 group.

53. C is correct. This is a High Yield MCAT fact: rough ER contains ribosomes, which serve as the site for protein synthesis. Smooth ER is responsible for cell detoxification and lipid synthesis. The mitochondrion is the "powerhouse" of the cell and lysosomes serve as organelles that carry out digestion.

54. C is correct. This is a High Yield MCAT fact: by definition a secondary protein structure is composed of numerous local conformations like beta-sheets and alpha-helixes. As a general rule, secondary conformations are stabilized by hydrogen bonds.

55. A is correct. Glycolysis produces ATP and NADH and is regulated by negative feedback (end-product) inhibition. A high level of ATP or NADH would *decrease* the rate of glycolysis to prevent product accumulation. ATP is the only glycolysis product among the answer choices. AMP and glucose both serve as glycolytic reactants and would therefore increase the rate of glycolysis. Fructose has no direct impact on glycolysis. FYI: glycolysis takes place in the cytoplasm.

56. C is correct. Isozymes are different forms of the same enzyme that catalyze the same reaction but have different chemical / physical properties and display variable catalytic rates. Different chemical properties (i.e., different primary amino acid structure) cause isozymes to display different stabilities and denaturation profiles. However, isozymes do catalyze the same reaction and will bind identical substrates with great specificity. The correct answer choice is C.

57. C is correct. Cyclic nucleotides, cAMP and cGMP, are *second messengers* that carry signals from the cell membrane to proteins within the cell, and are found widely in eukaryotes. The second messenger system is utilized primarily by protein hormones (i.e., ACTH) that cannot freely diffuse across the cell membrane. Lipid soluble steroid hormones (i.e., testosterone) do not depend on the second messenger system.

Passage 107 (Questions 58-63)

58. A is correct. This is a High Yield MCAT Topic. Glycolysis takes place in the cytoplasm and converts one mole of glucose into two moles of pyruvate. A hexose is a six-carbon sugar. Fructose (hexose) and galactose (hexose) can enter glycolysis mid-cycle as fructose 6-phosphate and glucose 6-phosphate respectively, but are NOT considered to be reactants of glycolysis. Bottom line, glucose (hexose) is the only glycolytic reactant you need to know for the MCAT.

59. C is correct. Lack of available oxygen will decrease the overall production of ATP by the electron transport chain. Glycolysis, however, is anaerobic and does not require oxygen to function. There will therefore be an increase in the rate of glycolysis (and therefore increased levels of pyruvate) to meet tissue ATP demand. Because no oxygen is available for the electron transport chain, pyruvate will be shunted into the lactic acid cycle instead. Lactic acid levels would increase as levels of fermentation (conversion of pyruvate to lactic acid) increase.

60. B is correct. This is a High Yield MCAT fact: red blood cells lack all organelles, including a nucleus. Therefore, the electron transport chain, fatty acid oxidation, and citric acid cycle do not occur in erythrocytes. These processes require the presence of mitochondria. The Na^+/K^+ pump, however, functions in EVERY cell in the human body, including RBCs, to maintain proper osmotic gradient and prevent lysis. FYI: red blood cells do not divide and are produced by the bone marrow.

61. C is correct. According to Table 1, McArdle's disease and Hers' disease are similar in etiology because both are deficient in a *phosphorylase* enzyme.

62. D is correct. This is High Yield MCAT information: pyruvate has a three-carbon backbone and glucose is a hexose, a 6-carbon sugar. Three pyruvic acids and a glucose yield: $3 + 3 + 3 + 6 = 15$ carbon backbone.

63. D is correct. This is a High Yield MCAT fact: glycolysis occurs in the cytosol or cytoplasm (regardless of whether the person has a GSD or not!) Smooth ER is responsible for cellular detoxification and steroid synthesis. Mitochondria are the powerhouses of the cell, constantly synthesizing ATP under aerobic conditions.

Passage 108 (Questions 64-70)

64. A is correct. According to the passage, two carbons enter the citric acid cycle as acetyl CoA and two carbons are lost as carbon dioxide. Therefore, citric acid cycle does not show a NET gain in the carbon backbone. Furthermore, all biological reactions display conservation when it comes to the length of the carbon skeleton; meaning whatever one puts in will eventually come out.

65. C is correct. To answer this question, examine Mechanism 1: high glucose concentration will cause an increase in pyruvate synthesis.

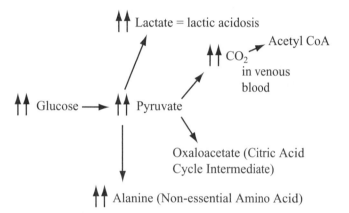

66. C is correct. Bile is produced in the liver and stored in the gall bladder. Based on the information provided in the question stem, a diet high in dandelion root will improve liver bile flow. Increased bile flow out of the liver may *decrease* liver congestion and relieve some symptoms of liver disease due to increased flow, but it may distend the bile duct, which leaves the liver into the gall bladder. As bile flow increases, however, the chance of gallstone formation decreases, not increases. Gallstones form when fluid is stagnant, unmoving. Increased bile flow would reduce stasis and therefore lessen the likelihood of stone formation.

67. C is correct. This is a typical MCAT application question. Enzyme classification allows one to deduce that alpha-ketoglutarate and pyruvate DEHYDROGE-NASES most likely utilize the same set of cofactors. The correct answer choice is C.

68. B is correct. The citric acid cycle produces ATP INDI-RECTLY, through reducing equivalents such as NADH, $FADH_2$, and GTP. NADPH is needed for lipid synthesis and is produced in the pentose phosphate pathway.

69. D is correct. According to the passage, choices A, B, and C are all intermediates of the citric acid cycle. acetyl CoA, however, is a Krebs cycle reactant that condenses with oxaloacetate to form citrate.

70. A is correct. This is a High Yield MCAT topic. Symmetric molecules are optically inactive and there-fore fail to rotate a plane of polarized light. Asymmetric compounds are optically active. Thus, citrate conversion

will cause the production of an optically active isoci-trate.

Passage 109 (Questions 71-77)

71. B is correct. According to the passage, isozymes of *malate dehydrogenase* are found in both the mitochon-dria and the cytoplasm and allow for oxaloacetate/malate interconversion. *RNA Polymerase* (which func-tions in RNA transcription) and *gyrase* (which functions to prevent DNA supercoiling during replication) are both found in the cell nucleus. Substance P is a GI neuropeptide that you do not need to worry about for the MCAT.

72. D is correct. According to the passage, gluconeogenesis is essential for the maintenance of constant blood glucose levels, not amino acid levels, between meals. Gluconeogenesis is a process in which glucose is gener-ated when blood glucose levels are low, i.e., during periods of fasting. Glycolysis is a process in which glucose is converted into pyruvate and subsequently metabolized. It occurs when glucose levels are high, i.e., after meals.

73. B is correct. The passage states that any gluconeogene-sis precursor must contain a minimum of three carbons in its backbone. Free fatty acids are broken down to acetyl CoA, which is a two-carbon molecule that cannot enter gluconeogenesis. FYI: free fatty acids are energy rich and, when oxidized, yield twice as much ATP as glucose. Lipid stores do provide organ padding; however, that does not explain their inability to enter glycolysis.

74. D is correct. This is a High Yield MCAT fact. Glycolysis is an anaerobic process that converts 1 mole-cule of glucose into 2 molecules of pyruvate. Glycolysis occurs in the cell cytoplasm.

75. B is correct. According to the passage, liver, kidney, and skeletal muscle all have the ability to synthesize glycogen. Involuntary smooth muscle lines the GI tract—it is unable to produce glycogen. Answer this question by the process of elimination.

76. B is correct. The passage states that, while both the liver and kidneys are capable of gluconeogenesis, the liver is the main site for gluconeogenic function.

77. C is correct. Peripheral proteins, located on the cell membrane surface, usually serve as surface receptors and never as channels. Integral proteins that span the entire cell membrane do function as transport channels. Answer choice D is incorrect because *malate* binds the channel receptor, not oxaloacetate. The passage does not provide any evidence to support answer choice B.

78. **B is correct.** The question is simply asking which of the listed amino acids is capable of forming disulfide bonds. **A High Yield MCAT fact:** cysteine is the only amino acid capable of forming disulfide bonds.

Every amino acid contains a carboxyl group, an amino group, and a side chain, all attached to an alpha-carbon.

79. **C is correct.** Enzyme prosthetic groups attach via strong molecular forces (i.e., covalent bonds). Thus, the correct answer is C. Hydrogen bonds and dipole/dipole interactions are examples of weak molecular forces. Ionic bonds are incredibly strong but are not used by prosthetic groups.

80. **B is correct.** Helium is a noble gas, but not a cofactor. NADPH is organic and synthesized by the body to function as a reducing agent for biosynthesis. Iron (Fe) is necessary for proper hemoglobin function and is a more likely answer choice than Francium (Fr), which does not naturally occur in nature.

81. **B is correct. This is a High Yield MCAT fact:** the three basic amino acids are *arginine, lysine*, and *histidine*. Proline, an *imino acid,* is also known as a "helix breaker." It has a double bond to the amino group nitrogen.

82. **D is correct. This is a High Yield MCAT fact:** each turn of the Krebs cycle consumes 1 acetyl CoA, 3 moles of NAD^+, 1 mole of FAD^+, and 1 mole of GDP. Each turn produces 3 moles of NADH, 1 mole of GTP, 1 mole of $FADH_2$, and *2 moles of CO_2*. Glycolysis consumes glucose to produce pyruvate. Essential amino acids are obtained from diet. The body synthesizes all other non-essential amino acids.

83. **C is correct. This is a High Yield MCAT fact:** in eukaryotes, the TCA cycle occurs in the mitochondrial matrix.

84. **B is correct. Mitochondrial function is a High Yield MCAT topic.** The mitochondrial ATPase uses a proton (H^+) gradient to generate ATP. The question stem informs that oligomycin *inhibits* proton re-entry into the mitochondrial matrix from the intermembrane space and therefore prevents ATP production. The proton concentration (and therefore acidity) in the intermembrane space will increase due to lack of proton re-entry. Thus, choice A is eliminated. Protein synthesis will not be affected by oligomycin.

85. **C is correct. This is a High Yield MCAT topic.** Fetal hemoglobin has a higher O_2 affinity than adult hemoglobin, since it must "steal" O_2 from the maternal circulation. CO poisoning occurs because this odorless gas has a very high hemoglobin affinity and binds tightly to it, preventing oxygen from binding. The question stem informs that choice B is incorrect. Positive cooperative binding: hemoglobin does exhibit this.

When O_2 binds to the first of four hemoglobin subunits, this increases the affinity of the three remaining subunits for oxygen. Similarly, once the first oxygen molecule is unloaded, the others are more easily unloaded. This aids hemoglobin in its proper tissue supply.

Passage 110 (Questions 86-91)

86. **B is correct. This is High Yield information.** All mitochondrial genes are inherited solely from the mother. Therefore, any defects in any of the enzymes or proteins involved with the mitochondria must come from the mother.

87. **C is correct.** According to the passage, the pyruvate dehydrogenase complex directly produces acetyl CoA. It therefore directly affects the amount of acetyl CoA available. While glycolysis produces pyruvate, it does not produce acetyl CoA; pyruvate may or may not be converted to acetyl CoA after glycolysis is finished. Thus, the correct answer choice must be B or C. The Krebs cycle utilizes acetyl CoA in its first reaction to form citrate. Therefore, both the pyruvate dehydrogenase complex and the Krebs cycle directly increase and decrease levels of acetyl CoA, respectively.

88. **B is correct.** According to Mechanism 1, the mitochondrial reaction between acetyl CoA and oxaloacetate forms citrate, which is then transported out of the mitochondria and into the cytoplasm. If the citrate shuttle is inhibited, acetyl CoA and oxaloacetate will accumulate in the mitochondria, not the cytoplasm. There will be no glucose accumulation because glucose oxidation occurs in the cytoplasm; this is known as glycolysis.

89. **B is correct.** Some enzymes require a *prosthetic group* in order to function properly. The key to a prosthetic group is that it is covalently attached to the enzyme. Under normal circumstances, weak molecular forces (i.e., hydrogen bonds) are utilized when binding to an enzyme.

90. **D is correct.** This question is best answered using the process of elimination. According to the passage, acetyl CoA is the main *reactant* needed for fatty acid synthesis. NADPH, a reactant for fatty acid synthesis, is produced during the conversion of oxaloacetate (which is not involved with fatty acid synthesis at all) to pyruvate. The only possible answer choice is D, water.

91. **B is correct. This is a High Yield MCAT fact:** lipid synthesis and modification occur in the smooth endoplasmic reticulum. Smooth ER is also involved in cell detoxification and calcium storage. Calcium is utilized in order to achieve contraction in muscle cells.

Rough ER is the site of protein synthesis. Lysosomes are organelles of digestion.

92. **A is correct.** According to the passage, pentose phosphate pathway (PPP) uses glucose 6-phosphate and $NADP^+$ as *reactants* in order to produce NADPH and ribose 5′-phosphate. There is no mention in the passage that ATP is a *direct* product of PPP.

93. **C is correct. This is a High Yield MCAT fact:** the first sentence of the first paragraph informs that PPP occurs in the cytoplasm. Glycolysis, the anaerobic conversion of glucose to pyruvate, also occurs in the cytoplasm. The citric acid cycle and the electron transport chain are all mitochondrial processes. Transcription is the production of RNA and it takes place in the nucleus.

94. **C is correct.** According to the passage, *glucose 6-phosphate (G-6-P)* is converted to a lactone ring, then *ribulose 5-phosphate* will be directly converted to *ribose 5-phosphate*. Thus the correct answer is C, G-6-P → Ribulose-5-P → Ribose-5-P → Seduheptulose-7-P.

95. **C is correct. This is a High Yield MCAT question.** The passage informs that the extra phosphate is a signal to prevent $NADP^+$ from being used by the Krebs cycle and other cellular respiration cascades that occur in the mitochondria.

96. **C is correct. Review of Circulation:** Left Heart → Aorta → Arteries → Arterioles → Capillaries → Venules → Veins → Vena Cava → Right Heart. Arterioles are the vessels that directly control the amount of blood received by each capillary bed. The reason for this is because arterioles are anatomically closer to capillaries than any other arterial vessel.

97. **B is correct.** The passage states that PPP supplies reduced equivalents for synthetic pathways, which are *anabolic* in nature. Glycolysis is an example of a catabolic pathway, which breaks down compounds to release energy. Phosphorylation is used for enzyme activation/deactivation and hydrolysis is the breaking of a bond with water.

98. **D is correct.** The passage states that glucose-6-phosphate is a pentose phosphate pathway reactant. Choice C is incorrect because ribose-5-phosphate is a PPP product. This is a classic MCAT question where careful reading of the passage provides the answer.

Passage 112 (Questions 99-104)

99. **C is correct.** According to the question stem ACE inhibitors inhibit *bradykinase* and thus increase tissue levels of *bradykinin*. The passage states that *bradykinin* increases vascular permeability. An increase in vascular permeability (meaning fluid can leak out of blood vessels because of poor tight junction mechanism) is a primary cause of edema (fluid accumulation in a space between blood vessels and cells – known as interstitial space). *Bradykinin* also causes pain. The *kinins* are important mediators of inflammatory responses; they are not anti-inflammation.

Inflammation is the response of living tissue to damage. Acute inflammation is short lasting, lasting only a few days. Various examples of acute inflammation that you may be aware of are sore throat, reactions in the skin to a scratch, or a burn or insect bite, etc.

100. **C is correct.** The passage states that the Hageman factor is an important plasma protein that can cause the production of inflammatory mediators and proteins for other cascades. According to the passage and Diagram 1, Hageman factor is involved in clotting, kallikrein, and inflammatory cascades. The correct answer must be C. **This is a High Yield MCAT fact:** The renin-angiotensin system plays an important role in regulating blood pressure. The most important site for renin release is the kidney. This is in no way associated with the Hageman factor. Why? It is not mentioned in the passage. If it is not in the passage, it is incorrect.

101. **D is correct.** The body responds in two general ways to chemical changes. **Reaction: A → B.** In *negative feedback*, the reaction product, in this case **B**, inhibits its own synthesis. The second type of response is positive feedback. In *positive feedback*, the product, once again **B**, further stimulates its own synthesis. So synthesis of **B** stimulates even more synthesis of **B**. According to the question stem, kallikrein serves to further activate the Hageman factor, which would cause more kallikrein synthesis. This is an example of positive feedback.

102. **A is correct.** The process being described in the question stem involving fibrin, plasmin, and platelets is clotting. When blood vessels are cut or damaged, the loss of blood from the system must be stopped before shock and possible death occur. This is accomplished by solidification of the blood, a process called coagulation or clotting.

103. **D is correct.** A protease is an enzyme involved in protein or peptide digestion or cleavage. According to the passage, kallikrein is a protease. The pancreas produces trypsin and chymotrypsin, two proteases involved in peptide digestion. Lipase is another pancreatic product. Lipase, however, is not a protease because it is involved in dietary lipid breakdown.

104. **C is correct.** The answer to this question can be derived from the passage. Fibrin is the product of an activated coagulation system and is the most important component of a blood clot. Plasminogen is cleaved into plasmin, which breaks down formed clots. This is a very important control point that prevents the entire blood volume from clotting. Platelets, not red blood cells, are necessary for proper coagulation.

105. D is correct. This is a High Yield MCAT topic. Quaternary protein structure is defined as two or more peptide chains linked together via a number of weak and strong molecular forces. According to the question stem, adult hemoglobin consists of four polypeptide chains. The correct answer must be D.

106. B is correct. This question is best answered using the process of elimination. According to the question stem, hexokinase and glucokinase catalyze the same reaction and are therefore isozymes. Answer choice C is eliminated. Fructose is not a glycolysis reactant, making choice A incorrect. Like most control point enzymes, it is safe to assume that hexokinase is controlled by negative feedback inhibition. Glucokinase is not a zymogen; zymogens carry a -ogen suffix (i.e., pepsinogen). The question stem further informs that glucokinase has a higher *Michaelis constant* (K_m), which means that this enzyme has a lower affinity for glucose (the reactant). This, however, has nothing to do with answering the question and is provided solely as a distraction.

107. D is correct. The addition of a 3′ poly-A tail aids in mRNA stability and is a *post transcription* event. Answer choices A, B, and C are all examples of protein modification.

108. C is correct. According to the question stem, penicillin binds the enzyme active site with a covalent bond. This is characteristic of an *irreversible* (covalent bond is a strong permanent attachment) *competitive* (competes with the substrate for the active site) inhibitor. *Reversible competitive* inhibitors utilize weak molecular attachment (i.e., hydrogen bonds) in order to attach to the enzyme active site. A non-competitive inhibitor binds to sites other than the active site; these other sites are called allosteric sites.

109. D is correct. You do not need to memorize the entire Krebs cycle schematic for the MCAT. You should be familiar with the fact that glucose, NADH, and $FADH_2$ are not considered intermediates of the cycle. Glucose is a glycolysis reactant. NADH and $FADH_2$ are both products of the cycle. So by the process of elimination, the correct answer choice is D.

110. B is correct. This is a High Yield MCAT topic. Citric acid cycle operates in an OXIDATIVE mode to accomplish ATP production to supply tissue needs. Each turn of the cycle yields three moles of NADH, and one mole of $FADH_2$ for use by the electron transport chain. Moreover, 2 molecules of CO_2 are released with every turn of the citric acid cycle. NADPH is required for lipid synthesis and is produced by the pentose phosphate pathway.

111. A is correct. The liver is the largest gland in the body and performs the following functions: 1) production of bile needed for the emulsification of fat; 2) detoxification and removal of toxic substances (i.e., alcohol and drugs); 3) storage of fat-soluble vitamins (A, E, D, K); 4) lipid and steroid synthesis; 5) production of urea; 6) cholesterol metabolism.

112. B is correct. According to the question stem, Type 1 diabetes is associated with an insulin deficiency. Insulin is produced by the pancreas, not the thyroid gland, and decreases blood glucose level. Without sufficient insulin, blood glucose rises to dangerously high levels and even appears in urine. In fact the presence of glucose in urine was how the diagnosis of diabetes was made in the early 1900s. Diabetes is not associated with the dysfunction of red blood cells.

113. B is correct. Lipids are not water-soluble and require carrier proteins in order to be transported in the hydrophilic blood plasma. The complication arises in the fact that these carrier molecules, known as chylomicrons, are too large to fit into tiny arterioles. As a result, absorbed lipids are initially dumped into *lacteals* of the lymphatic system, which carries lipids and dumps them into large veins of the cardiovascular system.

LECTURE 2

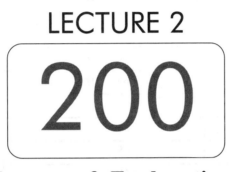

200

Answers & Explanations
Questions 114–221

ANSWERS TO LECTURE 2

114.	C	150.	A	186.	C
115.	B	151.	B	187.	A
116.	B	152.	C	188.	C
117.	B	153.	B	189.	C
118.	B	154.	D	190.	C
119.	D	155.	B	191.	A
120.	D	156.	B	192.	A
121.	C	157.	A	193.	B
122.	D	158.	A	194.	C
123.	B	159.	C	195.	A
124.	B	160.	D	196.	A
125.	C	161.	D	197.	B
126.	A	162.	C	198.	D
127.	C	163.	C	199.	A
128.	D	164.	A	200.	D
129.	C	165.	B	201.	B
130.	A	166.	C	202.	C
131.	D	167.	D	203.	B
132.	D	168.	D	204.	B
133.	B	169.	D	205.	C
134.	C	170.	D	206.	B
135.	B	171.	B	207.	C
136.	B	172.	C	208.	C
137.	B	173.	C	209.	D
138.	B	174.	C	210.	B
139.	C	175.	B	211.	B
140.	D	176.	B	212.	B
141.	D	177.	A	213.	C
142.	D	178.	C	214.	D
143.	B	179.	B	215.	B
144.	B	180.	B	216.	C
145.	C	181.	A	217.	C
146.	A	182.	B	218.	D
147.	B	183.	D	219.	A
148.	C	184.	C	220.	B
149.	C	185.	D	221.	D

114. C is correct. It is stated in the third paragraph that z-DNA has a zigzag appearance that may be involved in *gene expression*. Gene expression involves the activity of RNA polymerase biding to the promoter and catalyzing the synthesis of RNA and eventually protein.

115. B is correct. Codons are read by release factors and when the ribosome reaches the AUG, the start codon, which codes for methionine, causes protein translation to begin. Out of the 64 possible codons, 61 correspond to an amino acid. The remaining three (UAA, UAG, UGA) are stop codons that cause protein synthesis termination.

116. B is correct. The question stem describes the formation of a dinucleotide, which is held together by a phosphodiester bond. Single strands of DNA and/or RNA are formed by repetition of this phosphodiester linkage. Due to the negative charges of the phosphate groups in the phosphodiester bond, nucleic acids are negatively charged ions (anions). Histones, proteins attached to DNA, are positively charged and as a result are attracted to negatively charged phosphate groups.

Glycosidic bonds are seen in disaccharides. Amide (peptide) bonds link amino acids together and lead to the creation of a polypeptide. Hydrogen bonds allow base pairing to occur between complementary DNA strands. Recall: adenine binds with thymine and guanine pairs with cytosine.

117. B is correct. The answer to this question is obtained directly out of the third paragraph. a-DNA displays a right-handed helix that is shorter and wider than b-DNA. Thus answer choice D is incorrect. z-DNA forms a left-handed helix that is slimmer than the b-form. Therefore the b-form must be wider than the z-form.

118. B is correct. This is a High Yield MCAT fact. The nucleus houses one or more nucleoli. The nucleolus is a dark spherical mass of densely stained granules. It consists of nucleolar organizers, specialized regions of ten chromosomes with multiple copies of genes necessary for the production of ribosomal RNA (rRNA). An average, healthy cell can produce up to 9,000 ribosomes per minute.

119. D is correct. For some traits, two alleles can be codominant. This results when neither allele can "hide" the presence of its homologue. Thus, both alleles are expressed in heterozygous individuals. A classic MCAT example is the AB blood type that occurs with the ABO blood system. When they are tested, these individuals actually have the characteristics of both type A and type B blood. Their phenotype is not intermediate between the two. Codominance is one of several exceptions to Mendelian inheritance.

120. D is correct. According to the passage, the outer nuclear membrane is continuous with the endoplasmic reticulum. Therefore it is safe to assume that the lumen of both organelles are environmentally similar. In fact, the space between the outer and inner nuclear membranes is continuous with rough endoplasmic reticulum. It fills up with newly synthesized proteins just as the rough endoplasmic reticulum does. The cytoplasmic environment differs quite a bit from the inside of the nuclear and ER lumens.

121. C is correct. The basic reaction of protein synthesis is the controlled formation of a peptide bond between two amino acids. Protein synthesis takes place: 1) on free ribosomes in the cytoplasm; 2) on ribosomes embedded into the membrane of the rough ER; 3) according to the passage, on ribosomes embedded in the outer nuclear membrane. The correct answer is therefore C. Smooth ER is involved in steroid synthesis and cell detoxification.

122. D is correct. Red blood cells are the only eukaryotic cells that do not have nuclei. Remember this fact for the MCAT. RBCs are made in the bone marrow. Initially they have a nucleus, like other eukaryotic cells. However, as the red blood cell fills up with hemoglobin, the nucleus is pushed to the periphery of the cell and eventually disappears. Without a nucleus, red blood cells cannot divide. They survive roughly 120 days before they are degraded by the spleen, while bone marrow replenishes the supply.

123. B is correct. According to the passage, euchromatin is found only in transcriptionally active cells. Neurons and heart muscle cells are considered permanent and are forever arrested in the G_0 phase of the cell cycle. Therefore, they are not considered to be transcriptionally active cells. These permanent cells are expected to have a high concentration of heterochromatin instead. Viruses do not have euchromatin. Euchromatin is uncoiled at the several origins of replication that eukaryotic DNA has, where the enzyme machinery binds to begin replication or transcription. Only actively dividing cells (i.e., mucus-producing goblet cells, epithelial cells) have a high nuclear concentration of euchromatin.

124. B is correct. Mitochondria provide the power for each cell. They are double-membrane organelles that are usually rod-shaped (but they can also be round). The inner membrane is folded into shelf-like projections that extend inward. These are called cristae. While mitochondria were once independent cells that were engulfed by a larger one, after many thousands of years, a symbiotic relationship has resulted between a mitochondrion and its host cell. As a result, a substantial percentage of mitochondrial proteins are derived from nuclear mRNA.

125. C is correct. Please refer to figure 1 in the passage. The nucleus (not shown in the diagram) is the brain of the eukaryotic cell. Usually, the nucleus is round and is the largest organelle in the cell; it is much larger than a mitochondrion.

Organelle # 1—rough ER studded with ribosomes

Organelle # 2—mitochondrion

Organelle # 3—storage vacuole

Organelle # 4—identity uncertain, but not a nucleus

Passage 203 (Questions 126-131)

126. A is correct. According to the passage, the 2 major mitochondrial diseases, LHON and MELAS, are characterized by the pathology of the eye (vision loss), brain, and muscle. The correct answer must be A.

127. C is correct. According to the passage, mitochondrial DNA (mtDNA) encodes for several respiratory enzymes utilized by the electron transport chain of the inner mitochondrial membrane, not the cell membrane (answer choice D can be eliminated). Such enzymes include cytochrome oxidase C, NADH dehydrogenase, etc. You should have a general understanding of the type of enzymes located in the mitochondria. However, on the MCAT it is far more beneficial to eliminate incorrect answer choices than to search for the correct ones. Glycolysis takes place in the cytoplasm and has nothing to do with the mitochondria. Primase is a nuclear enzyme necessary for DNA synthesis.

128. D is correct. The "new" MCAT loves genetic techniques. PCR is an acronym for polymerase chain reaction, which uses "primers" to copy and amplify specific regions of DNA. A DNA polymerase runs back and forth between the primers, copying the region of interest over and over again. Using PCR, a short stretch of DNA can be amplified a million times. *Southern blotting* is a technique used to analyze, not amplify, a genetic pattern of interest that may appear in the mtDNA. ELISA is used to locate the presence of antibodies to a particular infection. It is the primary test for an HIV infection.

129. C is correct. According to the passage, mtDNA is inherited only from the maternal cell line. The same mtDNA is passed on from the mother to every offspring the woman bears. Thus, mtDNA cannot be considered a unique identifier, because more than one individual can have the same mtDNA. In fact, even apparently unrelated individuals might share an unknown maternal relative at some point in the distant past, evidenced by common mtDNA.

130. A is correct. The likelihood of recovering mtDNA from a digested cellular sample is *much greater* than for nuclear DNA. Why? According to the passage, mtDNA is present in hundreds to thousands of copies per cell, in comparison to the nuclear complement of just two copies per cell. Thus, the correct answer choice is A. The size of the genome does NOT depend on the state of cellular function.

131. D is correct. According to the passage, a cell is *homoplasmic* when all the mitochondria in it have identical DNA, regardless of whether or not that DNA is normal or abnormal. Answer choices A, B, and C are examples of *heteroplasmic* mitochondrial cell lines.

Independent Questions (Questions 132-142)

132. D is correct. The complicated question stem is asking a simple question: what is the name of the bond that is formed between two nucleotides? Nucleotides are linked together via a *phosphodiester bond*. A *glycosidic bond* is used to link together monosaccharides (i.e., glucose molecules). London dispersion is the formation of a spontaneous dipole moment that weakly attracts molecules toward each other. There is no such thing as a coordinate ionic bond.

133. B is correct. The SSBP, single stranded binding protein, attaches to ssDNA (ss = single stranded) during replication and keeps the origin of replication open. Let's review the entire process. *Helicase* is an ATP-dependent enzyme that "unzips" the DNA helix exposing the origin of replication. If the DNA helix is not unzipped, DNA polymerases cannot replicate DNA. Once the origin of replication is open, it naturally wants to close back up. The binding of SSBPs prevents this from happening. The correct answer had to be A or B because the question stem is inquiring about replication. As you recall, replication is the copying of DNA.

134. C is correct. Every human somatic cell (not germ cells like ova and sperm) is diploid (2N) and therefore houses 46 chromosomes. Chromosomes are further subdivided into 22 pairs of autosomes (these are numbered 1 through 22) and a pair of sex chromosomes (the female pair is XX and the male pair is XY).

During the S phase of the cell cycle the cellular genetic material is copied in order to have enough information to pass on to daughter cells. However, the diploid (2N) somatic cell remains diploid (2N) and still has only 46 chromosomes; there are simply 2 sets of DNA. At no point do somatic cells have 23 or 92 chromosomes; these chromosome numbers are not compatible with life.

Definitions:

Human diploid cell: contains two sets of 23 chromosomes.

Human diploid number: number of chromosomes in a diploid cell, 2N.

Human haploid cell: contains a single set of 23 chromosomes.

Human haploid number: number of chromosomes in a haploid cell N.

135. **B is correct. This is a High Yield MCAT fact.** One molecule of $FADH_2$ is produced by each full turn of the citric acid cycle (also known as the Krebs cycle), which occurs in the mitochondrial matrix. The electron transport chain does allow a molecule of $FADH_2$ to be converted into 2 ATP. However, the question is asking which metabolic process synthesizes $FADH_2$. Glycolysis is an anaerobic process that takes place in the cytoplasm and does not produce $FADH_2$. Nucleotide synthesis is necessary for the production of DNA or RNA.

136. **B is correct.** According to the question stem, the bubble mechanism prevents the loss of the DNA coding region during replication. Thus, the bubble mechanism represents *telomere* function. Telomeres are chromosomal ends that consist of nucleotide repeats that provide stability and prevent the loss of the DNA coding region. Telomeres are maintained by *telomerase*, an enzyme that adds repeats to chromosomal ends. The *centromere* is a region of a chromosome that connects the two sister chromatids. It is the site where kinetochores attach during mitosis. Centrioles form the spindle apparatus to separate chromosomes during cellular division.

137. **B is correct. Here are some High Yield facts about RNA:**

    mRNA: is the largest single-stranded RNA molecule that is "read" by the ribosome and codes for a new protein.

    tRNA: is the smallest single-stranded RNA molecule and has a cloverleaf structure. tRNA functions to deliver amino acids to the growing peptide chain as the ribosome "reads" the mRNA.

    rRNA: is synthesized in the **nucleolus**, is the most numerous single-stranded RNA molecule. It is necessary for the proper function of ribosomes.

    hnRNA: is an RNA molecule that has not yet undergone post-transcriptional modification (i.e., capping, intron splicing, etc.). Once modified, hnRNA becomes a mature mRNA.

138. **B is correct. This is a High Yield for the MCAT fact:** the degree and type of DNA supercoiling is controlled by DNA *topoisomerases*. The *helicase* induces severe supercoiling when it unwinds DNA in order to expose the origin of replication. This supercoiling is relieved by the actions of *gyrase* (a type of topoisomerase). Gyrase induces breaks between nucleotides that relax DNA supercoils, and this action relieves the torsional pressure that occurs during DNA replication and RNA synthesis. Gyrase inhibitors serve as antibiotics by inhibiting bacterial replication.

139. **C is correct.** There are three ways to answer most MCAT questions. The intuitive way: there are 4 different nucleotides (adenine, cytosine, guanine, and thymine) that exist in nature. Because each codon is composed of 3 nucleotides then there must exist 64 (4^3) possible codons for the 20 amino acids found in polypeptides (the genetic code is said to be redundant or degenerate because several different codons code for the same amino acid). 61 codons code for amino acids and 3 codons serve to terminate translation.

140. **D is correct.** The information regarding mitochondrial mutation is not necessary in order to answer this question. The question is asking which of the listed tissues produces calcitonin. Thyroid gland synthesizes calcitonin in response to high blood calcium levels. The liver synthesizes bile, which is necessary for the emulsification of ingested lipids. The parathyroid gland produces the parathyroid hormone that increases blood calcium. The kidney secretes renin, which induces the release of aldosterone from the adrenal cortex.

141. **D is correct.** According to the question stem, a person with I-cell disease cannot properly direct newly synthesized peptides to their target organelles. So the question is which organelle functions to distribute proteins using targeting markers? The answer is the Golgi apparatus, which serves as a cellular distribution center. Smooth ER detoxifies the cell and synthesizes steroid hormones. The nucleus is the largest cellular organelle that houses genetic material.

142. **D is correct.** Codon-anticodon interaction occurs between mRNA (codon) and tRNA (anticodon) during protein synthesis. Thus, answer choice A can be eliminated.

Passage 204 (Questions 143-148)

143. **B is correct.** This is not a simple question. According to the passage, prokaryotic genes of similar function are transcribed as single polycistronic mRNA. All listed components in answer choice B are involved in prokaryotic ATP synthesis (oxidation of glucose), and therefore can be assumed to be transcribed as a single polycistronic mRNA. In prokaryotes ATP is produced both across the cell membrane (via ATPase) and in the cytosol by glycolysis. In prokaryotes, the ATPase and the electron transport chain are located inside the cytoplasmic membrane between the hydrophobic tails of the phospholipid membrane inner and outer walls.

Heart muscle tissue, tracheal cartilage tissue, and lung surfactant, are all made up of eukaryotic cells and answer choice A can be eliminated. Proteins listed in answer choice C have nothing in common and histones are only seen in eukaryotes. Enzymes in answer choice D do not perform the same function.

144. B is correct. Transcription proceeds in three distinct phases: initiation, elongation, and termination. Initiation involves the association between the RNA polymerase and DNA at a specific region called the *promoter*. An *operon* is a cluster of genes under the control of a single operator. An *operator* is a site in DNA near the promoter region where the *inhibitor* can bind and prevent transcription.

145. C is correct. According to the passage, RNA polymerase requires magnesium in order to function. The other necessary components are a DNA template to attach to and precursor nucleotides.

146. A is correct. DNA differs from RNA in that DNA uses nucleotides containing deoxyribose, while RNA's nucleotides contain a ribose sugar. The most important thing to realize is that RNA ribose has a hydroxyl group at the 2′ carbon position. See the diagrams below. Both ribose and deoxyribose sugars possess a 3′ hydroxyl group.

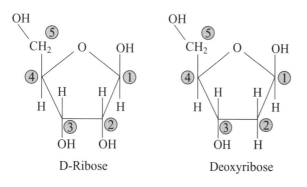

D-Ribose   Deoxyribose

147. B is correct. Because 3 hydrogen bonds are formed by the base pairing of guanine and cytosine, it is found to be more stable than the adenine/thymine 2 hydrogen bond pairing. Thus, if a DNA strand is found to be rich in guanine and cytosine, then more energy will be needed to denature the DNA. As a result, the guanine/cytosine-rich strand M should denature at a HIGHER temperature when compared to strand A.

148. C is correct. In DNA base pairing, adenine (A) pairs with thymine (T) and guanine (G) pairs with cytosine (C). The same rules apply to RNA except that in RNA, uracil (U) replaces thymine. According to the question stem, the deamination reaction did not occur because of a mutated enzyme, leaving cytosine unpaired. Thus, guanine will pair up with cytosine via 3 hydrogen bonds.

149. C is correct. According to the passage, the sk-loop of tRNA contains the anticodon sequence. The tRNA, carrying an appropriate amino acid, is brought to the ribosome by the pairing of its anticodon with the mRNA codon. The correct answer is therefore C.

Translation requires a large molecular machine comprised of tRNA, aminoacyl-tRNA synthetases, initiation, elongation, and termination factors, as well as rRNA and ribosomal proteins. These macromolecules interact in an ordered manner to ensure that proteins are accurately and efficiently synthesized according to the information that is encoded in mRNA.

150. A is correct. Knowledge regarding ribosomes is Very High Yield for the MCAT. Ribosomes are organelles that, along with their component parts, can be identified by sedimentation coefficients called Svedberg units, or S units. While that detail is not important for the MCAT, what is pertinent is that ribosomes consist of two subunits of unequal size, each containing both rRNA and proteins. Prokaryotic ribosomal subunits are 30S and 50S in size with a combined sedimentation coefficient of 70S. Eukaryotic cells possess 40S and 60S subunits with a combined sedimentation coefficient of 80S. (The combined values are not strictly additive). Ribosomes can self-assemble if the components are mixed in the proper order.

151. B is correct. According to the passage, the identity of the amino acids being added is not checked by the ribosome. Answer choice D is therefore eliminated. Because the A (aminoacyl) site is on the ribosome, answer choice A is also incorrect. According to the passage, some aminoacyl-tRNA synthetases are capable of a type of "proofreading" by checking certain tRNA sequences and activity.

152. C is correct. According to the passage, *aminoacylation* is catalyzed by a specific aminoacyl-tRNA synthetase and requires adenosine triphosphate (ATP). The correct answer can only be A or C. The reactions in the passage demonstrate that at first, the *aminoacyl-tRNA synthetase* catalyzes the formation of an intermediate between the amino acid and AMP (aminoacyl-AMP). The activated amino acid is then transferred to the tRNA (aminoacyl-tRNA).

153. B is correct. The question sounds complicated. It isn't. The reader is being asked to properly identify ribosomal structural components. Ribosomes consist of two subunits of unequal size, containing both rRNA and proteins. The rough ER synthesizes ribosomal protein components. The nucleolus, which is found in the nucleus, is responsible for rRNA synthesis.

Passage 205 (Questions 149-153)

Passage 206 (Questions 154-159)

154. D is correct. DNA synthesis begins at the *origin of replication* that is created by the unwinding of DNA by a *helicase. Single strand binding protein* (SSBP) keeps the replication fork open for the *primase* to attach and synthesize an RNA primer. Without a primer DNA polymerase has nothing to bind to. *DNA polymerase* binds to a single DNA strand. It moves along in the 3′ to 5′ direction while synthesizing a complementary DNA chain 5′ to 3′. The final step of DNA synthesis occurs when *ligase* stitches Okazaki fragments together.

155. B is correct. The question is asking the reader to pick a molecule that binds mRNA. Answer choice B is the only possibility. Each tRNA is defined by its 3-base anti-codon that binds only with its complementary codon on the mRNA. The first two positions of the mRNA codon observe Watson-Crick base pairing rules but the third position exhibits the *wobble*. Wobble occurs because the conformation of the tRNA anticodon loop permits flexibility at the first base of the anticodon.

156. B is correct. Both strands of DNA serve as templates for synthesis at the same time. The leading strand is synthesized *continuously* and grows in the direction of the replication fork. The lagging strand is synthesized *discontinuously* as small DNA fragments that are later joined together. Despite the differences in synthesis, both the leading and lagging strand finish DNA synthesis at the same time.

Thus replication of the chromosome involves semi-discontinuous synthesis of DNA at a speed about 1 kilobase per second.

157. A is correct. Primase is an *RNA polymerase* that synthesizes short stretches of RNA primer upon which the new DNA strand is made. DNA polymerases cannot initiate synthesis of a complementary strand of DNA on a totally single-stranded template. A double-stranded primer with a free OH group on the 3′ end is required. In DNA synthesis, the required primer is a short piece of RNA (an RNA oligonucleotide) complementary to the template DNA strand and having a free 3′-OH group. The RNA primers are later removed by the exonuclease activity of DNA polymerase I. RNA polymerase cannot synthesize DNA. The same holds true for a DNA polymerase—it cannot synthesize RNA.

158. A is correct. The question stem is inquiring about the function of DNA polymerase, not ligase. Thus, answer choice D can be eliminated. According to the passage, DNA polymerase III is responsible for polymerization of the leading and lagging strands. "ATP is only needed initially by the holoenzyme to clamp onto a primed template, but afterwards the holoenzyme is rapid and progresses without the need for additional ATP." The rate-limiting step must be the time needed for the polymerase to clamp to the template. The correct answer is A. Answer choice C is incorrect because, according to the passage, both the leading and lagging strand complete DNA synthesis at the same time.

159. C is correct. According to the passage, answer choices A and B are true. The end product of translation is protein, not RNA. Transcription (production of RNA) and replication (production of DNA) both occur in the nucleus. Translation takes place in the cytoplasm and its end product is protein, not RNA.

Independent Questions (Questions 160-170)

160. D is correct. *DNA dependent DNA polymerase* requires the following components in order to function: 1) 4 different nucleotides (A, C, G, and T), 2) a DNA template to copy, and 3) an RNA primer to attach to.

DNA polymerase begins replication by attaching to the template strand at a short segment of RNA known as a primer. Without a primer DNA synthesis cannot occur. The primer is synthesized by an *RNA primase*. The DNA polymerase (once it has reached its starting point as indicated by the primer) then adds nucleotides one by one in an exactly complementary manner, A to T and G to C. Basically, the DNA polymerase catalyzes the formation of hydrogen bonds between nucleotide bases.

161. D is correct. Once synthesized, RNA molecules undergo extensive post-transcriptional processing: 1) the *introns* (non-coding RNA regions) are removed and the coding *exons* (coding RNA regions) are spliced together; 2) **5′ RNA capping** increases RNA stability; 3) **3′ poly-A-tail** also functions to increase RNA stability.

162. C is correct. Polynucleotide (i.e., DNA) is the only macromolecule that is repaired rather than degraded. DNA repair is essential for maintaining cell function and is performed by a variety of biological repair systems (i.e., p53 protein). Uncontrolled cell growth may occur if somatic cell mutations are not repaired.

163. C is correct. MCAT writers ask a few stock questions about amino acids. Here are some **High Yield facts: Glycine** is the only optically INactive amino acid. Optical activity is measured by the ability to rotate a plane of polarized light and depends on the presence of a chiral center. (A chiral center is a central carbon that is bound to 4 DIFFERENT substituents.) **Valine** is a classic MCAT nonpolar amino acid. **Cysteine** is the only amino acids that is able to form disulfide bonds. **Proline** is the only *imino acid* (because it has two bonds to the amino group nitrogen) and is known as a helix breaker (because it does not allow for the proper formation of an alpha-helix).

164. A is correct. *Endopeptidases* are enzymes that cleave a polypeptide chain at a specific point in the middle of the chain. *Exopeptidases* cleave at the ends of the polypeptide chain. Zymogens are inactive peptidases (i.e., pepsinogen, trypsinogen, etc.). Ligases are en-

199

zymes needed to seal gaps between Okazaki fragments during DNA replication.

165. B is correct. MCAT writers love asking questions about frameshift mutations. A frameshift mutation occurs when there is an addition or deletion of 1 or 2 base pairs (a 3 base pair addition or deletion will cause an in-frame mutation, not a frameshift mutation, because each codon is coded by 3 nucleotides), which causes the ribosome to read all downstream codons in the wrong frame. Frameshift mutations usually result in truncated, non-functional proteins.

Altered base pairs (known as point mutations) do not cause the ribosome to read out of frame. Point mutations may cause silent, missense, or nonsense mutations. Answer choices A and C can be eliminated because both are examples of base pair deletion.

166. C is correct. A general understanding of blotting techniques is important for the MCAT. **Southern blotting** is used to identify DNA. **Northern blotting** is used on RNA and **western blotting** is used for proteins. There is no such thing as eastern blotting.

All blotting techniques rely on the use of gel electrophoresis to separate DNA, RNA, or proteins based on size. Then the gel is sandwiched between layers of blotting paper and probed by specific markers. Western blotting is the method of choice to confirm the presence of antibodies (proteins) to HIV.

167. D is correct. To answer this question one must realize that an antibody is just a protein. Thus, plasma cells are expected to have well developed protein synthesis machinery. Protein synthesis is carried out by the rough endoplasmic reticulum and/or free ribosomes. Answer choice D must be the correct answer. Smooth ER is responsible for steroid synthesis and is well developed for example in Leydig cells that synthesize testosterone. Mitochondria serve as the powerhouse of the cell.

168. D is correct. According to the question stem, in paper chromatography the rising nonpolar solvent will carry with it all nonpolar compounds. Propane ($CH_3CH_2CH_3$) is the only nonpolar compound listed in the answer choices. It will interact less strongly with the cellulose in the paper and move along with the mobile nonpolar solvent. Thus, less-polar compounds will move farther than more polar ones, resulting in separation.

169. D is correct. Each cellular ribosome is composed of a specific rRNA molecule and several different proteins. These organelles are identified by sedimentation coefficients called S units or Svedberg units (i.e., 30S, 50S, etc.). Lysosomes are digestive organelles full of enzymes that function in acidic (5.5 pH) environments. Cells that require a lot of ATP (i.e., muscle cells) contain many mitochondria, which serve as the site of cellular respiration. Peroxisomes are involved with peroxide, H_2O_2, synthesis and degradation. These organelles serve to detoxify the cell and possess *catalase*.

170. D is correct. Magnesium is a mineral, not a vitamin or a peptide. DNA and RNA polymerases use divalent (Mg^{2+}), not monovalent (K^+) metal ions for catalysis.

Passage 207 (IQuestions 171-176)

171. B is correct. According to the passage, the Shine-Delgarno is a short *purine-rich* sequence on the 5′ end of the AUG start codon on an mRNA. Adenine (A) and guanine (G) are the two DNA/RNA purines. The passage provides an example of a Shine-Delgarno sequence: $^A/_G{}^A/_G{}^A/_G{}^A/_G CC^A/_G{}^A/_G{}^A/_G{}^A/_G CCCAUG$. Based on the sequence it can be determined that four consecutive purines, either A or G ($^A/_G$), make up the Delgarno. The correct answer choice must therefore be B. Answer choice D has 5 consecutive purines; answer choice A has 3; and answer choice C displays 10 consecutive purines.

172. C is correct. Succinyl-CoA is a high potential energy molecule and an intermediate of the citric acid cycle (Krebs cycle). The energy stored in this molecule is used to form a high-energy phosphate bond, which produces 1 Guanine nucleotide triphosphate (GTP) molecule. Thus, every turn of the citric acid cycle produces 1 GTP molecule. No other listed pathway is capable of GTP synthesis.

173. C is correct. According to the first paragraph, prokaryote polypeptide synthesis begins with N-*formylmethionine*. An N-formylmethionine is a formylated methionine; formylation requires a *formylase*. (FYI: Eukaryotic methionine does not require formylation). The methionine that begins protein synthesis in prokaryotes is formylated (but not in eukaryotes). The codon for methionine is AUG, the initiation (start) codon. The three different stop codons are UAA, UAG and UGA.

174. C is correct. Translation can be subdivided into initiation, chain elongation, and termination. Rules for protein synthesis (or translation) are: 1) synthesis proceeds from the N-terminus to the C-terminus of the protein; 2) the ribosomes must "read" the mRNA molecule in the 5′ to 3′ direction; 3) translation requires the formation of a poly-ribosome in order to complete translation in a timely manner. It would take hours for a single ribosome to translate a long mRNA sequence.

175. B is correct. Taking the information from the question stem, $(GCAU)^4$ = GCAU GCAU GCAU GCAU. Each amino acid codon is composed of 3 nucleotides. However, where is the start codon (AUG)? GC **(AUG)**(CAU)(GCA)(UGC) AU. Thus, this nucleotide chain codes for 4 amino acids. The correct answer is B.

176. B is correct. Protein synthesis inhibitors are antibiotics that selectively inhibit prokaryotic protein synthesis while leaving the eukaryotic protein synthesis unaffected. The reason lies in that prokaryotic and eukaryotic ribosomes are very different. Prokaryotic ribosomes are 70S in size and are made of 50S and 30S subunits. Eukaryotic ribosomes are 80S in size and contain 60S and 40S subunits. Answer choice C and D are both true and this is an EXCEPT question. Antibiotics should not bind eukaryotic ribosomes, period. 40S is a component of the 80S eukaryotic ribosome.

Passage 208 (Questions 177-182)

177. **A is correct.** According to the first paragraph, chemotherapy is used to treat cancers that are spreading (metastasizing). Solid tumors are localized and are usually not metastatic in the early phases. Answer choices B, C, and D describe all solid, non-metastatic cancers. Answer choice A describes a lymphoma that is busy secreting white blood cells into the blood stream; chemotherapy is advised here.

178. **C is correct.** The answer to this question lies in the interphase mechanism 1. To start, answer choices A and D can be eliminated. Why? Because both mechanisms act on the same stage of the cell cycle (S-phase); both answers cannot be correct. As a result both are wrong. Learn this method of answer choice elimination. According to the question stem the neoplastic cell is slow growing; therefore it spends most of its time in the G_1 phase of the cell cycle. The correct answer choice is C.

Interphase:

G_1 phase: The period prior to the synthesis of DNA. In this phase, the cell increases in mass in preparation for cell division. It is the most variable phase of the cell cycle.

S phase: The period during which DNA is synthesized. In most cells, there is a narrow window of time during which DNA is synthesized.

G_2 phase: The period after DNA synthesis has occurred but prior to the start of mitosis. The cell synthesizes proteins and continues to increase in size.

179. **B is correct.** According to the passage, surgery is performed prior to chemotherapy or immunotherapy in order to "debulk" the tumor. "Debulking" a cancer—making it smaller—is thought to assist radiation and chemotherapy to get to the remaining pieces of the cancer and be more effective. A biopsy, not debulking, is used to accurately assess the nature and extent of the cancer. Answer choice C may be true, but it is describing a negative effect of debulking, not a benefit.

180. **B is correct.** According to Figure 1, remission induction occurs when tumor cell burden is below 1 gram.

181. **A is correct.** Purines and pyrimidines make up the two classes of nucleotides used for DNA and RNA synthesis. Adenine and guanine are two MCAT-relevant purines

found in both DNA and RNA. Uracil, thymine, and cytosine are pyrimidines, the concentration of which will be decrease in individuals on methotrexate.

182. **B is correct.** According to Figure 1, tumor mass is the variable that is most directly associated with death. Rapid cancer cell division will cause a tumor to increase in size. However, just because a tumor is rapidly dividing does not mean that it will grow very large. When the rate of cancer cell death is equal to the rate of cancer cell division the tumor remains the same size. The same applies for the number of cancer cell doublings. The correct answer is B.

Passage 209 (Questions 183-188)

183. **D is correct.** Detailed mitosis and meiosis knowledge is **High Yield information for the MCAT.** Meiosis is a type of cell division by which a diploid germ cell produces haploid gametes (spermatids and oocytes). Meiosis commences when homologous chromosomes (one from each parent) pair up and allow for a small exchange of genetic material between each other; this is known as crossing-over. Mitosis does NOT display homologue pairing and occurs in all somatic body cells.

During Anaphase I (of Meiosis I) homologous chromosomes, not centromeres, separate and migrate to the opposite poles of the cell. Centromere separation occurs in Mitosis I or Meiosis II. Once meiosis is initiated, the cell will not return to the normal cell cycle until both meiosis I and II have been completed. Therefore, there is NOT an S phase between meiosis I and II.

184. **C is correct.** According to the passage, prior to mitosis a cell will spend 95 percent of its time in a resting interval between divisions. This resting interval is known as interphase, which consists of G_1, a growth and preparation phase for chromosomal replication; **S**, a phase of DNA synthesis, in order to double all genetic material; and G_2, the final stage of interphase during which the cell is preparing to enter mitosis. **M**, is the mitotic phase of the cell cycle during which cell division occurs.

185. **D is correct.** The best way to answer this question is to associate each answer choice with a cell cycle phase. Organelle division usually occurs in the G_2 phase of the cell cycle. The cell is preparing to enter mitosis and must double all organelles to have something to pass on to all daughter cells. DNA polymerase activity occurs during S phase of the cell cycle. S phase correlates with nuclear chromosomal replication. Rate of nuclear degradation is important in prophase, the first of four mitotic phases. **Mitosis: Prophase → Metaphase → Anaphase → Telophase → Cytokinesis.** Quiescent phase nutrient requirement is important during G_1 phase. According to the passage, G_1 phase displays the most variability. "Quiescent cells are classified as being in G_0 phase, which

is a subdivision of the G_1 phase." The correct answer is D.

186. C is correct. *Permanent cells* are found in the central nervous system and heart. According to the passage, once they are destroyed, they cannot regenerate. New research indicates that the neurons of the olfactory nerve have some regenerative capacity, but they are the only neurons of the CNS that have been shown to have this ability. Liver hepatocytes (liver cells) are considered part of the *stable cell* population. Vessel mesothelium (epithelial cell) and hair follicle cells are *labile* and are constantly dividing. Labile cells are the ones most affected by chemotherapy utilized to treat malignancies. This is the reason cancer patients often lose their hair while undergoing treatment.

187. A is correct. According to the passage, *stable cells* are a subpopulation of cells that normally are replaced very slowly, but are capable of rapid renewal after tissue loss. This is most commonly seen in cells of the liver, which heal by regeneration, and in the cells of the proximal renal tubule of the nephron. Newly regenerated cells may require some time before they become fully functional.

Stable cells "show a post-adolescent decrease in ability to divide"; therefore these cells are fully active in a newborn and do not need to be properly stimulated. Thus, answer choice B can be eliminated. A cell that lacks division checkpoints is cancerous and divides out of control. Follicle stimulating hormone (FSH) serves as a constant source of "stimulation" and therefore acts on *labile cells*.

188. C is correct. There are a few **High Yield MCAT amino acid facts** that you should be familiar with:

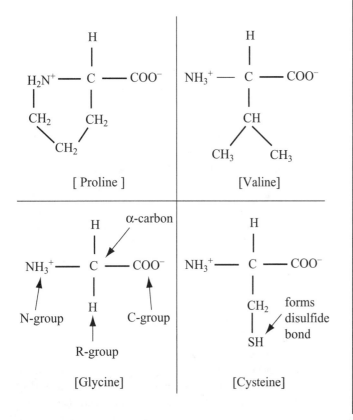

[Proline]

[Valine]

α-carbon

N-group

H

C-group

R-group

[Glycine]

forms disulfide bond

[Cysteine]

1) *Proline*—is a helix breaker because of its unusual cyclic side chain (R-group), which causes constraint and steric strain on critical hydrogen bonds along the peptide main chain necessary for secondary structure (helix) formation and stabilization. Proline is also an imino acid because of the R-group ring attachment to the amino nitrogen.

2) *Glycine*—is the only non-chiral amino acid; it contains 2 hydrogen atoms attached to the alpha-carbon.

3) *Cysteine*—is the only amino acid that can form disulfide bonds.

4) *Valine*—is a classic nonpolar amino acid used on the MCAT.

Independent Questions (Questions 189-199)

189. C is correct. According to the question stem, myoglobin is a single-chain peptide. Thus, it must by definition occupy a tertiary protein structure. If a protein is composed of 2 or more peptide chains it is by definition considered to be quaternary. A secondary protein structure has alpha-helixes and beta-sheets.

190. C is correct. According to the question stem, acid hydrolysis has several side effects: 1) partial destruction of tryptophan, which prevents the proper estimate of the tryptophan concentration; 2) the conversion of asparagine to aspartic acid, which prevents the direct measure of asparagine; 3) the conversion of glutamine to glutamic acid. Hence glutamic acid concentration is an indirect measure of glutamine. The correct answer choice must be C.

191. A is correct. According to the question stem *depurination* is the hydrolysis of a guanine glycosidic bond. Guanine is one of 2 purine nucleotides needed for DNA or RNA synthesis; the other purine nucleotide is adenine. The question is asking (in a complicated way) what macromolecule is composed of nucleotides. The correct answer choice is A.

192. A is correct. This is a very High Yield fact: because in the denatured condition only the primary structure is present, the primary structure is sufficient to take the protein back to the native (active) form. Primary structure determines protein secondary, tertiary, and quaternary structures.

193. B is correct. This is important to know: **anticipation** in a genetic disease is associated with an earlier onset of symptoms as well as an increase in disease severity with every generation. Anticipation is usually seen in autosomal dominant diseases associated with triple repeat expansion (i.e., Huntington's). The problem is believed to result because triple repeat sequences of increased length are unstable during cell division. **Heterozygous advantage** occurs when being a heterozygous carrier of a specific trait is a benefit; for example, individuals that are heterozygous for the sickle cell trait are less likely to catch malaria. **Penetrance** is used to explain the fact that some persons may carry a mutant allele but not show any sign of the disease.

194. **C is correct.** This is important because MCAT writers love to ask questions about cellular organelles. According to the question stem, attachment of glycoprotein side chains is a type of post-translational modification. Thus, the question is simply asking where in the cell can proteins undergo post-translational modification. The rough endoplasmic reticulum (rER) and the Golgi apparatus are the two cellular organelles that modify proteins. Lysosomes are digestive double-membrane organelles.

195. **A is correct. This is a very High Yield MCAT fact.** Ribosomal RNA (rRNA) binds to the large ribosomal subunit (i.e., 50S in prokaryotic cells) and creates a functional ribosome. Thus, ribosomes are complex assemblies of RNA molecules and other structural peptides. Furthermore, rRNAs are synthesized in the nuclear structure known as the nucleolus; rRNA is the only RNA molecule to be synthesized in the nucleolus.

196. **A is correct.** According to the question stem, *transversion* is a nucleotide interchange that replaces a purine with a pyrimidine or vice versa. To remember purine nucleotides use the mnemonic "**P**ure **A**s **G**old"; **A**denine and **G**uanine are the 2 purines. Cytosine, thymine, and uracil are the 3 pyrimidines. Answer choice A is the only example of a *transversion*.

197. **B is correct.** According to the question stem, leucine is nonpolar, thus hydrophobic and cannot form hydrogen bonds. Large hydrophobic side chain groups such as that of leucine can interact with each other through *hydrophobic interactions.* Cysteine is the only amino acid with a side chain that is capable of forming disulfide bonds. For the MCAT remember that ionic bonding is stronger than covalent interactions.

198. **D is correct.** Cell-mediated immunity depends on the proper function of T-cells. These are the cells that are destroyed by HIV and inhibit the development of an effective immune response. Humoral immunity relies on B-cells, which function to produce antibodies. Macrophages are part of innate immunity and destroy tissue invaders in a non-specific manner. Red blood cells are not part of the immune system.

199. **A is correct. This is a High Yield MCAT fact:** oxygen binding to hemoglobin displays positive cooperativity with an HC greater than 1. *Positive cooperativity* means that the first of four oxygens binds to the hemoglobin weakly. However, once the first oxygen binds, the affinity of the hemoglobin to fill up the remaining oxygen binding sites increases. *Negative cooperativity* exists where the binding of a ligand to the first site decreases the affinity of the protein for additional ligands.

Passage 210 (Questions 200-204)

200. **D is correct.** According to the passage, medium chain acyl-CoA dehydrogenase (MCAD) deficiency causes medium chain lipids to accumulate in the body, which leads to serious brain damage.

In order for the body to accumulate dietary lipids, they must first be absorbed from the small intestine. Lipid absorption requires the release of bile (synthesized in the liver) to emulsify the fat, rendering it accessible to pancreatic lipase. Lipase generates the formation of free fatty acids that are packed into micelles and absorbed by simple diffusion into the cells of the small intestine. Thus, in MCAD deficiency all lipid absorption mechanisms function normally. The mitochondrion is the site of lipid oxidation (breakdown). MCAD deficiency prevents the entry of medium chain lipids into the mitochondria and accumulation results.

201. **B is correct.** According to the passage, newborns are *screened* for diseases that are treatable if detected early. The correct answer choice is B, cancer. If the presence of cancer is detected early, the chances of recovery are twenty-fold better, thus morbidity and mortality would decrease. Screening for the common cold or undiagnosed fractures is far less beneficial because 1) these conditions are not life threatening and 2) even if found early, not much can be done to alleviate the disease progression. For example, if a screening test came back positive for a common cold, there is little to do but wait out the two weeks until the body can mount an effective immune response. FYI: Emotional difficulties can range from depression to schizophrenia.

202. **C is correct. This is a High Yield MCAT fact:** Protein digestion begins in the stomach with an enzyme called pepsin, which digests proteins into polypeptides. Protein digestion is completed in the small intestine. For the purposes of the MCAT, no digestion occurs in the esophagus.

203. **B is correct. The basics:**

[Glu$^+$] organism—can synthesize its own glucose, glucose is NOT essential for growth.

[Glu$^-$] organism—CANNOT synthesize its own glucose; glucose is essential for growth.

[Phe$^+$] organism—can synthesize its own phenylalanine; phenylalanine is NOT essential for growth.

[Phe] organism—CANNOT synthesize its own phenylalanine; phenylalanine is essential for growth.

Individuals with PKU have a high concentration of phenylalanine in their blood (and urine). According to the passage, *B. subtilis* cannot grow without a high concentration of phenylalanine, thus *B. subtilis* must be [Phe$^-$]. However, *B. subtilis* can survive on a glucose-free agar plate—this must mean that it has its own source of glucose. Thus it must be [Glu$^+$]. Lactose is presented solely as a distraction. If [Phe$^+$] organisms were used for PKU screening, then all the tests would come back positive and it would be impossible to tell which had PKU.

204. **B is correct.** Phenylalanine is normally converted into tyrosine by phenylalanine hydroxylase. In PKU, this enzyme is deficient, which causes an accumulation of phenylalanine (seen in both the blood and urine). In addition to this, no synthesis of tyrosine takes place in PKU, which means that tyrosine becomes an essential amino acid—that is, it can only be acquired through diet and not made in the body. Decreasing the consumption of other amino acids would not benefit PKU patients, because only one enzyme is missing. An all-vegetarian, strictly carbohydrate diet would be beneficial in preventing accidental phenylalanine intake. Fat is not converted to phenylalanine, thus limiting its intake would be of little value here.

Passage 211 (Questions 205-209)

205. **C is correct.** According to the passage, methylated or imprinted DNA is transcriptionally inactive. *Heterochromatin* is considered transcriptionally inactive and is abundant in non-dividing cells such as neurons. *Euchromatin* is unmethylated DNA found in actively dividing cells. There is no such thing as pseudochromatin or holo-DNA.

206. **B is correct.** What is a Barr body? It is a permanently inactivated X chromosome that forms a dense stainable nuclear mass. A normal female with XX inactivates one of her X's while expressing the other. She therefore has one Barr body. A normal male, who is XY, does not inactivate his only X chromosome, and therefore has no Barr bodies. A male who is XXY would inactivate his one extra X, giving him one Barr body.

The rule is that the number of X chromosomes is always 1 MORE than the number of Barr bodies. A person with 2 Barr bodies must have three X chromosomes.

207. **C is correct.** Paternal imprinting means that an allele inherited from the father is not expressed in offspring. Maternal imprinting means that an allele inherited from the mother is not expressed in offspring. According to the passage, Prader-Willi Syndrome exhibits maternal imprinting. The passage also states that the imprinted gene is methylated and inactive. In Prader-Willi, the normal allele inherited from the mother (the imprinted gene) is turned off, leaving the paternal gene to be expressed. Prader-Willi syndrome occurs because the paternal gene happens to be mutated, as described in the passage, and the offspring is born with the disease. The correct answer choice is C.

208. **C is correct.** According to the passage, genomic imprinting is found only in mammals. Of the answer choices, only an owl is not a mammal, as it does not carry its offspring inside of itself, but lays eggs.

209. **D is correct. This is a High Yield MCAT fact:** the primary protein structure is simply a linear sequence of amino acids held together by covalent peptide bonds. The presence of an alpha-helix or beta-sheet is seen in a secondary peptide structure. The tertiary structure refers to the three-dimensional (globular) arrangement of a peptide chain.

Independent Questions (Questions 210-221)

210. **B is correct.** According to the question stem, gout results when uric acid is not properly secreted and eliminated. Kidneys are the main organs that secrete, eliminate, filter, and reabsorb compounds in order to maintain homeostasis. Thus, gout may be caused by a renal (kidney) problem. Spleen filters blood for pathogens. The large intestine reabsorbs water and stores feces. The liver synthesizes blood proteins, produces bile, detoxifies the body, stores vitamins, etc.

211. **B is correct.** Autosomal dominant (AD) transmission is the most common type of inheritance. Here are some **High Yield MCAT facts about AD:**

- a person needs a single copy of the mutant gene to inherit the disease
- traits do not skip generations (called vertical transmission)
- there are usually equal numbers of affected males and females
- father to son transmission is observed

212. **B is correct.** Mutations may have three basic types of possible effects on protein, not carbohydrate, function: abnormal protein production, loss of protein function, or gain of protein function. Loss of function of a gene product may result from mutations in coding or regulatory elements or loss of critical sequences. Gain-of-function mutations are due to alterations of the protein that improves its function. There may be either an increase in the level of protein expression or an increase in each protein molecule's ability to perform its function.

213. **C is correct.** An X-linked gene mutation is more common in males (who have one X chromosome) than in females (who have two X chromosomes). The disease gene appears to skip generations because it is being transmitted through phenotypically normal heterozygous carrier females. Affected males transmit the gene to all their daughters and so all their daughters are carriers. There is no father to son transmission. Males that carry the mutant gene show the trait.

214. **D is correct.** *Gyrase*, not *ligase*, relaxes the positive su-

percoils that accumulate as the replication fork opens.

215. B is correct. Autosomal recessive (AR) inheritance is usually the product of mating of two heterozygous or carrier parents. From the mating of two heterozygotes carrying an autosomal recessive disease gene 1) there is a 25% (1/4) risk of having a homozygous normal child, 2) there is a 25% (1/4) risk of having a homozygous affected child, 3) there is a 50% (1/2) risk of having a heterozygous child. The heterozygous individual in AR inheritance is called a carrier. 75% of children appear phenotypically normal but may carry the mutant gene.

216. C is correct. The probability (p) of rolling any one number (i.e., 2) on a 6-sided die (one of a pair) is 1/6 since there are 6 sides and only one side carries a number 2. [p (of a 4) = 1/6]. Using two dice, what is the probability of rolling a pair of 2s? To answer the question, multiply the individual probabilities together: the probability of a 2 appearing on both dice is: [p (of two 2s) = 1/6 x 1/6 = 1/36].

217. C is correct. According to the question stem, severe combined immunodeficiency (SCID) causes abnormalities in T and B-cells. The question is simply asking which of the listed organs are involved in T and B-cell synthesis. B-cells are produced in the bone marrow. T-cells are produced in the bone marrow and mature in the thymus. Thus, an individual diagnosed with SCID is expected to have an underdeveloped thymus and bone marrow.

218. D is correct. Okazaki fragments are associated with the lagging DNA strand. They are synthesized in a 5′-3′ direction (just like all of DNA) by the DNA polymerase and are covalently linked by the *DNA ligase*, not *polymerase I*, forming a continuous DNA strand. Okazaki fragments are not synthesized to fill in gaps after the removal of the RNA primer.

219. A is correct. Accoridng to the question stem, myoglobin accepts oxygen from hemoglob—thus hemoglobin has a lower affinity for oxygen than myoglobin—and releases it to the cytochrome oxidase system—so the cytochrome oxidase system should have a higher affinity for oxygen than hemoglobin and myoglobin. Overall, myoglobin has a higher oxygen affinity than hemoglobin and lower oxygen affinity than cytochrome oxidase.

220. B is correct. According to the question stem, the semi-permeable membrane mimics the cell membrane in terms of function. Glucose cannot freely diffuse into cells. It requires a GLUT transporter and may need a sodium gradient. The cell membrane is freely diffusible by small hydrophobic molecules, gases (O_2, CO_2), and water.

221. D is correct.

	A	a
A	AA	Aa
a	Aa	aa

LECTURE 3

300

Answers & Explanations
Questions 222–332

222.	B	259.	C	296.	C
223.	B	260.	B	297.	C
224.	B	261.	D	298.	B
225.	C	262.	C	299.	B
226.	B	263.	D	300.	D
227.	D	264.	D	301.	A
228.	B	265.	C	302.	B
229.	C	266.	C	303.	C
230.	C	267.	A	304.	B
231.	D	268.	C	305.	B
232.	B	269.	B	306.	C
233.	A	270.	A	307.	D
234.	B	271.	A	308.	B
235.	C	272.	B	309.	D
236.	A	273.	A	310.	D
237.	B	274.	C	311.	C
238.	C	275.	A	312.	B
239.	A	276.	C	313.	D
240.	B	277.	C	314.	A
241.	A	278.	A	315.	B
242.	B	279.	C	316.	B
243.	D	280.	D	317.	D
244.	C	281.	B	318.	A
245.	D	282.	C	319.	C
246.	A	283.	C	320.	B
247.	C	284.	A	321.	C
248.	D	285.	D	322.	B
249.	D	286.	B	323.	A
250.	C	287.	C	324.	D
251.	D	288.	B	325.	C
252.	B	289.	D	326.	B
253.	B	290.	D	327.	B
254.	C	291.	D	328.	B
255.	D	292.	D	329.	B
256.	A	293.	A	330.	D
257.	C	294.	B	331.	D
258.	B	295.	B	332.	A

Passage 301 (Questions 222-228)

222. B is correct. According to the passage, *productive infection* occurs when the cell is permissive and thus allows for *viral integration*, replication, and virion release to occur. *Abortive infection* is non-permissive and does not allow viral genome to integrate into the host cell chromosome. During *restrictive* attacks viral production ceases *but the genome integration persists*. Therefore, the correct answer choice must be B.

223. B is correct. 0.1% of 10,000 is 10. Try not to miss these questions.

224. B is correct. This is important: most viruses acquire their envelopes from the **plasma membrane**, which is not available as an answer choice. Answer choice C can be eliminated because human cells lack a cell wall. Most viruses acquire their envelopes from the plasma membrane, which is not an answer choice. HSV-1 acquires its envelope from the **nuclear membrane**, a logical exception to the rule. Table 1 hints at the correct answer by informing that viral assembly occurs in the nucleus. The best way to answer this question is through the process of elimination.

225. C is correct. According to the passage, *abortive viral infection* occurs when cells are non-permissive and no virion particles are produced; basically the host does not get sick.

All invading particles (viruses, bacteria, fungi, etc.) possess surface markers (known as antigens) that allow them to be spotted by the host's immune system. If the influenza virus undergoes rapid random mutation, its virulence (ability to cause an infection) will increase because the immune system will have difficulty adapting to a rapidly evolving surface marker. This will lead to a *productive infection,* not *abortive.* All other answer choices are examples of abortive infection. Liver tissue, which lacks cell surfaces receptors, is not able to bind viral particles and will not be infected. Esophagus cells that lack DNA replication machinery cannot replicate and produce new virions. Viral surface markers (antigens) that match host's antibodies will be picked up by the immune system and will not cause an infection.

226. B is correct. Table 1 maps out steps of HSV-1 infection and provides the answer to this question. Table 1 states that, immediately prior to re-infecting the skin, HSV-1 leaves a **nervous system ganglion** (usually the trigeminal ganglion) to return to the skin surface. Latent HSV virus must be localized here. FYI: a ganglion is a collection of neuron cells bodies.

227. D is correct. According to the passage, tumor necrosis factors (TNF) are similar to viral growth factors, which bind the axon terminal receptors. Thus, it can be assumed that tumor necrosis factors also bind axon terminal receptors. Therefore, axon terminal injury will prevent TNF transport.

228. B is correct. You should not miss this question. According to the passage and Table 2, the tegument is a protein-filled area that is located between the capsid and the envelope. Radioactive tegument dye would adhere here.

Passage 302 (Questions 229-235)

229. C is correct. According to the question stem, virulence and infectivity are characteristics of an agent's ability to infect and cause disease. However, this information does not really assist in answering the question. The best way to answer this question is by the process of elimination. Answer choice C, bone-penetration through the periosteum, will serve as the *least* likely route used by a virus to cause an infection (bone is dense, tightly covered by periosteum, therefore difficult to penetrate). Bone infections do occur, but they are rare in comparison to those of the 1) respiratory tract (i.e., common cold) 2) GI tract (i.e., food poisoning) 3) excretory system (i.e., herpes). Moreover, answer choices A, B, and D are all lumenal structures, with a direct opening to the external environment.

230. C is correct. According to the passage, *host cytoplasm* is used to convert the viral RNA core, which is complexed with a *reverse transcriptase* (normal eukaryotic cells do not produce this enzyme) into DNA. The site of host chromosome integration by the virus has a tremendous influence on the expression of host genes (thus, answer choice B is eliminated). For example, if the virus happens to integrate near an oncogene, a cancer may develop in the host.

231. D is correct. According to the passage, *nondividing cells* are resistant to retroviral infection. Nerve cells are not destined to divide again and are arrested in the G_0 phase of the cell cycle—the transition from G_0 to G_1 commits the cell to complete the cell cycle and divide. Epithelial, epidermal, and helper T-cellss are all rapidly dividing cells and are therefore not resistant to retroviral infection.

232. B is correct. The central dogma is a High Yield MCAT topic. DNA → DNA conversion is known as **replication**. Conversion of DNA → RNA is **transcription**. Converting RNA → Protein is known as **translation**. Therefore, retroviral RNA is not *translated* but *transcribed* into DNA. The DNA form of the retroviral genome is called a provirus. **Translocation** is the polypeptide switch between ribosomal A and P sites during translation.

233. A is correct. According to the passage, the retroviral core, not the envelope, contains 2 copies of single-stranded RNA linked by the activity of the reverse transcriptase (eliminating answer choice D). Because retroviruses have 2 copies of single-stranded RNA they are diploid. By definition, a diploid cell contains two copies of each chromosomal set. Gametes are haploid and contain a single chromosomal set. Viruses are obligate intracellular parasites and by definition cannot make their own ATP.

234. B is correct. For a drug to be effective, it must be delivered – requires **solubility** in body fluids—to target tissue without being overly **toxic** to the host. Thus, answer choices A and D are eliminated. A crippling disease like HIV requires potent medication with an extended half-life in order to diminish the possibility of drug resistance. A drug with a short half-life is rapidly cleared from the body and is not as effective at preventing viral load increase. Medication cost is always an issue; however, it is the least important one during drug development.

235. C is correct. DiGeorge syndrome (DGS) is a disorder caused by the underdevelopment of the thymus, a gland where T-cells mature and multiply. Immature T-cells migrate to the thymus (located in the upper chest) from the bone marrow. B-cells mature in the bone marrow. The spleen filters the circulatory system in search of invaders. The thyroid gland produces thyroid hormone, which regulates overall body metabolism, and calcitonin, which lowers blood Ca^{2+} levels.

Passage 303 (Questions 236-241)

236. A is correct. Adipose (fat) tissue—made up of adipocytes, which are lipid-filled cells—is a specialized connective tissue that functions as the major storage site for fat in the form of triglycerides. Fat is used as padding and for ATP synthesis. Erythrocytes, also known as red blood cells, lack organelles and are not used for storage. Rather, red blood cells deliver oxygen to peripheral tissue. Epithelial cells—provide lining to all luminal body surfaces—and cardiac cells are highly active and only function in storage under pathological conditions.

237. B is correct. According to the passage, increased membrane fluidity is achieved by increasing membrane cholesterol concentration. Therefore, if cholesterol concentration decreases so will membrane fluidity. The correct answer choice must be B. Integral proteins serve as channels and carrier molecules but have little effect on membrane fluidity.

238. C is correct. Surfactant is a mixture of lipids and proteins that coat the inner surface of the *lungs*. This coating is a must in order to reduce the alveolar surface tension and allow for proper gas exchange. Respiratory distress syndrome occurs in premature neonates who lack proper surfactant concentration.

239. A is correct. According to tables 1 and 2, organism A shows the highest growth index difference $(8 - 2 = 6)$ between experiments one (temp. 25° C) and two (temp. 37° C). Therefore, organism A prefers higher temperatures in order to achieve maximum growth. Organism C has the highest overall growth index at 37° C, but this organism grew well during the course of experiment 1 (temp. 25° C) as well.

240. B is correct. The first paragraph explains the types of motion achieved by phospholipid molecules in the cell membrane. Membrane proteins are part of the cell membrane and are expected to display similar locomotion characteristics seen with phospholipids. Membrane phospholipids rotate (spin) on their axis and show lateral rotation (drift to the left and to the right). However, proteins do not flip-flop in the membrane. Receptor proteins cannot flip-flop; otherwise surface receptors will end up facing the cytoplasm rather than the extracellular environment.

241. A is correct. According to the passage, increase in temperature will cause an increase in both membrane fluidity and degree of fatty acid unsaturation. Therefore, unsaturated/saturated fatty acid ratio will be *lowest* at lower temperature. The correct answer must be A. Note: answer choices B and C can both be eliminated because the correct answer had to be one of the extremes.

Independent Questions (Questions 242-251)

242. B is correct. According to the question stem, a naked capsid virus is protected by the nucleocapsid from drying, acids and bile; as a result, naked capsid viruses are very resistant to conditions in the gastrointestinal tract. It can therefore be assumed that naked capsid virus infects the GI tract via an oral (mouth) route, otherwise known as the fecal oral route. The esophagus is the proximal portion of the digestive tract.

243. D is correct. This is High Yield MCAT information. When a virus infects a target cell, one of three things will happen: 1) a failed infection, 2) lytic infection that rapidly kills the host cell via lysis, or 3) lysogenic infection that causes the invading virus to integrate itself into the host genome. At any moment a lysogenic infection can become lytic.

Lysogenic phages are in a quiescent (non-active) state in the cell; most of the phage genes are not being transcribed, but the integrated virus is being passed on to daughter cells. Following stressful stimuli (i.e., UV light), lytic phase occurs, during which the virus rapidly multiplies in the host cell, inducing lysis at the end of the viral life cycle. Therefore, prior to UV exposure the virus was in a lysogenic phase.

244. C is correct. The S-shaped bacterial growth curve is a High Yield MCAT topic. The four-phase growth cycle: 1) lag phase → 2) exponential growth phase → 3) stationary phase (plateau) → 4) bacterial death phase.

245. D is correct. Blood plasma is defined as all components that remain in the mixture following red blood cell co-agulation (blood clot formation). Stated another way, blood plasma is blood and all of its components minus the red blood cells. Answer choices A-C are all normally present in blood plasma, as are Na^+, Ca^{+2}, Cl^-, HCO^{3-}, etc.

246. A is correct. This is the chronological order of events that occur during a viral infection:

1. Target cell binding: each virus is known to follow patterns of tissue tropism meaning a virus has a specific target tissue preference.

2. Attachment: the virus attaches to the target cell via specific surface receptors.

3. Penetration: the virus is internalized into the host following virus/host cell interaction.

4. Uncoating: the outer viral coat is removed, which allows for viral replication to begin.

5. Viral synthesis: the virus synthesizes mRNA, protein, and identical copies of its genome.

247. C is correct. This is a High Yield MCAT topic. Transformation involves the acquisition of DNA from the environment; bacteria simply "see and grab" all encountered DNA. Conjugation is the acquisition of DNA directly from another bacterium via sex pili. This is the main mechanism used by bacteria to pass along antibiotic resistance. Transduction is defined as DNA acquisition via a bacteriophage intermediate; a virus transfers DNA between host cells. Each of these mechanisms will allow bacteria to undergo genetic recombination. Translocation is the rejoining of broken chromosome ends and does not increase genetic variability.

248. D is correct. Knowledge regarding cellular organelles is High Yield for the MCAT. The inter-cristal space or the mitochondrial matrix houses a low H^+ ion concentration. H^+ ions are pumped out of the matrix into the intermembrane space by the electron transport chain. So, the intermembrane space has a high H^+ ion concentration and thus low pH. Mitochondrion is a double-membrane organelle with an infolded inner membrane that forms cristae. FYI: Red blood cells lack all cellular organelles and rely solely on glycolysis, which occurs in the cytoplasm, for ATP production.

249. D is correct. Under anaerobic conditions, glycolysis yields 2 net ATP and 2 molecules of pyruvate, which is routed into lactic acid or alcohol fermentation.

When oxygen is present (aerobic conditions), organisms carry out glycolysis followed by the Krebs cycle and the electron transport chain. In eukaryotes, the Krebs cycle and the electron transport chain occur in the mitochondrial matrix. Thus, glycolysis followed by aerobic respiration allows for the highest yield of ATP.

250. C is correct. This is a High Yield MCAT topic. Prokaryotes DO NOT have a nucleus or membrane-bound organelles and thus are much simpler anatomically than eukaryotic plant or animal cells. Prokaryotes come in different shapes and sizes and possess a peptidoglycan, not chitin, cell wall (a chitin-derived cell wall is seen in fungi). Their cytoplasm is not organized into compartments meaning enzymes and ribosomes exist freely in the cytoplasm.

251. D is correct. According to the question stem, all listed answer choices are either organelles or inclusions. An **organelle** is a small internal cellular organ with a distinct function and morphology, for example a lysosome, mitochondria, and smooth ER. An **inclusion** is a lifeless accumulation of cell products, for example pigment, glycogen, etc. Fat is a macromolecule that may accumulate in cells. However, this accumulation occurs in a vacuole. Thus, the correct answer choice must be D.

Passage 304 (Questions 252-257)

252. B is correct. According to the question stem, all molecules, even those in solids, display random movement. To simplify, the question is asking which of the listed movements will most likely occur in solids. Atoms that make up solid structures experience atomic vibration (oscillation) within the material. However, liquid and/or gas molecular units are capable of actual linear movement, with measurable displacement.

253. B is correct. According to the passage, cell membrane diffusion depends on Fick's Law: $J = pA ([S_1] - [S_2])$. Thus, diffusion is expected to increase with 1) an increase in the concentration gradient ($[S_1] - [S_2]$), 2) an increase in the cell membrane surface area and/or 3) increase in the cell membrane constant.

Membrane thickness is also an important factor in controlling rate of diffusion. For example, an increase in the membrane thickness will decrease overall membrane diffusion.

Surfactant is a lipid molecule, produced by pneumocytes (lung cells), that decreases the surface tension within the alveolar walls and prevents alveoli collapse. Alveolar collapse would inhibit an effective exchange of air. However, surfactant does not directly fit into Fick's equation and thus has no effect on the rate of diffusion.

254. C is correct. According to the passage, there are three types of biological work: active transport (H^+ ATPase activity), movement (flagella activity), and biosynthesis (albumin production). Osmosis is defined as *simple diffusion* of water, requiring no energy, and therefore does not qualify as biological work.

255. D is correct. This is a High Yield MCAT topic. Endocytosis requires the presence of a cell surface receptor to initiate an ATP-dependent recognition sequence, which utilizes cell membrane–derived vesicles to package ingested goods. Lysosomes will digest these vesicles to release nutrient monomers and other items necessary for cellular growth and development.

256. A is correct. According to the passage, the *partition coefficient* (K) = solubility in oil/solubility in water. Lipid-soluble substances (posses a high K) undergo a rapid rate of diffusion because they can dissolve in the hydrophobic lipid bilayer. According to Table 1, molecule A displays the highest K.

257. C is correct. The question being posed is this: which of the listed compounds is lipid soluble? **This is a High Yield MCAT topic.** All anterior pituitary hormones (i.e., prolactin, TSH, ACTH, etc.) are of peptide origin and are not lipid soluble. These will bind to cell membrane receptors and rely on second messengers (i.e., cAMP) to exert necessary nuclear effect. Pancreas also produces peptide hormones (i.e., insulin and glucagon). Aldosterone, which is cholesterol derived and therefore lipid soluble, will diffuse across the cell membrane and bind directly to nuclear receptors. The correct answer choice is C. FYI: other lipid-soluble hormones are estrogen, testosterone, and cortisol.

Passage 305 (Questions 258-264)

258. B is correct. A poor oxidizing agent must be a strong reducer. By definition, a reducing agent is an electron donor. Based on Table 1, compounds at the top of the table are strong oxidizing agents and compounds on the bottom are strong reducing agents. Choices A and C should be immediately eliminated because they are in the middle of the table; the correct answer choice has to be one of the extremes.

259. C is correct. This is an MCAT application question. According to the question stem, atractyloside will inhibit the ATP/ADP exchanger, which will indirectly inhibit the FoF_1 ATPase. So, the decrease in the available ADP for the FoF_1 ATPase will inhibit ATP synthesis. ATP synthesis relies on the movement of hydrogen ions from the intermembrane space into the mitochondrial matrix, which will also be inhibited causing increased acidity in the intermembrane space. This bottleneck will cause a decrease in oxygen consumption, since oxygen acts as the final electron acceptor in the electron transport chain.

260. B is correct. According to the passage, the reactive functionality of nicotinamide occurs on carbon 4, and two ribose rings, pyrophosphate, adenine, and adenosines 29-phosphate determine specificity and binding properties. Diphosphate is the only compound not mentioned in the passage. The correct answer choice is B.

261. D is correct. This is a High Yield MCAT fact. Oxygen serves as the final electron acceptor in the mitochondrial electron transport chain and is converted to water. High levels of oxygen consumption by cardiac cells will be linked with high levels of water production.

262. C is correct. Study the equation carefully. The equation displays a redox reaction, where one compound is being reduced as the other is oxidized. Specifically, flavin (in FMN) is being reduced while NADPH is oxidized (answer choice C). Be aware that if a topic in the answer choice is not mentioned in the passage, it rarely is the correct answer choice.

263. D is correct. According to the passage, production of one mole of ATP requires the translocation of a little more than three hydrogen ions. Thus, the correct answer must be greater than 18.

264. D is correct. The conditions that would have the maximum effect on oxidative phosphorylation would also affect the citric acid cycle in the same way, because the two processes are linked. The last paragraph states that high ADP and low intermembrane pH stimulate oxidative phosphorylation. If ADP levels are high then ATP levels must be low.

Passage 306 (Questions 265-270)

265. C is correct. According to the passage, lipopolysaccharide (LPS) layer is composed of lipid A, oligosaccharide core, and an O-antigen. **Read carefully and mark the passage for important information as you go along.**

266. C is correct. Refer to Figure 1. When the G-protein is stimulated, the expected ATP consumption would *increase* to produce more cAMP. Answer choice A is eliminated. As ATP is being consumed to produce cAMP, ADP levels would *increase*, eliminating answer choice B. Based on the information provided in the passage, there is no way for the reader to predict what would happen to the normal bacterial flora. FYI: the normal bacterial flora is composed of all microorganisms normally found in the small intestine. This eliminates answer choice D. The question stem states that an *E. coli* infection causes a dramatic secretion of water into the lumen of the small intestine. By definition, secretory diarrhea is caused by the oversecretion of water into the lumen of the small intestine.

267. **A is correct. This is a classic MCAT question.** Out of the four answer choices listed only one is an example of a *weak molecular bond or interaction.* The correct answer choice is A. You must be aware that hydrophobic interactions occur when hydrophobic compounds clump together to avoid hydrophilic ones and form weak molecular bonds. Ionic, covalent, and amide (type of a covalent bond) represent strong molecular bonding.

268. **C is correct.** As arteries and arterioles dilate (widen), there is more room for blood to flow through, which *decreases* the overall resistance to blood flow. This eliminates answer choice A. When the circulatory system undergoes vasodilation of arteries and arterioles, overall resistance is decreased, which also reduces the pressure at which blood flows (results in decreased blood pressure). This eliminates answer choice B. Vasodilation of capillary beds would increase perfusion (delivery of oxygen and nutrients) of those tissues due to increased blood flow. This eliminates answer choice D.

Summary:

Blood pressure drops when:

1. arteries or arterioles dilate
2. heart function (i.e., heart rate) decreases
3. there is a decrease in blood volume

269. **B is correct.** The hypothalamus is a major control center for the maintenance of basal body temperature. However, this answer could also be derived via the process of elimination. The cerebral cortex is primarily involved with higher mental functions such as speech, comprehension, and memory. The adrenal medulla produces hormones such as epinephrine and norepinephrine. The other three choices have nothing to do with temperature homeostasis. Smooth muscle is involved in maintaining visceral tone and vasodilation.

270. **A is correct.** Upon examining the pre and post values for LPS administration, one sees that hemoglobin values remain virtually unchanged throughout. Therefore, hemoglobin must be relatively unaffected by LPS. After 24 hours post-LPS administration, WBC counts have returned to normal while all other values (RBC, hematocrit, and WBC differential) remain well below normal.

The answer is based on results derived from Table 1. **Application questions like this one should not be missed.**

Independent Questions (Questions 271-280)

271. **A is correct. This is High Yield MCAT fact:** DNA (deoxyribonucleic acid) is negatively charged, because of the presence of phosphate groups on the ribose, and acidic. For electrostatic interactions to occur and chromatin to form, histones must be positively charged and basic. As a result, histones are composed of a high concentration of lysine and arginine, 2 basic amino acids. FYI: the 3rd basic amino acid is histidine.

272. **B is correct.** According to the question stem, a defect in oxidative phosphorylation will increase the level of anaerobic respiration. Anaerobic respiration occurs in the cytoplasm and involves 2 metabolic pathways: glycolysis and fermentation. Glycolysis converts 1 molecule of glucose into 2 molecules of pyruvate; as a result glucose accumulation is not expected. Fermentation converts pyruvate into lactic acid (lactate). FYI: Fermentation in non-animal cells produces ethanol. Thus, the expected result of a coenzyme Q deficiency is the accumulation of lactate. Oxidative phosphorylation produces ATP; if inhibited, ATP levels are expected to be low.

273. **A is correct.** MCAT writers enjoy asking questions about fungi. This is what is important to know: 1) Fungal cells are generally found in a haploid state, unlike most eukaryotic cells, which are usually diploid. 2) Most fungi contain a *chitin cell wall*; bacteria have a peptidoglycan cell wall. 3) Fungi can reproduce sexually and/or asexually and are NOT responsive to antibiotic therapy. The correct answer choice is A. Fungal infections are difficult to treat because these cells are eukaryotic and their annihilation often causes severe host toxicity.

274. **C is correct.** According to the question stem, thermogenin inhibits ATP synthesis by allowing protons to return into the mitochondrial matrix without going through the ATP synthase. Lactic acid and/or glucose accumulation is not expected because neither the Krebs cycle nor the electron transport chain is inhibited. Thus, through the process of elimination, the correct answer must be choice C. FYI: Neonates keep themselves warm by utilizing a mechanism similar to the one induced by thermogenin; the body temperature increases because the electron transport chain produces two forms of energy, ATP and heat. Thus, when ATP is not being produced there is an increase in the production of heat.

275. **A is correct.** Lysosomes are double membrane-covered organelles that act as cellular garbage disposal systems. They degrade most products of ingestion, as well as aging organelles.

Lysosomes are full of different digestive enzymes that only function at an acidic pH, just like stomach enzymes (i.e., pepsin). Thus, the correct answer choice is A.

276. **C is correct.** Somatic cell division involves two successive steps: mitosis and cytokinesis. Cytokinesis entails

the formation of a cleavage furrow by the contraction of actin and myosin microfilaments at the cellular equator. The cell cycle is a sequence of events that occur between mitotic cell divisions. The cell cycle phases include G_1 → growth and development, S → DNA synthesis, G_2 → pre-mitosis growth and development, and M → mitosis. Thus, the correct answer choice is C.

277. C is correct. Acetylcholine is a neurotransmitter used to stimulate: 1) the parasympathetic nervous system and 2) somatic muscular system. FYI: The parasympathetic nervous system acts to decrease the heart rate. According to the question stem, cobra venom inhibits acetylcholine activity. Thus, answer choice A is incorrect. However, when acetylcholine receptor function is blocked muscle paralysis does result. If respiratory muscles (i.e., diaphragm) cease to function, death from respiratory failure occurs. FYI: Rapid heart rate is stimulated by norepinephrine, a sympathetic nervous system neurotransmitter.

278. A is correct. According to the question stem, local anesthetics inhibit membrane-bound proteins. The sodium channel is essential for nerve conduction and is inhibited by the local anesthetics in a nonspecific process, resulting in blockage of nerve conduction.

279. C is correct. According to the question stem, vitamin A is a lipid. For the MCAT, lipid digestion begins in the small intestine, not in the mouth, and requires liver synthesized bile salts and pancreas synthesized lipase. Lipid absorption takes place mostly in the jejunum and the ileum of the small intestine. The stomach absorbs water and alcohol but NOT lipids. Pancreatic amylase is involved in carbohydrate digestion. If vitamin A is unavailable through diet, "night blindness" may result ("Night blindness" occurs in South American riverboat pilots.

280. D is correct. For the MCAT it is important to know that the retina of the eye is composed of 2 cell types: rod and cone cells. There are many more rod cells than cone cells that make up the retina of the eye. Rod cells are responsible for night vision and respond best to non-colored light. Cones cells are responsible for visual acuity and respond best to colored light.

Passage 307 (Questions 281-287)

281. B is correct. MCAT writers love to ask chemical bond questions. According to the passage, peptidoglycan lattices that are interconnected by amino acid bridges and therefore must be linked via peptide or amide bonds. Peptide bonds are found between amino acid residues and can be broken by hydrolysis. Phosphodiester bonds are found in DNA between nucleic acids. Hydrogen bonds are considered to be molecularly weak but there is

no mention of them in the passage.

282. C is correct. The question stem provides a clue to correctly answering this question. *S. pyogenes* M-protein mediates attachment to the upper GI tract. Answer choice B can be eliminated because the intestine is NOT a part of the upper GI tract. Therefore, any mutation in the gene for this protein will have a direct effect on surface attachment properties. Esophageal goblet cells produce mucus to prevent particles from entering lung alveoli. M-protein mutation is not expected to have an effect on goblet cell mucus production. Thus, answer choice A can be eliminated. Normal flora (normal bacterial population housed in the GI tract) is not expected to relocate because of an *S. pyogenes* mutation (*S. pyogenes* is not a part of the natural bacterial flora). The most likely outcome will be *S. pyogenes* overattaching to the upper GI tract and causing an infection.

283. C is correct. The last sentence of the second paragraph informs that muramic acid, D-amino acids, and diaminopimelic acid are not found in fungi. Therefore, these compounds will not be obtained by an omnivore (meat and plant eater) that consumes fungus.

284. A is correct. This is important: The anterior pituitary gland is responsible for the production of peptide hormones only (i.e., GH, FSH, LH, Prolactin, etc), and therefore does not carry out steroid or fatty acid synthesis. The adrenal cortex (produces cortisol and aldosterone) and the liver (Low Density Lipoprotein or LDL synthesis) are involved in cholesterol-based lipid synthesis. A lactating mammary gland is constantly active with milk production. Lipids make up high percentage of milk.

285. D is correct. According to the question stem, *Mycoplasma* lacks peptidoglycan molecules, which according to the passage are necessary for cell wall synthesis. As a result, *Mycoplasma's* lack of peptidoglycans strongly suggests that it must not have a cell wall but only a cell membrane.

286. B is correct. According to the passage, peptidoglycan synthesis occurs in the cytoplasm. Krebs cycle enzymes are found in the mitochondrial matrix, making answer choice B the correct answer. Glycolysis occurs in the cytoplasm and is an anaerobic process. **This is a High-Yield MCAT fact.** Fatty acid production (therefore steroid synthesis) takes place in the cytoplasm as well. Answer choices C and D describe the same metabolic process; both answer choices can be eliminated as a result.

287. C is correct. This is High Yield MCAT fact: penicillin inhibits bacterial cell wall synthesis. If you were not familiar with this fact, the passage provides enough information to answer the question correctly. "The cell wall is composed of overlapping peptidoglycan lattices…peptidoglycan synthesis depends on muramyl penta-peptide attaching to UDP…*Penicillin-binding pro-*

teins function to cross-link the inserted penta-peptide subunits."

Passage 308 (Questions 288-293)

288. **B is correct.** According to the passage, **bacteriophage tail fibers** are involved in reversible surface binding that is Mg^{+2} and Ca^{+2} dependent. This information strongly suggests that the interaction between a phage and host cell is due to **electrostatic interactions**. **Hydrophobic interactions** involve non-polar compounds (i.e., lipids) attempting to minimize exposure to polar compounds (i.e., water). **Covalent bonding** forms a strong attachment between two surfaces and is rarely reversible.

289. **D is correct. This is a High Yield MCAT topic.** In eukaryotic cells, proteins are synthesized by ribosomes that are either free or attached to the *rough endoplasmic reticulum.* However, protein modification (i.e., addition of tetra-saccharide residues) ordinarily occurs in the *Golgi apparatus.* The *smooth ER* is responsible for lipid synthesis and cell detoxification. The cell nucleus houses genetic material.

290. **D is correct.** This question is best answered via the process of elimination. Nerve cells are unable to divide; answer choice A is eliminated. Cardiac muscle contraction relies on muscle cells uptaking calcium and contracting. Muscle contraction is in no way linked to glycosaminoglycans. **Peristalsis** is the propulsion of food along the digestive tract via smooth muscle contraction. Thus the correct answer choice is D. Because proteoglycans are involved in cell-to-cell adhesion, high amounts of *hyaluron* would be needed in wound healing.

291. **D is correct.** FYI: Every cell on the MCAT has a cellular membrane, ribosomes (for protein synthesis), and genetic material. The first line of the first passage states that gram-negative bacteria have an internal membrane… and often (not always) a polysaccharide-based capsule. The correct answer is D. Bacterial genome is composed of naked DNA and is often referred to as the **bacterial nucleoid.** Unlike the eukaryotic cellular nucleus, the bacterial nucleoid has no nuclear envelope or nucleolus.

292. **D is correct. This is important:** Steroid hormones (i.e., aldosterone, testosterone) DO NOT bind to cell membrane receptors. Steroids are lipid soluble and therefore can enter the cell directly by simple diffusion. Thus, answer choice C is incorrect. Answer choice B is incorrect as well: bacteriophages DO NOT attack animal cells (only bacterial cells, hence the term bacteriophage). According to the passage, proteoglycans do trap water, but they are *extra*cellular compounds (outside of the cell) and do not serve to dehydrate the cell. Moreover, no cell would need to dehydrate itself. Therefore, by the process of elimination, answer choice D is correct. Proteoglycans are used in cell-to-cell adhesion. The pas-

sage hints at this by informing that GAG compounds are involved in surface protein binding.

293. **A is correct.** The passage states that heparan sulfate gives GAGs a negative charge at physiologic pH. A negative charge barrier would prevent the filtration of negatively charged ions. The correct answer choice is A. The renal filtration membrane (barrier) consists of slits to prevent filtration of large substances such as red blood cells. These filtration slits, not the negatively charged barrier, prevent the unwanted filtration of neutral and needed substances such as platelets.

Passage 309 (Questions 294-300)

294. **B is correct. This is a High Yield MCAT question.** The four most common and characteristic bacterial shapes you must be aware of for the MCAT are: 1) **cocci** (spherical), 2) **bacilli** (rods), 3) **vibrio** (shaped like a comma) and 4) **spiral.**

295. **B is correct. This is a High Yield MCAT topic.** Bacterial conjugation is the transfer of DNA to a recipient cell through a pilus (bridge). The donor replicates its chromosome and injects the newly made copy into the recipient. If and when the pilus breaks the gene transfer stops. Transduction involves DNA being accidentally packaged into newly synthesized viruses. When the virus infects its next target DNA transfer may occur. Transformation occurs when bacteria are induced to pick up small pieces of circular DNA from a medium or the environment. Answer choices A, C, and D are all caused by genetic recombination via conjugation, transformation, or transduction. The only reason for a cell to have cellular DNAases is to degrade incoming DNA. Answer choice B is incorrect based on the fact that at one point all cells in a colony have the potential to be F^+ males; that is impossible.

296. **C is correct.** Inclusions function as storage sites for energy or as reservoirs for structural building blocks (i.e., amino acids). A flagellum is a long appendage capable of rotation and responsible for cellular motility. A plasmid is a small piece of bacterial DNA outside the main cellular genome. Fimbriae are straighter, thinner, and shorter than flagella. They enable adhesion of bacterial cells to tissue surfaces, and thereby promote colonization and invasion of those sites.

297. **C is correct.** Conjugation is a favorite MCAT topic. It involves the transfer of genetic information from one cell to the next. What happens after conjugation is anyone's guess. The newly acquired plasmid may transfer resistance to the recipient cell or the newly acquired plasmid may be completely incompatible with the recipient's genome and will be degraded or lost during subsequent cellular replications. The correct answer

choice is C because conjugation does not guarantee plasmid compatibility. Conjugation, however, requires cell-to-cell contact (pilus formation) and DNA transfer is unidirectional (from F^+ to F^- cell types only). According to the passage, conjugation is used to predict the location of the origin of replication and a helicase is used to unwind DNA at the origin of replication.

298. **B is correct.** Genetic conservation serves to describe the newly synthesized piece of DNA as: 1) completely original or conservative, which occurs when the cell maintains a complete original copy of its DNA, passing on the newly synthesized DNA to the daughter cell or some other recipient; 2) half original/half newly synthesized or semiconservative, which occurs when the cell maintains genetic material that is half original and half newly synthesized. Conjugation is conservative because the donor (F^+) retains a complete original copy of the plasmid after the transfer is complete. DNA replication is semi-conservative (**a High Yield MCAT fact**) because following replication one-half of each new DNA molecule is original while the other half is newly synthesized.

299. **B is correct.** According to the passage, episomes (F') are NOT genome associated. Thus, answer choices A and D are eliminated. By definition, bacterial DNA has a *single* origin of replication. The passage hints at the answer to this question. The reader is informed that the efficient conjugation is due to the small length of the transferred DNA, which must cross before the pilus can break.

300. **D is correct.** According to the passage, F^+ is a male bacterium; it can be safely assumed that F^- bacterium must be a female. The correct answer is D. A wild-type category includes all species without a mutation, any mutation.

Independent Questions (Questions 301-310)

301. **A is correct.** The release of any neurotransmitter occurs at the axon terminal and requires the influx of Ca^{+2}. Sodium influx causes neuron depolarization. Potassium efflux determines the neuron resting membrane potential and may cause hyperpolarization. Gap junctions do NOT link neurons together nor are they involved in neurotransmitter release. FYI: Gap junctions are found in the heart.

302. **B is correct. This is a topic one should be comfortable with for the MCAT.** Passive transport is driven by the concentration gradient (from regions of greater concentration to regions of lesser concentration) and requires no ATP hydrolysis. Simple and facilitated diffusion are both examples of passive transport.

Active transport requires ATP hydrolysis and functions against the concentration gradient. *Primary active transport* consumes ATP directly (i.e., Na⁺/K⁺ pump). In *secondary active transport,* ATP consumption is used to create a concentration gradient, which is then used to co-transport compounds like glucose from the small intestine.

303. **C is correct.** The cell membrane is a mostly hydrophobic structure composed of phospholipids and proteins. Integral proteins, which span the entire thickness of the membrane, function as carriers and must form hydrophobic interactions with the surrounding membrane hydrophobic fatty acids. Membrane phospholipid phosphate groups are hydrophilic and interact well with polar compounds like water.

304. **B is correct. This is a High Yield MCAT topic.** A virus cannot grow, produce ATP, or reproduce apart from a living host cell. Hence it is an obligate intracellular parasite that invades living cells and uses a host's chemical machinery to keep itself alive. Viruses may contain either DNA or RNA as their genetic material.

305. **B is correct. These are High Yield MCAT facts:** Aldosterone is the only steroid hormone (cholesterol-derived) listed in the question stem and is produced by the adrenal gland. Thyroid hormone is amino acid, tyrosine, derived and regulates the basal metabolic rate. Thyroid hormone is produced by the thyroid gland. Insulin is a peptide hormone product of the pancreas and functions to reduce blood glucose levels after meals.

306. **C is correct.** Surfactant, a lipid compound, is secreted by lung pneumocytes to forms a layer over the alveolar surface. This layer reduces alveolar collapse by decreasing surface tension within the alveoli.

307. **D is correct.** Viral infection is highly specific for a selected target host or host tissue. However, in order for a viral infection to occur numerous innate and active defense mechanisms must be overcome, for example, physical barriers (i.e., skin), local temperature, pH, and non-specific body secretions. Furthermore, the host must be able to support a viral replication with ATP and necessary enzymes. If digestive enzymes and bile are lacking, any virus will be able to cause a GI system infection because tissue defense and therefore specificity is compromised.

308. **B is correct. This is a favorite topic of MCAT writers.** Glycolysis is an anaerobic process that takes place in the cytoplasm only. The Krebs cycle and the electron transport chain are both localized to the mitochondria only. Thus, by the process of elimination, the correct answer is B.

309. **D is correct.** This is a classic MCAT question that tests your understanding of basic cellular glucose metabolism. Glucose is oxidized during glycolysis into two molecules of pyruvate. Pyruvate can enter fermentation (during anaerobic conditions) or the TCA cycle (during aerobic conditions). According to the question stem, flu-

oroacetate inhibits the TCA cycle and indirectly the electron transport chain. Thus, pyruvate has no choice but to enter fermentation and produce lactic acid (in animal cells) or ethanol (in yeast); answer choice C is eliminated. The TCA cycle produces NADH and $FADH_2$, which are shuttled through the electron transport chain to produce ATP. The inhibition of the TCA cycle inhibits ATP production.

310. **D is correct.** Microtubules are organelles that 1) serve ascytoskeletal structural components, 2) are responsible for chromosome segregation during cell division, 3) take part in intracellular transport and organelle positioning, and 4) guide cellular movement via cilia and flagella. Actin is a thin microfilament, not a microtubule, that is part of the muscular contractile apparatus.

Passage 310 (Questions 311-317)

311. **C is correct.** According to the passage, fungal cells are eukaryotic—possessing a nucleus and internal organelles—and therefore are much larger than prokaryotic bacterial cells. **Fungi contain a *chitin* cell wall, while bacteria rely on peptidoglycan for cell wall synthesis.** Thus, answer choice B is eliminated. While some fungi can infect humans and cause disease (i.e., Athlete's foot, vaginal yeast infections), bacteria is a much more significant animal pathogen.

312. **B is correct.** According to the passage, temperature-dependent fungal growth time (X) vs. temperature (Y) relationship is steeper (therefore has a **greater slope**) than initially thought. It is also not quite so log-linear; choice D is eliminated. Answer choices A and C have nothing to do with the passage.

313. **D is correct.** According to the passage, fungal infections occur on outer body surfaces. Fungal infection can also occur on epithelial surfaces of lumenal structures, such as esophagus, GI tract, large intestine, etc. By the process of elimination, the correct answer choice must be D. Liver is not a lumenal surface structure but a glandular solid accessory organ.

314. **A is correct.** According to the passage, colony growth rate will double for each 4° C temperature increase. Therefore, 300 colonies at 10° F → 600 colonies at 14° F → 1,200 colonies at 18° F → 2,400 colonies at 22° F. Answer choice A is the closest number.

315. **B is correct.** This is an outside knowledge question. Only two bacterial species have the ability to form spores. (You are not concerned with which ones for the MCAT.) Be careful of extreme statements (i.e., All, Every, Always, Never, etc.) on the MCAT; never say never in science. **Spores form when nutrient supply is low or environmental conditions are harsh and can survive for thousands of years on minimal metabo-**

lism. Answer choice D is false because autoclave is the preferred method for eliminating spores, via pressurized steam.

316. **B is correct.** According to the passage, mold grows well at below room temperature (below 20-25° C). According to Table 1, only P. type B decreases its growth rate as the temperature increases above 20-25° C. Choices C and D are incorrect because yeast is not a mold. The passage provides no information regarding P. type C.

317. **D is correct.** Fungi are heterotrophic single-celled, multinucleated, or multicellular organisms (answer choice A is eliminated) that include yeasts, molds, and mushrooms. These organisms live as parasites, symbionts, or saprophytes. ***Fungi are not plants.*** Heterotrophs are organisms that obtain energy from an external carbon source (i.e., dead organic material). Autotrophs, on the other hand, do not require an external carbon source to make ATP. All animals, most bacteria, and fungi are heterotrophic.

Passage 311 (Questions 318-323)

318. **A is correct.** According to the passage, "animals developed from colonial protists after a division of labor among the cells…Next came a process that is unique… to all animals. Some of the cells folded inwards to produce a blastopore, which continued to fold inward until it formed a digestive tract." Thus, the digestive tract is unique to the animal kingdom. The correct answer choice is A. Answer choices B, C, and D are contradicted by the passage. The first line of the passage states that "the first fungi were multicellular organisms that developed from colonial protists independently of plants."

319. **C is correct. This is a High Yield MCAT fact:** members of the kingdom Protista are the simplest eukaryotes. This means that they have a nucleus, membrane-bound organelles (i.e., lysosomes), and 80S ribosomes. FYI: Prokaryotic cells have smaller, 70S, ribosomes.

320. **B is correct.** According to the passage, Mycorrhizal fungus "makes these nutrients available to the plant, and the plant nourishes the fungus in exchange." This by definition is an example of mutualism. Mutualism is an interaction between two organisms where both species benefit from the relationship. Symbiosis is an interaction between two organisms where at least one of the species benefits from the relationship. Commensalism is an interaction between two species in which only one species benefits and the other one is not affected. Parasitism results when one species benefits from the interaction while the other organism is harmed.

321. **C is correct.** The cell membrane is composed of phospholipids, protein, and cholesterol. Its functions include

1) regulation of cell-cell interaction, 2) maintenance of cellular structural integrity, and 3) ligand (i.e., hormone, neurotransmitter) recognition. Carbohydrate synthesis is an anabolic process that does not occur at the cell membrane.

322. **B is correct.** According to the passage, sponges of the phylum Porifera digested their food inside their cells. Lysosomes are intracellular organelles responsible for macromolecule digestion. Therefore, Porifera sponges must have had a high concentration of well-developed lysosomes in order to carry out intracellular digestion. Peroxisomes contain hydrogen peroxide and are involved in cellular detoxification. Endoplasmic reticulum synthesizes protein and steroids.

323. **A is correct.** According to the question stem, endoparasites live in the digestive tract; to simplify, the question is asking which of the listed organs are part the digestive system. The correct answer choice is A. The gall bladder is an accessory organ of the digestive system, along with the liver and the pancreas. FYI: The gall bladder stores and concentrates bile salts. The spleen is part of the cardiovascular system and functions to filter blood, eliminating invaders and old blood cells. The adrenal gland is part of the endocrine system and produces hormones such as cortisol and aldosterone. The trachea is part of the respiratory system and delivers oxygen to the lungs.

Independent Questions (Questions 324-332)

324. **D is correct.** The kidney secretes renin when blood volume is low. Renin cleaves angiotensinogen into angiotensin I. Angiotensin I is converted into angiotensin II by the angiotensin-converting enzyme (ACE). Angiotensin II stimulates the release of aldosterone from the adrenal cortex.

325. **C is correct.** According to the question stem, Giardiasis is a disease that presents with non-bloody diarrhea, abdominal pain, cramps, and weight loss. Let us focus on the diarrhea, which is a problem with what organ system? The correct answer choice is C, the digestive system. The digestive system is a tubular structure that begins at the mouth and ends with the anus. Diarrhea results when the digestive system fails to properly reabsorb water, causing fecal matter to become dilute and watery.

326. **B is correct.** The cell is the basic unit of life. Based on the organization of their cellular structures, all living cells can be divided into two groups: prokaryotic and eukaryotic. Animals, plants, fungi, protozoans, and algae all possess eukaryotic cell types. Only bacteria of the kingdom Monera have prokaryotic cell types.

327. **B is correct. Transcription** is the conversion of DNA

into RNA and occurs in the nucleus. **Reverse transcription** is the conversion of RNA into DNA. According to the question stem, activated T-cells are very effective at carrying out the reverse transcription reaction. As a result one expects a high rate of DNA synthesis from an RNA genome in activated T-cells when compared to resting T-cells. The correct answer choice is B. **Translation,** which occurs in the cytoplasm, is the conversion of RNA into protein. Answer choice D is describing reverse translation. Answer choice D is incorrect.

328. **B is correct.** According to the question stem, surfactant prefers and is capable of forming micelles. Micelle formation requires numerous hydrophobic interactions to occur and is designed to minimize exposure to hydrophilic surfaces. Thus, surfactant must be a lipid-based compound. By definition, most lipids are hydrophobic. The correct answer choice is B. FYI: micelle formation is a must during the absorption of dietary lipids by the small intestine. Lack of Micelle formation may result in lipid-soluble vitamin deficiency.

329. **B is correct.** The autonomic nervous system is composed of sympathetic and parasympathetic components. Both components rely on a 2-neuron motor pathway away from the spinal cord and a 2-neuron sensory pathway toward the spinal cord. The sympathetic nervous system has a short preganglionic neuron and a long postganglionic neuron. The parasympathetic nervous system has a long preganglionic neuron and a short postganglionic neuron. This information is a must know for the MCAT.

330. **D is correct.** The parasympathetic nervous system relies on acetylcholine as the neurotransmitter of choice to carry out its function. This information is of no help in answering this question. **However, it is very High Yield overall for the MCAT.** Parasympathetic nerves: 1) decrease the heart rate, 2) constrict the eye, and 3) stimulate salivation and overall digestion. Recall the feeling that one experiences after consuming a large meal...that is your parasympathetic system at work. Cortisol release by the adrenal gland is mediated by the pituitary gland via ACTH. Parasympathetics have no effect on the adrenal gland.

331. **D is correct.** According to the question stem, a prion infection (England's mad cow disease) does NOT generate an immune response. So pick the only non-immune cell listed, the red blood cell. Red blood cells deliver oxygen to peripheral organs. The correct answer choice is D. T-cells are produced by the bone marrow, mature in the thymus, and generate a cell-mediated immune response. Macrophages are phagocytic cells that are part of innate (non-specific) immunity. Plasma cells are mature B-cells converted to produce antibodies. B-cells are made in the bone marrow and are part of the humoral immune response.

332. A is correct. According to the question stem, insulin is a peptide. A peptide is a collection of amino acid residues linked via peptide or amide bonds. Thus, in order to degrade insulin one would need to break a few peptide bonds. Peptide bonds are broken via hydrolysis, otherwise known as the addition of an H_2O molecule. Dehydration is a loss of water molecules and occurs during peptide synthesis. Evaporation is defined as the conversion from a liquid to a gas phase and does not apply to protein degradation. Esterification is the synthesis of an ester bond; the correct answer must be an example of bond degradation, not synthesis.

LECTURE 4

400

Answers & Explanations
Questions 333–445

ANSWERS TO LECTURE 4

333.	B	371.	C	409.	A
334.	A	372.	B	410.	B
335.	C	373.	D	411.	A
336.	C	374.	B	412.	B
337.	B	375.	D	413.	D
338.	C	376.	C	414.	C
339.	D	377.	B	415.	B
340.	B	378.	D	416.	B
341.	B	379.	A	417.	C
342.	C	380.	B	418.	C
343.	A	381.	C	419.	B
344.	C	382.	B	420.	C
345.	D	383.	C	421.	A
346.	C	384.	A	422.	A
347.	D	385.	D	423.	C
348.	A	386.	B	424.	B
349.	B	387.	A	425.	D
350.	C	388.	B	426.	A
351.	A	389.	A	427.	C
352.	B	390.	C	428.	A
353.	B	391.	A	429.	D
354.	A	392.	C	430.	D
355.	D	393.	B	431.	B
356.	C	394.	C	432.	C
357.	C	395.	B	433.	C
358.	C	396.	D	434.	D
359.	A	397.	C	435.	C
360.	B	398.	C	436.	D
361.	D	399.	B	437.	C
362.	D	400.	B	438.	D
363.	D	401.	D	439.	B
364.	C	402.	A	440.	A
365.	D	403.	A	441.	D
366.	B	404.	B	442.	B
367.	B	405.	A	443.	C
368.	B	406.	C	444.	B
369.	C	407.	C	445.	B
370.	C	408.	D		

Passage 401 (Questions 333-339)

333. B is correct. The answer to the question lies in the 3rd paragraph. According to the passage, *radial spokes* connect the central core microtubule doublet to nine peripheral doublets. Answer choice D can be eliminated because radial spokes do not stabilize peripheral doublets. Peripheral doublets possess nexin arms, which link and hold microtubule columns together. Answer choice B is correct. *Dynein* (kinesin is a type of dynein) is an ATPase and according to the passage has nothing to do with microtubule stability.

334. A is correct. According to the question stem, *nocadazol* binds tubulin and thus completely blocks microtubule formation. This would most likely result in a lack of tubulin polymerization and ultimately microtubule destabilization. However, the best approach to answer this question is via the process of elimination. Cilium synthesis requires microtubule polymerization. As a result cilium synthesis would NOT occur in a patient following a *nocadazol* injection. Dynein ATPase and nexin structure/function will not be affected by inhibited microtubule polymerization because these peptides rest on microtubules but are not made of tubulin.

335. C is correct. Sperm use flagella to propel themselves. Drugs that inhibit flagellar activity will cause sterility in males. According to Table 1, drug C is optimal for cilia inhibition with limited flagellar paralysis. Drug A is more efficient at ciliary paralysis but severely cripples flagellar function as well. Thus, answer choice A is eliminated. Note that 1=highly efficient and 5=least efficient.

336. C is correct. According to the passage, **the cell propels in the direction perpendicular to cilia and parallel to flagella's beating patterns.** The question stem informs that the organism is heading north. Therefore, cilia are expected to point in a direction perpendicular to the north, that being either east or west. Flagella, on the other hand, must be parallel to the north axis. Since flagella are located in rear of the cell, they are facing south to create propulsion north. Answer choice C is correct.

337. B is correct. According to the passage, dynein requires Mg^{+2} and ATP to function. Thus, answer choices C and D are eliminated. It is implied that dynein requires an ion of divalent oxidation state (i.e., Ca^{+2}) to function. The correct answer choice must be B.

338. C is correct. This is a High Yield MCAT fact. Water, accounting for roughly 75% of total body weight, is the most abundant compound in the human body and its cells.

339. D is correct. Charcot-Marie-Tooth disease (CMT) is a degenerative peripheral nerve disorder, which affects kinesin, a protein similar to dynein (this information was presented in the question stem). CMT patients therefore suffer from microtubule paralysis, which leads to nerve degeneration and causes muscle weakness and atrophy. Answer choices A, B, and C have nothing to do with microtubule function and/or paralysis.

Passage 402 (Questions 340-346)

340. B is correct. Macrophages are cells that search and ingest (phagocytize) invaders as part of the non-specific immune response. After macrophages complete their meal they inform local T lymphocytes (T-cells) of a possible infection. **T-cells**, mature in the thymus, serve to recognize surface markers on bacterial cells and label them for destruction. T-cells, however, do not physically engulf foreign invaders. **Liver cells** are not involved in phagocytosis; however, a population of liver macrophages known as Kupffer cells protects the organ from invaders.

341. B is correct. This is a difficult question that is best answered using the information in the passage and process of elimination. According to the passage (3rd paragraph), hydrolases are active at an acidic pH created by the endosomal H$^+$ ATPases. A high intracellular concentration of H$^+$ causes an acidic pH (below 7). Because the cytoplasm of any cell has a pH of about 7.2, accidental rupture of a lysosome can cause spillage of hydrolases, but they will become inactivated in the higher pH without causing any damage to the cell. This is nature's protective mechanism.

342. C is correct. This is a High Yield MCAT fact: glycolysis is an anaerobic process and it occurs in the cytoplasm. For this reason one expects to find glycolytic enzymes in the cytoplasm. The **Krebs cycle** occurs in the mitochondria. It is an aerobic process that produces reduced substrates for the electron transport chain. Thus, answer choice B can be eliminated. Mammalian eukaryotic cells lack a cell wall and therefore do not need enzymes for its synthesis. **RNA polymerase** functions in transcription and is housed in the nucleus, not the cytoplasm.

343. A is correct. Lysosomes are responsible for the digestion of material in food vacuoles and the dissolution of bacterial particles that enter. A phagosome containing bacteria fuses with a late lysosome to produce a phagolysosome. Lysosomes also take part in cellular auto-death (also known as apoptosis) and *autophagy*, whereby lysosomes engulf and digest damaged or old intracellular organelles. According to the passage, lysosomes receive products of receptor-mediated endocytosis.

344. C is correct. According to the passage, lysosomal storage diseases cause lysosomes to increase in size and number. The correct answer choice is C. Answer choice

A is eliminated based on information provided in Table 1: hexosaminidase A is deficient in Tay-Sachs, not glucocerebrosidase. Lysosomal storage diseases have nothing to do with the rough ER. FYI: The rough ER is an organelle responsible for protein synthesis.

345. D is correct. Based on Table 1, *L-iduronosulfate sulfatase* and *L-iduronidase* must be enzymes involved in the same metabolic pathway since mutation of either one leads to the buildup of the same product, heparan, and dermatan sulfate.

346. C is correct. According to the passage, peroxisomes detoxify the body of hydrogen peroxide (H_2O_2) and other metabolites. **This is a High Yield MCAT fact:** the liver detoxifies by extracting and excreting many harmful materials (i.e., hormones, toxins, hemoglobin, etc.) from the blood. Liver also regulates blood sugar, lipids, and amino acids; forms cholesterol, and serves as a site for blood and vitamin storage. Pancreas is an exocrine/endocrine organ that synthesize digestive enzymes and hormones that control blood glucose concentration.

Passage 403 (Questions 347-353)

347. D is correct. According to the passage, ion gradients, open "leaky" potassium channels, and the action of the sodium/potassium ATPase all set up the resting membrane potential. The number of channels and their open/closed status will most certainly contribute and affect the resting membrane potential.

348. A is correct. A neuron will be used to describe the answer to this question but the stated concepts apply to all cells. A neuron cell can exist in one of two phases, *resting* (also known as polarized or hyperpolarized) and *depolarized*. The next important piece of information is that sodium channels are ALWAYS closed unless the cell is being depolarized. "At rest, leaky potassium channels display the greatest permeability and consequently determine the resting membrane potential."

During the *resting phase,* a negative resting membrane potential is established with closed Na^+ and Cl^- channels and open ("leaky") K^+ channels. During *depolarization,* Na^+ channels open rapidly to make the cell membrane potential less negative.

349. B is correct. This is a High Yield MCAT fact: *facilitated transport* is similar to simple diffusion in the sense that it allows ions (K^+) and other hydrophilic molecules to cross the cell membrane down the concentration gradient and without ATP expenditure. *Active transport* requires the use of ATP to force ions or small hydrophilic molecules against their concentration gradient. According to the passage, an existing concentration gra-

dient powers K^+ ions through "leaky" membrane channels to establish the resting membrane potential. Simple diffusion does NOT rely on channels to transport molecules down the concentration gradient.

350. C is correct. This is a difficult question. According to Table 1, normal extracellular K^+ concentration is very low. According to the question stem, in a patient with hyperkalemia the extracellular concentration of K^+ is significantly increased. This will prevent K^+, and therefore (+) charge, from leaking out of the cell. Why can't K^+ leak out? Because the K^+ concentration gradient has been decreased and there is nothing powering the flow of ions. Potassium will remain in the cell, making the cell interior more positive, which lowers the action potential threshold.

For example, a cell has a resting membrane potential of -70mV, with a -30mV threshold for an action potential. If the cell interior has a buildup of (+) charge the resting membrane potential moves from -70 mV to -55mV and closer to the threshold. The closer the cell is to the threshold the easier it is to stimulate an action potential.

351. A is correct. According to Table 1, the intracellular compartment has the lower pH. Recall, low pH is associated with a high $[H^+]$ concentration.

352. B is correct. According to the passage, "potassium channels display the greatest permeability and consequently determine the resting membrane potential."

353. B is correct. Let's use the process of elimination. According to the passage, Na^+ channels must swing open to function and therefore must be gated. Ca^{+2} and Cl^- channels are also gated. The correct answer choice is B. "Leaky" (ungated) potassium channels determine the resting membrane potential and should be present at a greater concentration compared to all other channel types.

Independent Questions (Questions 354-363)

354. A is correct. Parasympathetic nervous system uses *only acetylcholine* as the neurotransmitter of choice. This is a **High Yield MCAT fact.** The sympathetic nervous system relies on *norepinephrine* for communication across the synaptic cleft. Glutamate is a central nervous system neurotransmitter (no need to memorize). **Gastrin** is a hormone produced by the stomach that stimulates the release of HCl.

355. D is correct. Almost every cell in the human body relies on sodium channels to maintain osmotic gradients to prevent lysis. Read the question stem carefully. The reader is being asked to select a NON-excitable cell from the answer choices. Nerve, skeletal, cardiac, and smooth muscle cells are all examples of Na^+ dependent excitable cells. These cells are excitable because when sodium enters they become *depolarized*. Epithelial cells line all lumenal structures (i.e., blood vessels, GI tract, excretory system, etc.) in the human body. They are NON-excitable because they are not able to depolarize.

356. **C is correct.** This is an outside knowledge question. A group of similar cells united to perform a specific function, which is essential to life, make up a **body tissue** (i.e., muscle tissue). An **organ** (i.e., liver) is a collection of several tissues, one of which predominates, and determines the primary organ function. For example, the liver is made up of vascular tissue (blood vessels), lymphatic tissue, etc. A group of organs constitute an organ system (i.e., the digestive system).

357. **C is correct. This question is a popular one on the MCAT.** It is best to answer via the process of elimination. **Cilia** occur in large numbers and line the small intestine, lungs, and the fallopian tubes to help move and absorb nutrients, move and bring up mucus, and propel ova and semen, respectively.

Sperm rely on a flagellum for movement. Males who produce sperm with a paralyzed flagellum may be sterile. The urinary tract does not have surface structures (i.e., cilia), which would impede the flow of urine.

Review: Cilia-Covered Surfaces

- trachea and bronchi of the respiratory tract
- the lumen of the small intestine
- the fallopian tubes

358. **C is correct. This is a tough question, best answered via the process of elimination.** To start, pretend you cut your finger and are currently experiencing pain. Now let's go through the list of answer choices: *Mechanoreceptors* sense touch—mechanical pressure on skin. *Thermoreceptors* sense changes in temperature— hot/cold. *Chemoreceptors* are used to distinguish taste and smell—odorous (chemical) particles bind nasal receptors and cause action potentials to occur. Therefore, nociceptors must be used to sense pain.

359. **A is correct. Obligate anaerobes** are absolutely unable to grow in oxygen. For example, the old fashioned treatment for gangrene, a disease caused by an obligate anaerobe, was to flush the wound with oxygen. Most organisms are **facultative anaerobes** and are capable of growth in the presence or absence of oxygen. They have metabolic machinery for both conditions. **Microaerophilic organisms** (-philic means loving) require low levels of oxygen. They derive their energy solely from reactions that occur without oxygen, but some of their intermediate metabolic steps may require it. **Obligate aerobes** must have oxygen to survive.

360. **B is correct.** According to the question stem, cardiac purkinje fibers have large diameters and short axons.

Conduction velocity directly correlates with the diameter and inversely correlates with the length. A large diameter means more space for the action potential to maneuver in. An increase in the diameter and/or decrease in axon length cause an increase in the conduction velocity.

Cardiac purkinje cell conduction must be fast and Na^+ channel dependent. Conduction is always channel dependent.

361. **D is correct.** Neurotransmitters act on postsynaptic receptors to change the membrane potential. This change can be either 1) a direct depolarization, which causes an action potential, 2) a direct hyperpolarization, which prevents an action potential, or 3) the activation of a second messenger that eventually leads to changes in the neuron firing rate. Why a second messenger? Remember, protein neurotransmitters are hydrophilic and cannot freely diffuse across the cell membrane. They require a second messenger (i.e., cAMP) to get their signal from the cell membrane to the nucleus.

362. **D is correct.** According to the question stem, *B. fragilis'* capsule inhibits phagocytosis. What immune system cell engulfs invaders? The correct answer choice is D. **Macrophages** are non-specific immune system cells involved in phagocytosis of foreign matter. **Platelets** are produced by the bone marrow and are part of the clotting cascade. **T-cells** are part of the cell-mediated immune response but do NOT phagocytize other cells. T-cells "mark" invaders for destruction by macrophages.

363. **D is correct. This is a High Yield MCAT topic.** The **central nervous system** consists of the brain and the spinal cord. The **peripheral nervous system** is composed of the somatic and autonomic nervous systems. The **autonomic nervous system** is involuntary and divides into sympathetic and parasympathetic components. The **somatic nervous system** is voluntary and moves all skeletal musculature. Move your arm. That is the somatic nervous system at work.

Passage 404 (Questions 364-370)

364. **C is correct.** According to the question stem, gray matter is composed of unmyelinated nervous system structures. The white matter, on the other hand, is composed of myelinated elements (myelin itself is whitish in color). The passage states that axons are myelinated and axon terminals and dendrites are not. FYI: The central nervous system axons are myelinated by oligodendrocytes. Axons of the peripheral nervous system are myelinated by Schwann cells.

365. **D is correct.** The passage indicates that muscarinic receptors predominate at higher levels of the central nervous system, for example, the cerebral cortex,

medulla, or cerebellum. Answer choices A and B are all part of the autonomic peripheral nervous system. As per passage, cholinergic neurons function as part of the parasympathetic (not sympathetic) nervous system. Answer choice C is incorrect.

366. **B is correct.** According to the question stem, GABA is an inhibitory neurotransmitter. Hyperpolarization moves the cell away from the depolarization threshold, making it difficult to stimulate an action potential. Any neurotransmitter that hyperpolarizes the cell would cause an inhibitory effect on the CNS. A depolarized cell, on the other hand, is excited, and anything that causes depolarization of the cell would be a excitatory neurotransmitter.

367. **B is correct. This is important for the MCAT:** the greatest concentration of sodium channels is found at the nodes of Ranvier. The axon terminal is full of calcium channels needed to release neurotransmitters into the synaptic cleft. The rough ER is an organelle responsible for protein synthesis and does not have any membrane channels. The best way to answer this question is through the process of elimination.

368. **B is correct. This is a High Yield MCAT topic.** The sympathetic nervous system utilizes norepinephrine as the neurotransmitter of choice. Release of norepinephrine during the "flight or fight" response increases the heart rate, raises blood glucose, raises blood pressure, dilates the pupils, opens up the trachea and bronchi, and shunts blood away from the GI tract to skeletal muscles, brain, and heart. All of these responses prepare the body to "defend" itself by heightening visual, muscular, and cardiovascular activity while inhibiting digestive and "rest" functions.

369. **C is correct. This is High Yield MCAT information:** resistance is inversely proportional to the radius. As the radius decreases, resistance increases, not proportionally, but exponentially (to the fourth power). This means that even a small decrease in radius can have significant effects in terms of increasing the resistance of that conduit, thus slowing the action potential down. A high resistance makes it difficult for an action potential to spread. Myelination, on the other hand, makes it easier to conduct APs because there is less leakage of the AP through the axon itself. According to the passage, dendrites are both thinner than axons and never myelinated, thereby having the slowest rate of AP conduction.

370. **C is correct.** According to the passage, there are two types of cholinergic receptors: nicotinic and muscarinic. Cholinergic receptors bind acetylcholine (ACh) and are part of the parasympathetic nervous system - answer choice A is eliminated. Muscarinic receptors predominate at higher levels of the central nervous system (i.e. brain), while nicotinic receptors are concentrated in the peripheral postganglionic neurons. Beta-adrenergic receptors do not bind ACh and are not mentioned in the passage. Answer choice B must be incorrect.

Passage 405 (Questions 371-377)

371. **C is correct.** According to the passage, uncoupling agents are amphipathic weak acids. The answer must therefore be a weak acid. NaOH is the strong base, eliminating choice B. H_2SO_4 and HCl are strong acids that, by definition, completely dissociate in solution. Carbonic acid, H_2CO_3, is a weak acid used to buffer the pH of blood. By definition, a weak acid does NOT completely dissociate in solution.

372. **B is correct.** According to the passage, cyanide completely inhibits oxidative phosphorylation and therefore halts ATP synthesis. Answer choice C is incorrect. Oxygen serves as a final electron acceptor in the electron transport chain. The consumption of oxygen is decreased when oxidative phosphorylation is inhibited. Answer choice A is eliminated. When oxidative phosphorylation ATP synthesis is decreased, the body will attempt to increase ATP synthesis by stimulating the rate of glycolysis. FYI: Glycolysis synthesizes a net of 2 ATP per 1 glucose molecule.

373. **D is correct.** According to the passage, uncoupling agents accumulate in the membrane and dissolve the transmembrane proton gradient, preventing ATP synthesis. Uncouplers must be hydrophobic based on the ease with which they diffuse across the mitochondrial membrane. The correct answer choice is D. Uncouplers promote proton transport, not inhibit it. They do not inhibit ATP synthase or the ETC. Uncouplers do not directly inhibit ATP synthesis like cyanide does. They simply decrease the hydrogen ion concentration gradient needed to feed the ATP-synthase.

374. **B is correct.** According to the passage, the chemiosmotic theory describes how oxygen consumption allows for the generation of the intermembrane hydrogen ion gradient. H^+ ions are pumped into the mitochondrial intermembrane space, producing a 1) pH and 2) electrical potential gradient (positive charges in the intermembrane space and negative charges in the mitochondrial matrix). **This is High Yield information for the MCAT:** the intermembrane space is more acidic (because of the increased H^+ ions) and has a higher concentration of positive charge compared to the mitochondrial matrix. Glycolysis and the Krebs cycle supply reduced substrates (NADH and $FADH_2$) to the electron transport chain, but this is not a component of Mitchell's theory.

375. **D is correct.** Boiling point is reached when the vapor pressure of a solution is equal to the atmospheric pressure. The higher the vapor pressure, the easier it is for a liquid to evaporate; the higher the vapor pressure, the lower the boiling point. According to Table 1, hydrogen cyanide (AC) has a lower vapor pressure and a higher boiling point than cyanogen chloride (CK). Answer choice B is eliminated. CK undergoes complete solubility at a lower temperature, thus eliminating answer

choice A. CK has a higher digit of volatility and is therefore more reactive and hazardous in comparison to hydrogen cyanide. FYI: Distillation is a method of separating compounds based on difference in boiling points. cyanogen chloride and hydrogen cyanide display drastically different boiling points and therefore can be separated by distillation.

376. **C is correct.** The retina of the eye has a high rate of oxidative metabolism because it requires high levels of ATP to function. A lack of ATP will result in blindness. According to the passage, 2,4-dinitrophenol pokes holes in the mitochondrial membrane, disrupting H^+ gradient and decreasing ATP synthesis. Overabundance of ATP is never a problem. Answer choices B and D are incorrect because data to support these statements is lacking.

377. **B is correct.** According to the passage, uncouplers increase body temperature; therefore, an overdose of uncouplers would result in fever. Although aspirin prevents blood clotting and may lead to gastric and duodenal ulcers with chronic use, these facts are not relevant to the fact that aspirin is a mild uncoupler. It is stated in the passage that uncouplers decrease intermembrane acidity by disrupting H^+ gradient. Therefore answer choice D is incorrect.

Passage 406 (Questions 378-383)

378. **D is correct.** This is an outside knowledge question. Many, many microorganisms normally live on or in the human body. Most are non-disease causing (non-pathogenic) and are known as the normal flora. The normal flora is of benefit to humans by aiding in digestion and because by their mere presence they crowd out potential invaders that can cause infection. Disease causers are also present on the human body and are kept in check by the immune system. When the immune system weakens these pathogenic organism grow out of control and cause disease.

379. **A is correct.** Mitosis is a reproductive method that produces 2 offsprings identical to the parent cell. Anti-mitotic agents inhibit mitosis and have the greatest effect on rapidly dividing cells. Strain A pathogen will be devastated by an anti-mitotic agent in comparison to other less division oriented strains.

Anti-cancer drugs rely on this principle to inhibit neoplastic growth while attempting to spare normal cells.

380. **B is correct.** Toxoplasmosis is a disease found in cats and is caused by a parasitic protozoan, Toxoplasma gondii. The best way to answer this question is through the process of elimination. When was the last time you saw elephants and snakes in major U.S. cities? These are rare exotic animal that are found in the plains of Africa. Trees are not animals.

381. **C is correct.** Eliminating the host would prevent the spread of disease. However, such measures are not an option when fighting a disease that attacks humans, for example. Answer choice D is incorrect. Vaccinating against the parasite, eliminating the tick that spreads the parasite, and using an anti-tick repellant are all reasonable methods to prevent the spread of a disease.

382. **B is correct.** If the parasite infects a host and the host dies without spreading the disease the parasite dies as well. This is the struggle for survival faced by the 3 strains described in the passage. According to the passage, "death of the host is unimportant…to a highly virulent parasite…" Why? The most virulent strain (strain A) wins by reproducing rapidly and passing the most genes to new hosts. By similar reasoning, strain C wins when the transmission is difficult, requiring live, mobile hosts who can serve as vectors as long as possible. A situation with most hosts being immune to the disease favors strain C. An established reservoir (i.e., open sewer) allows for easy spread favoring strain A. A situation when all hosts are infected does not favor anyone: both the host and the parasite will become extinct.

383. **C is correct.** The passage hints at the definition of a vector: any agent that carries and transmits a disease. Accroding to Diagram 1, mosquitos are vectors of plasmodium. Humans are the hosts.

Independent Questions (Questions 384-393)

384. **A is correct. This is High Yield MCAT information.** What is oxidative phosphorylation? It is another name for the electron transport chain (ETC) and the ATP-synthase that is located in the inner mitochondrial membrane. The ETC accepts 2 reduced substrates, NADH and $FADH_2$. NAD^+ is an oxidized molecule that does not serve as a substrate for ETC. (NAD^+ is a substrate for glycolysis and the Krebs cycle.) ATP is a product of oxidative phosphorylation. Glucose is a substrate for glycolysis. Where does glycolysis take place? In the cell cytoplasm.

385. **D is correct.** The question stem informs that *tubulin* is a globular heterodimer, meaning that it is composed of 2 different peptide chains. **This is a High Yield MCAT topic.** *Quaternary protein structure* is formed when two or more polypeptide chains make up a protein. Proteins composed of identical polypeptide chains are termed as *homodimers*, while those containing different chains are known as *heterodimers*.

386. B is correct. Peroxisomes are organelles involved in cellular detoxification and lipid breakdown. They form and degrade hydrogen peroxide, a compound needed to destroy infectious agents like bacteria. *Catalase* is mainly found in the peroxisomes. Lysosomes are full of digestive enzymes used to degrade macromolecules.

387. A is correct. This is a must know for the MCAT. Ca^{+2} binds **troponin C**, causing **tropomyosin** to shift, which allows the actin-myosin interaction to occur. **Myosin** (thick filament) has a high affinity for **actin** (thin filament). When myosin binds actin the muscle cell contracts.

Blood calcium levels are tightly regulated via parathyroid hormone (which raises calcium levels) and calcitonin (which lowers calcium levels).

388. B is correct. To answer this question one must select the only structure that is not a part of the respiratory tract. The respiratory tract begins with the **trachea**, which divides into **two main bronchi**. The main bronchi further subdivide into **bronchioles**, which eventually lead to **alveoli**. The **esophagus** is part of the digestive tract and leads to the stomach.

389. A is correct. Nodes of Ranvier are gaps along the length of the axon, formed *between* myelin-producing Schwann cells—answer choice D is eliminated. The myelin sheath speeds up the action potential transmission from the cell body to the axon terminal. Electrical impulses regenerate and "jump" from one node to the next; this is known as *saltatory conduction*. Acetylcholine receptors are located on the dendrite of a postsynaptic neuron.

390. C is correct. According to the question stem, apoptosis is cell death. Apoptotic programmed cell death occurs during 1) development and 2) aging. The formation of fingers in a fetus, synaptic cleft development, and tadpole tail resorption are all examples of developmental apoptosis. The synthesis of the uterine lining is an anabolic process that requires mitosis, not cell death. The correct answer choice must be C.

391. A is correct. This is a high yield MCAT fact. Schwann cells produce myelin in the peripheral nervous system. Myelin acts as an insulator around the nerve axon and speeds up the conduction of an action potential. Hepatocytes (liver cells) and leukocytes (immune system cells) do not produce myelin. Lymphatic system fluid (lymph) carries lipids and plays a role in the immune response to infection.

392. C is correct. Microtubules, intermediate filaments, and microfilaments are 3 non-membrane bound organelles. **FYI:** The 4th non-membrane bound organelle is a ribosome. **Microtubules** are hollow protein tubes made of *tubulin*. Microtubules are a must for 1) the formation of the **spindle apparatus** that separates chromosomes during cell division, 2) the synthesis of cilia and flagella, 3) the formation of a sturdy cytoskeleton. Myosin and actin

are found in muscle cells and are microfilament, not microtubules.

393. B is correct. The immune system can be subdivided into 2 major components, non-specific (innate) and acquired immunity. The **non-specific immune system** consists of barrier (i.e., skin, mucous membranes) and cells that non-specifically remove invaders (i.e., macrophages, neutrophils, etc.). The **acquired immune system** synthesizes cells directed against a *specific* invader. It has the capacity to remember past infections and responds rapidly in case of recurrence. The non-specific system does not have this ability and always responds in the same way to every infection.

T and B-cells make up the acquired immunity system, which has humoral and cell-mediated divisions. According to the question stem, the acquired immunodeficiency syndrome (AIDS) infects and kills T-cells, resulting in a loss of **cell-mediated immunity**. The destruction of B-cells would cause a loss of **humoral immunity**.

Passage 407 (Questions 394-399)

394. C is correct. The synthesis and movement of secretory proteins through the cell follows the following sequence: protein synthesis by the rough ER → transition vesicle → Golgi apparatus for packaging → exocytosis. RNA leaves the nucleus to direct protein synthesis. Smooth ER is responsible for lipid (steroid synthesis) and cell detoxification. Therefore, lipid-producing cells display large concentrations of smooth ER.

395. B is correct. The resting membrane potential is the voltage across the cell membrane when the cell is not being stimulated: a typical cell has a resting membrane potential of –70mV. Ions, K^+ and Na^+, determine the resting cell membrane potential.

Glucose is a neutral compound and has nothing to do with the resting membrane potential. FYI: Influx of sodium causes cellular depolarization and efflux of potassium causes hyperpolarization.

396. D is correct. The Na^+ / K^+ pump transfers 3 Na^+ ions out of cell for every 2 K^+ ions into the cell. This causes a negative charge buildup across the cell membrane (sets up the resting membrane potential of –70 mV) and maintains the resting membrane potential. Roughly 35% of all cellular ATP is consumed by the Na^+ / K^+ pump.

397. C is correct. Neurotransmitter exocytosis is an active process that requires a great deal of ATP to fuel plasma membrane vesicle fusion. High concentration of mitochondria, the location of cellular respiration, will be necessary to supply needed ATP. According to the passage, rough ER is found in the soma—answer choice A is eliminated. Smooth ER is involved in lipid synthesis and is also located in the soma. Lysosomes are digestion organelles.

398. C is correct. According to the passage, secretion set is the only signal transfer component to not display a change in the electric properties of the cell membrane. Answer choices A, B, and D all discuss changes in the electric properties of the cell membrane. Ca^{+2} influx is necessary for neurotransmitter release into the synaptic cleft. As a result, Ca^+ levels are very tightly monitored by the parathyroid gland.

399. B is correct. The sympathetic nervous system is responsible for the "fight or flight" response. Therefore, it causes pupil dilation (better vision), increased heart rate (to supply blood to muscle instead of the GI organs), etc. Blood flow to kidneys is also expected to decrease to supply muscle tissue instead. .

Passage 408 (Questions 400-405)

400. B is correct. The question is asking the reader to pick out a cell population that is continuously dividing. Cells of the skin, the tympanic membrane, and the GI tract are routinely exposed to the external environment and are in constant need of division to replace the damaged cell population. These types of cells are called labile. Two other cell types exist: stable and permanent. Stable cells (i.e., stem, pancreatic, and liver cells) are normally arrested in G_0 phase of the cell cycle but can re-enter cell division if properly stimulated or damaged. Permanent cells (i.e., nerve and cardiac cells) lose all mitotic activity during embryogenesis and are unable to divide even if damaged.

401. D is correct. According to the passage, tensor tympani and the stapedius insert onto the ossicles to protect the inner ear from extremely loud sounds: these 2 muscles only function during a loud explosion to protect the ear from damage. The tympanic membrane, external ear canal, malleus, incus, and stapes are all expected to function during every sound wave transmission, loud or not.

402. A is correct. This is important for the MCAT: an inward Na^+ current causes cellular depolarization. An outward K^+ current causes cellular hyperpolarization. This is always the case. If perilymph depolarizes the cell it must contain a high concentration of sodium.

403. A is correct. According to the passage, ossicles amplify the tympanic membrane vibrational force by twenty-fold. In order to do so, they must strike the oval window with increased force over a smaller surface area. FYI: Pressure = Force/Area. So let us review the process: 1) sound strikes the tympanic membrane, which begins to oscillate; 2) the mechanical energy of oscillation is amplified by the ossicles, which deliver a much more powerful input onto the oval window. The correct an-

swer choice is A. Increasing the surface area would result in a decrease in pressure. Answer choice B is therefore incorrect. One last thing; ossicles can inhibit the oscillation of the tympanic membrane to protect the nervous system from loud noises but ossicles cannot increase the oscillation of the tympanic membrane.

404. B is correct. According to the passage, "sound energy is transformed through the oval window onto...the inner ear." The correct answer choice is B. It is stated in the passage that sound enters the external ear canal and travels to the tympanic membrane, a structure that marks the beginning of the middle ear compartment. Answer choices A and D can be eliminated.

405. A is correct. A pure mechanical energy transfer occurs through the oval window. This information is obtained from the passage: when the membrane vibrates in response to sound (mechanical energy), the malleus oscillates in concert (mechanical energy). The stapes inserts into the oval window, which delivers sound vibrations to the fluid-filled inner ear (mechanical energy).

Passage 409 (Questions 406-412)

406. C is correct. So what is myasthenia gravis (MG)? It is a disease that decreases the number of receptors available to bind acetylcholine. Because acetylcholine stimulates the contraction of voluntary muscles, individuals diagnosed with MG experience paralysis. While there is no cure for myasthenia gravis, there are a number of treatments: 1) increasing acetylcholine production and release, 2) preventing postsynaptic acetylcholine receptor destruction (this effectively controls symptoms in most people). Anti-cholinesterase medications prolong the effect of acetylcholine in the synaptic cleft and as a result increase muscle strength. Furthermore, preventing autoantibody receptor destruction and/or endocytosis will further decrease disease symptoms. The correct answer choice must be C.

407. C is correct. T-tubules are invaginations of the plasma membrane that are only found in striated muscle (skeletal and cardiac). Depolarization of the T-tubule membrane triggers the release of calcium from the sarcoplasmic reticulum and eventually muscle contraction.

Summary:

Muscle Type	Properties
Skeletal	voluntary, *striated,* with T-tubules
Cardiac	involuntary, *striated*, with T-tubules, are auto-stimulatory
Smooth	involuntary, *non-striated*, with myosin light chain kinase, without T-tubules

408. D is correct. The parasympathetic nervous system uses only acetylcholine as the neurotransmitter of choice. **This is a High Yield MCAT fact.** The sympathetic nervous system relies on norepinephrine to move information across the synaptic cleft. Release of norepinephrine shunts blood away from the skin and viscera to skeletal muscles and causes vasodilation. Sympathetic stimulation (involuntary) of the autonomic nervous system allows the body to deal with stress (the "fight or flight" response).

409. A is correct. According to the passage, myasthenia gravis (not a demyelination disease) is an acetylcholine receptor disease. MG patients display normal acetylcholine production and release (answer choices B and C are eliminated). Increasing the acetylcholine level in the synaptic cleft will not cause myasthenia gravis (MG) symptoms. However, inducing improper function of the postsynaptic nicotinic acetylcholine receptors is a possible way to induce MG in laboratory animals.

410. B is correct. The acquired immune system can be divided into 2 components: cell mediated and humoral. Cell mediated immunity is made up of T-cells that are produced in the bone marrow and mature in the thymus. Humoral immunity is made up of B-cells that are synthesized by the bone marrow. **This is a High Yield MCAT fact:** B-cells produce antibodies and/or autoantibodies that bind foreign surface receptors (antigens) to mark them for destruction by the immune system. *T-cells*, on the other hand, regulate the complex system of immune response and most component cells.

411. A is correct. According to the question stem, severity of MG skeletal muscle symptoms (answer choice D is incorrect) worsens as the day progresses. How long does it take you to get over a cold? Days, right? That is how long it takes the body to synthesize antibodies. Answer choice B is eliminated.

The passage mentions nothing regarding anticholinesterase side effects. If it is not mentioned it cannot be correct. MG symptoms must worsen after prolonged use of affected muscle tissue. The correct answer choice is A.

412. B is correct. Based on the information presented in Table 1, FXC-5 has T-tubules. Therefore, it must be either a skeletal (voluntary) or cardiac (involuntary) muscle cell. Smooth muscle cells are the only ones that lack T-tubules. Because FXC-5 can be either skeletal or cardiac, answer choices A, C, and D are eliminated. A hyperpolarized cell is more negative in comparison to the resting membrane potential.

Independent Questions (Questions 413-422)

413. D is correct. Smooth Muscle:

- involuntary
- without T-tubules
- without troponin and tropomyosin
- without striations
- unicellular

The contraction of smooth muscle cells is involuntary and occurs 1) in blood vessels to manipulate blood pressure, 2) in the gastrointestinal tract to propel food forward, and 3) in the bladder to excrete urine.

414. C is correct. The **liver** is the largest and most metabolically complex organ in the body. It detoxifies the organism by extracting and excreting many harmful materials (i.e., hormones, toxins, hemoglobin, etc.) from the blood. Liver also regulates blood sugar, lipids, and amino acids; forms cholesterol; and serves as a site for blood and vitamin storage. The **lysosome** is the stomach of the cell that digests all ingested components. The **Golgi apparatus** coupled with exocytosis excretes metabolic waste. The brain of the cell is the nucleus.

415. B is correct. This is a High Yield MCAT topic. The 4 phases of mitosis (prophase, metaphase, anaphase, and telophase) and cytokinesis divide a mother cell into 2 identical daughter cells. The condensed chromosomes are aligned along the equatorial plane in mitotic **metaphase**. This arrangement ensures that chromosomes are properly separated.

416. B is correct. This is a High Yield MCAT fact: cortisol is a glucocorticoid produced by the cortex of the adrenal gland. Secreted cortisol is not water-soluble and circulates bound to a protein. Cortisol a) increases blood glucose level, b) inhibits pituitary ACTH secretion via negative feedback, and c) suppresses the immune system.

417. C is correct. This is a High Yield MCAT topic. The bone marrow synthesizes two major classes of lymphocytes: B and T-cells. B-cells go on to mature in the bone marrow, while T-cells are relocated to the thymus to complete their development. Answer choice A is eliminated.

T-cells carry out three functions: 1) they activate B-cells to respond to invaders, 2) stimulate the growth of macrophages (phagocytic cells), and 3) destroy foreign invaders and abnormal tissue (i.e., cancers). For this reason, the thymus plays an important immunity role in children as well as adults.

418. C is correct. As an overview, **endocytosis** is an ATP-dependent transport of "goods" INTO the cell. Both phagocytosis and pinocytosis are forms of endocytosis. **Phagocytosis** is the process by which foreign particles invading the body or minute food particles are engulfed and broken down by the cell. The cell membrane of the phagocyte invaginates to capture the particle and then closes around it to form a sac or vacuole. The vacuole coalesces with a lysosome, which contains enzymes that break down the particle. **Pinocytosis** is the process by which living cells engulf *minute droplets* of liquid. Specifics about pinocytosis are less understood. **Exocytosis** is the transport of "goods" OUT of the cell. There is no such thing as phago-engulfing.

419. B is correct. According to the question stem, NMDA receptor activation must be inhibited in order to prevent cell death. NMDA inhibition can be accomplished by: 1) inhibiting the synthesis of glutamate, which is an NMDA receptor agonist, 2) blocking the NMDA receptor to prevent cell death, and/or 3) preventing the degradation of NMDA *regulatory* molecule. Thus, the correct answer choice is B.

420. C is correct. The question is asking in a sneaky way where protein synthesis takes place. According to the question stem, substance P is a neuro-*peptide* and protein synthesis is mediated by free ribosomes and/or ribosomes embedded in the **rough ER. Peroxisomes** produce H_2O_2 and function in cellular detoxification. Mitochondria are the powerhouses of the cell; they have nothing to do with protein synthesis.

421. A is correct. What does a current do to a nerve cell? It will stimulate the opening of sodium channels and depolarize the nerve. The depolarization will rapidly move away from the cell body toward the axon terminal (always unidirectionally), where the neurotransmitters are stored. Once the exon terminal is depolarized, calcium will cause the release of neurotransmitters into the synaptic cleft. What happens to the neurotransmitter in the synaptic cleft? Some will stimulate postsynaptic receptors, some will be broken down by *neurotransmitterases* (i.e., *acetylcholinesterases*), and some will be carried away by the bloodstream. The electrical current has nothing to do with neurotransmitter degradation in the synaptic cleft.

422. A is correct. This is a High Yield MCAT topic. Cell cytoskeleton is a complex mesh of microfilaments, intermediate filaments, and microtubules. It establishes cellular shape, provides mechanical strength, allows locomotion (via cilia and flagella), and is needed for chromosome separation during mitosis and meiosis (remember those microtubules make up the spindle apparatus). Recall, nerve cells are arrested in G_0 phase of the cell cycle and DO NOT replicate.

Passage 410 (Questions 423-429)

423. C is correct. According to the passage, efferents are spinal cord motor neurons, which coordinate voluntary/involuntary muscle movement. Answer choices A and D both describe afferent sensory neurons and thus are eliminated. Interneurons transfer signals between neurons.

424. B is correct. According to the passage, cervical nerve roots are named for the vertebrae directly below the root. However, the reader is informed that C8 is an exception to the rule because it passes between C7 and T1. Therefore, answer choice C can be eliminated. FYI: There are only 7 cervical vertebrae: a C8 vertebra does not exist.

425. D is correct. A very important piece of information: a muscle reflex does NOT require brain involvement. A reflex is a rapid response designed to prevent injury, for example burning your hand. Involving the brain would take too much time. The brain will be informed of what has happened only after the limb has been retracted from the open flame. Answer choices A, B, and C are all true.

426. A is correct. According to the passage, afferents are spinal cord sensory neurons, which enter the spinal cord by posterior nerve roots. Efferents are spinal cord motor neurons and the denticulate ligament is a surgical landmark that holds the spinal cord in place within the vertebral column.

427. C is correct. It is stated in the passage that an adult spinal cord extends until the first lumbar vertebrae (L1). The question stem informs the reader that a newborn will have a spinal cord of greater relative length. Therefore, the answer choice must be below L1: answer choice C is the only one to fit that description.

428. A is correct. According to the passage, motor information from the brain causes individual effector muscles to contract or relax. Medulla is an organ within the brain, not a muscle. The correct answer choice is A. **This is a High Yield MCAT topic.** The autonomic nervous system (ANS) regulates homeostasis and is not subject to voluntary control. (It is subdivided into the sympathetic and parasympathetic nervous systems.) The ANS regulates the heart rate (i.e., cardiac tissue), constricts and dilates blood vessels, contracts and relaxes smooth muscle in various organs, and secretes products from various glands.

429. D is correct. Here is what you need to know about the brain for the MCAT: the cerebellum is responsible for motor coordination and balance (i.e., catching a baseball, tying a shoe while standing on one leg). Cats have well-developed cerebellums and as a result always land on their feet. The medulla is needed to control the respiratory and heart rates. If you're running to catch the bus and your respiratory and heart rates increase, that is the medulla at work. The hypothalamus synthesizes hormones (ADH and oxytocin) and controls hormone release from the anterior pituitary. The cerebrum (cerebral cortex) is responsible for higher thought and memory.

Passage 411 (Questions 430-436)

430. D is correct. These are High Yield MCAT facts: prolactin is one of six major peptide hormones produced by the anterior pituitary gland and controlled by dopamine (information regarding dopamine is provided in the question stem). Prolactin initiates and sustains lactation (milk production). Oxytocin is synthesized in the hypothalamus and stored in the posterior pituitary, same as ADH.

431. B is correct. According to Mechanism 1, L-dopa → dopamine conversion prevention will result in precursor accumulation of phenylalanine, tyrosine, and L-dopa. The only correct answer choices possible are B and C. Dopa decarboxylase denaturation will also inhibit the production of dopamine, norepinephrine, and epinephrine.

432. C is correct. According to the question stem, both parents are heterozygous carrierss for phenylketonuria—represented by Pp; 50% of their children will be expected to carry the PKU gene.

	P	p
P	PP	*Pp*
p	*Pp*	pp

433. C is correct. The question is asking about polarity and hydrogen bonding. Are the two related? The answer is yes. Polar compounds are hydrophilic (they bond with a very polar compound, water) and are usually able to form hydrogen bonds. Nonpolar compounds (i.e., lipids) are hydrophobic and usually do not form hydrogen bonds. One more piece of information: COOH is a very strong organic acid.

According to the passage, the formation of biogenic amines causes a loss of hydroxyl (OH-) and/or carboxyl (COOH) functional groups: hydroxyl and carboxyl functional groups are notorious hydrogen bond formers. The loss of COOH functional groups causes the new compound to be less acidic. As a result, hydrogen bond formation, acidity, water solubility (therefore, biogenic amines become more hydrophobic), and reactivity all decrease. The correct answer choice is C.

434. D is correct. This is a High Yield MCAT topic: acetylcholine must be released to move any voluntary muscle. Knowing this, there are two ways to inhibit muscle contraction or induce muscle relaxation: 1) prevent acetylcholine synthesis or release, 2) prevent acetylcholine from binding to its receptors on the postsynaptic membrane.

A destruction of acetylcholine receptors will cause permanent paralysis. **ADH** (anti-diuretic hormone) is produced by the hypothalamus, stored in the posterior pituitary, and causes water reuptake by the kidney.

435. C is correct. This is important: the *adrenal medulla*, located above the kidney, produces and releases epinephrine and norepinephrine (according to Table 1, both are tyrosine derived) into the bloodstream. The *adrenal cortex* produces steroid hormones like glucocorticoids (i.e., cortisol) and mineralocorticoids (i.e., aldosterone).

Mnemonic: "AMEN"

A – Adrenal
M – Medulla
E – Epinephrine
N – Norepinephrine

436. D is correct. According to the passage, the blood-brain barrier prevents hydrophilic substances, those possessing a dipole moment, from entering the brain (i.e., dopamine). Thus, answer choice B is eliminated. Dopamine *agonists*, not antagonists, bind and stimulate receptors in place of dopamine.

Independent Questions (Questions 437-445)

437. C is correct. This is a High Yield MCAT topic. The **sympathetic nervous system** is a division of the *involuntary* autonomic nervous system. **Norepinephrine** stimulates the sympathetic "fight and flight" response. (The parasympathetic division of the autonomic nervous system uses **acetylcholine**). The release of norepinephrine dilates pupils (so you can see); further opens the trachea and bronchi (so you can take in more oxygen); shunts blood away from the skin and viscera to skeletal muscles (so you can run away), brain (so you can think), and heart (so you can deliver oxygen to all those muscles).

438. D is correct. This is a High Yield MCAT fact: Na^+/K^+ ATPase pushes two potassium ions (K^+) into the cell for every three sodium ions (Na^+) it pumps out; so its activity causes a net loss of a positive charge from within the cell. This is the reason why the inside of any cell is negative (i.e., −70 mV).

This question is best answered via the process of elimination. According to the question stem, glycosides inhibit the Na^+/K^+ pump. If the pump were not working the consumption of ATP would decrease, Na^+ would build up within the cell (the pump is not taking any sodium out of the cell), while K^+ concentration would increase in the extracellular environment (the pump is not bringing any potassium in).

The buildup of Na^+ based positive charge in the cell would eventually cause the cell to spontaneously depolarize. Why? As the inside of the cell becomes more positive it will eventually reach the action potential threshold, therefore depolarization.

439. **B is correct.** Mitochondria are able to self-replicate in order to meet the energy needs of the cell. Be careful. DNA is not an organelle. Ribosomes are not self-replicating, they are peptides synthesized by the cellular machinery.

440. **A is correct.** Most fungi are haploid, and only spend a small percentage of their life cycle in a diploid phase.

441. **D is correct.** Minerals (i.e., magnesium and calcium) are obtained from diet and serve as cofactors for enzymes. They are not digested by lysosomes. Nucleotides, lipids, and proteins are all degraded into monomers for cellular use.

442. **B is correct. This is a High Yield MCAT topic**. The Golgi apparatus controls protein trafficking via numerous post-translational modifications. Once released from the Golgi, protein have 2 general paths to take. Some peptides are secreted out of the cell, while others are translocated to various cell locations.

443. **C is correct.** Cilia and flagella are microtubule, derived cellular projections. They are motile and designed to move the cell itself or to move substances over or around the cell. Cilia and flagella have similar internal structures. The major difference is in their length. Only the flagellum is found on sperm and is responsible for their propulsion. The correct answer is C.

444. **B is correct.** According to the question stem, monoamine oxidase inhibitors increase blood concentration of catecholamines like epinephrine (adrenalin). The sympathetic nervous system utilizes catecholamines to dilate pupils,; to increase heart and respiratory rates; and to shunt blood away from the skin and viscera to skeletal muscles, brain, and heart. Sympathetic stimulation is involuntary and allows the body to deal with stress ("fight or flight").

445. **B is correct. This is High Yield for the MCAT.** A wave is a disturbance that travels through a medium, transporting ONLY ENERGY from one location to another location. The medium is simply the material through which the disturbance is moving.

LECTURE 5

Answers & Explanations
Questions 446–556

446.	D	483.	B	520.	B
447.	C	484.	C	521.	A
448.	C	485.	A	522.	B
449.	C	486.	B	523.	B
450.	A	487.	C	524.	C
451.	A	488.	D	525.	B
452.	C	489.	A	526.	C
453.	D	490.	B	527.	A
454.	D	491.	C	528.	B
455.	B	492.	D	529.	D
456.	C	493.	B	530.	D
457.	A	494.	B	531.	A
458.	C	495.	D	532.	C
459.	B	496.	C	533.	A
460.	A	497.	D	534.	C
461.	B	498.	B	535.	B
462.	D	499.	D	536.	A
463.	A	500.	A	537.	D
464.	B	501.	B	538.	B
465.	B	502.	D	539.	B
466.	A	503.	A	540.	B
467.	C	504.	C	541.	B
468.	D	505.	C	542.	B
469.	A	506.	C	543.	B
470.	B	507.	B	544.	D
471.	A	508.	D	545.	B
472.	C	509.	C	546.	B
473.	B	510.	B	547.	C
474.	C	511.	A	548.	C
475.	C	512.	A	549.	B
476.	D	513.	C	550.	C
477.	B	514.	C	551.	C
478.	B	515.	C	552.	A
479.	A	516.	C	553.	B
480.	D	517.	C	554.	C
481.	B	518.	C	555.	D
482.	D	519.	B	556.	A

446. D is correct. According to the passage, trophic hormones stimulate *other* glands to secrete hormones. The correct answer is TSH, which stimulates the thyroid gland to release thyroxine (T_3/T_4). When pituitary hormone production is impaired, target gland hormone production is reduced because of a lack of trophic stimulus.

447. C is correct. How to decide the answer to this question? Well, according to the second sentence in the passage, "hormones are always present in *minute* concentrations." The correct answer to this type of MCAT question can only be one of the two extremes; it is either the highest or lowest number. 101 nanomoles (10^{-9}) per liter is the smallest concentration listed; the correct answer is C. 713 moles per liter is quite a concentrated solution and therefore incorrect.

448. C is correct. This is High Yield MCAT information: The Na^+/K^+ ATPase transports 3 sodium ions out of the cell and 2 potassium ions into the cell. So the pump lowers that intracellular sodium concentration. When digitalis is administered, the intracellular sodium concentration will increase and intracellular potassium concentration will decrease. Moreover, extracellular sodium concentration will decrease as well and unaffected cells will not have any sodium to reabsorb. If the Na^+/K^+ ATPase activity is inhibited, so will be the ATP consumption.

449. C is correct. According to the passage, major hormones are capable of exerting local as well as distant effects on target organs. The question stem is describing a local paracrine effect of testosterone on the seminiferous tubules. An autocrine effect occurs when a cell signals itself through a self-binding compound. The *endocrine system* secretes hormones directly into the bloodstream that have an effect on distant organs. The *exocrine system* utilizes ducts in order to release its active compounds.

450. A is correct. The pancreas has four major anatomical divisions, which include the head, neck, body, and tail. Its structure and function is commonly tested on the MCAT. The pancreas is comprised of both exocrine and endocrine cells, each with different functions. The exocrine pancreas synthesizes and secretes a variety of enzymes into the duodenum (first portion of the small intestine) in order to digest food. The endocrine pancreas produces a multitude of hormones that not only contribute to the digestion of food but also play an important role in the metabolism of the body. The liver is not considered to be an endocrine organ by definition.

451. A is correct. Plasma is the transporting medium for a myriad of hormones, electrolytes, sugars, waste products, and other substances. It contains three major proteins: albumin (5 grams), gammaglobulins or antibodies (2.5 grams), and fibrinogen (0.4 grams). Myosin and actin are proteins that compose the muscle contractile unit.

---

452. C is correct. This EXCEPT question is best answered by eliminating a few answer choices. According to the question stem, *human placental lactogen* is structurally similar to growth hormone. According to the first paragraph, growth hormone is a *single-chain polypeptide* and therefore CANNOT occupy a quaternary protein structure, which requires two or more polypeptide chains to form. The correct answer must be C. **FYI:** primary protein structure is simply a collection of amino acids linked via peptide bonds. Secondary protein structure always consists of alpha-helices and/or beta sheets. Tertiary protein structure is a 3D globular protein made up of a single polypeptide.

453. D is correct. According to the passage, growth hormone reaches its physiological maximum during *sleep*, puberty, starvation and stress. The correct answer choice is D. The body conducts most tissue growth and repair while the person is sleeping.

454. D is correct. What do the numbers in Table 1 mean? 5 = baseline, this is what the normal level should be. According to Table 1, as levels of growth hormone increase, insulin levels increase and blood glucose levels decrease. What disease is associated with abnormal insulin concentration leading to problems will blood glucose? The answer is diabetes mellitus.

Patients with **diabetes mellitus** have a problem regulating their blood glucose because their bodies fail to produce or properly respond to insulin. **Down's syndrome** and **muscular dystrophy** are genetic diseases that have nothing to do with insulin or blood glucose. **Osteoporosis** is the wasting of bones seen in postmenopausal women: it is believed to be caused by estrogen abnormalities.

455. B is correct. Two major systems maintain homeostasis, the endocrine system and the nervous system. The endocrine system has a slow onset (hormones need to be synthesized and released) but its effects are long lasting. The nervous system has a rapid onset but is short acting.

456. C is correct. Answer this question via the process of elimination. According to Table 1, high concentration of growth hormone a) increases mRNA production and therefore transcription; b) increases glucose consumption. The question stem states that growth hormone also inhibits the breakdown of protein. Thus, answer choices A, B, and D are eliminated.

457. A is correct. Question stem lab values show an elevated concentration of calcium. **This is High Yield MCAT information:** blood calcium concentration is tightly regulated by the thyroid and parathyroid glands. **Parathyroid hormone** is the most important elevator of calcium and a depressor of phosphorus. The gland responsible for the elevated blood calcium must be the parathyroid. The thyroid gland produces calcitonin, which decreases blood calcium level. The **adrenal gland** produces cortisol, aldosterone, epinephrine, and norepinephrine, none of which have anything to do with calcium.

458. C is correct. According to the passage, growth hormone reaches its physiological maximum during starvation. In an individual with Kwashiorkor syndrome, low levels of protein will stimulate the release of growth hormone in an attempt to return to homeostasis by consuming lipids for fuel.

Passage 503 (Questions 459-464)

459. B is correct. The cell membrane is impermeable to all charged particles; charged calcium salts would never be able to enter a cell by simple diffusion across the hydrophobic cell membrane. Calcium ions are capable of entering the cell utilizing a channel or a carrier molecule. Thus, II is correct. Albumin is a large plasma protein that is too big to enter the intracellular space. The same is true for any compound directly attached to albumin. The correct answer choice must be B.

460. A is correct. Neuron depolarization occurs when sodium rushes into the cell, down its concentration gradient, through hundreds of open voltage-gated sodium channels. According to the question stem, low calcium concentration increases neuron permeability to sodium, stimulating unnecessary spontaneous depolarizations and causing overall hyperexcitability. Muscle tetany is a frequent contraction of muscle that is usually caused by low levels of calcium, which increase the action potential frequency. **Neuron hyperpolarization** is caused by excessive efflux of potassium out of the cell. So, sodium depolarizes and potassium hyperpolarizes. Parathyroid hormone regulates blood calcium levels by stimulating the breakdown of bones. Low calcium concentration stimulates the release of parathyroid hormone.

461. B is correct. The *parathyroid hormone* increases plasma calcium concentration by stimulating the resorption of bone. **Osteoclasts** are cells that actively reabsorb bone and release calcium into the bloodstream. **Osteoblast**s are stimulated by *calcitonin* to increase bone synthesis and lower blood calcium concentration. Adipocyte is a fat cell.

462. D is correct. An **endocrine gland** secretes hormones directly into the bloodstream (without the use of ducts) for distribution to distant target organs throughout the body. An example of an endocrine gland is the parathyroid gland. It synthesizes parathyroid hormone, which serves to increase blood calcium level. An **exocrine gland** secretes its product into a system of ducts. An example of an exocrine gland is the pancreas, which secretes digestive juices into the duodenum via two pancreatic ducts. A **paracrine hormone** is designed to stimulate nearby cells: it is not carried by the bloodstream to distant target organs. A **neurocrine hormone** is simply synthesized by the nervous system.

463. A is correct. The parathyroid hormone does three important things: 1) stimulates osteoclasts to reabsorb bone in order to increase blood calcium concentration; 2) increases calcium absorption from the small intestine; 3) inhibits the loss of calcium in urine, thus conserving calcium in the blood. PTH also stimulates the loss of phosphate in urine. So, PTH increases blood calcium and decreases blood phosphate.

464. B is correct. This is important MCAT information: Vitamin D hormone increases calcium absorption from the intestine and promotes normal bone formation and mineralization. The critical 1-hydroxylation of the inactive form of vitamin D (25-(OH) D$_3$) is strongly stimulated by parathyroid hormone (PTH). Without proper levels of PTH, vitamin D remains inactive and is eliminated by the liver.

Independent Questions (Questions 465-475)

465. B is correct. This is a high yield MCAT fact. Digestion of fat requires bile salts that are produced in the **liver** and stored and concentrated in the **gall bladder**. Presence of fat in the duodenum, the first third of the small intestine, stimulates the release of bile salts from the gall bladder.

466. A is correct. Catecholamines, norepinephrine and epinephrine, are neurotransmitters synthesized by chromaffin cells of the *adrenal medulla*. They are released in times of stress. **Cortisol** is a steroid hormone produced by the *adrenal cortex*. It inhibits the immune system, increases blood glucose, and is necessary when the body is dealing with stress. **Thyroxine** or thyroid hormone is tyrosine derived (tyrosine is an amino acid) and increases the basal metabolic rate. You do not need to know what substance P is.

467. C is correct. A patient with Type I diabetes cannot make insulin because most of the insulin-producing beta-cells are destroyed by autoimmune antibodies.

Insulin is secreted by pancreatic beta-cells to stimulate most body cells to take up glucose from the blood stream. A shortage of insulin will cause the blood-glucose level to *increase* and glycolysis to *decrease* because glucose remains in the bloodstream and cannot be used for metabolism.

A decrease in the rate of glycolysis forces the body to metabolize fat to keep up with body ATP demands. High levels of fat metabolism elevate ketone bodies in the blood. Ketone bodies are end products of fat metabolism.

468. D is correct. There are 2 hormones that regulate urine volume, ADH and aldosterone. The only one listed in the answer choices is ADH.

The condition being described in the question stem is known as *diabetes insipidus*, which results from a decrease in the production of **antidiuretic hormone** (ADH). ADH is produced in the hypothalamus and is released by the posterior pituitary. It helps the kidneys to retain water, especially during periods of dehydration. Without ADH, excessive thirst with excessive urination of very dilute urine occurs. **Oxytocin** causes the uterus to contract during birth and milk release during breast feeding. **Prolactin** stimulates the synthesis of breast milk.

469. A is correct. Luteinizing hormone (LH) is released by the anterior pituitary and causes ovulation. The release of LH is stimulated by an increase in estrogen. **Progesterone** is secreted by the ovary and the corpus luteum and maintains the pregnancy by inhibiting the loss of the endometrial lining. FSH is also produced by the anterior pituitary and stimulates the maturation of the ova.

470. B is correct. The question stem is describing a **gap junction**, which is a protein channel that allows ions and small molecules to traverse between connected cells without encountering the extracellular environment. **Important for the MCAT:** gap junctions are found in the heart and smooth muscle.

471. A is correct. Some strategy: the answer choice must be one of the extremes—A or D—regarding velocity.

Oligodendrocytes and Schwann cells synthesize myelin, which serves as axon insulation. Myelinated axons transmit nerve signals *much faster* than unmyelinated ones. (Answer choices A and B are highly myelinated nerve fibers; they display a rapid rate of conduction.)

According to the question stem, multiple sclerosis is a demyelinating disease that is expected to have a devastating effect on highly myelinated, fast-conduction neurons. The correct answer choice is A.

472. C is correct. REVIEW: thyroid hormone increases the basal metabolic rate by stimulating protein synthesis and increasing the activity of the Na^+ / K^+ ATPase.

There are 2 types of thyroid dysfunction: gland overactivity (*hyperthyroidism*) and gland underactivity (*hypothyroidism*). Under normal circumstances, the **anterior pituitary gland** produces thyroid-stimulating hor-

mone (TSH), which binds to TSH receptors and stimulates the release of thyroid hormone. Auto-antibodies to TSH receptors will over-stimulate the thyroid gland and cause an abnormally elevated level of thyroid hormone.

473. B is correct. This is a High Yield MCAT fact: growth hormone is one of six major hormones produced by the anterior pituitary gland. The hypothalamus controls all secretions that come out of the pituitary. Hypothalamic hormones are referred to as *releasing* and *inhibiting hormones*, reflecting their influence on the anterior pituitary.

474. C is correct. What hormone controls the basal metabolic rate? The answer is the thyroid hormone. The basal metabolic rate depends on a variety of physiological processes including oxygen consumption, cardiovascular activity, and respiratory function. **Glucagon** is produced by the pancreas to increase blood glucose levels. Interestingly enough, insulin is also produced by the pancreas.

475. C is correct. According to the question stem, **atrial natiuretic peptide** decreases blood volume there by counteracting the actions of 2 hormones that increase blood volume, antidiuretic hormone (ADH) and aldosterone. **ADH** is released from the posterior pituitary and increases the amount of water reabsorbed by the nephron collecting duct. **Aldosterone** is secreted by the adrenal cortex and increases the reabsorption of sodium and water by the distal nephron.

Passage 504 (Questions 476-482)

476. D is correct. Cancer is cellular division out of control. When a synthesizing cell grows out of control it is expected to secrete an abnormally high concentration of product that may be used as a cancer marker.

According to the passage, thyroid parafollicular cells synthesize calcitonin. An elevated concentration of calcitonin would make a reasonable tumor marker. Abnormal cellular division cannot be used as a specific marker because it is seen in every type of cancerous growth. Answer choice A is incorrect because parafollicular cells do not secrete thyroid hormone.

477. B is correct. It is stated in the passage that calcitonin decreases plasma calcium by *directly* inhibiting the activity of cells that reabsorb bone; these cells are known as **osteoclasts**. When osteoclast activity is decreased osteoblasts rapidly build bone.

REVIEW: Calcitonin 1) blocks bone resorption by inhibiting osteoclasts, which prevents the release of calcium and phosphorous into the bloodstream; and 2) inhibits renal tubular reabsorption of calcium and phosphorous, causing them to be lost in urine.

478. B is correct. According to the passage, drug-X is calcitonin-like and must reduce blood calcium. The question stem informs that the methyl carbon chain has the maximum drug efficacy; it must be a full agonist. However, according to Table 2, the octyl carbon chain has almost no effect on blood calcium; octyl must be a competitive inhibitor. The competitive inhibitor competes with the agonist for the receptor. If the inhibitor finds the receptor first the agonist cannot bind. If the agonist cannot bind drug efficacy is non-existent. Methyl/octyl combination does produce a calcium reducing effect; answer choice C is eliminated.

479. A is correct. According to the passage, vitamin D promotes bone mineralization by elevating plasma calcium. In *osteomalacia* newly synthesized bone is not properly mineralized. Weight-bearing bones become soft and more likely to fracture.

480. D is correct. The vitamin D synthetic pathway is found in Table 1. According to Mechanism 1, vitamin D synthesis concludes with the production, *1, 25-dihydroxycholecalciferol* (cholecalciferol), which is the active form of vitamin D.

481. B is correct. Lanthanum, a calcium channel blocker, will cause a decrease in blood calcium by inhibiting absorption. A decrease in blood calcium stimulates the release of vitamin D and the parathyroid hormone (not an answer choice option). Both will attempt to return blood calcium concentration to baseline.

482. D is correct. Calcitonin, which functions to decrease blood calcium, is an effective treatment for hypercalcemia, a state during which blood levels of calcium are too high. The **parathyroid hormone** and **vitamin D** would further increase blood calcium, which can lead to death. **Growth hormone** is secreted by the anterior pituitary gland. It stimulates mitosis when the body needs to repair and increases blood glucose levels.

Passage 505 (Questions 483-488)

483. B is correct. MCAT writers love to ask about this. Glucocorticoid hormone, **cortisol**, is lipid soluble and easily diffuses through the plasma membrane into the cytoplasm where it binds a specific, high-affinity nuclear receptor. Inside the nucleus, the receptor complex binds to a specific DNA region to activate gene transcription.

There are 2 types of hormones, steroid and peptide. **All lipid-soluble hormones** (steroids) directly bind intracellular nuclear receptors. As a result they DO NOT require a second-messenger system (i.e., cAMP). **All peptide hormones** bind cell membrane receptors and require a second messenger to move their signal from the cell membrane to the nucleus.

484. C is correct. Norepinephrine is a *sympathetic neurotransmitter* that when released stimulates post synaptic

dendrites. According to the passage, norepinephrine alpha2-receptors are located on the presynaptic nerve terminal. So to obtain an accurate estimate of norepinephrine receptors, both pre- and post- synaptic terminals need to be evaluated.

485. A is correct. According to Figure 1, amphetamine and norepinephrine compete for the same receptor. Amphetamine is therefore a **competitive inhibitor** that binds to the same site as the substrate (in this case norepinephrine). An allosteric inhibitor binds to a site (known as the allosteric site) other than the one used by the substrate.

486. B is correct. According to the passage, amphetamine (also nicknamed "speed") mimics the action of the sympathetic nervous system. What does the sympathetic nervous system do? It stimulates the "fight or flight" response via the release of norepinephrine. Some short-term effects of the sympathetic nervous system are: **(memorize these)**

- Dilated pupils
- Flushing and sweating
- Constipation (because of inhibited GI peristalsis)
- Increased heart rate
- Increased respiratory rate
- Elevated blood pressure
- Basically everything that happens to you when you are busy running away from a bear

487. C is correct. The autonomic nervous system has both afferent (sensory) and efferent (motor) components and is absolutely essential for life. It is involuntary and is divided into the parasympathetic and sympathetic divisions. The **sympathetic division** responds to stress by releasing norepinephrine. The **parasympathetic nervous system** maintains the resting state and releases acetylcholine.

488. D is correct. According to the passage, under normal circumstances the alpha2-presynaptic carrier functions to remove norepinephrine from the synaptic cleft.

Passage 506 (Questions 489-494)

489. A is correct. An adrenal gland, with an outer cortex and an inner medulla, can be located atop of each kidney. ACTH and renin stimulate the adrenal cortex to release cortisol and aldosterone, respectively. **Cortisol** controls the body's use of fat, protein, and carbohydrates, as well as response to overall "stress." **Aldosterone** stimulates sodium reabsorption by the kidney in an effort to increase blood volume.

490. B is correct. In order to completely inhibit the release of cortisol, the entire endocrine **hypothalamo-pituitary**

axis must be shut down. What is the hypothalamo-pituitary axis? Here it is: the hypothalamus secretes CRH to stimulate the anterior pituitary gland. The anterior pituitary then releases ACTH, which stimulates the adrenal cortex to release cortisol.

To fully inhibit the release of cortisol, direct negative feedback would need to be placed on: 1) the hypothalamus (which releases CRH) and 2) the anterior pituitary (which releases ACTH).

491. **C is correct.** Use the process of elimination to answer this question. According to the question stem, the woman has low levels of ACTH. This may be caused by an ACTH under-production by the anterior pituitary gland. Answer choice B is incorrect.

According to Figure 1, the posterior pituitary releases **ADH** and **oxytocin**. It has nothing to do with ACTH.

The adrenal gland is stimulated by ACTH to release cortisol. When cortisol levels are elevated there will be a negative feedback system that inhibits the release of ACTH. The woman described in the question stem has a high sugar level and demonstrates significant muscle wasting. These are classic signs of excess cortisol being present in the blood. The question remains as to why there is excess cortisol in the blood. This woman is over-injecting exogenous cortisol that is causing her present symptoms.

492. **D is correct.** According to the 1st paragraph, diabetes can be caused by a problem with the adrenal gland, the pituitary gland, and the pancreas.

An **endocrine gland** secretes its contents directly into the bloodstream without the use of any ducts. The pituitary, the adrenal, and the pancreas are all endocrine organs. However, the pancreas is also partly exocrine. An **exocrine organ** utilizes a system of ducts to deliver its contents to the target site. Pancreatic digestive enzymes are propelled through the pancreatic duct to reach the small intestine.

The pituitary gland is found in the brain but it is part of the endocrine system.

493. **B is correct.** According to the passage, high cortisol levels cause muscle wasting to keep the liver supplied with amino acids. A short-term treatment option is to increase the dietary intake of protein to prevent the deterioration of large muscles. Removal of the adrenal cortex would prevent cortisol synthesis and muscle wasting but surgery is not a short-term treatment option.

The posterior pituitary has nothing to do with cortisol synthesis. It produces ADH and oxytocin. ACTH injection will stimulate the adrenal gland to release even more cortisol and further complicate the situation. The correct answer choice is B.

494. **B is correct.** According to the passage, elevated blood amino acids stimulate the liver to synthesize protein. Protein synthesis occurs in 2 organelles, ribosomes and the rough endoplasmic reticulum. The **mitochondrion** is the powerhouse of the cell. **Lysosomes** are digestive organelles full of hydrolytic enzymes. **Peroxisomes** are involved in cellular detoxification and hydrogen peroxide degradation via *catalase*.

Independent Questions (Questions 495-505)

495. **D is correct.** There are 4 hormones that increase blood glucose levels, glucagon, cortisol, growth hormone, and epinephrine. **Cortisol** is produced by the adrenal cortex; **glucagon** is released by the pancreas; **growth hormone** (GH) is released from the anterior pituitary.

Prolactin stimulates milk production and breast development. Thus, the correct answer choice to this EXCEPT question is D.

496. **C is correct.** Only the thyroid gland uses iodine to synthesize its hormone. In fact an iodine deficiency will cause a severe disruption in thyroid function and the overall metabolic rate. The parathyroid gland regulates blood calcium concentration. The ovary secretes estrogen.

497. **D is correct. This is a High Yield MCAT topic**: protein digestion is initiated in the stomach by the release of **pepsin**. The pancreas releases other peptide-digesting enzymes (known as proteases) such as **trypsin**, and **chymotrypsin**. These proteases cleave peptides into amino acids, which are absorbed by the small intestine. **Bile** (produced by the liver) and **pancreatic lipase** are both involved in lipid digestion, while **amylases** break down carbohydrates.

498. **B is correct.** A **metabolic process** begins with a substrate, passes it through a unique network of interconnected chemical reaction, and releases a product. An example of a metabolic process is glycolysis. Glycolysis converts glucose (a substrate) into pyruvate (the product) via a series of ten reactions.

499. **D is correct.** In **endocrine function** a hormone is carried by blood to a distant target organ. Schematic 1 does not demonstrate an endocrine response. During **paracrine function** the hormone stimulates an adjacent cell a short distance away. Cell A releasing a hormone that stimulates a nearby cell B is an example of a paracrine function. During an **autocrine response** the hormone signal acts back on the cell of origin. Schematic 1 demonstrates both autocrine and paracrine responses.

500. **A is correct.** All anterior pituitary hormones are peptides, including growth hormone. Peptide hormones are

hydrophilic (cannot diffuse across the hydrophobic phospholipid bilayer) and therefore bind cell membrane receptors. The destruction of a cell membrane would greatly decrease the concentration of growth hormone receptors.

501. B is correct. According to the question stem, scars can sometimes form in the reproductive tract and prevent the ova from reaching the uterus. These situations are quite common and lead to infertility. Hormone levels would not be altered by scars. Ovulation would still occur but the ova would have difficulty migrating.

502. D is correct. This is High Yield MCAT information. Insulin (decreases blood glucose) is produced by beta cells of the pancreas, while **aldosterone** is synthesized by the adrenal gland to increase the reabsorption of Na^+ and water by distal convoluted tubules in the kidney.

503. A is correct. The **parathyroid gland** functions with the **thyroid** to regulate blood calcium levels. The thyroid gland is located in the middle of the lower neck, below the larynx (the voice box) and just above the clavicles (collarbones). Imbedded in the thyroid are 4 small parathyroid glands. The adrenal gland is located above the kidney.

504. C is correct. Facilitated diffusion relies on a channel protein to move items down the concentration gradient. **Simple diffusion** also translocates items down the concentration gradient but without the use of a channel protein. **Active transport** uses ATP to move compounds against the concentration gradient. **Endocytosis** is an ATP dependent process of bringing extracellular compounds into the cell.

505. C is correct. The **intrinsic factor** is secreted by *parietal cells* along with HCl. *Chief cells* release pepsinogen, while mucus cells protect the stomach lining from irritation.

Passage 507 (Questions 506-511)

506. C is correct. On average, hormone concentration ranges from 1 picogram to values no greater than a few micrograms/ml. These are tiny numbers. So tiny, in fact, that some hormones cannot even be detected in the blood. The rates of hormone production are correspondingly low, ranging from as little as a few micrograms per day to at most a few milligrams per day.

507. B is correct. It is stated in the passage that epinephrine is derived from tyrosine, a non-essential amino acid. If administered in a pill form, epinephrine will be digested as any other protein by peptidases present in the stomach and the small intestine. Intravenous injections have an instantaneous effect because the medicine is delivered directly into the bloodstream. The alpha group is the control for the experiment because the delta group was given epinephrine and not a placebo.

508. D is correct. The reader is being asked to pick an answer choice that is not a part of the endocrine system. **The salivary gland** (i.e., parotid gland) is an exocrine gland because it uses a system of ducts to release its contents into the mouth.

The endocrine system secretes its hormones directly into the bloodstream and is composed of the following glands: the hypothalamus of the brain, the anterior and posterior parts of the pituitary gland, the thyroid and parathyroid glands, the medulla and cortex of the adrenal gland, the islets of Langerhans in the pancreas, the testes in males, and the ovaries in females. In addition, the pineal gland of the brain is often considered an endocrine organ that secretes melatonin.

509. C is correct. According to the passage, peptide hormones are synthesized in the rough endoplasmic reticulum followed by further processing in the Golgi apparatus. Thus, the Golgi apparatus must modify or cleave the *prohormone* to yield the final active hormone product. The correct answer choice is C.

Review: peptide hormones are typically synthesized as large *preprohormones* (with no hormonal activity) that are cleaved to yield smaller *prohormones* (also with little hormonal activity) while still being synthesized in the rough ER. The *prohormone* is then packaged into vesicles and transported to the Golgi, where final protein modification occurs.

510. B is correct. According to the passage, hormones (i.e., testosterone) that are transported in the blood are *loosely* bound to albumin. Thus, the correct answer must be a weak molecular interaction that allows for easy binding and unbinding. B is the correct answer choice.

Covalent bonds are strong and usually permanent. A **disulfide bond** is a type of covalent bond that occurs between 2 cysteine amino acids. Consider an ionic bond to be stronger than any covalent interaction.

511. A is correct. This is important for the MCAT: Amines or derivatives of the amino acid tyrosine are a group of endocrine hormones that include: 1) **thyroid hormone** (synthesized by the thyroid gland) and 2) **epinephrine** and **norepinephrine** (secreted by the adrenal medulla). (Epinephrine and norepinephrine are also known as catecholamines.) **Oxytocin** is a peptide hormone produced by the hypothalamus. **Aldosterone** is a cholesterol-derived steroid that is synthesized by the adrenal cortex. **Acetylcholine** is a neurotransmitter utilized by the parasympathetic nervous system.

---

512. A is correct. The passage informs that the muscarinic receptor is a cell membrane protein that carries out its action through a second messenger. **Peptide hormones** cannot diffuse across the cell membrane and must utilize second messengers (i.e., cAMP, cGMP) to exert their effect. All products of the anterior pituitary gland, including prolactin, are peptide in nature.

Steroid hormones—cortisol, aldosterone, progesterone, and testosterone—bind to nuclear or cytoplasmic receptors and do not need a second-messenger system.

513. C is correct. As per Table 1, a low dose (20-70 mg/minute) infusion of acetylcholine produces a *decrease* in blood pressure and an *increase* in the heart rate. Answer choices A and B are incorrect. Infusion of a large dose (80-150 mg/minute) causes a decrease in the heart rate as well as the blood pressure.

514. C is correct. The transmission of a signal requires the translocation of neurotransmitters from the presynaptic to the postsynaptic neuron.

What makes a neurotransmitter a neurotransmitter?

- the presynaptic neuron must be able to synthesize the neurotransmitter.
- enzymes that destroy the neurotransmitter may be present in the synaptic cleft.
- administration of the neurotransmitter under experimental conditions must reproduce the expected signal transfer.
- the postsynaptic neurotransmitter receptor may be blocked, thus inhibiting signal transfer.

515. C is correct. Hypertension is elevated blood pressure and the question is asking us to lower it. According to Table 1, any dose of acetylcholine will lower the blood pressure. However, the correct answer must not increase the heart rate, which would increase the strain on the cardiac muscle. A dose of 80 mg/minute is the correct answer because it lowers the heart rate as well as the blood pressure. No information is available on the 170 mg/minute dose. It might be lethal?

516. C is correct. The **vena cava** delivers deoxygenated blood from large veins to the right atrium. **Pulmonary arteries**, however, have the pleasure of carrying the *most deoxygenated* blood that is pumped by the right ventricle into the lungs. **Pulmonary veins** return oxygenated blood from the lungs to the left atrium of the heart. **Aorta** (the largest artery of the body) carries oxygenated blood from the left ventricle into systemic circulation.

517. C is correct. According to the passage, *nicotine* and *muscarine* stimulate acetylcholine receptors. The question is simply asking which of the listed nervous system components rely on acetylcholine as the stimulating neurotransmitter. **This is High Yield MCAT informa-**

tion: acetylcholine is used 1) by the parasympathetic nervous system and 2) at neuromuscular junctions to stimulate voluntary muscles. The sympathetic nervous system uses norepinephrine, not epinephrine, to stimulate components of the "fight or flight" response. The correct answer choice is C.

---

518. C is correct. This is a High Yield MCAT fact: the sudden surge of **luteinizing hormone** (LH) stimulates ovulation and the formation of the **corpus luteum**. The corpus luteum secretes progesterone, which maintains the uterine lining and keeps it suitable for implantation of the ova.

A sudden rise in urine LH level is diagnostic for ovulation. Oral contraceptives inhibit the LH surge by the anterior pituitary and thereby suppress ovulation. FSH is also released from the anterior pituitary and stimulates the maturation of the ova.

FYI: In males FSH stimulates the maturation of sperm.

519. B is correct. Synthetics are being used for a reason. They must be better in some way in comparison to natural hormones.

Synthetic estrogen/progesterone are utilized in oral contraception because natural hormones are quickly removed from circulation and degraded by the liver. Synthetics are devised to have a longer biological half-life, with better efficacy at pregnancy prevention.

Estrogen and progesterone DO NOT bind LH receptors: LH binds to LH receptors.

520. B is correct. Endocrine glands rely on negative and positive feedback mechanisms to maintain homeostasis. **Positive feedback** increases the deviation from some normal value by making more product. For example, a positive increase in estrogen directly correlates with a positive increase in cellular FSH and LH receptors. **Negative feedback** decreases the deviation from some normal value. **Desensitization** is a reduction in sensitivity to a particular stimulus.

521. A is correct. This is a tough question. As per the passage, there are four phases of the menstrual cycle: menstruation, the follicular phase, ovulation and the luteal phase. The follicular (proliferative) phase is hormone regulated and can vary in duration. What hormones regulate the follicular phase? The answer is estrogen, LH, FSH, etc. The endometrial lining is regulated by the same hormones that control the follicular phase. It does not have its own signal system. Answer choice B may be accurate but does not answer the question. The luteal (secretory) phase is genetically controlled and is always 14 days in length.

522. B is correct. According to the question stem, in endometriosis uterine endometrial lining grows outside the woman's uterus, usually in the fallopian tubes. This results in severe pelvic pain and infertility most likely do to an obstruction of the fallopian tubes. When the fallopian tubes are blocked sperm cannot reach the egg and the egg cannot reach the uterus to implant.

523. B is correct. Cyclic events of the female menstrual cycle occur every 28–30 days: **Menstruation** (day 0–5) → **Follicular (Proliferative) phase** (day 5–15, may be longer) → Ovulation (24 hours) → **Luteal (Secretory) phase** (constant 14 days in duration).

Independent Questions (Questions 524-534)

524. C is correct. Luteinizing hormone stimulates testosterone release in males. Testosterone is necessary for the proper development of testes, as well as the penis and seminal vesicles. It is also important for secondary male sex characteristics. Testosterone inadequacy would be high on the list as the primary cause for cryptochordism. FSH stimulates sperm/ova maturation. Cortisol suppresses the immune system and elevates blood glucose during stress.

525. B is correct. Glucagon is one of four hormones (the other three being cortisol, growth hormone, and epinephrine) that raise blood glucose levels. **Insulin** lowers blood glucose by increasing fat production and glucose reuptake from circulation. **Acetylcholine** is a parasympathetic neurotransmitter. **Testosterone** is needed for proper overall male/female sexual development.

526. C is correct. Peristalsis propels food down the GI tract and occurs in both the small and large intestine. For the MCAT you must be aware that the large intestine performs 2 important tasks, water reabsorption (to concentrate fecal matter) and potassium secretion. All nutrient absorption is completed by the time food enters the large intestine.

527. A is correct. Growth hormone is one of six peptide hormones synthesized and secreted by the **anterior pituitary** gland. The **posterior pituitary** secretes both vasopressin (ADH) and oxytocin, which are synthesized in the hypothalamus. The hippocampus has a role in emotion and sexuality.

528. B is correct. Hormones are classified chemically as **steroids** (cholesterol derived – i.e., cortisol), **proteins or peptides** (amino acid derived – i.e., prolactin) and **amines** (tyrosine derived – i.e., thyroid hormone).

529. D is correct. Glucose, amino acids, and phosphate are all reabsorbed in the proximal convoluted tubule through secondary active transport. Urea is a waste product that may or may not be reabsorbed by the kidney; if reabsorbed, it is never through active transport.

530. D is correct. Crossing over (recombination) occurs during meiosis to produce combinations of alleles not present in either parent. **Cytokinesis** is the final stage of mitosis during which material within the parent cell is equally cleaved into two daughter cells. **Chromatin condensation** is a method utilized to inactivate genes. **Chromatid splitting** is a normal anaphase occurrence that does not increase genetic variability.

531. A is correct. The Golgi apparatus modifies all peptides synthesized by the rough ER. Most peptides acquire carbohydrate groups. Lysosomes are digestive organelles and peroxisomes detoxify the cell.

532. C is correct. Oxytocin and prolactin are both *agonists* of the same process, specifically the production of milk by the mammary gland. Vitamin D and parathyroid hormone make up the second set of *agonists*: both increase blood calcium levels. ACTH and TSH are not at all related: ACTH stimulates the adrenal gland, while TSH activates the thyroid. Insulin and glucagon have an *antagonistic relationship*. Both are made by the pancreas but insulin lowers blood glucose, while glucagon raises it.

533. A is correct. The anterior pituitary secretes 2 gonadotropic hormones, FSH and LH. **FSH** causes ova to mature and enlarge, while LH stimulates ovulation. Oxytocin is produced by the hypothalamus and stimulates uterine contractions during birth.

534. C is correct. All anterior pituitary (i.e., TSH) and pancreatic (i.e., insulin) hormones are peptides. Peptide hormones are hydrophilic and cannot cross the hydrophobic phospholipid bilayer. As a result, these endocrine mediators are forced to bind cell membrane receptors and activate intracellular second-messenger (i.e., cAMP) cascades. Cholesterol-derived steroid hormones (i.e., estrogen) bind nuclear receptors and do not depend on a second-messenger system.

Passage 510 (Questions 535-340)

535. B is correct. The passage informs that radioactive ^{86}Rb was used to measure the activity of the Na$^+$/K$^+$ ATPase. ^{86}Rb had to use the Na$^+$/K$^+$ ATPase to exit the aortic cell. All pumps that excreted ^{86}Rb were labeled as ^{86}Rb/K ATPases. **Active transport** utilizes a pump to move substituents against the gradient with the help of ATP. **Exocytosis** implies the fusion of vesicles with the cell membrane to release certain contents into the extracellular environment. **Facilitated transport** uses channels, not pumps, to translocate hydrophilic compounds across the hydrophobic cell membrane.

536. A is correct. Renin is synthesized by the kidneys when the body is low on fluids. Renin stimulates the release of aldosterone, which elevates the blood volume. However, elevated aldosterone levels negatively inhibit further release of renin.

An individual with Conn's syndrome will have an over-abundance of aldosterone. What does aldosterone do? According to Figure 1, aldosterone stimulates the release of sodium and water into blood vessels, which increases the blood pressure. Aldosterone also decreases the H^+ concentration in the blood. A decrease in H^+ ions causes alkalosis (an increase in the pH). The potassium concentration will be altered by the imbalance of K^+ entering and leaving the blood vessel.

537. D is correct. In the passage it is stated that actinomycin D inhibits gene transcription. **Transcription** is the synthesis of RNA from DNA and occurs in the nucleus. The drug must enter the nucleus to be therapeutic.

538. B is correct. This is a High Yield MCAT fact: aldosterone increases the reabsorption of sodium and water in the distal convoluted tubule and the collecting duct. Aldosterone is secreted by the adrenal cortex after being stimulated by renin-induced angiotensin II.

539. B is correct. What does aldosterone do? It *increases* blood volume by removing sodium and water from urine.

It *increases* urine potassium by activating the Na^+/K^+ ATPase that dumps potassium into the nephron lumen while reabsorbing sodium.

It *decreases* urine volume by reabsorbing water.

As per the question stem, *eplerenone* is a mineralocorticoid antagonist that inhibits the activity of aldosterone. The correct answer choice is B.

540. B is correct. Hormones are almost always delivered to their target tissue by blood. The answer can also be found in Figure 1, where aldosterone is shown to activate the blood side sodium/potassium pump. Hormones found in urine are being excreted. The lymphatic system may contain hormones but it is not their main delivery system. There is no such thing as interstitial hormone fluid.

Passage 511 (Questions 541-546)

541. B is correct. The answer to the question is in the equations. An *increase* in plasma hormone concentration will increase the *metabolic clearance rate* (MCR). An increase in MCR will decrease the hormone half-life. Answer choices C and D are incorrect to this EXCEPT question. A decrease in the total hormone in the body would decrease the *volume of distribution* (VD), thereby decreasing the half-life. The correct answer choice is B.

542. B is correct. According to the passage, a water insoluble steroid travels bounded to a protein and has a longer half-life as a result. **This is important.** Lipid-soluble hormones (i.e., progesterone and other steroids) have a slow onset but a long duration of action. Following their release, steroid hormones require several hours to several days before their initial activity can be detected, but their effect can persist for up to 6 to 8 weeks.

On the other hand, water-soluble hormones (ACTH and other anterior pituitary hormones) are quickly released, have a rapid course of action, but are immediately eliminated by the liver.

543. B is correct. *Clearance* is a direct measure of kidney function. It is the only organ listed that actually clears or removes. The rate at which a particular chemical (i.e., aspirin) is removed from the blood indicates kidney efficiency. This rate of removal is called the renal clearance. This is the identical concept seen in hormone removal.

544. D is correct. The **proximal convoluted tubule** reabsorbs almost all amino acids, glucose, ions, water, etc. that enter the nephron. The **glomerulus** and the **bowman's capsule** make up the kidney filter system: nothing is reabsorbed here. The **collecting duct** reabsorbs water when stimulated by ADH.

545. B is correct. This is a tough question. Receptor properties are important to proper metabolic function because they provide a **high degree of specificity** for a particular ligand (i.e., hormone, neurotransmitter). This makes it possible for a hormone to be secreted at one site in the body and have very specific effects on a distant target organ with a proper receptor. However, the receptor never modifies the ligand because doing so would destroy the ligand specificity.

A receptor also **amplifies** the stimulating signal. This is why hormones that are present in extremely minute concentrations can exert such a powerful control over bodily processes.

546. B is correct. Oxytocin is produced in the hypothalamus, stored in the posterior pituitary, and its target is the uterus. It stimulate uterine contractions during birth and causes the release of milk during breastfeeding.

Independent Questions (Questions 547-556)

547. C is correct. Two hormones are involved in milk production and letdown, prolactin and oxytocin. The correct answer choice is C. **Prolactin** is produced by the anterior pituitary and stimulates the production of milk. **Oxytocin** is produced by the hypothalamus and causes the ejection of milk. **Estrogen** stimulates the development of mammary glands. **ADH** (vasopressin) increases the reabsorption of water in the nephron collecting duct.

548. C is correct. To answer this question select the only component that should never interact with blood. Blood contains RBC, WBC, platelets and proteins. The 3 most important blood proteins are albumin (which maintains the osmotic gradient, globulin (antibody component), and fibrin (needed for coagulation).

The renal artery is in constant contact with moving blood. Sperm are protected by the blood-testes barrier and never interact with blood. Sperm may spill into the blood following an injury to the groin area. The immune system will respond to them as foreign invaders and sterility may result.

549. B is correct. Spermatogenesis, the production of sperm, begins with a **spermatogonium cell** that becomes a **primary spermatocyte** (cell line M). After 24 days, each primary spermatocyte undergoes *the first meiotic division* and becomes two **secondary spermatocytes** (cell line N). Two to three days after that, the 2 secondary spermatocytes undergo *the second meiotic division* and emerge as **4 spermatids**. The entire process from spermatogonial cell to newly released spermatozoa takes about 74 days.

Meiosis has converted a diploid cell (the primary spermatocyte) into haploid spermatids.

550. C is correct. ADH and its analogs stimulate the production and endocytosis of aquaporin channels in nephron collecting ducts. These aquaporins allow the reabsorption of water during the concentration of urine. Renin stimulates the release of aldosterone, which reabsorbs sodium in the kidney.

551. C is correct. Aldosterone is produced by the adrenal gland in response to *low sodium or elevated potassium*. The hormone increases blood sodium levels and decreases blood potassium concentration. This ionic shift is achieved by the aldosterone-stimulated sodium-potassium pump that eliminates potassium into urine.

552. A is correct. This is a High Yield MCAT topic. Thyroid-stimulating hormone (TSH) is the chief stimulator of the thyroid gland and thyroid hormone synthesis. TSH is produced by the anterior pituitary and enhances all components needed for thyroid hormone synthesis, like the iodide transporter, thyroid peroxidase, and thyroglobulin.

The **posterior pituitary** stores ADH and oxytocin, which are synthesized by the hypothalamus. The **parathyroid gland** secretes a hormone by the same name that elevates blood calcium levels.

553. B is correct. Growth hormone is produced by the anterior pituitary and stimulates tissue growth through the synthesis of IGF-1. A deletion of both IGF-1 genes would cause a growth deficiency. Brittle bones and decreased calcium level occurs in animals deficient in parathyroid hormone. Inability to digest lipids may be caused by a lack of pancreatic lipase or bile salts. **FYI:** Anemia is an abnormally low level of hemoglobin in the blood.

554. C is correct. Mitosis produces 2 identical daughter cells. It occurs in all somatic cells to grow, repair, and replace tissue when necessary. (Tissue repair may cause the formation of scar tissue.) **Viral transduction** is one of three methods (the other 2 being conjugation and transformation) bacterial cells use to introduce genetic variability into their genomes. Specifically, transduction depends on a virus injecting novel genetic material while infecting the host.

555. D is correct. The synthesis of sperm begins in the **seminiferous tubules** of the testes. Sperm undergo maturation in the **epididymis** and are expelled through the **vas deferens** during ejaculation. **Seminal vesicles** are a pair of male accessory glands that provide nutrients for sperm.

Mnemonic: "SEVEN UP"—tracks the path sperm take during ejaculation.

- Seminiferous tubules
- Epididymis
- Vas deferens
- Ejaculatory duct
- Nothing
- Urethra
- Penis

556. A is correct. The menstrual cycle is controlled by a variety of glands: the hypothalamus, the anterior pituitary, and the ovaries. The **anterior pituitary** releases FSH, which stimulates the maturation of the ova. **Progesterone** is synthesized by the ovary and the corpus luteum. It regulates the development and shedding of the uterine endometrial lining.

"AMEN"—The **A**drenal **M**edulla produces **E**pinephrine and **N**orepinephrine, which are not involved in the menstrual cycle. They assist the sympathetic nervous system in stimulating the "fight or flight" response.

LECTURE 6

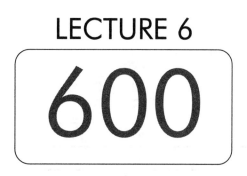

600

Answers & Explanations
Questions 557–667

ANSWERS TO LECTURE 6

557.	C	594.	A	631.	A
558.	B	595.	B	632.	C
559.	C	596.	C	633.	C
560.	B	597.	B	634.	B
561.	D	598.	B	635.	C
562.	A	599.	A	636.	D
563.	B	600.	D	637.	D
564.	B	601.	A	638.	A
565.	B	602.	B	639.	A
566.	B	603.	B	640.	A
567.	C	604.	D	641.	A
568.	A	605.	C	642.	B
569.	D	606.	D	643.	A
570.	C	607.	B	644.	A
571.	B	608.	B	645.	C
572.	A	609.	B	646.	D
573.	D	610.	D	647.	B
574.	B	611.	C	648.	C
575.	A	612.	B	649.	C
576.	C	613.	C	650.	C
577.	B	614.	C	651.	D
578.	D	615.	A	652.	C
579.	B	616.	A	653.	C
580.	B	617.	B	654.	B
581.	A	618.	A	655.	B
582.	C	619.	B	656.	D
583.	B	620.	D	657.	D
584.	B	621.	B	658.	B
585.	C	622.	D	659.	B
586.	A	623.	B	660.	D
587.	B	624.	D	661.	B
588.	C	625.	C	662.	C
589.	D	626.	B	663.	B
590.	A	627.	A	664.	D
591.	D	628.	C	665.	B
592.	A	629.	B	666.	B
593.	A	630.	D	667.	B

Passasge 601 (Questions 557-563)

557. C is correct. Hydrochloric acid is produced by **parietal cells** and gives stomach contents the pH of 2.0. **Chief cells** synthesize pepsinogen, which is designed to digest protein. Pancreatic cells do not secrete pepsinogen. S-cells are found in the duodenum and secrete **secretin**, a natural antacid that neutralizes acidic duodenal contents.

558. B is correct. According to the question stem, vagotomy abolishes the vagal nerve stimulation to the stomach. The vagus nerve is one of the main nerves of the parasympathetic nervous system. Acetylcholine (ACh) is the neurotransmitter for all neurons of the parasympathetic nervous system.

559. C is correct. What is the most important intracellular ion? The answer is **potassium**. The sodium-potassium ATPase pump maintains the ion gradient across a cell membrane by continuously pumping sodium out of the cell (making intracellular sodium concentrations low) and potassium into the cell (making the intracellular potassium concentration high). **Sodium** is the most important extracellular ion.

Ion	Extracellular mmol/L	Intracellular mmol/L
K^+	5	150
Ca^{+2}	110	10
Na^+	140	4

Table 1 Ion Concentrations

560. B is correct. The small intestine is the longest section of the digestive tract and is divided into three segments. The **duodenum** is the first and shortest segment. It receives secretions from the pancreas and liver via the pancreatic and common bile ducts. From the duodenum, food enters the **jejunum** and then the **ileum** before emptying into the first segment of the large intestine. The appendix is a small out-pouching of the large intestine that is prone to infection.

561. D is correct. According to the passage, gastrin, acetylcholine, and histamine are all parietal cell stimulators. All three stimulate the proton pump to secrete acid into the stomach. Blocking each one individually would only partially reduce the secretion of HCl. So the best way to inhibit acid synthesis and release would be to inhibit the proton pump. Proton pump inhibitors are used to treat diseases in which HCl damaged the digestive tract.

562. A is correct. Mechanism 1 is missing leaky potassium channels. Both pumps are pumping potassium into the parietal cell. As a result, potassium will certainly build up in the intracellular environment.

The **sodium-potassium pump** maintains the ion gradient of low intracellular sodium and high intracellular potassium. Adenosine triphosphate (ATP) powers the sodium-potassium pump to transport 3 sodium molecules out of the cell while bringing 2 potassium molecules in.

All peptides bind to cell membrane receptors and exert their effect via a second-messenger system. Steroid hormones are free to diffuse across the cellular membrane and bind to nuclear receptors. According to the passage, HCl secretion is an active process that requires ATP.

563. B is correct. As per the question stem and Mechanism 1, the Cl^-—HCO_3^- exchanger is dumping **bicarbonate** into the bloodstream. Bicarbonate is a base that will increase blood pH and cause an "alkaline tide." The normal blood pH range is 7.35- 7.45. If the blood pH ever reaches 7.0, the person is most likely dead.

Passasge 602 (Questions 564-569)

564. B is correct. Carefully think about the respiratory system. It is a dead-end, a blind tube entering the celom via the trachea. The trachea further progresses into the celom to become the bronchi and the lungs grow around these structures. It is therefore a blind-end structure.

The digestive system is a tube within a tube that has a beginning and an end: it begins at the mouth and ends at the rectum. The digestive system is therefore not a blind tube.

The vascular system is a closed tube. It has no start or finish; rather, blood that circulates the vascular system loops around the same course all day.

565. B is correct. The cells of the three germ layers are able to divide, migrate, and differentiate into various cells, tissues, and organs. You will see at least one 'derived from what?' question on the MCAT.

Derivatives of the three germ layers

Ectoderm:
a. central and peripheral nervous systems
b. epidermis, hair, and nails of the skin
c. lens of the eye

Endoderm:
a. epithelial lining of all the major lumenal surfaces in the body—i.e., gastrointestinal and respiratory tracts
b. liver, pancreas, gall bladder—accessory GI organs

Mesoderm: derives into everything else not already listed
a. cardiovascular system
b. muscular system
c. skeletal system
d. excretory system

566. B is correct. The question stem states that an organ that doesn't move much is difficult to repair. According to the passage, the liver is imbedded in the posterior abdominal wall. The heart was never mentioned in the passage, but it is a relatively mobile structure in comparison to the liver or kidney. Its non-mention in the passage is a clue that it is not the correct answer choice.

567. C is correct. It is stated in the passage that all organs are contained within the celom. External to the *celom* is the head and neck, the muscular portion of the trunk, and the upper and lower limbs.

568. A is correct. Glomeruli are found in the kidneys. They, along with the Bowman's capsule, make up the main nephron filter. The kidneys are situated in the abdominal region and must be surrounded by the abdominal (peritoneal) celom.

569. D is correct. This is very High Yield for the MCAT: In fetal circulation, blood coming through the umbilical vein is shunted around the liver through the **ductus venosus**. Upon birth, the ductus venosus closes off, and the adult remnant is called the *ligamentum venosum*.

In an embryo, blood is shunted around the lungs two ways: the **foramen ovale** allows blood to flow from the right atrium into the left atrium, bypassing the ventricles. Later in the circulation, the **ductus arteriosus** shunts blood from the pulmonary artery (coming out of the right ventricle) directly into the aorta.

Passage 603 (Questions 570-576)

570. C is correct. According to the passage, phenopropylolamine alters hormone levels in the hypothalamus. The question is simply asking which of the listed answer choices is associated with the hypothalamus and thereby will be affected by any drug that affects the hypothalamus. The correct answer is B. **Oxytocin** is synthesized by the hypothalamus and is stored in the posterior pituitary. Its principal actions include the stimulation of uterine contractions during birth and the release of milk when the baby begins to suckle.

The following is High Yield MCAT information: testosterone is made by the testes and is necessary for genital development and secondary sexual characteristics. **Prolactin** is the product of the anterior pituitary and stimulates breast milk synthesis. **Epinephrine** is produced by the adrenal medulla to stimulate the "fight or flight" response in conjunction with the sympathetic nervous system.

571. B is correct. Of the answer choices, *Beta-cells* are the only ones not found in the stomach, but rather in the pancreas. These cells synthesize insulin, which lowers blood sugar levels. All other answer choices are found in the stomach and would therefore be affected by gastric stapling. **Chief cells** are the most numerous of gastric cell types—hence the name. They produce pepsinogen, which is a precursor to pepsin. Pepsin is used to digest protein. **Parietal cells** secrete hydrochloric acid, which activates pepsinogen and effectively sterilizes the contents of the stomach. Parietal cells also secrete intrinsic factor, which is necessary for the resorption of vitamin B_{12}. **Mucous neck cells** protect the stomach from acidic pH by secreting mucous, which helps buffer the acidity.

572. A is correct. This is very High Yield MCAT neuroscience information. The main function of the **hypothalamus** is to maintain *homeostasis*. The gland holds such factors as blood pressure, body temperature, fluid and electrolyte balance, and body weight at a precise "set-point."

The **medulla oblongata** is a swollen upper tip of the spinal cord. It contains the breathing centers that control the rate of breathing by controlling the diaphragm.

The **cerebellum** coordinates balance and body movements during walking, running, etc. People with damage to the cerebellum display jerky and uncoordinated movements.

573. D is correct. According to the passage, orlistat inhibits pancreatic lipase. **Lipase** is an enzyme that is used by the body to break down dietary fats. With insufficient break down of dietary fats, greasy, light-colored stool ensues. There are four lipid-soluble vitamins, A, D, E, and K, that rely on bile and pancreatic lipase for absorption. Long-term lipase inhibition would deplete the body stores of these vitamins because of inhibited intestinal uptake.

574. B is correct. According to the passage, "Slim Tea" causes hepato-renal failure in some people. Thus, the correct answer is B. The renal system does contain the kidneys; however, kidneys are NOT digestive accessory organs; they do not aid digestion in any way.

Hepatocytes (liver cells) make up the largest and most important digestive accessory organ, the liver. (The other 2 digestive accessory organs are the gall bladder and the pancreas.) The stomach is part of the digestive tract but it is not an accessory organ; rather, it is a primary digestive organ.

575. A is correct. Cortisol is a cholesterol derived steroid produced by the adrenal gland. Its principal physiological action is to increase blood glucose levels, thus decreasing glycolysis. Glycolysis occurs in cells that are full of glucose. Cortisol inhibits cellular glucose uptake leaving the sugar in the blood. **Insulin**, on the other hand, functions to decrease blood glucose levels, increase glucose cell reuptake, and increase the rate of glycolysis. Cortisol concentrations show diurnal variation, with its highest concentration being after waking and declining throughout the day.

576. **C is correct.** Stomach stapling is a procedure that makes the stomach smaller and less able to store undigested food. Following stapling, one feels fuller faster so the intake of food decreases. The esophagus is simply a pipe connecting the pharynx to the stomach. No digestion occurs in the esophagus. Lipase is produced by the pancreas and released into the small intestine. The enzyme would not be affected by a smaller stomach.

Independent Questions (Questions 577-587)

577. **B is correct.** The digestive tract is subdivided into compartments by muscular sphincters that occur at the esophagus-stomach (lower esophageal sphincter), stomach-duodenum (pyloric sphincter), and ileum-colon (ileocecal sphincter) junction sites. A high concentration of villi is only present in the small intestine. The propagative process that moves food along the GI tract, known as peristalsis, occurs along the entire length of the digestive system.

578. **D is correct.** As per the question stem, the sodium-hydrogen exchange carrier moves Na^+ ions out of the urine into epithelial cells and H^+ ions, in the opposite direction (an anti-port carrier), into the urine. Because H^+ ions are moving out of epithelial cells (the pH inside the cells would be basic, 7.4 or higher) and into the urine, the expected urine pH should be acidic. The only answer choice with an acidic pH is D.

579. **B is correct.** Pancreatic **lipase** (digests lipids), **colipase** (needed for proper lipase function), and **amylase** (digests carbohydrates) are secreted as active enzymes whereas, like **pepsinogen**, pancreatic proteases (trypsinogen, chymotrypsinogen) are secreted as inactive precursors. Proteases must be inactive while being secreted, otherwise they would digest the pancreas itself and the GI tract along with it.

Also, any enzyme ending in *-ogen* is a zymogen, an inactive enzyme precursor.

580. **B is correct.** The main enzyme found is saliva is amylase. **Amylase** digests carbohydrates and is also produced by the pancreas. **Trypsin** and **chymotrypsin** are only secreted by the pancreas to digest proteins. **Pepsin** is produced by gastric chief cells to initiate the breakdown of protein.

581. **A is correct.** More of the positively charged dextran and less of the negatively charged dextran will be filtered compared to a neutral dextran of the same molecular weight. This is because of the *negative charge* on the renal filtration membrane which attracts positively

charged compounds and repels negatively charged ones.

582. **C is correct.** The small intestine in approximately 6 to 8 m in length and functions to digest food and absorb water, electrolytes, and nutrients. It is divided into the short duodenum, jejunum, and ileum.

583. **B is correct.** According to the question stem, the kidneys and the respiratory system maintain the pH of the body fluids near 7.4. Each system alters a different variable. The respiratory system regulates the level of carbon dioxide (CO_2), while the kidneys control the concentration of bicarbonate (HCO_3^-).

The equation: $CO_2 + H_2O \rightarrow H_2CO_3 \rightarrow H^+ + HCO_3^-$

When carbon dioxide levels increase, the reaction shifts to the right, increasing the concentration of hydrogen ions in the blood. An increase in the concentration of hydrogen ions will decrease the pH. The lungs serve to blow off excess carbon dioxide to maintain blood pH.

584. **B is correct.** Use the process of elimination to answer this question. **Pepsin** is secreted by stomach chief cells to digest protein. **Cortisol**, an endocrine hormone, is released by the adrenal cortex in response to stress. **Trypsin** is an exocrine pancreatic product necessary for digestion of protein.

The endocrine islets of Langerhans account for only 2% of the pancreatic mass. They secrete insulin to lower blood sugar, glucagon to raise blood sugar, and **somatostatin** to inhibit the release of both insulin and glucagon.

585. **C is correct.** Renal conservation of water is an absolute necessity for survival. The nephron, the functional renal unit, is composed of the proximal convoluted tubule, the descending and ascending loop of Henle, the distal convoluted tubule, and the collecting duct. The following renal sites are permeable to water:

- the proximal convoluted tubule—reabsorbs 2/3 of all water entering the nephron
- the descending loop of Henle—passively reabsorbs water
- the distal convoluted tubule—only when stimulated by aldosterone
- the collecting duct—only when stimulated by antidiuretic hormone (ADH)

586. **A is correct.** Three germ layers are present during embryological development: ectoderm, mesoderm, and endoderm. **Ectoderm** is the most external layer and gives rise to the skin, fingernails, and the nervous system including the eye. **Endoderm**, the innermost layer, gives rise to the epithelial lining of all luminal structures and accessory organs of digestion: liver, gall bladder, and pancreas. The **mesoderm** gives rise to all remaining organ systems including the cardiovascular, musculoskeletal, excretory, and reproductive systems.

587. B is correct. Lactic acid is the product of fermentation, which occurs under anaerobic conditions. Glycolysis is also an anaerobic process that produces **pyruvic acid**. The electron transport chain converts reduced substrates, like NADH, into ATP.

Passage 604 (Questions 588-593)

588. C is correct. Be familiar with every major hormone for the MCAT.

Gland	Hormone	Function
Adrenal Medulla	Epinephrine	Stimulates glucose release and "Fight or Flight"
Pancreas (alpha cells)	Glucagon	Raises blood glucose concentration
Adrenal Cortex	Cortisol	Raise blood glucose level and adaptation to long-term stress
Thyroid gland	Calcitonin	Lowers blood calcium level

Of the listed hormones, only calcitonin is unrelated to blood glucose levels.

589. D is correct. The body exists in either a well-fed or fasting state. The well-fed state occurs right after a consumption of a meal. Glucose enters the cell by facilitated diffusion, which is stimulated by insulin. In a well-fed state, the following is seen:

1. high insulin/low glucagon
2. high insulin promotes glucose uptake by muscle and fat
3. glucose in liver is used for glycogen deposition
4. organ glucose oxidation leads to the production of pyruvate and/or lactate via glycolysis and/or fermentation
5. adipose tissue converts excess glucose into fat

590. A is correct. According to the passage, Type 1 diabetes mellitus results from a cell-mediated *autoimmune destruction* of the insulin-secreting pancreatic ß-cells. The most useful markers of autoimmunity are circulating self-antibodies that can be detected in body fluids many years before the disease can be detected by increased glucose concentrations. An insulin receptor count may be useful in Type II insulin-resistant diabetes.

591. D is correct. The salivary glands, liver, gallbladder, and pancreas are not part of the primary digestive tract, but they have a role in digestive activities and are considered to be accessory digestive organs. The two solid accessory organs are the liver and the pancreas. They produce digestive juices that reach the intestine through a system of ducts. The gallbladder contains digestive juices that reach the intestine through a duct. However, it is a hollow sac-like structure (hence the term 'bladder') that only stores the bile made in the liver.

592. A is correct. According to the diabetic ketoacidosis mechanism, muscle tissue is degraded to produce alanine (an amino acid) that is converted to pyruvate and results in hyperglycemia. If the production of glycerol-3-phosphate is inhibited, glycerol, not DHAP, will accumulate in cells.

593. A is correct. It is stated in the passage that diabetes is the #1 cause of non-traumatic amputations (due to damage to peripheral lower limb vessels), blindness (damage to the retina of the eye), and kidney failure (damage to the nephron Bowman's capsule). By the process of elimination, A is correct answer choice B.

Passage 605 (Questions 594-599)

594. A is correct. According to Table 1, alcohol causes cancer of the digestive system and its accessory glands. This makes sense because the GI tract is directly exposed to and most likely to be irritated by the consumption of alcohol.

595. B is correct. A screening test is never diagnostic! Diagnostic tests are used to *confirm* cancer screenings. For example, an abnormal Pap smear is not necessarily indicative of cervical cancer. A biopsy must be performed and evaluated for the possible diagnosis of cancer. (A biopsy is a procedure to obtain a tissue specimen for a microscopic analysis to establish a *precise diagnosis*.) The same goes for a mammography—it's a screening test, not a diagnostic test. A screening test simply serves to identify those individuals with a higher likelihood of developing cancer. Carcinogen exposure does not necessarily mean that cancer is present or will result.

596. C is correct. Use the process of elimination to answer this question. The liver synthesizes but does NOT store bile. Bile is stored and concentrated in the gallbladder. The liver is an accessory organ of the digestive system, not cardiovascular. Anything ending is –itis describes an infection; *meningitis*- infection of the meninges in the brain, *gastritis*- infection of the stomach, *laryngitis* – infection of the larynx. Hepatitis is a viral infection of the liver that may lead to cancer.

597. B is correct. Table 2 demonstrates that residents of different countries have different risks for various cancers. According to the data, citizens of Japan demonstrate a high incidence of stomach cancer, while those of the U.S. have a much lower incidence. If someone from Japan moves to the United States, where there is a relatively low incidence of stomach cancer, his/her risk of developing stomach cancer is likely to *decrease*. Why? It is believed that cancer is caused by an exposure to some unknown agent. If or when the exposure is minimized or eliminated, the risk of associated cancer decreases as well. According to Table 1, stomach cancer is not associated with the consumption of alcohol. Thus, answer choice D can be eliminated.

598. B is correct. According to the question stem, radon causes alveolar cancer, which is associated with the lungs. It can therefore be assumed that radon is a *gas* that is inhaled. Radon is considered to be the second leading cause of lung cancer in the U.S. today. It comes up through the soil under buildings and enters through gaps and cracks in the foundation or insulation.

599. A is correct. According to the table, a nonsmoker/non-asbestos exposed person has a mortality ratio equal to 1. A nonsmoker, asbestos-exposed person has a mortality ratio of 5.2. A smoker that has also been exposed to asbestos has a mortality ratio of 53.2. This data clearly demonstrates that exposure to more than one carcinogen (i.e., cigarette smoke and asbestos) causes much more than a simple additive-affect. The effect is synergistic, or more than the sum of all the parts. The association between smoking and cancer is very strong.

Passage 606 (Questions 600-605)

600. D is correct. According to Figure 1, the colon epithelial cells are involved in the secretion of potassium and reabsorption of sodium and water. The colon does not secrete 230mL of water; that is the volume of water not reabsorbed by the large intestine. This water volume is needed to soften the stool. **Aldosterone** is produced and secreted by the adrenal gland. While it binds receptors in the intestine, it is not secreted from there. Aldosterone stimulates the reabsorption of sodium and water from the kidneys and the large intestine.

601. A is correct. According to the passage, the right colon (cecum and ascending colon) plays a major role in sugar fermentation. Sugar fermentation is the conversion of pyruvate (formed by glycolysis) into lactic acid (lactate) during *anaerobic conditions* via lactate dehydrogenase.

If plenty of oxygen is available, pyruvate is converted into acetyl CoA, which enters the mitochondrial Krebs cycle (citric acid cycle).

602. B is correct. The major target for aldosterone is the distal convoluted tubule of the kidney, where it stimulates three physiologic processes:

1. an increase in the reabsorption of sodium;
2. an increase in the reabsorption of water;
3. an increase in the renal excretion of potassium.

According to the question stem, aldosterone will have the identical effect on the colon. The effects of aldosterone (i.e., the retention of sodium and water) increase overall blood volume and therefore cause an increase in blood pressure.

603. B is correct. According to the question stem, cholera has a flagellum; it is therefore motile. Answer choice A can therefore be eliminated. According to Figure 1, cholera toxin *activates* the adenylate cyclase enzyme in the intestinal cell. This causes an increase in the intracellular second messenger, cAMP, which stimulates a massive release of Cl^-. The high concentration of Cl^- in the lumen drags water out of the cells causing a massive, osmotic diarrhea. Cholera has no effect on ligand binding.

604. D is correct. ACTH is a hormone secreted by the anterior pituitary gland, which then acts directly on the adrenal gland to increase the secretion of cortisol. In stressful situations, ACTH levels rise, causing an elevation in cortisol levels. ACTH release from the anterior pituitary is controlled by a hypothalamus releasing factor, CRH (corticotropin releasing hormone).

In women, **FSH** from the anterior pituitary stimulates the maturation of an oocyte. **Epinephrine** is secreted by the adrenal medulla. **Aldosterone** release from the adrenal cortex is stimulated by angiotensin II.

605. C is correct. According to the question stem, Hirschsprung's disease occurs when the innervation to a segment of the colon is absent. As a result, that portion of the colon constricts (the innervation normally keeps the colon open and moving) not allowing the passage of stool, causes an intestinal obstruction and constipation. Hirschsprung's is present at birth and must be corrected surgically. The Na^+/K^+ pump is unaffected in Hirschsprung's disease; thus changes in potassium secretion are not expected.

Independent Questions (Quesitons 606-616)

606. D is correct. The conversion of **vitamin D** to its active form, synthesis of renin, and the release of erythropoietin all occur in the kidney. Vitamin D helps to increase blood calcium concentration. **Renin** stimulates the adrenal gland to release aldosterone. **Erythropoietin** activates the bone marrow to produce red blood cells.

607. B is correct. The follicle-stimulating hormone (FSH) is secreted by the anterior pituitary. It binds testicular receptors and causes the maturation of sperm in males. In females, FSH governs the maturation of an oocyte prior to ovulation.

608. B is correct. As per the question stem, CCK stimulates the release of enzymes needed to digest fat (i.e., bile and lipase) and protein (i.e., chymotrypsin). **Salivary**

amylase digests carbohydrates and is produced in the mouth. CCK is released in the small intestine and is in no way associated with salivary amylase.

609. B is correct. **Primary active transport** moves compounds against their concentration gradient, uses a pump (i.e., sodium-potassium pump), and requires ATP. **Secondary active transport** is a little more complicated because it is a 2-step mechanism that is used to move compounds like glucose, amino acids, and calcium. The 1st step is to set up a sodium gradient by the use of the sodium-potassium pump (this is primary active transport). Once the sodium gradient is in place, it is used to move glucose against the concentration gradient.

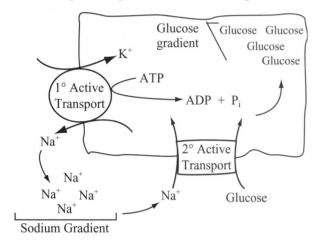

610. D is correct. The renal system is composed of the kidneys and all associated plumbing. (The endocrine glands that sit atop the kidneys are called the *adrenals*.) The organ composed of *hepatocytes* is the liver.

611. C is correct. **Aldosterone** is secreted by the adrenal cortex after being stimulated by the renin-angiotensin system. Renin is released by the kidneys when a decrease in blood volume is sensed. Renin activates angiotensin I, which in turn gets converted into angiotensin II. **Angiotensin II** is a potent stimulator of the adrenal gland. **ACTH** is released by the anterior pituitary to stimulate the release of **cortisol** from the adrenal gland.

612. B is correct. Bicarbonate (HCO_3^-) is a very important biological buffer that buffers the blood as well as the GI tract. It is also a weak base that increases the pH of the GI tract. If the GI tract is too acidic, pancreatic enzymes denature and cannot digest luminal contents. However, bicarbonate is NOT a digestive enzyme.

Bicarbonate synthesis:

$$H_2O + CO_2 \times H_2CO_3 \times HCO_3^- + H^+$$

613. C is correct. The surge of **luteinizing hormone (LH)** causes ovulation. The anterior pituitary may be under-secreting LH, which inhibits the release of an oocyte and causes infertility. In fact, oral contraceptives are designed to inhibit the release of LH by altering estro-

gen/progesterone levels. The **follicle-stimulating hormone (FSH)** stimulates oocyte maturation.

614. C is correct. Bile is synthesized in the liver to emulsify the ingested fat. Bile is stored and concentrated, by the absorption of water and electrolytes, in the **gall bladder**. The spleen is part of the cardiovascular system. It filters blood for invaders and removes old red blood cells.

615. A is correct. The anatomy of the **excretory system** starting from the urethra and moving into the body:

Opening to the urethra → urethra → bladder → opening to the ureter → ureter → kidney renal pelvis

The anatomy of the **male reproductive system** starting from the urethra and moving into the body:

Opening to the urethra → urethra → prostate → ejaculatory duct → vas deferens → epididymis → seminiferous tubules

616. A is correct. Kidney stones in the ureter can cause an obstruction of urine flow out of the nephron. The result is an increase in the hydrostatic pressure in the Bowman's capsule because of the fluid backup. This will interfere with the filtration of blood because of decreased renal function.

The human body does have 2 kidneys but a kidney stone in the urethra, the only tube out of the bladder, will cause a fluid backup in both kidneys.

Passage 607 (Questions 617-622)

617. B is correct. According to the passage, acinar cells secrete pancreatic digestive enzymes. Gyrase (type-II topoisomerase) breaks the transient double-strand DNA in order to relax and prevent DNA supercoiling during DNA replication. Proteases (trypsin, chymotrypsin), amylase and lipase are all secreted by the pancreas and are essential for breaking down and absorbing nutrients. Hydrochloric acid (HCl) is produced by the stomach, not the pancreas. Bicarbonate, also secreted by the pancreas, neutralizes the acidic chyme that enters the duodenum from the stomach.

618. A is correct. The **autonomic nervous system** is divided into sympathetic and parasympathetic divisions. The **parasympathetic system** relies on *acetylcholine* (ACh) as its main neurotransmitter. As a whole, it functions to "rest and digest": it promotes energy conservation by reducing the heart rate and blood pressure, and facilitates digestion by stimulating the digestive tract and all accessory organs (i.e., the pancreas).

The **sympathetic nervous system**, on the other hand, is used during periods of "fight or flight": it causes an increase in blood pressure and a decrease in GI function (since you can neither fight nor flight while digesting).

254

Norepinephrine is the neurotransmitter used by the sympathetic nervous system. **Autonomic nervous system neurotransmitters are very High Yield for the MCAT.**

619. B is correct. The pancreas produces digestive enzymes to breakdown protein, fat, and carbohydrates. When the pancreas is damaged by pancreatitis it may not be able to secrete lipases, amylases, peptidases, etc. Digestion of lipids, proteins, and carbohydrates would decrease and a deficiency in fat-soluble vitamins may follow.

620. D is correct. Insulin is a common MCAT topic. It is made in the pancreas and is released into the bloodstream to decrease blood sugar (cause hypoglycemia) by stimulating sugar uptake by body cells. When sugar enters a cell it is utilized in one of two ways: it can be oxidized by glycolysis into pyruvic acid or stored as glycogen. So insulin indirectly increases the rate of glycolysis and glycogen synthesis. Insulin does NOT stimulate protein synthesis.

621. B is correct. The **spleen** is located on the left side of the body, near the pancreas, and performs several functions. It filters incoming blood and digests old red blood cells and platelets. In addition, it houses nests of B and T-cells (white blood cells) that filter incoming blood for bacteria and infectious agents. With overactivity, the spleen may become swollen and rupture.

Insulin is produced by the pancreas to decrease blood glucose.

622. D is correct. According to the passage, secretin and cholecystokinin (CCK) *stimulate* pancreatic secretions, whereas somatostatin and pancreatic polypeptide *inhibit* enzyme release. The correct answer must be D. **Secretin** is released into the blood and stimulates the pancreas to discharge bicarbonate, which neutralizes the acidic contents entering the intestine from the stomach.

Passage 608 (Questions 623-628)

623. B is correct. The kidneys are two bean-shaped, reddish organs located in the lower back on either side of the vertebral column. They are responsible for

1. removing waste from the body by filtering blood at the glomerulus;
2. selectively reabsorbing metabolically important substances like amino acids, carbohydrates, and electrolytes;
3. excreting metabolic toxins;
4. regulating the electrolyte and acid-base balance;
5. regulating the blood pressure, and
6. stimulating red blood cell production.

Steroids hormones are produced by endocrine glands, not the kidneys.

624. D is correct. This is a straightforward question asked in a complicated way. Where is ADH synthesized? ADH is synthesized in the **hypothalamus** and is stored in the posterior pituitary. ADH is a peptide with a major role in regulating the water balance.

ADH is also known as vasopressin because of the vasopressor response to pharmacological doses. You may see the same hormone referred to by either name.

625. C is correct. The final disaccharide digestion and absorption occurs at the microvilli (also known as a "brush border") of the small intestine. Incorporated into the brush border are enzymes that complete disaccharide digestion: *maltase*—hydrolyzes maltose into glucose; *sucrase*—hydrolyzes sucrose into glucose and fructose; and *lactase*—hydrolyzes lactose into glucose and galactose. Carbohydrate digestion begins in the mouth. However, tiny disaccharides are not produced until chyme (food mass leaving the stomach) enters the small intestine. The large intestine (colon) is responsible for water reuptake.

626. B is correct. Brush border is composed of microvilli, which are extensions of the lumenal wall that increase the absorptive surface area. Unlike cilia, microvilli are not motile.

627. A is correct. Renal gross anatomy: Kidney → Ureter → Bladder → Urethra. The most common source of a renal infection is bacteria that live on the skin and enter the urinary tract through the urethra. Note that the urethra is the tube that extends from the outside of the body to the bladder, while the ureter connects the bladder to the kidneys (and thus has no direct contact with the outside surface). Women have very short (4 cm) urethras when compared to males, whose urethras are about 20 cm in length. As a result, once bacteria enter the female urethra, they have a much shorter distance to travel before reaching the bladder and sometimes the kidneys. The ureters, on the other hand, which take urine from the kidneys into the bladder, are smooth muscle tubes that are identical in length in both sexes. Women have smaller bladders in order to accommodate a uterus in that space.

628. C is correct. The anatomy of the excretory system starting from the urethra and moving into the body:

Opening to the urethra → urethra → bladder → opening to the ureter → ureter → kidney renal pelvis

According to the passage, infection of the excretory system begins at the urethra and migrates into the body to spread bacteria to the bladder (causing cystitis) or the kidney (causing pyelonephritis). In order for pyelonephritis to occur, bacteria must invade the ureter to reach the kidney. That is not the case with cystitis because the bladder is situated before the ureter. The correct answer choice is C. The urethra and the bladder are usually infected in both cystitis and pyelonephritis. The urethra runs through the prostate, which is part of the reproductive system. In males, the prostate would also be infected in both cystitis and pyelonephritis.

Passage 609 (Questions 629-634)

629. B is correct. According to the passage, 67% of filtered sodium is reabsorbed by the proximal convoluted tubule (PCT). So, 67% of the 62 mg/ml of sodium filtered through the nephron will be reabsorbed by the PCT. 62 mg/ml was rounded to 60 mg/ml to allow for an easier calculation: *2/3 × 60 = 40 mg/ml*. Always round figures on the MCAT..

630. D is correct. Chloride (Cl⁻) is the only *anion* listed in the answer choices.

Ion	Extracell. Conc. mmol/L	Intracell. Conc. mmol/L
K^+	5	150
Ca^{2+}	110	10
Na^+	140	4

Table 1 Ion Concentrations

631. A is correct. According to the passage, the sodium-hydrogen pump excretes hydrogen ions out of the tubular cell and into the nephron lumen. A higher H^+ concentration in the lumen will increase lumenal acidity, or cause a decrease in the pH. The reverse is also true; as the lumen becomes more acidic, the tubular cell cytoplasm must become more basic as it loses protons. Only answer choices A and D demonstrate a basic tubular cell pH; but answer choice D is too extreme. No biological cell has a pH of 13.

632. C is correct. Antidiuretic hormone, or ADH, is one of the important regulators of body volume. It is produced by the hypothalamus and stored in the posterior pituitary. It stimulates the nephron collecting duct to reabsorb water (and thus have an antidiuretic effect). A person with SIADH, or inappropriately high secretion of ADH, is absorbing every last drop of water from the collecting tubule. This results in extremely concentrated, low volume urine. Alcohol is a potent ADH *inhibitor* – this explains the long bathroom lines in bars.

633. C is correct. A Type I diabetic does not synthesize any insulin, a hormone needed to lower blood sugar. Because the concentration of blood glucose is very high in an uncontrolled diabetic, high amount of glucose is filtered (glucose is never secreted!) into the nephron lumen. Under normal physiologic conditions, the proximal convoluted tubule reabsorbs every last glucose

molecule via a transporter, such that no glucose is lost in the urine. In a diabetic individual, however, the amount of glucose filtered through the kidneys is so high that it saturates all the carriers. When this occurs, glucose will begin to appear in urine. Note that glucose would never, under any circumstances, be secreted or transported deliberately into the urine.

634. B is correct. GI digestion is a High Yield MCAT topic. Food placed in the mouth is chewed into smaller particles, moistened and lubricated by saliva, and worked on by **salivary amylase**. The amylase initiates the digestion of starch. Therefore, carbohydrate digestion begins in the mouth. Protein digestion starts in the stomach and is completed in the small intestine. For the purposes of the MCAT, lipid digestion occurs only in the small intestine. No digestion of any kind takes place in the esophagus.

Independent Questions (Questions 635-645)

635. C is correct. For the MCAT, foods high in triglycerides are digested only in the small intestine by the pancreatic lipase. (Lipase is also produced in the mouth but this information is never tested on the MCAT.) The digestion of carbohydrates begins in the mouth. The stomach initiates protein digestion. No digestion takes place in the esophagus.

636. D is correct. Antidiuretic hormone (ADH) is released from the posterior pituitary and stimulates the renal collecting duct to reabsorb water in order to concentrate the urine. As per the question stem, persons with *diabetes insipidus* do not respond to ADH despite having normal blood concentration of the hormone. Their urine remains diluted because the collecting duct fails to reabsorb water. *Diabetes mellitus* is a disease of the pancreas that elevates blood glucose levels.

637. D is correct. The renal loop of Henle, specifically the descending limb, concentrates urine by reabsorbing water. (The ascending limb of the loop of Henle is impermeable to water.) According to Table 1, juxtamedullary nephrons have longer loops of Henle in comparison to cortical nephrons. A kidney with the highest concentration of juxtamedullary nephrons is expected to be better at concentrating urine. The correct answer choice is D.

638. A is correct. The exocrine pancreas is one of three accessory GI organs (the other 2 being the liver and gall bladder). Its function is essential for digestion. Unlike the enzymes secreted by the mouth (amylase) and stomach (pepsin), pancreatic enzymes are absolutely essential for normal digestion and nutrient absorption. One cannot digest food without a functioning pancreas. This is why pancreatic cancer has such a poor prognosis.

The colon does not secrete digestive enzymes. It functions to reabsorb water and secrete potassium.

639. A is correct. Glycolysis is an anaerobic process that occurs in the cytoplasm. It converts a molecule of glucose into 2 molecules of pyruvic acid, 2 molecules of NADH, and 2 net ATP.

640. A is correct. According to the question stem, clinical manifestations of a pheochromocytoma are caused by an excessive production of epinephrine. **Epinephrine** (also known as adrenalin) mediates a sympathetic nervous system "fight or flight" response. The biological effects of epinephrine include: 1) an increase in blood pressure, 2) an increase in heart rate, 3) pupil dilation, and 4) the inhibition of the GI system.

641. A is correct. Gastric **parietal cells** produce hydrochloric acid when properly stimulated. As per the question stem, cimetidine inhibits parietal cells from releasing HCl and as a result the gastric pH would increase. Pepsin is designed to digest protein and is produced by gastric **chief cells**.

642. B is correct. This is important. The digestive tract is lined with **involuntary smooth muscle** that is controlled by the autonomic nervous system. Can you make yourself digest? The only exception is the esophagus: with the upper 1/3 being voluntary skeletal muscle (to allow for swallowing), middle 1/3 being a mixture of both skeletal and smooth muscle, and the lower 1/3 being pure smooth muscle.

643. A is correct. The proper digestion of macromolecules is required for adequate absorption of nutrients out of the small intestine. Carbohydrates must be broken down into monosaccharides like glucose, fructose, and galactose. Sucrose is a disaccharide composed of glucose and a fructose. Disaccharide digestion occurs at the intestinal brush border via enzymes like sucrases, lactases, and maltases. Peptides are broken into amino acids in order to be absorbed. Triglycerides are degraded into free fatty acids and monoglycerides.

644. A is correct. Aldosterone is produced by the adrenal cortex. It stimulates the reabsorption of sodium and the excretion of potassium by the kidney. When sodium is reabsorbed water follows passively into the blood and increases the blood pressure.

645. C is correct. Protein synthesis is carried out by **ribosomes**, which are either free-floating or embedded in the rough endoplasmic reticulum (rough ER). Free-floating ribosomes synthesize proteins (i.e., enzymes) needed by the cell itself, while the rough ER usually produces proteins for secretion into the extracellular space (i.e., peptide hormones). The **smooth ER** is involved in steroid synthesis and cellular detoxification. **Lysosomes** are digestive organelles.

Passage 610 (Questions 646-651)

646. D is correct. It is stated in the passage that angiotensin I is a deca-peptide; a deca-peptide is composed of 10 amino acids. (Familiarity with chain prefixes is important for the MCAT: meth- is 1, eth- is 2, prop- is 3…octyl- is 8, non- 9, deca- 10.) ACE then catalyzes a two-amino acid cleavage from angiotensin I to produce angiotensin II. Therefore, angiotensin II must be 8 amino acids long.

647. B is correct. According to Table 1, percentage of sodium absorbed from the proximal convoluted tubule is identical to the percentage of water absorbed. The reabsorbed fluid must therefore be isosmotic with the nephron lumenal contents because the concentration gradient across the renal cell membrane does not change.

Definitions: A *hyperosmotic solution* has a greater solute concentration in comparison to another solution. A *hypoosmotic solution* has a lower solute concentration in comparison to another solution. An *isosmotic solution* has an equal solute concentration in comparison to another solution.

648. C is correct. According to the passage, angiotensin-converting enzyme (ACE) is a protease that stimulates the production of angiotensin II (ATII). ATII then stimulates the adrenal cortex to release **aldosterone**, and promotes the constriction of arterioles: these actions increase the blood pressure.

An ACE inhibitor such as captopril reverses all of these effects, thus decreasing the blood pressure. It does so by preventing the formation of ATII, which prevents the release of aldosterone. It also causes vasodilation of arterioles instead of vasoconstriction. But it does not exert any competitive inhibition on angiotensin II receptors.

649. B is correct. According to the passage, the macula densa releases rennin when stimulated by low levels of NaCl entering the distal nephron. The nephron is the functional unit of the kidney. Review of nephron anatomy: the glomerulus → Bowman's capsule → proximal convoluted tubule → Loop of Henle (descending and ascending limbs) → distal convoluted tubule (this is where the macula densa is located) → collecting ducts → minor calyx → major calyx → renal pelvis → out of the kidney into the ureter.

The macula densa responds to NaCl changes that occur before the distal convoluted tubule. Thus, answer choices A, C and D can all be eliminated. According to Table 1, the proximal convoluted tubule (PCT) reabsorbs the most Na+; low sodium here is most likely to stimulate the release of renin downstream.

650. C is correct. The information to answer this question is found in Table 1. The loop of Henle uses a sodium countercurrent mechanism to establish extremely hypertonic conditions (up to 1200 mmol/l); this allows for maximal water reabsorption and the production of highly concentrated urine. Inhibition of water reabsorption by the loop (as with a diuretic) will result in rapid water loss from the body. For this reason, **loop diuretics are the most powerful.**

651. **D is correct.** According to the passage, angiotensinogen is a peptide. Peptides are synthesized by the rough endoplasmic reticulum. The smooth endoplasmic reticulum synthesizes hormones and detoxifies the cell. Lysosomes are digestive organelles that break down ingested macromolecules.

Passage 611 (Questions 652-657)

652. **C is correct.** According to the passage, the basement membrane is the most selective part of the filtration barrier and is *negatively charged* at physiological pH because of all those attached anions. Large negatively charged particles will be repelled by the basement membrane, while positively charged and neutral particles will enter the nephron.

Glucose and amino acids are tiny and are normally freely filtered by the kidneys. After being filtered into the nephron, glucose and amino acids are reabsorbed by the proximal convoluted tubule and returned to circulation.

653. **C is correct.** Two hormones regulate body volume: antidiuretic hormone (ADH) and aldosterone. **ADH** is made in the hypothalamus and stored in the posterior pituitary. **Aldosterone**, which is stimulated by angiotensin II, is made in the adrenal cortex. Dehydration or the loss of body water causes both the release of *renin* from the kidneys and the stimulation of osmoreceptors in the hypothalamus. The release of renin begins a series of reactions, beginning with the conversion of angiotensinogen to angiotensin I, ultimately leading to the release of aldosterone from the adrenal cortex. In the hypothalamus, stimulation of osmoreceptors causes the release of ADH from the posterior pituitary. ADH then promotes increased water reabsorption from the kidneys. Together, the effects of ADH and aldosterone result in an increase of body fluids and an increase in blood pressure.

654. **B is correct. Endothelium** is a specialized type of epithelium that lines blood vessels and capillaries. Epithelium is derived from embryonic endoderm and lines all lumenal body surfaces. It is stated in the passage that pores in the capillary wall are called *endothelial fenestrae*. On the MCAT, be sure to read every word and pay attention to small details that may be hidden in the text.

655. **B is correct.** T_3 is the active form of *thyroid hormone*, which increases the basal metabolic rate by stimulating protein synthesis in virtually every body tissue. In addition, T_3 elevates oxygen consumption by increasing the activity of the Na^+ / K^+ ATPase. A person with *hypothyroidism* has abnormally low levels of thyroid hormone, which decreases the metabolism of all nutrients, including cholesterol, triglycerides, and phospholipids. This may lead to accelerated clogging of arteries with lipids (arteriosclerosis).

656. **D is correct. This is a High Yield MCAT fact:** ADH acts on receptors of the *collecting tubule or duct*, to allow them to reabsorb more water. These cells are impermeable to water in the absence of ADH.

657. **D is correct.** Approximately 10% of the filtered water and 25% of filtered Na^+ and Cl^- are reabsorbed by the loop of Henle. Under normal circumstances, the *descending limb* of the loop of Henle is permeable to water and impermeable to ions. The *ascending limb,* on the other hand, is impermeable to water but allows for the transport of Na^+, K^+, and Cl^-.

Independent Questions (Questions 658-667)

658. **B is correct.** The cardiac conduction pathway begins with the **SA node** that is located in the right atrium. The signal then travels to the **AV node** (located between the atria and the ventricles), down the **bundle of His**, which splits into the right/left **Purkinje fibers**. The Purkinje fibers spread the conduction signal to the 2 ventricles, which contract simultaneously to expel blood.

Summary: SA node → AV node → bundle of His → Purkinje fibers

659. **B is correct.** Excretory system anatomy: the **collecting ducts** empty into a much larger duct, called the minor calyx. Several **minor calyces** join to form a **major calyx**. The major calyces join to form the **renal pelvis**. A single **ureter** originates from the renal pelvis and extends to the **urinary bladder**. The bladder stores urine and is emptied by **the urethra**, which carries urine from the bladder out of the body.

660. **D is correct.** Methionine is the first amino acid incorporated into every eukaryotic protein. **Cysteine** is the sole amino acid capable of forming disulfide bonds. Valine and alanine are 2 nonpolar amino acids.

661. **B is correct.** There are only 2 anions listed in the answer choices, chlorine and oxygen. Answer choices A and C are eliminated. Sodium (Na^+) carries a 1^+ change. So the most appropriate anion of choice would be chlorine (Cl^-), which carries a 1^- charge. Oxygen (O^{-2}) has a 2^- charge and is not the best option.

662. C is correct. The Na^+/K^+ ATPase transports 3 sodium ions out of the cell for every 2 potassium moving into the cell. When the pump is inhibited, the intracellular sodium concentration *increases* and intracellular potassium concentration *decreases*. When the intracellular sodium is elevated, the extracellular sodium should be decreased.

663. B is correct. Gastrin, intrinsic factor, and pepsin are all secreted by the stomach. Gastrin stimulates the stomach to release HCl. Intrinsic factor is needed for the absorption of vitamin B_{12}. Pepsin is produced by stomach chief cells to digest ingested protein.

664. D is correct. The normal urine volume is 1-2 L/day, which is less than 2 percent of the fluid that enters the kidneys. To figure out the answer to this question consider this: the total human blood volume is about 5 liters or 11 pints.

25 % of 180 = 45 liters

11 % of 180 = 20 liters

5 % of 180 = 9 liters

Any other answer choice, with the exception of D, assumes that one urinates out more fluid than his/her entire blood volume. That would be impossible.

665. B is correct. Based on the information in the question stem it is safe to assume that at all rates of secretion, pancreatic juice is essentially isotonic with plasma.

666. B is correct. Organ A is the liver, which synthesizes bile salts. Bile salts are stored in the gallbladder and are released when fat is present in the small intestine (Organ B). Bile salts emulsify lipids and increase the surface area for pancreatic lipase to bind to. Pancreatic lipase is the actual enzyme that digests ingested fats.

667. B is correct. The small intestine is divided into 3 parts: **the duodenum, the jejunum, and the ileum**. (The cecum is the beginning of the large intestine.) All the pancreatic digestive enzymes and liver's bile are dumped into the "mixing pot," otherwise known as the duodenum. It is the shortest segment of the small intestine and does not have the extensively developed folding seen in the jejunum. This may have to do with the fact that relatively little nutrient absorption occurs in this area.

LECTURE 7

700

Answers & Explanations
Questions 668–781

668. B	706. A	744. B
669. C	707. D	745. D
670. B	708. B	746. B
671. C	709. C	747. B
672. B	710. D	748. A
673. A	711. D	749. B
674. B	712. C	750. D
675. B	713. D	751. B
676. C	714. D	752. D
677. B	715. B	753. B
678. D	716. D	754. A
679. A	717. D	755. C
680. A	718. D	756. D
681. C	719. B	757. C
682. B	720. D	758. D
683. B	721. C	759. B
684. D	722. D	760. D
685. B	723. B	761. B
686. B	724. B	762. B
687. D	725. D	763. C
688. B	726. A	764. C
689. D	727. B	765. A
690. D	728. A	766. C
691. C	729. C	767. A
692. C	730. C	768. A
693. B	731. D	769. B
694. B	732. A	770. A
695. A	733. B	771. D
696. C	734. A	772. C
697. A	735. C	773. D
698. B	736. D	774. C
699. B	737. B	775. D
700. A	738. B	776. C
701. D	739. B	777. C
702. C	740. C	778. A
703. C	741. C	779. C
704. A	742. C	780. C
705. B	743. C	781. B

668. B is correct. The heart has 4 valves:

1. **Tricuspid valve** separates the right atria from the right ventricle.

2. **Bicuspid (mitral) valve** separates the left atria from the left ventricle.

3. **Pulmonic valve** separates the right ventricle from pulmonary arteries.

4. **Aortic valve** separates the left ventricle from the aorta.

The normal cardiac blood flow:

The **vena cava** brings blood into the **right atria** → tricuspid valve → **right ventricle** → pulmonic valve → pulmonary artery → **lungs** → pulmonary vein → **left atria** → mitral valve → **left ventricle** → aortic valve → aortic arch.

669. C is correct. Use the process of elimination to answer this question. According to the passage, the Starling's laws describes the way *preload*, influencing myocardial stretching, determines the blood volume pumped by the heart. The parasympathetic nervous system is never mentioned in the passage. As per the passage, a decrease in the *afterload* decreases the resistance to blood flow, thereby decreasing the work on the heart. Also, an increase in the heart rate decreases the *preload*.

670. B is correct. According to the passage, the left ventricular blood volume is known as the *preload*. The question stem informs that *end-diastolic volume* is the amount of blood found in the left ventricle at the end of diastole. Thus, end-diastolic volume is equivalent to the *preload* of the heart. *Afterload* is not a volume at all; rather it is a measure of the aortic resistance to blood flow.

671. C is correct. The sympathetic nervous system increases the heart rate by stimulating cardiac receptors with **norepinephrine** (sympathetic neurotransmitter) or with **epinephrine** (adrenal medulla catecholamine). **Acetylcholine** is a parasympathetic neurotransmitter. The parasympathetic nervous system decreases the heart rate.

672. B is correct. In order to maximize oxygen delivery, the heart needs to pump blood against minimal resistance. In order to do so, the *preload* (volume in the left ventricle before it contracts) must increase and the *afterload* (resistance to blood flow) must decrease. Increasing the heart rate is always a sensible method to increase oxygen delivery to tissue. However, in order to maximize the amount of oxygen delivered for any given heart rate, resistance to flow must be low.

673. A is correct. According to the question stem, varicose veins prevent an effective return of blood to the heart. Law 1 deals with venous return and its effect on the heart. The correct answer choice is A. Law 2 describes how cardiac function depends on aortic resistance to

blood flow. Law 3 examines the heart rate and cardiac function.

---

674. B is correct. As per the passage, trained athletes (i.e., marathon runners) have a high pulse pressure because of a very low peripheral resistance, which decreases the diastolic blood pressure. Pulse pressure is the difference between systolic and diastolic pressures: when the systolic pressure remains the same but diastolic pressure decreases, the pulse pressure increases.

675. B is correct. According to the question stem, stored blood pressure is considered to be potential energy, which would then propel blood along the circulatory system. As blood (under pressure) changes from standing to flowing, there is a decrease in the potential energy and an increase in the kinetic energy. Kinetic energy would eventually be converted to thermal energy by the friction of blood rubbing against the walls of blood vessels. Electrical energy is used during the cardiac action potential to stimulate muscle contraction.

Potential energy exists whenever an object with a mass is in the "position" to be converted to kinetic energy. **Kinetic energy** exists whenever an object with a mass is in motion with some velocity. Everything moving has kinetic energy.

Potential Energy = (mass)(gravitational acceleration of the earth)(height)

Kinetic Energy = → (mass)(velocity^2)

676. C is correct. Under normal circumstances, glucose and its oxidation product, ATP, supply the chemical energy to feed the heart. Nucleic acids are the building blocks of DNA and do not supply chemical energy.

677. B is correct. The blood is ejected from the heart and must return there; the ideal receptive area is the heart itself, specifically the right atrium, which has a blood pressure of almost zero. The capillaries do have a low blood pressure, however, they cannot serve as a receptive area because blood would pool there and not return to the heart. Blood pooling in the lungs is a medical emergency and can cause death by inhibiting proper gas exchange.

678. D is correct. Blood pressure is controlled by several functional and structural properties of the cardiovascular, endocrine, nervous, and renal systems—all of which are complexly regulated. Let us assess of few of these factors:

Blood volume: is regulated by the kidneys and correlates directly with blood pressure. If the blood volume increases, the blood pressure will increase because of the need to accommodate the extra fluid.

Blood vessel compliance: determines the degree to which blood vessels can stretch in order to accommodate the flowing blood. As compliance decreases, the blood pressure increases.

Peripheral resistance: is determined by the sympathetic nervous system. When elevated it causes an increase in blood pressure because blood has a difficult time flowing through narrow vessels.

679.   A is correct. According to the passage, pulse pressure is the difference between systolic and diastolic pressures. For instance, in an individual with an ideal blood pressure of 120/80:

- 120 mm Hg is the systolic pressure during *contraction* of the ventricles

- 80 mm Hg is the diastolic pressure when the ventricles are *relaxed*

- 40 mm Hg is the pulse pressure, or the difference between the two (120 – 80 = 40 mm Hg)

Maximum pulse pressure would result when systolic pressure is highest and diastolic pressure is lowest.

Passage 703 (Questions 680-685)

680.   A is correct. According to the cardiac output equation, Cardiac Output = HR x Stroke Volume, an animal can maximize its cardiac output by increasing the heart rate and the stroke volume. (Stroke volume is the volume ejected per cardiac contraction.) Decreasing physical exertion does not maximize cardiac output. Increasing the red blood cell concentration would not have any direct effect on cardiac output.

681.   C is correct. It can be inferred from the 1st paragraph that since the oxygen carrying capacity of blood is similar, small animals must have hearts that pump blood at a higher rate. In other words, small animals have a higher cardiac output to supply the needs of the body. This perhaps explains their overall shorter life spans.

682.   B is correct. To determine how long it takes to circulate 5 liters of blood, it is first necessary to determine the cardiac output. Taking the data from the question stem: (heart rate of 72) (ejection volume of 70 ml) = 5,040 ml or 5.040 liters. Comparing the total blood volume with the cardiac output you can see that the entire blood volume passes through the heart on the average once every minute. All of the output from the right heart goes through the lungs (5 liters/min). The output from the left heart goes through different systemic organs.

683.   B is correct. The renin-angiotensin system plays an important role in regulating blood volume and, as a result, blood pressure: when the blood volume increases so does the blood pressure.

The kidneys release renin in response to decreased blood volume. Renin catalyzes the conversion of angiotensinogen to angiotensin I (ATI). Angiotensin Converting Enzyme (ACE) then converts ATI into angiotensin II (ATII). Angiotensin II stimulates the adrenal cortex to release aldosterone, which in turn acts upon the kidneys to increase sodium and fluid retention. This increases blood volume and blood pressure. MCAT writers frequently ask questions regarding this pathway and blood pressure.

684.   D is correct. According to data in Table 1, not all medium-sized animals adjust to increased activity in the same way. An active mammal increases cardiac output by increasing the heart rate (there is almost a 6 fold increase). Ejection volume actually decreases in an active mammal (see the –0.9). In contrast, a swimming fish increases cardiac output by increasing the ejection volume, with only a minor increase in the heart rate (only a 35% increase).

685.   B is correct. This question tests one's deduction skills. According to the last sentence in the passage, reptiles and amphibians cannot take oxygen through the skin. Answer choices C and D are eliminated.

Also the question stem suggests that the early ancestors of vertebrates took oxygen up through their skin because they used their gills to feed. (Fish have gills to take up oxygen, not to feed.) These early ancestors also lacked jaws to feed. Today's vertebrates (including all backboned creatures such as fish, amphibians, and reptiles) are not capable of oxygen uptake through the skin because they have gills or lungs to breathe with and jaws with which to feed. Only hagfish and lampreys lack jaws, like their invertebrate ancestors, and therefore must take up oxygen though their skin.

Independent Questions (Questions 686-695)

686.   B is correct. The normal cardiac blood flow:

The **vena cava** brings blood into the **right atria** → tricuspid valve → **right ventricle** → pulmonic valve → pulmonary artery → **lungs** → pulmonary vein → **left atria** → mitral valve → **left ventricle** → aortic valve → aorta. The vena cava is located before the right atrium.

687.   D is correct. Review of the circulatory system:

Right atrium **(deoxygenated blood)** → Right Ventricle **(deoxygenated blood)** → Pulmonary artery **(deoxygenated blood)** → Lungs → Pulmonary vein **(oxygenated blood)** → Left atrium **(oxygenated blood)** → Left Ventricle **(oxygenated blood)** → Aorta **(oxygenated blood)** → Arteries **(oxygenated blood)** → Arterioles **(oxygenated blood)** → Capillaries **(oxygenated blood)** → Venules **(deoxygenated blood)** →

Veins **(deoxygenated blood)** → Vena Cava **(deoxygenated blood)** → Right atrium **(deoxygenated blood)**

The **pulmonary artery** carries deoxygenated blood from the right ventricle to the lungs. To answer this question the reader must select a vessel that also carries deoxygenated blood. The correct answer choice is D.

688. B is correct. Hypertension (high blood pressure), atherosclerosis, and stroke are all cardiovascular disorders because all three are associated with problems with blood vessels. A stroke does happen in the brain but it is caused by an occluded vessel.

689. D is correct. The minute-to-minute regulation of blood pressure is a multifactorial process. The major factors that influence blood pressure are blood volume, heart rate, and peripheral resistance to blood flow.

An increase in the muscle tone around blood vessels or scarring *increases* the peripheral resistance and the blood pressure. Why? Because blood is forced to flow through a narrow space.

An increase in the number of blood vessels increases the area available for blood flow and decreases the blood pressure.

The number of epithelial cells (cells that line all lumenal surfaces in the body), however, has no effect on the blood pressure.

690. D is correct. The **thymus**, along with the bone marrow, is a primary central lymphoid organ that replenishes the T-cell population of the immune system. (The **bone marrow** replenishes the B-cell population.) Lymph nodes, the spleen, and tonsils are peripheral lymphoid tissues that house immune system cells but do not replenish aged ones.

691. C is correct. Adenosine triphosphate (ATP) is an energy molecule that contains a ribose sugar (5-member ring), a nitrogen base, and 3 phosphate groups. **Nucleotides** are the building blocks of DNA. They also have a ribose sugar, a nitrogen base, but a single phosphate group.

692. C is correct. Lung alveoli are designed for rapid gas exchange. Here are some things to remember:

Each lung is composed of millions of alveolar sacs. This arrangement produces an enormous surface area for gas exchange.

Gas exchange occurs by **simple diffusion** down the concentration gradient.

The diffusion distance traveled by gas molecules from the alveoli into the blood is very short. An increase in the diffusion distance decreases the efficacy of the gas exchange.

693. B is correct. The respiratory system begins with either the **nose** or the **mouth**. Then oxygen is propelled into the **pharynx** and then the **larynx**, which houses the voice box. The **larynx** continues into the **trachea**, which divides into 2 main bronchi.

Review: nose → pharynx → larynx → trachea → main bronchi

694. B is correct. This is an example of **autoimmunity**, where an inappropriate immune response is targeted against a non-diseased self-tissue. An **allergy** is the immune system overreacting to a foreign substance (i.e., pollen) that is of little threat to the host. Pancreatitis (just like any other *–itis*) is a bacterial or viral infection of the pancreas.

695. A is correct. The heart has 4 valves:

Right Side Heart Valves:

1. The **Tricuspid valve** separates the right atria from the right ventricle.
2. The **Pulmonic valve** separates the right ventricle from pulmonary arteries.

Left Side Heart Valves:

3. The **Bicuspid (mitral) valve** separates the left atria from the left ventricle.
4. The **Aortic valve** separates the left ventricle from the aorta.

Passage 704 (Questions 696-701)

696. C is correct. The cardiovascular system is the heart and associated plumbing that supplies blood to the body. *Oxygenated blood* leaves the heart through the **aorta** and passes into a branching system of **arteries** that flow into **arterioles** and then into a system of **capillaries**, where the functional gas exchange occurs. The blood that flows out of the capillaries into **venules** is *deoxygenated*. The **venules** drain into **veins**, which eventually drain into the **superior and inferior vena cavas**. The vena cavas empty into the right atrium. The blood remains deoxygenated until re-oxygenation can occur in the lungs. The **pulmonary vein** carries freshly oxygenated blood to the left atrium.

Deoxygenated blood is found in:

• venous system

• vena cava

• right atrium and ventricle

• pulmonary artery

697. A is correct. The aortic valve separates the left ventricle from the aorta. Aortic stenosis or narrowing of the aortic valve would prevent the proper flow of blood out of the ventricle and decrease the expected stroke volume. (Stroke volume is the volume of blood pumped by the left ventricle with every heartbeat.) According to the passage, the normal stroke volume ranges from 70-140 ml. The correct answer choice would be a stroke volume under 70 ml.

698. B is correct. The only listed metabolic pathway that produces carbon dioxide is the Krebs cycle. **Glycolysis** converts a molecule of glucose into 2 molecules of pyruvate, 2 molecules of NADH, and 2 net ATP. Pyruvate is converted into **acetyl CoA**, which enters the **Krebs cycle** to produce 3 NADH, 1 FADH$_2$, and carbon dioxide. The electron transport chain synthesizes ATP by oxidizing NADH and FADH$_2$ molecules. Protein synthesis is conducted by ribosomes without the release of carbon dioxide.

699. B is correct. According to the passage, cardiac output is equal to the stroke volume (SV) multiplied by number of beats per minute. (CO = SV × Heart Rate) As per the question stem, the heart rate is 130 beats per minute. The maximal stroke volume is 140ml. Cardiac output = (130) (140) = 18,200 ml per minute or 18.2 liters per minute.

700. A is correct. The pressure gradient is the main force that drives the flow of blood. The aorta is an area of high blood pressure and the vena cava is an area of low blood pressure. The heart just gives the blood a little push.

701. D is correct. The MCAT loves to test heart valves. There are four valves all together. The valve that separates the right atrium from the right ventricle is called the **tricuspid valve**. The valve that separates the left atrium from the left ventricle is called the **mitral or bicuspid valve**. The valve that separates the right ventricle from the pulmonary trunk is called the **pulmonic valve**. The **aortic valve** separates the left ventricle from the aorta.

Passsage 705 (Questions 702-708)

702. C is correct. At high altitudes oxygen concentration is decreased. Low oxygen concentration is sensed by chemoreceptors and **hyperventilation** (increased breathing) results in an attempt to increase oxygen delivery to tissues.

In addition to hyperventilation as a coping mechanism for high altitude breathing, the kidneys also release **erythropoietin**. This hormone stimulates the bone marrow to produce more red blood cells in order to increase the oxygen-carrying capacity of the blood.

The MCAT loves to ask questions about the oxygen dissociation curve. The shift to the RIGHT of the O$_2$ dissociation curve reflects a decrease in affinity of hemoglobin for oxygen, which promotes oxygen release to the tissues. (2,3-biphosphoglycerated [BPG] stimulates a right shift.) The shift to the LEFT of the oxygen disso-

ciation curve increases the affinity of hemoglobin for oxygen. The famous example is fetal hemoglobin, which stimulates a left shift in the dissociation curve.

703. C is correct. According to the passage, central chemoreceptors have the strongest effect on breathing movements. Central chemoreceptors are not affected by oxygen (answer choice B is eliminated) but respond best to changes in the carbon dioxide concentration.

704. A is correct. As per the passage, the medulla and the pons are part of the *brain* stem. The spinal cord, the brain, and its stem are part of the central nervous system. The **peripheral nervous system** contains all nerves coming off the spinal cord and is divided into the somatic and autonomic divisions. The **somatic division** is voluntary and regulates the movement of all skeletal muscles. The **autonomic division** is involuntary with sympathetic and parasympathetic subdivisions.

705. B is correct. According to the second paragraph, peripheral chemoreceptors are located in the *walls of the circulatory system*. The only structure listed in the answer choices that belongs to the circulatory system is the aorta and its arch. The correct answer must be B.

706. A is correct. According to the question stem, lung stretch receptors are stimulated by distention of the lungs. This implies that lung stretch receptors are designed to prevent overbreathing. Therefore, once stretch receptors are stimulated, the medulla will send an inhibitory signal to decrease respiratory rate and depth.

707. D is correct. According to the passage, central chemoreceptors are primarily stimulated by changes in the arterial CO$_2$ concentration. The receptors actually sense changes in the hydrogen ion concentration, generated by the breakdown of carbonic acid (H$_2$CO$_3$). CO$_2$ + H$_2$O → H$_2$CO$_3$ → H$^+$ + HCO$_3^-$. Because a high [H$^+$] will cause a decrease in the pH, answer choices A, B, and C can all be eliminated.

708. B is correct. According the passage, the central chemoreceptor exerts control over the breathing rate. Its cardiovascular counterpart would have to be the pacemaker of the heart, the SA node, which regulates the rhythmic beating of the heart.

Passage 706 (Questions 709-715)

709. C is correct. The heart works to pump blood to nourish every cell. It has 4 chambers: 2 atria and 2 ventricles. Both ventricles pump the same amount of blood.

The right ventricle is smaller and weaker in comparison to the left because the pulmonary circulation is a lot less resistant to blood flow. As a result, the right ventricle does not have to pump as hard as the left one.

710. D is correct. As per the question stem, **pulmonary edema** is the accumulation of fluid in the lungs. What can cause edema? Edema can result from an *increase* in the hydrostatic pressure when the heart is really pumping hard. Edema can also be caused by an *increase* in the capillary wall permeability, which allows fluid to escape out of the capillaries into the lungs. A *decrease* in the pulmonary pressure or systemic pressure is caused by an increase in the resistance to blood flow. A decrease in blood flow does not cause edema. The correct answer choice is D.

711. D is correct. According to the question stem, bronchial circulation supplies blood to "feed" the lung itself but *not* to exchange gases. Furthermore, **bronchial arteries** are blood vessels that branch off the aorta. The aorta comes off the left side of the heart (specifically the left ventricle) and is part of systemic circulation, which is higher in pressure in comparison to the pulmonary circulation.

The **pulmonary artery** carries *deoxygenated* blood from the right ventricle to the lungs.

712. C is correct. According to the last line in the passage, pulmonary arteries balloon during ventricular contraction (systole). The correct answer choice is either A or C. The passage also informs that 5 liters (1000ml) of blood are pumped by the heart every minute. How many times per minute does the heart undergo a systolic contraction? The average heart rate is 75 beats per minute. 5000ml / 75 = 67 ml per systole. The correct answer choice is C.

713. D is correct. The 2 lungs are located on each side of the chest, protected from both sides by the rib cage, and separated by the heart. The top, or apex, of the lung extends into the lowest part of the neck, while the bottom or the lung base contacts the diaphragm. The **diaphragm** is the major breathing-associated muscle that separates the chest from the abdominal cavity.

714. D is correct. According to Table 1, only statement D is correct. Clara cells exist in the bronchioles, which do not have type III collagen. Furthermore, clara cells exist in cilia-free regions, which makes answer choice B untrue.

715. B is correct. To decrease resistance requires an increase in the ease of blood flow. Increasing the number of pulmonary capillaries would increase the overall area and the number of pathways that pulmonary blood can flow through: this would decrease resistance. Narrowing or hardening of pulmonary vessels would increase resistance because blood would have a difficult time flowing. Narrowing of the mitral valve, which separates the left atrium from the left ventricle, would cause blood to accumulate in the left atrium and back up into pulmonary veins and the lungs. This would serve to increase resistance to blood flow.

Independent Questions (Questions 716-725)

716. D is correct. During quiet breathing, **the predominant muscle of respiration is the diaphragm.** As the diaphragm contracts, pleural pressure drops creating *negative thoracic pressure*, which draws air into the lungs. **Expiration** during quiet breathing is a passive phenomenon. As for the lung anatomy, the left lung is smaller (only has two lobes) in order to accommodate the left-sided heart.

717. D is correct. A **zymogen** is an *inactive* enzyme that must be cleaved to gain activity. (Any enzyme ending in –ogen is a zymogen.) All *peptidases* designed to digest proteins are secreted as zymogens to prevent autodigestion of the secreting organ. For instance, the stomach secretes inactive pepsinogen that is activated by HCl into pepsin, which then aids in protein digestion. (The pancreas does not produce pepsin.) Trypsinogen and chymotrypsinogen are the 2 major pancreatic zymogens.

718. D is correct. Carbon dioxide, a waste product of metabolism, is transported to the lungs predominantly in the form of bicarbonate (approximately 70%), with a lesser amount as hemoglobin-attached CO_2 (25%), and the remaining 5% transported as a dissolved gas.

719. B is correct. The **nephron** is the functional unit of the kidney that is subdivided into the proximal convoluted tubule, the loop of Henle, the distal convoluted tubule, and the collecting duct. The **proximal convoluted tubule** reabsorbs most of the peptides, sugars, and electrolytes (i.e., sodium) that enter the nephron.

The **glomerulus/Bowman's capsule junction** is the renal filter that rids the blood of metabolic waste. The **loop of Henle** is the major site for water reabsorption. The **collecting duct** is regulated by the antidiuretic hormone (ADH), which stimulates water reabsorption.

720. D is correct. The human body is capable of both *primary* and *secondary* immune responses. A *primary* immune response occurs when a NEW invader gains access into the human body. It is a slow response that requires about 10 days to develop. (This explains why the common cold usually lasts about 10 days.)

A *secondary* immune response occurs when memory cells respond to an invader that has been seen before. The *secondary* immune response is so fast (requires 1-3 days) that most of the time the host is not even aware that his body is fighting off an infection.

721. C is correct. As per the question stem, the macrophage is able to engulf *listeria*, which implies that the macrophage is much larger in size. In fact a macrophage can engulf numerous bacterial cells at the same time.

Macrophages are part of innate, nonspecific immunity. They do not form attack units in an attempt to halt an infection.

722. D is correct. The small intestine is made up of the duodenum, jejunum, and ileum. Duodenum receives food from the stomach and is the shortest part of the small intestine. The ileum connects to the large intestine and is the longest part of the small intestine. Peyer's patches are found in the ileum.

723. B is correct. The right side of the heart pumps blood to the lungs to pick up oxygen. If the blood goes to the left side of the heart without first entering the lungs, the patient will experience *cyanosis* (the individual will look blue because of a lack of oxygen). **Sickle cell anemia** is a genetic disease that causes red blood cells to collapse when they are not carrying oxygen.

724. B is correct. As per the question stem, a gastrin over-secreting tumor stimulates stomach **parietal cells** to release hydrochloric acid (HCl) into the lumen of the stomach. A constant secretion of HCl would erode the lining of the stomach causing ulcers. Pepsin is a protease secreted by stomach **chief cells**. Mucus is synthesized by mucus-secreting cells to protect the stomach from acidic insult.

725. D is correct. There are two main fluid systems in the body that transport immune system cells: blood and lymph. The **cardiovascular system** is a closed loop; both arterial and venous blood transports immune cells. The **lymphatic system** is an open system that dumps all of its contents into the cardiovascular system.

Passage 707 (Questions 726-731)

726. A is correct. The best way to answer this question is to draw a brief schematic of a few branch points (see the diagram below). According to the passage, there are seventeen generations before the air reaches terminal bronchioles. In order to obtain 17 generations, 16 branch points must occur, one fewer than the total segments needed.

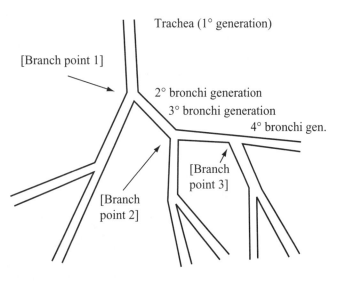

727. B is correct. The **larynx** consists of cartilage, intrinsic and extrinsic muscles, and a mucosal lining. Laryngeal cartilage houses the vocal cords, or the voice box. The intrinsic muscles of the larynx alter the position, shape, and tension of the vocal folds to allow for the production of various sounds.

728. A is correct. According to the passage, gas exchange requires 0.25 seconds, which is 1/3 of the total transit time for a red blood cell: a red blood cell requires .75 seconds for transit time through the lungs. Gas exchange occurs by *simple diffusion*, a transport method powered by the concentration gradient. The rate of simple diffusion can never be increased because the concentration of oxygen in the atmosphere remains constant. The correct answer choices must be A or B. However, the red blood cell transit time can decrease by increasing the heart rate, which would propel blood through the vascular system with greater speed. Answer choice B would be seen in an individual at rest.

729. C is correct. According to the passage, the upper and middle lobes are anterior, while the lower lobes are posterior. **Anterior** is the front of the body including the chest and the abdomen. **Posterior** is the back of the body including the powerful musculature around the spine and the buttocks region. As per the question stem, the injury occurred in the back and would most likely cause damage to the lower lung lobes.

730. C is correct. According to the question stem, upper airway causes atmospheric air to be humidified. **Humidification** increases the partial pressure of water vapor in the inspired air. Because the body's only source of oxygen is the atmosphere, under no circumstances can the alveolar oxygen concentration be higher than the oxygen concentration in the atmosphere. Carbon monoxide is not normally found in significant amounts in either the atmosphere or the alveoli. The atmospheric concentration of carbon dioxide is almost nonexistent. Because the body exchanges carbon dioxide for atmospheric oxygen, alveolar carbon dioxide levels can be expected to be many times higher than that of the atmosphere.

GAS	ATMOSPHERE PARTIAL PRESSURE
Oxygen	.21
Nitrogen	.78
Carbon Dioxide	.0003
Hydrogen	.0090
Total	**1.00**

Table 1 Gas Partial Pressures

731. D is correct. The right lung is larger than the left because the left side of the chest has to accommodate the heart. According to the passage, the average weight of 2 lungs is 300-400 grams. 350 grams / 2 = 175 grams. The right lung must weigh more than 175 grams. The correct answer choice is D.

Passage 708 (Questions 732-737)

732. **A is correct.** According to the passage, the majority of plasma proteins are synthesized by the liver. As a result, liver disease can result in decreased levels of plasma proteins, which may lead to edema and clotting problems. The liver is an accessory organ to the digestive system. It synthesizes bile that is needed to emulsify ingested fats.

733. **B is correct.** All blood cells (i.e. red blood cells, white blood cells, platelets) are non-dividing. They are synthesized by the bone marrow, have a set lifespan, and when aged are removed by the spleen. The researcher should only see bacterial cells dividing in the blood. This type of infection is very serious and requires hospitalization. FYI: the blood is a sterile fluid under normal circumstances.

734. **A is correct. Red blood cells** (erythrocytes) make up 45% of the blood and are the most numerous blood cells. Erythrocytes are devoid of a nucleus, shaped like a biconcave lens, and are rich in hemoglobin. Plasma makes up 55% of the blood but it is mostly water. Platelets are part of the "buffy coat."

735. **C is correct.** According to the passage, blood can be separated into 3 layers with the uppermost being the plasma layer, beneath it the "buffy coat" layer, and the red blood cell layer all the way on the bottom. Before the 2% glutaraldehyde buffer is added to the test tube, the plasma layer is removed, exposing the "buffy coat" layer directly beneath. So the 2% glutaraldehyde buffer is layered on top of the buffy coat and will seep through it first.

736. **D is correct. Anemia** is a condition in which the red blood cell concentration (also known as hematocrit) is decreased below the normal range. Anemia makes it difficult for the body to move oxygen. According to the passage, red blood cells normally make up 45 percent of the blood. An anemic individual is expected to have a red blood cell concentration below 45 percent. The correct answer choice is D.

737. **B is correct.** Platelets are synthesized by **megakaryocytes** and are crucial for human hemostasis. Megakaryocytes are developed from the hematopoietic stem cells just like all other blood cells. Use the process of elimination to answer this question. **Erythrocytes** are red blood cells. Platelets are involved in blood clotting. They are not phagocytic cells like **monocytes**, which give rise to macrophages.

Passage 709 (Questions 738-743)

738. **B is correct.** What does Experiment 1 demonstrate? Surgical reduction of the tumor burden allowed the host to achieve a full recovery. The decrease in the number of cancer cells allowed the immune system to mount an effective immune response. Under normal circumstances, there is a "race" going on between the growing tumor and the immune system. In a patient suffering from a full-blown cancer, the immune system becomes overwhelmed and the patient dies.

739. **B is correct.** According to Experiment 3, the immune system can mount an immune response against cancerous growth without attacking normal tissue. This implies that cancer cells have a unique receptor profile that allows them to be separated from normal cells. However, because cancer cells were once normal tissue, their receptors cannot be completely different from those on healthy tissue. Answer choice C is too extreme: most "never" answer choices on the MCAT are incorrect. The immune system constantly combats cancerous growth, even in end-stage cancers.

740. **C is correct.** Using two different mice with unequal genetic makeup would severely compromise the validity of the study. The results of the experiment would only be valid if the mice displayed identical immune responses to cancer.

Using identical cancer cells in each experiment is critical to its validity, eliminating answer choice A. The increase in the tumor burden in Experiment 2 is part of the study and does not diminish the validity of the experiment.

741. **C is correct.** Antibodies are produced by a **plasma cell**, which is a specific type of a B-cell. **B-cells** are synthesized by the bone marrow and are converted into plasma cells during an active infection. Antibodies bind invading bacteria making them easier to be ingested by phagocytic cells.

742. **C is correct.** In Experiment 2, the untreated mouse died from the alpha-tumor in 264 days. The alpha-tumor must be fast growing and aggressive in nature. It is not a benign mass that can be lived with because of its slow growth.

743. **C is correct.** According to Experiment 3, when T-cells were injected into a mouse the alpha-tumor was eradicated. T-cells are part of the cell-mediated immunity. **Cell-mediated immunity** (CMI) is a specific immune response that does not involve antibodies (antibodies are part of the **humoral response**) and is directed primarily against viral infections and cancer.

In Experiment 1, surgery to decrease the cancer cell burden was performed and the mouse lived. In experiment 2, the cell burden was not decreased and the mouse died from cancer. Roman numeral III is a method to combat cancer.

744. B is correct. The aortic valve separates the left ventricle from the aorta. Aortic stenosis or narrowing of the aortic valve would prevent the proper flow of blood out of the ventricle. As a result, the left ventricle would expand from all the accumulated blood. The heart, especially the left ventricle, would have to work harder to force the same amount of blood through a narrowed passageway. Like any muscle, the overworked ventricle would eventually enlarge, resulting in a condition known as ventricular hypertrophy.

745. D is correct. Cartilage is avascular tissue composed of chondrocytes embedded in collagen. Because it is avascular, nutrients reach cartilage by simple diffusion. Bone, on the other hand, is highly vascular and full of Haversian canal systems that supply nutrients and oxygen.

Strong, healthy bone is continually maintained via remodeling, which has two phases: resorption and formation. Bone-resorbing cells called **osteoclasts** remove old bone by releasing acids and enzymes to remove minerals and collagen. Once the osteoclasts have done their job, protein-secreting cells called **osteoblasts** cause the synthesis of new bone.

746. B is correct. As per the question stem, *shock* is caused by inadequate blood flow throughout the body. What does blood do? Blood carries oxygen to all metabolically active cells. Without oxygen organs begin to fail and die. Shock results when the heart cannot adequately pump blood or a vessel that carried blood is occluded. Shock can also be caused by a low blood volume (which means low blood pressure). An elevated blood pressure is least likely to result in shock.

747. B is correct. The immune system combats infection by stimulating the synthesis of white blood cells (WBC). As a result, an increase in the WBC concentration can be used to detect the presence of an underlying infection. An increase or decrease in the platelet concentration can be used to assess an individual's clotting status. Red blood cell concentration is important to assess the presence of anemia.

748. A is correct. The body has 2 methods of regulating homeostasis, the endocrine system and the nervous system. The nervous system is always a short-term solution that utilizes neurotransmitters and nerves. The endocrine system, however, is capable of maintaining homeostasis over a long period of time by relying on hormones. The **medulla** regulates the respiratory rate and is part of the nervous system.

749. B is correct. Aldosterone is produced by the adrenal cortex and binds the distal convoluted tubule to stimulate the reabsorption of sodium and water. **Cortisol** is also a product of the adrenal cortex. It is released in times of stress but does not bind nephron receptors.

ADH is produced by the hypothalamus and binds the collecting duct to increase the reabsorption of water. **Epinephrine** is synthesized by the adrenal medulla to assist in stimulating the sympathetic "fight or flight" response.

750. D is correct. Anaerobic respiration occurs when oxygen is unavailable and involves 2 metabolic processes: glycolysis and fermentation. Glycolysis converts a molecule of glucose into 2 molecules of pyruvate. Pyruvate is converted into lactic acid and ATP by fermentation. Fermentation taking place in non-animal cells would yield ethanol and ATP.

751. B is correct. Platelets are synthesized in the bone marrow by megakaryocytes. **Red blood cells** also have no nucleus but are derived from erythrocyte precursors.

752. D is correct. The **autonomic nervous system** is composed of sympathetic and parasympathetic divisions. The sympathetic nervous system uses **norepinephrine** as a neurotransmitter and may influence the immune system. The parasympathetic nervous system uses acetylcholine as a neurotransmitter and has no influence on the immune system.

Passage 710 (Questions 753-759)

753. B is correct. The immune (lymphoid) system relies on the following component organs: lymph nodes, thymus, spleen, and tonsils. These organs are filled with B and T-cells that protect the body against foreign molecules, bacteria, viruses, and other antigens. The thyroid gland is an endocrine organ that regulates the metabolic rate. The **thymus** produces mature T-cells. The **spleen** filters blood and removes all foreign agents that may cause infection or disease.

754. A is correct. The liver synthesizes all lipoproteins: low density lipoprotein (LDL), high density lipoprotein (HDL), very-low density lipoprotein (VLDL). Lipoproteins deliver cholesterol from the liver to peripheral tissue and back. **LDL** is known as the bad cholesterol because it takes fats away from the liver and deposits them into arterial walls. This leads to atherosclerosis and heart disease. **HDL** is the good cholesterol that returns fats to the liver and causes their excretion through feces. Cortisol is produced by the adrenal gland in times of stress. Erythropoietin and renin are both secreted by the kidneys. **Erythropoietin** stimulates the bone marrow to secrete red blood cells. **Renin** initiates a cascade to release aldosterone from the adrenal gland.

755. C is correct. According to the passage, complement plasma proteins must be capable of both hydrophobic and hydrophilic attachments to form membrane-attack complexes (MAC) that lyse infecting cells. **Hydrophobic interactions** are necessary for MAC to penetrate the hydrophobic cell membranes that protect invading cells. At the same time, complement proteins must be hydrophilic enough to dissolve in the blood and react with the hydrophilic bacterial extracellular surface.

756. D is correct. According to the information in the passage, the innate immune system protects the body using phagocytic cells like macrophages, neutrophils, and natural killer cells (NK). The **humoral immune response** relies on B-cells and is part of acquired immunity.

B-cells are produced in the bone marrow and differentiate into **plasma cells**, which synthesize antibodies. Cells of the innate immune system are not specific, killing any and all cells that appear foreign.

757. C is correct. According to the passage, the complement system lyses foreign invaders. Patients with a C3 deficiency are expected to have recurrent bacterial infections because of an inability to formulate MAC. Despite the low level of C3, the rest of the T and B-cells function normally, and complete crippling of the immune system does not occur.

758. D is correct. The complement system currently is known to contain at least 30 different proteins, which are primarily formed in the liver and circulate in their inactive form. These proteins, when activated, produce various complexes that play a major role in the natural defense mechanisms of the human body. According to the passage, complement is involved with: the formation of membrane-attack complexes, opsonization and phagocytosis enhancement, and receptor-mediated endocytosis. As both statements I and III are correct, the correct answer must be D.

759. B is correct. According to Table 1, neutrophils have a life span of just a few days and must be constantly removed by the spleen. Red blood cells and monocytes live for up to 4 months and are less frequently cleared by the spleen. Neutrophils cause a larger energy drain on the spleen in comparison to other cell types.

Passage 711 (Questions 760-766)

760. D is correct. According to the question stem, innate immunity serves as a barrier by preventing the entry of microorganisms into tissue. The **integumentary system** (aka. the skin) is the largest organ in the body and the most important component of innate immunity. It also has roles in homeostasis, temperature regulation, and sensory reception. (Infection is a great concern in burn patients who have extensive damage to their skin.) Beating of cilia is another important barrier that prevents infections. Organisms are trapped in mucus and expelled by the beating cilia or coughed out. Other components of innate immunity include secretion of antibacterial substances (i.e., HCl, lysozyme, lactoferrin), low stomach pH, and vomiting.

FYI: innate immunity is

1. present from birth,
2. nonspecific,
3. not made more efficient upon subsequent exposures to same organism.

761. B is correct. What organelle synthesizes antibodies? Antibodies are proteins and protein synthesis takes place in the rough endoplasmic reticulum and on free ribosomes. One more thing to realize is that neither the liver, nor the bone marrow or the thymus are organelles. All three are tissue organs. Answer choice B is the only organelle.

762. B is correct. The T-lymphocyte, specifically the T-helper cell, controls the immune system response to every antigen. Without T-cells there is no immune response. HIV infection destroys all T-helper cells and the host cannot fight off a simple cold and may die as a result.

The mounting of an immune response: macrophages and other cells of nonspecific immunity find foreign antigens and "show" them to T-helper cells, which decide whether or not to activate the immune system. If an immune response is necessary, T-helper cells stimulate B-lymphocytes to initiate humoral immunity, which involves the conversion of B-lymphocytes into plasma cells, which secrete antibodies.

763. C is correct. According to the passage, macrophages are derived from monocytes and are activated to become phagocytic. The correct answer choice is C.

764. C is correct. The thymus is located below the thyroid gland and is the primary site for T-cell maturation. T-cells make up the **cell-mediated division** of acquired immunity. Without a thymus, T-cells would not develop properly and cell-mediated immunity would be compromised. Patients with thymic hypoplasia should have normal B-cell levels and antibody production since B-cells are synthesized in the bone marrow.

765. A is correct. Invading microorganisms are phagocytized by macrophages but are not always easily killed. Some bacteria can even interfere with phagocytosis or elude lysosomal digestion while in the phagocytic cell. They begin to multiply inside the phagocyte and behave like intracellular parasites. The intracellular environment guards the bacteria against activities of extracellular immune cells, antibodies, and drugs.

766. C is correct. According to Figure 1, the antigen is digested by the lysosome *before* being presented to the T-lymphocyte; answer choice A is incorrect. The MHC II receptor, not MHC I, is synthesized by the macrophage. The T-lymphocyte synthesizes the CD4+ peptide arm, which is used to complete the multi-site attachment with the MHC II receptor. (The second attachment point is between the T-cell receptor and the processed antigen.)

Passage 712 (Questions 767-772)

767. **A is correct.** According to the passage, inflammation is a white blood cell (leukocyte) response to a bacterial infection. Leukocytes reach the infection because of an increase in vascular permeability of the cardiovascular system. The second sentence states that the main characteristic of inflammation is the formation of an exudate.

    FYI: Ever been stung by a bee? The after-affects of a bee sting are a good example of an inflammatory response. The site of the sting swells up, becomes red, and itches because of an increase in the local blood flow and vascular permeability.

768. **A is correct.** According to the diagram in the passage, natural killer cells are the first to respond to a viral infection.

    The immune system has 2 major divisions, innate and acquired. **Innate immunity** is the one every individual is born with. It is *nonspecific* and includes barriers (i.e., skin), bodily secretions, (i.e., stomach acid), and cells like macrophages and natural killers (NK). **Natural killer cells** attack a variety of foreign antigens in order to prevent infection. **Acquired immunity** is *very specific*, designed to combat particular invaders, and develops as the individual matures. It has 2 subdivisions: cell-mediated and humoral. **Cell-mediated immunity** is composed of T-cells that mature in the thymus. **Humoral immunity** is made of B-cells and antibodies.

769. **B is correct.** It is stated in the passage that during an inflammatory response, leukocytes must leave the circulatory system and gain access to the site of injury. It can therefore be inferred that under normal circumstances, leukocytes are being pumped through the cardiovascular system.

    While the liver and bone marrow are involved with leukocyte production and storage, these stored leukocytes are "immature" and are not yet ready to respond to infection. Mature leukocytes circulate throughout the body, looking for potentially dangerous invaders to tag and attack.

770. **A is correct.** The vascular fluid is always experiencing 2 types of pressure: hydrostatic and oncotic. *Capillary hydrostatic pressure* causes the fluid to leave the cardiovascular system. (Hydrostatic pressure increases with increased contraction of the heart.) *Tissue hydrostatic pressure* forces the fluid back into the vascular system but it is normally 0. *Capillary osmotic pressure* is created by albumin or other plasma proteins forcing the fluid back into the vascular system. (Diseases that cause a decrease in albumin and/or osmotic pressure can result in lower limb swelling or edema.)

771. **D is correct.** According to the passage, a phagocytic cell (i.e., macrophage) engulfs a bacterial cell, enclosing its prey in a vacuole known as a *phagosome*. The *phagosome* fuses with a lysosome to form a *phagolysosome*, which digests engulfed bacteria. **Lysosomes** are membrane-bound organelles that contain hydrogen peroxide, free radicals, and numerous hydrolytic enzymes. The **Golgi apparatus** performs post-translational protein modification and is considered to be the distribution center for proteins and lipids.

772. **C is correct.** According to the graphed data presented, neutrophils bind E-selectins during an inflammatory response. Levels of both E-selectins and neutrophils increase proportionally during inflammation. Antibodies are not required to initiate an inflammatory response. Inflammation has already occurred and they are still being synthesized. Macrophages make up the second cell line on the scene, not third. T-cells are the second cell line to respond to a viral stimulus.

Indendent Questions (Questions 773-781)

773. **D is correct. This is High Yield information for the MCAT. Lymphocytes** are a special type of white blood cells that come in 2 varieties, B-cells and T-cells. Both originate in the bone marrow from stem cells. **B-cells** go on to maturity in the bone marrow, while immature T-cells are translocated to the thymus to complete their maturation process.

774. **C is correct.** Asthma is a perfect example of a respiratory allergic reaction that causes excessive mucus secretion, smooth muscle spasms, and inflammatory swelling of the bronchial lining. These changes cause obstruction to airflow by increasing resistance. Persons suffering from an asthma attack are unable to move air well, which decreases their arterial oxygen concentration.

775. **D is correct.** The involuntary autonomic nervous system has 2 divisions, the sympathetic and the parasympathetic. The sympathetic system increases the heart rate in times of stress or during "fight or flight". The parasympathetic system decreases the heart rate and has the most dominant affect on the heart. Why? The answer lies in the fact that the heart rate is normally low and only increases in time of stress or exertion. This means that the cardiac baseline is determine by the parasympathetic stimulation. The somatic nervous system is voluntary and does not fall under the heading of autonomic nervous system. The enteric nervous system regulates the GI tract and digestion.

776. **C is correct.** The question diagram contains numerous alveoli, a vein, and an artery. **Alveoli** are areas of gas exchange found in the lungs. The **spleen** is a cardiovas-

cular system organ that filters blood for foreign pathogens and old red blood cells.

777. **C is correct. Lymph nodes** are small bean shaped structures that lie along the lymphatic system. They are full of β-cells, T-cells, and macrophages that filter lymph for foreign invaders. The lymphatic system does have valves to prevent the back flow of lymph, but these valves are not bean-shaped. The interconnection between the lymphatic and venous systems occurs only in the upper chest.

778. **A is correct. Blood pH is slightly alkaline at 7.4.** It is tightly monitored and regulated by both the kidneys and lungs. The skin pH is an acidic 5.6. The skin is part of innate immunity and the acidic pH makes it difficult for pathogens to enter the body. So in comparison, the blood is more alkaline than the skin.

779. **C is correct.** The air inhaled by the respiratory system is warmed and humidified by the countercurrent vasculature of the nose. The nose also filters the incoming air for major particles and allergens, trapping them in the mucus. Humidification elevates the water vapor concentration in the air, making it less irritating for the respiratory tract.

780. **C is correct.** When any valve narrows, blood begins to collect behind the valve. The mitral valve is located between the left atrium and the left ventricle; if narrowed, blood would accumulate in the left atrium. The **aortic valve** separates the left ventricle from the aorta. When the aortic valve narrows, blood cannot adequately drain out of the chamber and accumulates in the left ventricle. The **pulmonic valve** separates the right ventricle from the pulmonary artery. The tricuspid valve forms a barrier between the right atrium and the right ventricle.

781. **B is correct.** As per the question stem, the complement system is composed of proteins that must be synthesized by the **rough endoplasmic reticulum**. Protein synthesis can also occur on free **ribosomes**, but this is not an answer option. The nucleus, the largest cellular organelle, is enclosed by a nuclear envelope and contains most of the DNA possessed by the cell. **Peroxisomes** are small membrane-bound organelles that synthesize hydrogen peroxide (H_2O_2) to detoxify the cell.

LECTURE 8

800

Answers & Explanations
Questions 782–888

ANSWERS TO LECTURE 8

782.	A	818.	B	854.	A
783.	D	819.	C	855.	B
784.	A	820.	A	856.	A
785.	B	821.	B	857.	C
786.	B	822.	C	858.	C
787.	C	823.	A	859.	C
788.	A	824.	B	860.	C
789.	B	825.	B	861.	B
790.	C	826.	C	862.	B
791.	A	827.	A	863.	D
792.	D	828.	C	864.	D
793.	D	829.	B	865.	C
794.	D	830.	B	866.	A
795.	D	831.	C	867.	B
796.	B	832.	B	868.	B
797.	A	833.	A	869.	B
798.	C	834.	C	870.	C
799.	B	835.	D	871.	C
800.	B	836.	C	872.	B
801.	B	837.	D	873.	D
802.	C	838.	D	874.	B
803.	D	839.	D	875.	C
804.	B	840.	B	876.	B
805.	C	841.	A	877.	C
806.	C	842.	C	878.	B
807.	B	843.	B	879.	D
808.	B	844.	B	880.	B
809.	B	845.	B	881.	B
810.	B	846.	C	882.	A
811.	C	847.	B	883.	B
812.	D	848.	B	884.	A
813.	D	849.	B	885.	C
814.	C	850.	B	886.	A
815.	B	851.	B	887.	B
816.	B	852.	A	888.	B
817.	C	853.	A		

782. A is correct. A normal skeletal muscle is pink to red in color because of its rich vascular supply and the presence of **myoglobin**, an oxygen-transporting protein that resembles hemoglobin.

According to Table 1, red muscle fibers are rich in myoglobin and mitochondria. Mitochondria are powerhouses of the cell that supply a ton of ATP. Mitochondria also have enzymes of the Krebs cycle, an aerobic process that converts acetyl CoA into NADH and $FADH_2$. It is safe to assume that red muscle fibers require high levels of oxygen and ATP in order to function properly.

Glucose is stored intracellularly as **glycogen**. A cell that has a low concentration of glycogen does not store glucose for ATP synthesis and must rely on glucose delivery or other anaplerotic processes in times of need.

783. D is correct. On the MCAT, extreme statements like "all muscle tissue…" should not be selected as an answer choice. In science only a handful of concepts are absolute.

Red fibers are slow to contract but are full of mitochondria. The Krebs cycle and ATPases of the electron transport chain are housed in the mitochondria, the "powerhouse" of the cell. As a result, red muscle fibers are not easily fatigued. White fibers are fast acting but are mitochondria poor. They derive their ATP primarily from glycolysis.

784. A is correct. According to the passage, fibroblasts lay down *endomysium*, which surrounds each individual muscle cell filament: the highest concentration of fibroblasts is expected on the muscle filament. The muscle tendon is composed of the e*pimysium*. *Perimysium* surrounds the fascicle.

785. B is correct. According to the passage, fascicles are located inside the *epimysium*. Each fascicle is surrounded by *perimysium*.

786. B is correct. As per the passage, *epimysium* surrounds all body muscles and continues as a **tendon** that attaches muscle to bone. **Ligaments** attach bones to other bones.

787. C is correct. According to the passage, local injury stimulates satellite cells to divide in an effort to repair the damaged muscle. Myoblasts are precursors to skeletal muscle cells and are most likely to be derived from satellite cells. Nowhere in the passage does it say that satellite cells repair the basement membrane. They are not a part of the contractile apparatus. Answer choice B is true but it does not answer the question.

788. A is correct. A short-distance sprinter needs to rapidly accelerate. As a result he/she would most likely have muscle fibers with a fast contractile velocity. (A long-distance runner would benefit from a slower contractile velocity because the muscle would not tire as easily.) As per Table 1, white and intermediate muscle fibers have fast contractile velocity. Answer choices B and D are eliminated. However, intermediate muscle fibers have some properties of red fibers, which would be of no benefit to a sprinter. The correct answer choice is A. **FYI:** White fibers rapidly burn glucose to release ATP needed to supply musculature. Mitochondrial ATP production yields much more ATP but it is a much slower process and is of little benefit to a sprinter.

Passage 802 (Questions 789-795)

789. B is correct. As per the passage, it is safe to assume that actin myofilaments originate from the Z-disk, to which they are attached by α-*actinin*. The A-band contains myosin and actin, but actin does not originate from there. Myosin grips actin during a muscular contraction but actin does not originate from myosin.

790. C is correct. Myosin is the thick muscle myofilament. Its globular heads have actin-binding sites that must be located in the A-band. When stimulated, myosin "grabs" actin myofilaments and contracts the sarcomere. According to Figure 1, A-band represents the length of the myosin myofilament. The dark A-band contains both myosin and actin. The only FALSE statement is roman numeral III.

791. A is correct. The **somatic nervous system** carries out voluntary actions, such as moving a limb. Skeletal muscle is the only voluntary muscle group listed in the answer choices. The **autonomic nervous system** controls most involuntary actions, like the heart rate, digestive functions, hormone release, etc. (The autonomic nervous system has parasympathetic and sympathetic components.) Smooth, cardiac, and intestinal muscles are all involuntary.

792. D is correct. What happens to a sarcomere (muscle cell) during a muscular contraction? Both H and I-bands become smaller. "Say HI to the muscle." Z-lines move closer together, approaching the A and I-band interphase. The width of the A-band remains unchanged. During a sarcomere relaxation everything occurs in reverse.

Band	Muscle Contracts	Muscle Relaxes
A	unaltered	unaltered
H	shortens	lengthens
I	shortens	lengthens
Z	move closer	move apart

Changes in sarcomere bands is Very High Yield for the MCAT.

793. D is correct. The muscle cell obtains calcium from 2 sources: 1) the extracellular space and 2) the sarcoplasmic reticulum. The **sarcoplasmic reticulum** is tightly associated with the system of T-tubules, which stimulate the release of calcium. The **Golgi apparatus** is a distribution center that does not store calcium. **Lysosomes** are digestive organelles.

794. D is correct. The correct answer to this EXCEPT question is an anabolic reaction that synthesizes something. The correct answer choice is D because **fatty acid synthesis** uses ATP to form long-chain fatty acids. Glycolysis, cellular respiration, and the breakdown of creatine phosphate are all catabolic processes that release energy. **Creatine phosphate** donates a phosphate group to form ATP. (Creatine shakes are what most weightlifters drink.) **Glycolysis** and cellular respiration (i.e., electron transport chain) both generate ATP.

795. D is correct. According to the passage, myosin is made of 2 meromyosin monomers. By definition, myosin occupies a **quaternary peptide structure**, which is composed of at least 2 peptide chains. A single chain, globular protein that occupies a 3-dimensional configuration is known as a **tertiary peptide structure**. A **secondary peptide structure** is made out of alpha-helixes and beta-sheets. A **primary peptide structure** is simply a collection of amino acids linked in a long chain.

Passage 803 (Questions 796-802)

796. B is correct. According to the passage, the Golgi tendon organ is sensitive to changes in *tension*, while the muscle spindle is sensitive to changes in the *muscle length*. Translocating any weight from point A to point B does NOT cause a change in tension but does cause a change in the muscle length. (To practice, flex the bicep. The muscle gets shorter as the arm approaches the chest.) The tension remains constant because the weight amount translocated remains the same. (The 20-pound weight at point A remains the same 20 pounds at point B.)

797. A is correct. According to the passage, the mechanosensory hairs deliver information to the central nervous system, not the body. In experiment 1, when the mechanosensory hairs were rendered motionless, the fly could no longer sense that the head was turned. The body does not sense what the head is doing; rather it receives stimulation from the nervous system to act.

798. C is correct. According to the passage, if the prosternal organ would be shaved on the one side (right or left) the fly would tilt its head to the opposite side of the shaved hair plate. The correct answer choice is C.

799. B is correct. According to the passage, the *prosternal organ* is one of the main proprioceptors located in the head that inputs into the central nervous system. The

central nervous system is composed of the brain and spinal cord. The correct answer choice is B. The **peripheral nervous system** is broken down into somatic (voluntary) and autonomic (involuntary) components. The **notochord** is an embryologic structure that induces the formation of the central nervous system and the spine.

800. B is correct. As per the passage, the Golgi tendon organ lies in *series* with the muscle, while the muscle spindle lies in *parallel* with the muscle. Answer choices A and D display the muscle spindle proprioceptor in parallel with the muscle. Answer choice C is a proprioceptor lying perpendicular to the muscle. The correct answer choice is B.

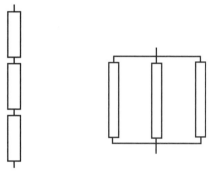

Items in Series   Items in Parallel

801. B is correct. As per experiment 2, if hairs on the left hair plate were shaved, the fly would roll its head to the right during flight, compensating for the *overexcitation* of the left prosternal organ. Overexcitation would result in a higher frequency of action potential. The correct answer choice is B.

802. C is correct. As per the question stem, gamma neurons are motor in nature, meaning they stimulate the contraction of muscle. On the MCAT, all muscle-stimulating neurons produce the neurotransmitter **acetylcholine**. **Cortisol** is a hormone made by the adrenal gland in times of stress. **Epinephrine** is also made by the adrenal medulla to assist the sympathetic nervous system with the "fight or flight" response. **Norepinephrine** is a neurotransmitter used by the sympathetic nervous system.

Independent Questions (Questions 803-811)

803. D is correct. F-actin, tropomyosin, and troponin C are *thin myofilaments*. **Myosin** is a *thick myofilament*. **F-actin** has an active site that myosin binds to during a muscular contraction. When the muscle is not contracting, **tropomyosin** blocks the active site on the F-actin. **Troponin C** has calcium binding sites, which when occupied, cause tropomyosin to shift the active site on actin, which myosin to bind to.

804. B is correct. Transverse tubules (T-tubules) are found in skeletal and cardiac muscle cells only. Acetylcholine, a neurotransmitter responsible for most muscle contractions, attaches to postsynaptic receptors and spreads an action potential across the entire muscle cell surface. Currents also travel deep into the muscle cell, carried by T-tubules to stimulate the release of calcium from the sarcoplasmic reticulum. Unicellular smooth muscle cells have no need for T-tubules.

805. C is correct. A normal heart has 2 major heart sounds, both correlating with the *closing* of the valves. The first heart sound (lub) is the closing of the atrioventricular (mitral and tricuspid) valves. The second heart sound (dup) occurs during the closing of the aortic/pulmonic valves.

806. C is correct. Adenosine triphosphate (ATP) supplies energy to drive thermodynamically unfavored reactions. It works by losing the endmost (gamma) phosphate group, which is catalyzed by an enzyme. The reaction releases energy and its product is **adenosine diphosphate (ADP)** and a phosphate group. Even more energy can be extracted by removing the second phosphate group to produce **adenosine monophosphate (AMP)**.

807. B is correct. Scientists use terms, such as *proximal* and *distal*, to describe 3D anatomy. *Distal* structures are farther away from a preset point of origin, while *proximal* ones are closer to a present point of origin. For example, the elbow is distal to the shoulder, the wrist is distal to the elbow, and fingers are distal to the wrist.

808. B is correct. Osteoblasts synthesize new bone. **Osteocytes** are mature osteoblasts that have been trapped in bone they recently synthesized. Every working osteoblast eventually becomes an osteocyte and sits in a space called the **lacuna. Chondrocytes** are cells that synthesize cartilage. **Fibroblasts** synthesize muscle tissue. **Keratinocytes** are found in the keratinized layer of the skin.

809. B is correct. Every cell has a **resting membrane potential** with the intracellular compartment usually carrying a negative charge (i.e., –70 mV). The resting membrane potential is part of the overall cellular homeostasis and is maintained by the sodium-potassium pump.

An **action potential** is a rapid change in the resting membrane potential from negative (i.e., –70 mV) to positive (+50 mV). It is elicited by a stimulus that opens certain ion channels. This is an important feature of all "excitable" cells. The **voltage threshold** is a preset membrane potential value (i.e., +10 mV) beyond which further stimulus generates an action potential. **Depolarization** is an electrical process that makes the membrane potential *more* positive than its previous value.

810. B is correct. There are 3 unique structures that pertain to the fetal cardiovascular system:

The **foramen ovale** is an opening in the interatrial wall that allows right atrial blood to bypass the developing lungs and enter directly into the left atrium. The foramen closes at birth to yield a fossa ovale.

The **ductus arteriosus** is another lung bypass that allows blood to leave the pulmonary artery (which leads to the lungs) to enter directly into the aorta. It too seals at birth.

The **ductus venosus** is designed to bypass the developing liver by routing blood around the organ but not through it.

There is no such thing as ductus vena cavas.

811. C is correct. The blood vessels are lined with smooth muscle. Smooth muscle is involuntary and is under the control of the **autonomic nervous system**, which is a division of the peripheral nervous system. The **somatic nervous system** controls voluntary skeletal muscle movements. The **central nervous system** is composed of the brain and spinal cord. It gives rise to the peripheral nervous system.

Passage 804 (Questions 812-818)

812. D is correct. As per Figure 1, four distortions appear on the "heart sounds" plot. Each distortion correlated with the closure of one of the four (tricuspid, mitral, pulmonic, aortic) heart valves. A trained cardiologist can hear four distinct heart sounds when examining a normal individual. **Important:** Each heart sound correlates with the CLOSING of a heart valve.

813. D is correct. According to the passage, skeletal muscles rely on sodium and potassium to generate an action potential. Answer choices A and B can be eliminated because the question stem asks to exclude ions involved in the excitation of skeletal muscles. **FYI:** Cardiac depolarization utilizes calcium ions to enter the cell and cause membrane depolarization.

814. C is correct. A systolic event is the contraction of the ventricles. The closing of the mitral and the tricuspid valves creates the **1st heart sound** and happens at the *beginning* of systole. The closing of the aortic and pulmonic valves creates the **2nd heart sound** and happens at the end of systole. The correct answer choice is C.

815. B is correct. As per the passage, the heart generates electrical activity that stimulates cardiac muscle cells (myocytes) to contract and expel blood. The electrical activity is first to occur: it must begin with the opening of ion channels, which cause an action potential to occur. If the action potential is large enough, myocytes will depolarize and contract.

816. B is correct. Use the process of elimination to answer this question. According to the passage, an *inward current* is the movement of positive ions into the cell or the movement of negative ions out of the cell; this makes the cell more positive. Which ions move into the cell? The answer is sodium (+1) and calcium (+2), which are designed to depolarize the cell.

An *outward current* is generated by the movement of positive ions out of the cell or negative ions into the cell: this makes the cell more negative. The correct answer choice is B. I has both inward and outward currents. III is an example of an inward current.

817. C is correct. According to the passage, peptide gates create voltage dependence. **Important:** All living cells (skeletal muscle cells, red blood cells, etc.) have gated sodium—potassium ATPases and/or other pumps that are voltage dependent.

A **leaky potassium channel** is always open because it is ungated. It allows potassium to freely flow out of the cell, down a concentration gradient, and it is not voltage dependent.

818. B is correct. According to the diagram, LVEDV is the blood volume in the left ventricle before it contracts; this means LVEDV represents a point just before the onset of systole (a period of ventricular contraction). Because LVEDV is taken at the end of phase 2 and the beginning of phase 3, phase 3 must be the first phase of systole. Phase 2 is the last phase of diastole (a period of ventricular relaxation) and phases 5 and 6 correlate with the end of systole and the beginning of diastole.

Passage 805 (Questions 819-824)

819. C is correct. The heart has 2 atrial and 2 ventricular chambers. The ventricular musculature is much thicker in comparison to the atrium. The ventricle must generate a tremendous amount of pressure to force blood throughout the entire body. The left ventricle is the thickest overall chamber because it must force blood against a higher systemic resistance, while the right ventricle pumps against a low resistance of the pulmonary circulation.

820. A is correct. Scientists use terms, such as *proximal* and *distal*, to describe 3D anatomy. As per the first paragraph, *distal* structures are farther away from a preset point of origin, while *proximal* ones are closer to a present point of origin. In regards to the digestive system, the stomach is the most proximal structure to the mouth. The pancreas and small and large intestines are more distal from the mouth in comparison to the stomach.

Review of the digestive tract (from the mouth to the rectum): the mouth → esophagus → stomach → small intestine (pancreatic ducts join the GI tract here) → large intestine → rectum.

821. B is correct. According to the passage, atrial natriuretic factor (ANF) stimulates the elimination of sodium and water by the kidneys. Which hormone causes the reabsorption of sodium and water by the kidney? The answer is **aldosterone**, which is released by the *renin → angiotensin I → angiotensin II → aldosterone* system. **Antidiuretic hormone (ADH)** is produced by the hypothalamus and stimulates the reabsorption of water only by the renal collecting duct.

822. C is correct. According to the passage, cardiac tissue is composed of 3 layers: inner *endocardium*, middle, and most prominent *myocardium* and the outermost *epicardium*. The *endocardium* is lined with an *endothelium*, which is in direct contact with all the blood being pumped by the heart. Cardiac valves, papillary muscles, and chordae tendinae are all within heart chambers and just like the *endocardium* are covered with an anti-clotting *endothelium*. **FYI:** Papillary muscles and chordae tendinae are attached to cardiac valves and force them closed during systole.

823. A is correct. As per the passage, the distention of the atrial chamber induces the release of ANF into circulation, which stimulates the loss of water by the kidneys. Water loss is a method the body utilizes to lower the blood pressure. Elevated blood pressure would flood the heart with blood and distend the atria. The correct answer choice is A.

824. B is correct. Two major sets of vessels come directly off the heart. The **right ventricle** gives off several pulmonary arteries, which deliver blood to the lungs for oxygenation. The **left ventricle** gives rise to the aorta, the largest artery in the human body. **Coronary arteries** supply oxygen and nutrients to the cardiac muscle itself but they do not come off the heart itself. Rather, they are the first branches of the aorta. The hepatic artery is associated with the liver.

Passage 806 (Questions 825-830)

825. B is correct. As per the passage, the migration of smooth muscle cells (from the media layer) causes the proliferation of the intima layer. If the media layer were nonexistent, intimal proliferation would not occur.

826. C is correct. The constriction of blood vessels *decreases* the amount of space in the cardiovascular system, which increases the blood pressure. The reverse is also true: dilation of blood vessels decreases the blood pressure. Answer choices A and D are incorrect.

High Yield for the MCAT: the heart and the kidneys regulate blood pressure. A heart attack diminished the heart's ability to pump blood, which decreases the blood pressure. As a compensatory response, blood vessels would be expected to constrict.

827. **A is correct.** As per the passage, the coronary artery has 3 distinct layers: the inner intima, middle media, and outer adventitia layers (serosa is never mentioned in the passage, which implies it is NOT the correct answer). The intima is closest to the blood because it is lined with **endothelial cells**: endothelium is a type of **epithelium**, which lines all blood vessels in the human body. **FYI:** Epithelium lines all lumenal structures in the body.

828. **C is correct.** As per the question stem, a heart rate above 100 beats per minute is considered to be an arrhythmia. Answer choice C is the only one with the heart rate above 100 beats per minute—determined by counting the total number of beats in the answer choices and multiplying by 4 (there are 60 sec. in 1 minute and all answer choices represent a 15 sec. time duration).

Answer choice A: $18 \times 4 = 72$

Answer choice B: $22 \times 4 = 88$

Answer choice C: $26 \times 4 = 104$ Arrhythmia

Answer choice D: $16 \times 4 = 64$

829. **B is correct.** As per the passage, the media layer of the coronary artery is primarily smooth muscle. **Smooth muscle** is involuntary, non-striated, single nucleated, and unicellular. It has no T-tubules or troponin. Myofilaments, actin and myosin, are necessary for the contractile apparatus and are present in all types of muscle cells.

830. **B is correct.** As per the passage, atherosclerotic plaque grows to accumulate calcium, a positively charged ion. Calcium concentration is decreased by **calcitonin**, which is produced by the thyroid gland. **Testosterone** is needed for sexual development. **Glucagon** is produced by the pancreas to increase blood glucose concentration. **Thyroid hormone** increases the basal metabolic rate.

Independent Questions (Questions 824-832)

831. **C is correct.** The release of **acetylcholine** stimulates the contraction of most body musculature. **Norepinephrine** is a neurotransmitter of the sympathetic nervous system and the "fight or flight" response. **Epinephrine** is released from the adrenal medulla to assist the nervous system with the sympathetic response. **Acetylcholinsterase** is an enzyme that breaks down acetylcholine in the synaptic cleft.

832. **B is correct.** A **ligament** attaches bone to bone. A **tendon** attaches muscle to bone.

833. **A is correct.** There are 2 types of bone, mature and immature. **Woven bone** is immature, mechanically weak,

with a disorganized infrastructure of coarse collagen fibers. It is the first bone to form during development and in fracture repair. **Lamellar bone** is mature, strong, with layers of highly organized parallel collagen fibers. There are 2 types of lamellar bone, compact and spongy. Most fully developed bones have a rigid, outer compact shell and an inner spongy zone.

834. **C is correct.** Muscle contraction requires a great deal of calcium, which is obtained 1) from the extracellular environment via calcium-gated channels and 2) from the sarcoplasmic reticulum (muscle cell smooth ER). Sodium-gated channels open during the depolarization of nerves, while most muscle cells, including skeletal, cardiac, and smooth, rely on calcium-gated channels.

835. **D is correct. Adenosine triphosphate (ATP)** is one of the better understood methods used to store energy. Cleaving one ATP phosphate group liberates 7.3 kcal/mole. **Nicotinamide adenine dinucleotide (NADH)** is produced by glycolysis and the Krebs cycle. Through the mitochondrial electron transport chain, NADH can transfer two electrons and a hydrogen ion to oxygen (the final electron acceptor), liberating 52.6 kcal/mole. **Creatine phosphate** is used by muscle cells to store energy: this is what weightlifters consume before working out. Large muscles rapidly burn energy and rely on the hydrolysis of creatine phosphate to release 10.3 kcal/mole. When reduced, **flavin adenine dinucleotide (FADH$_2$)** is an energy-rich substrate produced by the Krebs cycle. However, FAD$^+$ is an energy-poor, oxidized compound that must be converted into FADH$_2$.

836. **C is correct.** The sympathetic and parasympathetic divisions of the autonomic nervous system regulate the heart rate and the force of contraction. **Acetylcholine** is the neurotransmitter utilized by the parasympathetic nervous system, which *decreases* the heart rate and the force of contraction. The sympathetic nervous system relies on **norepinephrine** to *increase* the heart rate and the force of myocardial contraction.

837. **D is correct. This is High Yield information for the MCAT.** Nucleic acids are the building blocks for DNA and RNA and are very similar in structure to ATP. Each nucleic acid has a ribose sugar, a nitrogen base, and a phosphate group. DNA is converted to RNA via **transcription**. **Translation** is the conversion of RNA into protein.

838. **D is correct.** There are 4 main cell lines that occupy bone tissue:

- **Stem cells** (osteoprogenitor cells) are precursor cells that differentiate into osteoblasts and other cell populations. These are the cells replaced by a bone marrow transplant.

- **Osteoblasts** decrease blood calcium concentration by actively depositing bone.

- **Osteocytes** are relatively inactive, mature cells derived from osteoblasts. They are trapped within the mineralized bony matrix, which they maintain.
- **Osteoclasts** are similar to macrophages. They brea down bone and increase the calcium concentration in the blood.

839. D is correct. Diseases are categorized as acquired or inherited. An *inherited disease* is one a person is born with or predisposed to, for example hair loss in early adolescence. An *acquired disease* happens as a result of an external stressor, for example the treatment of gastric cancer causes the patient to lose his hair. Answer choices A-C are all examples of an acquired disease process.

Passage 807 (Questions 840-845)

840. B is correct. The myosin light chain kinase (MLCK) catalyses Reaction 1:

$$light\ chain\text{-}OH + Mg\text{-}ATP^{2-} \rightarrow\rightarrow light\ chain\text{-}O\text{-}PO_3^{2-} + Mg\text{-}ADP^- + H^+$$

The reaction degrades alcohol (light chain-OH becomes light chain-O-PO_3^{2-}), does not consume magnesium (the concentration of magnesium is equal on both reactant and product sides), and releases hydrogen ions into the cytoplasm. An increase in the hydrogen ion concentration causes the cytoplasm to become more acidic. The correct answer choice is B.

841. A is correct. As per the passage, smooth muscle cells contain much less protein than skeletal muscle cells. Based on this information it is safe to assume that skeletal muscle cells have a *higher* concentration of free ribosomes, organelles of protein synthesis, in comparison to smooth muscle cells. It is also safe to assume that skeletal muscle cells consume more ATP for protein synthesis in comparison to smooth muscle cells.

842. C is correct. Smooth muscle is responsible for the contractility of hollow organs, such as blood vessels, the stomach and the rest of the gastrointestinal tract, the urinary bladder, or the uterus. The liver is the largest solid organ in the human body.

843. B is correct. The contraction of the left atrium is performed by a cardiac muscle. Answer choice A can be eliminated. As per the question stem, phasic contraction is not continual: answer choice C is incorrect. Flexion of the wrist is a voluntary process performed by skeletal muscles. **Peristalsis** is the movement of food down the GI tract. It relies on a phasic contraction of smooth muscles. The correct answer choice is B.

844. B is correct. Acetylcholine is a neurotransmitter, not a hormone. It is released by neurons to stimulate the contraction of most major muscles. **Glucagon** is a hormone

produced by the pancreas to increase the blood glucose concentration. It has absolutely no effect on smooth muscles. Aldosterone is a hormone that does not alter muscle function. It stimulates the reabsorption of sodium and water in the kidneys and the large intestine. Oxytocin is released by the posterior pituitary to stimulate uterine contractions during labor. The first sentence in the passage states that the uterus is a smooth muscle organ.

845. B is correct. According to the passage, the myosin light chain kinase (MLCK) transfers a terminal phosphate group to a serine. Adenosine triphosphate (ATP) is the only compound listed in the answer choices able to donate a terminal phosphate group. Adenosine monophosphate (AMP) is depleted of all active phosphate groups.

Passage 808 (Questions 846-851)

846. C is correct. As per the passage, primary endochondral bone forms in ossification centers, which are located within the mesenchymal tissue or in the cartilaginous model. The correct answer choice is C.

847. B is correct. According to the passage, the availability of *vasculature* determines which type of bone development takes place. What items fall under the category of vasculature? The answer is anything that delivers blood to tissue, for example arteries, capillaries, and veins (vessels that carry deoxygenated blood). The lymphatic system does not deliver blood to tissue. Rather, it drains the extracellular environment, returning water, protein, nutrients, etc. back into circulation.

848. B is correct. According to the question stem, osteoprogenitor cells differentiate into osteoblasts, cells that synthesize bone. A growing embryo, with a developing musculoskeletal system, is expected to have a high concentration of osteoblasts.

849. B is correct. According to the passage, **intramembranous ossification** occurs in the *mandible*, as well as frontal, parietal, and maxillary bones. The mandible is one of the many flat bones of the face and skull. The correct answer choice is B. Bones found in the upper and lower extremities (arms and legs) are long bones formed by **endochondral ossification**. Cartilage is not bone. It is an avascular tissue that receives nutrients via simple diffusion. Cartilage makes up the nose and ears.

850. B is correct. Two hormones and vitamin D regulate bone homeostasis. The **parathyroid hormone** increases blood calcium by breaking down bone. The correct answer choice is B. **Vitamin D** also increases blood calcium by increasing the reabsorption of calcium from the digestive tract. **Calcitonin** is released by the thyroid gland to decrease blood calcium by increasing the synthesis of bone.

FYI: Osteoblasts have parathyroid hormone (PTH) receptors and when activated secrete osteoclast-stimulating factor that increases bone resorption in order to elevate blood calcium.

Thyroid hormone regulates the basal metabolic rate. **ACTH** stimulates the adrenal cortex to secrete cortisol.

851. **B is correct.** As per the passage, a cartilage model is converted into endochondral bone. What properties define cartilaginous tissue? Cartilage is made of collagen; it is avascular and "fed" by simple diffusion; it lacks a nerve supply. Cartilage may be palpated at the tip of the nose or the top of an ear. Hyaline cartilage rings are present in the tracheal wall, larynx, and conducting bronchi. The rings keep the airway from collapsing.

Passage 809 (Questions 852-858)

852. **A is correct.** As per the passage, persons with *osteopenia* have an excess of osteoid, which prevents the formation of the Haversian systems. All long bones depend on the **Haversian systems**, which house neurovascular central channels called **Haversian canals**. Haversian canals are interconnected by perpendicular **Volkmann's canals** and both systems supply bones with blood. Osteoid prevents the proper delivery of nutrients and oxygen to bone and bones begin to deteriorate. **Osteoblasts** are osteoclast counterparts that build bones. The bone marrow synthesizes blood cells (i.e., red blood cells, white blood cells, platelets, etc.) and if it wete destroyed, the patient would develop a disease of the blood (i.e., anemia, leukemia, etc.).

853. **A is correct.** According to the passage, 50% peak bone mass level is the established threshold for long bone fractures. The closer one is to the 50% peak bone mass, the higher the risk for a long bone fracture. The peak bone mass occurs 10 years after a person stops growing, after which both males and females lose 1% of their peak bone mass for each year of life. Women also experience a tremendous drop in bone mass at menopause ,which is caused by a decrease in estrogen, a hormone that is osteo-protective.

1. Male A is 57, growth stopped at 21 years of age, peak bone mass at approximately 31 years of age: bone mass is 74%.

2. Male B is 49, growth stopped at 17 years of age, peak bone mass at approximately 27 years of age: bone mass is 78%.

3. Male C is 51, growth stopped at 19 years of age, peak bone mass at approximately 29 years of age: bone mass is 78%.

4. Female A is 43, PREMENOPAUSAL, growth stopped at 18 years of age, peak bone mass at approximately 28 years of age: bone mass is 85%.

854. **A is correct.** Bone fractures occur when the musculoskeletal system is weak. With increasing age, bones weaken because certain hormone levels decrease, a calcium-rich diet is not maintained, exercise programs are not implemented, etc. All those factors lead to bone fragility, poor coordination, and poor eyesight, which invariably lead to accidents and fractures.

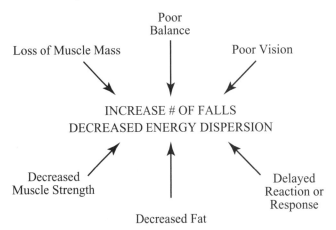

Factors that Contribute to Fractures

855. **B is correct.** The top line, line data A, represents the male pattern of bone density loss, while line data B displays the average female bone density loss. Note the sudden drop in the line data B curve: this signifies menopause, which accompanies a dramatic decrease in the bone mass. Also note that women never achieve the bone mass density men do.

856. **A is correct.** According to the passage, women have a higher risk of bone fractures after menopause. As women age, ovaries slowly decrease the production of estrogen and progesterone. However, following menopause, which occurs between the ages of 48 and 53, there is a drastic drop in estrogen, which causes an end to menstruation.

Estrogen hormone is osteo-protective because it inhibits the synthesis of potent osteoclast stimulators. (Recall, osteoclasts are cells that break down bone.) Following menopause estrogen decreases and so does the osteo-protection.

Parathyroid hormone (PTH) increases calcium levels in the bloodstream. If it were inhibited by estrogen, PTH could not perform its job. Answer choice C is incorrect.

Hormone/Factor	Target Cell Type	Bone Resorption	Bone Formation
Vitamin D	Osteoblast	+ + +	– –
Parathyroid Hormone (PTH)	Osteoblast	+ + + +	– – –
Estrogen	Osteoblast	– – – –	+ +
Thyroid Hormone	Osteoblast	– –	+ +
Calcitonin	Osteoclast	– – –	+ +

(+) = Stimulating   (–) = Inhibiting

Table 1 Hormones and Other Systemic Factors Acting on Bone Cells

857. C is correct. The first thing to realize is that a bone mass level under 83% is completely normal. In fact it is expected in middle-aged people. The next important piece of information is that, according to the passage, osteoporosis is definitely more severe in comparison to osteopenia. The correct answer choice is C. Low calcium levels are easily corrected with dietary supplements. However, a chronically low level of calcium may lead to the development of osteopenia.

858. C is correct. As per the passage, the peak bone mass occurs approximately ten years after a human being stops growing. In humans, growth stops between the ages of 19-23; add 10 to that number and the age range for the peak bone mass becomes 29-33.

Independent Questions (Questions 859-867)

859. C is correct. Use the process of elimination to answer this question. Smooth muscle does not have T-tubules (found in skeletal and cardiac muscle), troponin, or striations. The myosin light chain kinase is used by smooth muscle to overcome the lack of troponin. Smooth muscle contraction occurs when the myosin light chain kinase phosphorylates necessary components.

860. C is correct. MCAT writers love to ask this question. As per the question stem, troponin is a *globular protein* and by definition must have a tertiary structure. Why? A single chain, *globular protein* that occupies a 3-dimensional configuration is known as a **tertiary structure**. A **quaternary peptide structure** is composed of at least 2 peptide chains. A **secondary protein structure** is made out of alpha-helixes and beta-sheets. A **primary protein structure** is simply a collection of amino acids linked in a long chain.

861. B is correct. Amylase is an enzyme that degrades carbohydrates and is released in only 2 locations, the mouth and the small intestine. **Salivary amylase** in secreted by salivary glands to initiate carbohydrate digestion in the mouth. The pancreas supplies **pancreatic amylase**, which is released into the duodenum of the small intestine. Carbohydrate digestion is completed by brush border enzymes (i.e., lactase, maltase, etc.). The stomach releases **pepsin**, an enzyme that digests only protein.

862. B is correct. The Krebs cycle and the electron transport chain are both aerobic processes that occur in mitochondria. Prokaryotic cells lack organelles and as a result cannot carry out mitochondrial-based metabolism. Photosynthesis occurs only in select species of plants. Glycolysis is an anaerobic process that takes place in the cytoplasm of virtually every living cell.

863. D is correct. Smooth muscle is unicellular and involuntary. Can you move your tongue? The answer is yes, because the tongue is full of skeletal muscle cells, which are voluntary. Smooth muscle cells are found in the aorta, the uterus, and the bladder.

864. D is correct. The bone marrow is a blood cell factory. It makes **red blood cells** that carry oxygen and would be needed in an environment with a decreased concentration of oxygen. A chronic internal bleed needs to be controlled via a clotting cascade. The bone marrow would release **platelets** to bind the fibrin clot. An infection is battled with **white blood cells**, which are all released by the bone marrow. The correct answer choice is D.

865. C is correct. Cardiac and smooth muscle cells contract as a group. As a result, both cell types depend on gap junctions (channels that link cells together) to spread an excitatory action potential between cells. Skeletal muscle cells can contract independently and DO NOT have gap junctions. **FYI:** In cardiac muscle cells gap junctions are known as **intercalated disks**.

866. A is correct. Smooth muscle cells are involuntary and much smaller than skeletal muscle cells. Unlike skeletal muscle cells, smooth muscle has no T-tubules, no striations, no troponin, and no tropomyosin. Myosin and actin myofilaments are present but they are poorly developed and disorganized. **FYI: Troponin** binds calcium during a muscular contraction. Smooth muscle cells also use calcium to contract but rely on a different calcium-binding mechanism in comparison to skeletal muscle cells.

867. B is correct. The **sinoatrial (SA) node** is the main pacemaker of the heart. It determines the heart rate and undergoes auto-depolarization stimulated by the influx of calcium. If the SA node is damaged, the **AV node** would take over as the main pacemaker of the heart.

Cardiac conduction overview: the SA node → the AV node → the bundle of His → Purkinje fibers.

Passage 810 (Questions 868-874)

868. B is correct. Osteoblasts synthesize new bone. **Osteocytes** are mature osteoblasts that have been trapped in bone they recently synthesized. Every working osteoblast eventually becomes an osteocyte and sits in a space called the **lacuna**.

All other answer choices are not directly involved with bone. **Chondrocytes** are cells that synthesize cartilage. **Fibroblasts** synthesize muscle tissue. **Keratinocytes** are found in the keratinized layer of the skin.

869. B is correct. According to the passage and the question stem, both osteoclasts and macrophages are derived from monocytes. It is safe to assume that osteoclasts must be related to phagocytic cells like macrophages. B and T-cells are part of **acquired immunity**; they are not related to macrophages.

870. C is correct. Knowing endocrine function is important for the MCAT. According to the question stem, calcium and phosphate make up the main component of inorganic bone. The question is simply asking which hormones are involved in regulating blood calcium and phosphate levels. There are three of them:

Hormone	Secretory Gland	Serum Calcium	Serum Phosphate
Parathyroid hormone	Parathyroid gland	increases	decreases
Vitamin D	Diet + Sun Light	increases	increases
Calcitonin	Thyroid gland	decreases	minimal increase

Thyroid hormone regulates the basal metabolic rate. It is released when the thyroid gland is stimulated by TSH.

871. C is correct. Calcitonin is a hormone that decreases the blood calcium concentration by increasing bone synthesis. As per the passage, the bone-lining cell population regulates the movement of calcium and phosphate into and out of the bone. It is therefore safe to assume that a calcitonin analog would most likely bind the bone-lining cell population.

872. B is correct. As per the passage, osteoblasts DO NOT divide but rather convert into another cell population. Answer choices A and C can be eliminated. **Binary fission** is a type of cell division utilized by bacterial cells. By the process of elimination, the correct answer choice is B.

873. D is correct. According to the passage, osteoclasts seal onto bone and release *acids*. The correct answer choice must be D. Osteoclasts have *carbonic anhydrase* that catalyzes the following reaction:

$$CO_2 + H_2O \rightarrow H_2CO_3 \rightarrow HCO_3^- + H^+$$

This is a Very High Yield MCAT reaction. Later the proton pump releases H^+, with Cl following, into the Howship's lacuna, which causes bone resorption.

Ammonia (NH_3) is a polar compound that hydrogen bonds. It is also a common MCAT base. **Calcitonin** is produced by the thyroid gland and acts to decrease the blood calcium concentration.

874. B is correct. According to the passage, the diaphysis is the primary center of ossification. It is composed of mostly dense bone with a spongy lining in the medullary cavity.

Passage 811 (Questions 875-880)

875. C is correct. As per the passage, Paget's disease begins with active bone breakdown (resorption) during the osteolytic phase. The disease is better managed if the initial bone breakdown is stopped or delayed. The question stem states that a hormone is used to decrease the breakdown and stimulate growth of new bone.

Calcitonin is produced by the thyroid gland and is the current hormone treatment for Paget's. It lowers the blood calcium concentration by decreasing the breakdown of bone. **Parathyroid hormone (PTH)** increases the blood calcium concentration by increasing the breakdown of bone. PTH would speed up the destruction seen in Paget's disease. **Glucagon** is produced by the pancreas to increase the blood glucose level. **Cortisol** is released by the adrenal cortex in times of stress.

876. B is correct. As per the passage, an abundance of osteoclasts and osteoblasts accounts for the elevated level of *serum* alkaline phosphatase. Serum is blood.

877. C is correct. As per the passage, the *osteolytic phase* of Paget's disease involves a focus of active bone resorption (bone breakdown). **Osteoclasts** are cells that are responsible for the resorption of bone and must be active during the *osteolytic phase* of Paget's disease. **Osteoblasts** synthesize new bone and eventually are converted into **osteocytes**, which maintain healthy bone tissue during times of non-synthesis.

878. B is correct. The question stem informs that Paget's disease causes hearing loss. As per the passage, Paget's is a disease of bone, not nerves. Based on the 2 pieces of information it is safe to assume that hearing is a bone-dependent mechanism, which it is. The ear contains 3 ossicles (the incus, maleus, and stapes—the smallest bones in the body), which deliver sound from the external to the inner ear. **Hydroxyapatite** is the major mineral component, and an essential ingredient, of normal bone.

879. D is correct. As per the passage, the osteoblastic phase of Paget's disease can occur by itself or, more commonly, simultaneously with osteoclastic phase (when both phases occur together, it is known as a "mixed" phase). The bottom line, the osteoblastic phase always occurs; as a result, all 107 untreated individuals would be expected to go through the osteoblastic phase.

880. B is correct. As per the passage, hyperparathyroidism (an excess of parathyroid hormone) dominates the mixed phase of Paget's disease. **Parathyroid hormone** increases blood calcium concentration by increasing bone resorption (which releases calcium into the blood) and the reuptake of calcium by the kidneys.

Independent Questions (Questions 881-888)

881. B is correct. Glycolysis is an anaerobic process that converts a molecule of glucose into 2 molecules of pyruvate, produces 2 net molecules of ATP, and releases 2 NADH molecules. The Krebs cycle occurs in the mitochondria and converts acetyl CoA (obtained from pyruvate) into 3 molecules of NADH, 1 molecule of $FADH_2$, and 1 molecule of GTP (which can be converted to ATP). **Fermentation** is an anaerobic process that converts pyruvate into lactic acid. The **electron transport chain** converts reduced substrates (i.e., NADH) into ATP by establishing a hydrogen ion gradient.

882. A is correct. The **pulmonary vein** transports blood from the lungs to the left atrium. It is 1 of 2 veins in the body that carries *oxygenated* blood. (The other vein that transports *oxygenated* blood is the **umbilical vein**. It carries blood from the mother to the fetus. The **umbilical artery** carries deoxygenated blood from the fetus to the mother.) The **right atrium** receives blood from the largest vein in the body, **the vena cava**, as both structures deliver the *most deoxygenated* blood to the lungs.

883. B is correct. Cartilage is avascular connective tissue that receives all nutrients by simple diffusion. It has no blood vessels or Haversian or Volkmann's canals, which are only found in bone. Collagen is the main peptide found in cartilage.

Bone is very vascular and is constantly being supplied with blood. **Canaliculi** are microvascular spaces used by osteocytes to maintain nutrient supply to every bone cell.

884. A is correct. As per the question stem, smooth muscle constantly carries on glycolysis, which converts a molecule of glucose into 2 molecules of pyruvate. As a result it is safe to assume that a high rate of glycolysis would lead to a high concentration of pyruvate. **Lactate** is synthesized during fermentation, which occurs only in anaerobic conditions. Citrate is an intermediate of the mitochondrial Krebs cycle.

885. C is correct. Calcitonin is a hormone that decreases the blood calcium concentration by increasing bone synthesis. It is secreted by the thyroid gland. The **parathyroid hormone** increases the blood calcium concentration and is secreted by the parathyroid gland. The **pineal gland** is located in the brain. It produces melanin, which regulates circadian rhythms and the day/night cycle.

886. A is correct. The **spleen** is located on the left side of the body, is part of the cardiovascular system, and filters blood for aged cells. The **liver** also filters blood for aged cells, but it is located on the right side of the body. It is the largest body organ that performs other tasks like bile synthesis, hormone removal, blood glucose regulation, vitamin storage, etc. The stomach and the pancreas are part of the digestive system and are not involved in blood homeostasis.

887. B is correct. There are 3 unique structures that pertain to the fetal cardiovascular system:

The **ductus venosus** is designed to bypass the developing liver by routing blood around the organ but not through it.

The **foramen ovale** is an opening in the interatrial wall that allows right atrial blood to bypass the developing lungs and enter directly into the left atrium. The foramen closes at birth to yield a fossa ovale.

The **ductus arteriosus** is another lung bypass that allows blood to leave the pulmonary artery (which leads to the lungs) to enter directly into the aorta. It too seals at birth.

There is no such thing as ductus ovale.

888. B is correct. A muscle filament is divided by Z-lines into **sarcomeres**, which are functional muscle cell units. Sarcomeres have alternating light and dark bands, which make skeletal muscle look striated. The **sarcolemma** is the cell membrane found around the sarcomere. The **sarcoplasmic reticulum** is the muscle cell version of the endoplasmic reticulum, which stores calcium and synthesizes protein. Sarcoidosis is a rare disease seen in African Americans.

LECTURE 9

900

Answers & Explanations
Questions 889–1001

889. D	927. C	965. D
890. B	928. B	966. D
891. C	929. B	967. D
892. B	930. B	968. D
893. B	931. C	969. A
894. B	932. D	970. B
895. C	933. C	971. D
896. D	934. B	972. C
897. C	935. A	973. B
898. B	936. A	974. D
899. B	937. B	975. A
900. B	938. C	976. A
901. A	939. B	977. C
902. D	940. B	978. B
903. B	941. C	979. C
904. B	942. A	980. A
905. B	943. D	981. D
906. B	944. B	982. A
907. B	945. B	983. B
908. C	946. B	984. D
909. B	947. D	985. C
910. B	948. B	986. B
911. D	949. A	987. C
912. C	950. B	988. C
913. C	951. C	989. C
914. B	952. C	990. C
915. D	953. D	991. D
916. B	954. C	992. B
917. B	955. B	993. C
918. C	956. B	994. C
919. B	957. C	995. B
920. B	958. B	996. A
921. B	959. C	997. B
922. A	960. B	998. A
923. A	961. C	999. B
924. C	962. C	1000. D
925. C	963. B	1001. C
926. B	964. C	

889. D is correct. The **Hardy-Weinberg equilibrium** states that, under certain conditions, after one generation of random mating, the *genotype* frequencies will become fixed at a particular equilibrium value. MCAT writers will certainly ask about the list of assumptions that apply to the Hardy-Weinberg equilibrium. **They include:**

1. an infinitely large population
2. a population that mates randomly
3. a population free from mutation
4. a population free from migration
5. a population free from natural selection

890. B is correct. As per the passage, the occurrence of random mating can be checked by comparing the expected genotypic frequencies to obtained genotypic frequencies in a given population. If the data does not correlate, it can be assumed that random mating is not occurring. Any mating cross (i.e., WW × WW or Ww × Ww) can be used to assess random mating. Why? In a given population, a change in gene frequency of WW directly implies a change in gene frequency of Ww or ww as well.

891. C is correct. You don't need to understand the proof to answer this question. There are 2 equations that apply to the Hardy-Weinberg equilibrium: **p2 + 2pq + q2 = 1** and **p + q = 1.** Because p + q =1, q =1 − p. Answer choice A can be eliminated because it is found in the proof, which contradicts the parameters of the question stem.

892. B is correct. In humans, random mating would most likely occur for a trait like blood type. Individuals do not consciously select a mate according to their blood type. But for other traits, such as intelligence, physical appearance, or personality, this is the case. For these traits the population is not randomly mating.

893. B is correct. The Hardy-Weinberg equilibrium equation: $p2 + 2pq + q2 = 1$, with p^2 representing the homozygous dominant genotype, 2pq representing the heterozygous genotype, and q^2 representing homozygous recessive genotype.

894. B is correct. As per the passage, the Hardy-Weinberg equilibrium estimates *genotypic frequencies* in a population, during an absence of any factors that alter the allele frequency. The **genotype** is the genetic makeup of an individual in the form of DNA. It codes for the phenotype of that individual. The **phenotype** is the specific manifestation of a trait (i.e., hair color) as physical appearance. Phenotype is determined by the genotype.

895. C is correct. According to the question stem, a *hemizygous condition* is having only one gene instead of two: a haploid type state. Males (XY) are hemizygous because they only have one X or one Y chromosome. Females (XX) are not hemizygous because they have two X chromosomes. Answer choice B can be eliminated because females do not have a Y chromosome. Both males and females carry two copies of chromosomes 1-22.

896. D is correct. As per the passage, the WZz sex-determination system is found in birds, with females having 3 *different kinds* of chromosomes (i.e., WXz or WzX) and males having 2 of the same kind of chromosomes (i.e., ZZ, WW, zz). Answer choice A represents a male bird. Answer choices B and C can be eliminated because they do not have 3 *different kinds* of chromosomes.

897. C is correct. As per the passage, species of reptiles (i.e., alligators) have their sex determined by the temperature at which their eggs are incubated. Snails undergo a sex change with maturity. Insects rely on the WZz system, while bees sex-differentiate via a haploid-diploid system.

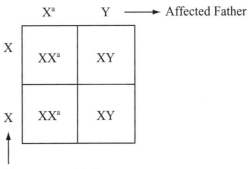

898. B is correct. In the passage, the reader is told that in the haploid-diploid system, daughters share 75% of their genes with their mother, which is not the case in the XY system. Thus, answer choice C can be eliminated. In the mammalian XY system, daughters share 50% of their genes with each parent.

899. B is correct. In pedigree 1, roman numeral II represents the second generation. In the second generation, female 2 is represented by a clear circle, which implies that she is NOT color blind: red/green colorblindness is an X-linked recessive disease, thus answer choice C can be eliminated.

To confirm the genotype of female 2, construct a Punnett square for the parents. According to the results, all female offspring are carriers of the red/green colorblindness gene. The correct answer choice is B.

900. B is correct. According to pedigree 1, an X-linked recessive disease can skip generations (look at generation II), while being transmitted through phenotypically normal heterozygous carrier females (female carriers have an X^AX^a genotype, while normal females are X^AX^A). Homozygous recessive females [X^aX^a] or hemizygous males [X^aY] are the only ones affected by an X-linked recessive disease.

The pedigree further demonstrates that three males are affected to one female. Hence, the incidence of an X-linked disease is much higher in males, who only have one X-chromosome.

MCAT Rules for an X- linked Recessive Inheritance:

1. X- linked recessive diseases are more common in males.

2. The disease can skip generations while being transmitted through heterozygous carrier females.

3. If a mother is a heterozygous carrier, her children have a 50% chance of inheriting the disease.

4. Affected males transmit the gene to all their daughters, who become carriers.

5. There is no father-to-son transmission.

6. Males that carry the mutant gene have the disease.

901. **A is correct.** In pedigree 1, first cousins make up the couple in the third generation. They are first cousins because their mothers are siblings.

Passage 903 (Questions 902-908)

902. **D is correct.** The question is asking to select an enzyme produced by the pancreas. Pancreatic juice contains two secretory products: digestive enzymes and bicarbonate. **Lipase** is a pancreatic product that digests fats. **Bile** is synthesized by the liver to emulsify fats. **Pepsin** is produced by the stomach to initiate the digestion of protein. **Aldosterone** is a steroid hormone produced by the adrenal cortex, which causes the reuptake of sodium and water by kidneys.

903. **B is correct.** There are 2 ways to answer this question: knowing that the **ileum** is the most distal and the longest part of the small intestine that leads into the **colon**, otherwise known as the **large intestine**. The second way to answer the question is per the information in the passage, which informs that the meconium ileus causes a plug at the junction between the ileum and the cecum. The cecum is the proximal portion of the colon. The kidneys are not part of the digestive tract. Both the stomach and the small intestine are situated before the plug and their functions should not be altered by the meconium ileus.

904. **B is correct.** Heterozygotes in some autosomal recessive diseases may have a slight increase in their biological fitness when compared to normal homozygotes. This is called the **heterozygote advantage**. The best-known example of the heterozygote advantage is

the sickle-cell disease, in which a heterozygous person's red blood cells are relatively immune to the malarial parasite because they are abnormally shaped and difficult to penetrate. **Penetrance** is the likelihood that a genetic condition will appear phenotypically when a given genotype known to produce the phenotype is present. For example, if every person with a gene for a dominant disorder has the mutant phenotype, then the gene is said to have 100% penetrance.

905. **B is correct.** According to the passage, cystic fibrosis is an autosomal recessive disease. The only way for two parents to have a child with cystic fibrosis is if both parents are heterozygous carriers of the recessive gene. No other possibilities exist because persons who are fully affected with disease are infertile.

MCAT Rules for Autosomal Recessive Inheritance:

1. 2 heterozygous parents (who are disease-free) can have a child with the disease.

2. Every time 2 heterozygous parents mate there is:

    a. a 1/4 risk of having a homozygous normal child.

    b. a 1/4 risk of having a homozygous affected child.

    c. a 1/2 risk of having a heterozygous child, who is disease-free but a carrier.

3. 1/2 of all children appear phenotypically normal (unaffected).

906. **B is correct.** To answer this question, consider only the phenotypically normal children, which make up 75% of all children born to parents who are carriers for cystic fibrosis. (Drawing a Punnett square may help.) There are 3 phenotypically normal genotypes: 1 homozygous dominant and 2 heterozygous carriers. Two of the three possible genotypes are heterozygotes, so the probability of a heterozygote is 2/3 or 67%.

One of three possible genotypes is homozygous normal, so the probability of a homozygous normal child is 1/3 or 33% of all phenotypically normal children.

907. **B is correct.** As per the passage, the lungs are one of the major organs affected by cystic fibrosis (CF). Answer choice B, conduction bronchioles, is the only one that belongs to the respiratory system. The other possibility is the pancreas, which is also damaged in persons with CF. However, none of the answer choices apply to the pancreas.

908. **C is correct.** As per the passage, the CFTR gene mutation causes the cell to misprocess the CFTR glycoprotein following protein synthesis. Based on this information it is safe to assume that the CFTR gene is able to replicate and transcribe RNA. The RNA is then translated into a protein by the rough endoplasmic reticulum. At this point, however, the CFTR glycoprotein fails to mature because of a problem with the post-trans-

lational modification, which normally occurs in the Golgi apparatus.

Independent Questions (Questions 909-918)

909. B is correct. Hemoglobin is an oxygen transporting molecule that is almost identical in every individual, as a result, it is not used to classify blood types. However, **ABO** and **Rh factor** are used to classify blood types in humans. ABO blood groups are inherited from both parents and are controlled by a single gene with three alleles: A, B, and i. A allele gives type A blood, B gives type B blood, and i gives type O blood.

The second characteristic of blood is the **Rhesus factor (Rh factor)**. A person either has it or not, which is indicated as (+) or (–) sign. The most common blood type is O+.

910. B is correct. Genetic drift is simply a change in the frequency of an allele in a population over time. The drift may be toward higher or lower values. Drifting alleles can disappear all together from the gene pool. When the number of individuals who carry an allele drifts to zero, so that no individuals are left to reproduce it, it disappears forever. Similarly, if all but one allele for a given gene disappears, the proportion of individuals who carry it will always be 100 percent, unless a **spontaneous mutation** or some other event reintroduces a new allele into the gene pool. When only 1 allele is present in a population, genetic drift cannot alter the allele frequency because it has no place to drift to.

The **Hardy-Weinberg equilibrium** is a mathematical relationship that *opposes* the introduction of new alleles into a population. It is used to calculate genotype frequencies in an ideal population that is 1) without mutation, 2) without migration, 3) without genetic drift, etc.

911. D is correct. There are 4 different nucleotides that make up all genetic material and are divided into **purines** and **pyrimidines** on the basis of their nitrogen rings. Purines have two-member nitrogen base rings, while pyrimidines carry one-member rings.

Mnemonic:

Purines: "**P**ure **A**s **G**old"

Adenine and **G**uanine are found in both DNA and RNA.

Pyrimidines:

Uracil is found only in RNA. **Thymine** is found only in DNA. **C**ytosine is found in both DNA and RNA.

912. C is correct. According to the family karyotype, all diseased individuals have an A/B genotype. The only affected person with a different genotype, A/A, is individual II-5. It is therefore safe to assume that a crossover event had to occur in individual II-5.

913. C is correct. DNA must be replicated before cell division can occur. Replication is carried out by DNA polymerases that both copy and proofread DNA for damage and/or errors that may be present. If and when DNA damage is discovered, the cell will immediately activate its **tumor suppressor genes** that halt the cell cycle in an attempt to repair the genetic lesion. If the genetic lesion is too extensive, an intracellular auto-death pathway, known as **apoptosis**, will be activated and cell self-digestion would follow. The attempt to carry out apoptosis may fail, perhaps because of a preexisting defect in the repair mechanism, which would increase the possibility for a malignancy to develop.

914. B is correct. The **gram stain** is used to distinguish between gram-positive and gram-negative bacteria, which have distinct and consistent differences in their **cell walls**. Gram-positive cells have thick cell walls and appear blue in color following a gram stain. Gram-negative cells are more virulent, have thinner cells walls, and appear pink following a gram stain.

915. D is correct. NAD^+/NADH (NAD^+ is the oxidized state; NADH is the reduced state) molecule has a pivotal role in metabolism because it is absolutely necessary for the breakdown of glucose. The 2 main catabolic pathways, glycolysis and the Krebs cycle, produce NADH (glycolysis produces 2 molecules of NADH per every molecule of glucose; every complete turn of the Krebs cycle produces 3 molecules of NADH), while the electron transport chain oxidizes NADH to generate ATP.

916. B is correct. A normal female has two X chromosomes. The Lyon's hypothesis introduces a concept of a **Barr body,** which states that one of two X chromosomes is randomly inactivated in every female cell. As a result, a genotypically normal female (XX) is expected to possess a single Barr body. A 47, XXX female is expected to have two Barr bodies.

917. B is correct. Sperm undergo maturation in the **epididymis**, which is analogous to the ovary and is housed in the scrotal sack. Just before an orgasmic climax, sperm are propelled from the epididymis and through the **vas deferens** (which is analogous to the fallopian tubes) while collecting fluid from the 1) prostate gland, 2) the Cowper's gland, and 3) the seminal vesicle. The fluid provided by these 3 glands mixes with sperm to create semen, which is then ejected through the urethra.

918. C is correct. A homozygous dominant population (AA) has only dominant alleles. A heterozygous population (Aa) has an equal proportion of dominant to recessive alleles. A homozygous recessive population (aa) has only recessive alleles. As per the question stem, if all recessive alleles disappear, the entire population would become homozygous dominant. The correct answer choice is C.

---

919. B is correct. As per the passage, sirtuin-activating compounds increased the life span of ethanol-producing cells. **Ethanol** (alcohol found in beer and wine) is produced under anaerobic conditions by yeast cells during the process of **fermentation**.

Yeast, mold, mildew, and mushrooms are all **fungi**. They are plantlike living things that contain no chlorophyll. Yeast is a one-celled fungi that reproduces by budding. Animal cells produce **lactic acid** during anaerobic conditions.

920. B is correct. As per the passage, sirtuins use NAD$^+$ to shut down unnecessary gene expression, which may increase the life span. So an increase in the concentration of NAD$^+$ would increase sirtuin activity and slow down the aging process. Increasing the concentration of histones would prevent excessive DNA replication, but without NAD$^+$, sirtuins would not be able to modify histones and keep DNA tightly coiled.

921. B is correct. According to the passage, cellular respiration "is the process of using *oxygen* to convert calories into energy." The **Krebs cycle** and the **electron transport chain** are mitochondrial-based processes that require oxygen (aerobic) to function. **FYI:** Oxygen is the final electron acceptor and is converted to water by the electron transport chain. **Glycolysis** is a cytoplasmic-based process that DOES NOT use oxygen (anaerobic). The correct answer choice is B.

922. A is correct. Brief Review of Biochemistry:

Glycolysis converts 1 molecule of ingested glucose into 2 molecules of **pyruvate**. Under aerobic conditions, pyruvate is converted into **acetyl CoA**, which enters the Krebs cycle. Under anaerobic conditions, pyruvate is converted into **lactic acid** (in animal cells) or **ethanol** (in bacterial cells).

As per the passage, sirtuins convert acetate into acetyl CoA, which feeds into the Krebs cycle. So cells missing sirtuins cannot live on acetate but still use the Krebs cycle as part of glucose metabolism.

Answer choice B is incorrect because when the electron transport chain is inactive, so is the Krebs cycle. Both metabolic processes are linked, with the Krebs cycle supplying reduced substrates (i.e., NADH) to the electron transport chain.

923. A is correct. As per the question stem, yeast cells are preferred for sirtuin research, which eliminates answer choices C and D. Moreover, bacterial cells are prokaryotic, lack membrane-bound organelles, and are very different from eukaryotic cells. Yeast cells are eukaryotic fungi, with membrane bound organelles, and for that reason their intracellular machinery more accurately reflects activity of eukaryotic animal cells. **FYI:** Fungi have a cell wall made of a material called **chitin**.

924. C is correct. Lysine is a basic amino acid. **High Yield MCAT amino acid facts: Glycine** is the smallest and the only achiral amino acid. It is achiral because it does not have 4 different substituents on the alpha-carbon. **Proline** is the sole *imino acid* because it has a double bond to the amino group nitrogen. Also, proline is known as a *helix breaker* because of its ability to disrupt secondary protein structures. **Cysteine** is the only amino acid that can form disulfide bonds.

---

925. C is correct. As per the passage, the *founder effect* occurs when the entire population gene pool is based on the genes of individuals that founded that population. Breeding within this small gene pool will amplify the alleles they carry; this is an example of **inbreeding**, which when practiced repeatedly reduces genetic diversity. Inbreeding occurs in animals. For example, the cheetah is a highly inbred species, probably because of a **population bottleneck** in the species' recent past.

The formal definition of a **population bottleneck** is an evolutionary event that wipes out a large percentage of a population, reducing genetic diversity by several orders of magnitude.

926. B is correct. According to the passage, **genetic drift** is a change in the gene frequency that occurs in a small group when separated from the main population. **Speciation** is an important MCAT concept. To achieve speciation, defined as the formation of two or more new species, usually requires an extensive period of geographic isolation, which allows natural selection to produce a distinctive gene pool in the new species. **Genetic disconnect** is extinction: a steady loss (known as background extinction) or abrupt, catastrophic loss (known as mass extinction) of a particular lineage. Regression is not something to be concerned about for the MCAT.

927. C is correct. According to the question stem, ethnic and religious groups are genetic isolates. As a result, answer choices A and D can be eliminated because they do not include the concept of isolation. The question is, does the *founder effect* fit into the presented scenario? According to the description of the *founder effect*, a founding member may carry a mutant allele that gets passed on to a large number of his/her descendants. Therefore, a high incidence of rare autosomal disorders in ethnic or religious groups can be explained by a combination of the *founder effect* and/or genetic isolation. **Genetic isolation** can be caused by social, religious, or geographic isolation. Some examples are the Amish, Ashkenazi Jewish groups, Mormons, and inhabitants of Iceland.

928. B is correct. The main concept of **natural selection** is that the environment determines how well a particular trait serves to improve survival and reproduction of an organism; organisms lacking a certain trait may die before reproducing. So the expectation is that an unsuccessful member of a population would leave fewer offspring, while successful members leave many offspring. As per the second paragraph in the passage, natural selection applies only to large populations.

929. B is correct. The Hardy-Weinberg equilibrium is a mathematical relationship that is used to calculate genotype frequencies based on the allele frequencies. The equilibrium only holds true in an ideal population that: 1) is excessively large, 2) has random mating (an unattractive male has the same probability of finding a wife as does an attractive male), 3) has no migration in or out of the population, 4) has no new mutations, and 5) experiences no natural selection.

The Hardy-Weinberg Law is:

$$p^2 + 2pq + q^2 = 1.00$$
$$p + q = 1.00$$

- p^2 represents the frequency of homozygous dominant genotype
- q^2 represents the frequency of homozygous recessive genotype
- $2pq$ represents the frequency of the heterozygous genotype

When allele frequencies, meaning p and q, remain constant, the population genotype frequencies remain constant, in a state of equilibrium, from one generation to the next. Even though many of the above Hardy-Weinberg assumptions do not apply in real-life situations, the equation still provides approximate estimates of gene frequencies in real populations.

930. B is correct. As per the passage, **gene flow** is the change in allele frequencies because of migration. Historical documents and archeological digs may be inaccurately interpreted, misunderstood, or nonexistent all together for a particular culture. Urine samples monitor bodily changes but do little to inform of evolutionary changes or background. The correct answer choice is B. Similar ABO blood types are found in Northern Africa, the Near East, and Southern Spain, for example. Another example is the correlation of frequency of certain ABO blood types in areas where Arab populations ruled.

931. C is correct. As per the passage, the allele frequency seen in the offspring (in this case the 37-year-old man) reflects a sampling of the alleles of the *preceding* generation (in this case the man's 47-year-old paternal uncle, his father's brother).

---

932. D is correct. The **Golgi apparatus** regulates the distributions of all newly synthesized components, including most extracellular secretion. The Golgi also carries out post-translational modifications (i.e., protein glycosylation) and can be converted into an acrosome. The **smooth ER** is involved in steroid synthesis and cell detoxification. The **lysosome** is a digestive organelle.

933. C is correct. The organelle being discussed in the question stem is the mitochondrion, which relies on a hydrogen ion gradient to generate ATP. According to the passage, a mature sperm cell body is densely packed with mitochondria. If mitochondrial rupture were to occur, hydrogen ions would be released into the cytoplasm and the sperm body pH would be the lowest.

934. B is correct. As per the passage, estrogen is synthesized from testosterone. As a result, an excess in testosterone is expected to cause an abnormal elevation of estrogen.

935. A is correct. In males, luteinizing hormone is released from the **anterior pituitary** into the blood and carried to the testes where it binds to **Leydig cells** and stimulates them to release testosterone. Testosterone is essential for the growth and division of the spermatogonial cells. **Follicle-stimulating hormone** (FSH) causes the maturation of sperm.

936. A is correct. This type of question has been asked frequently on the MCAT. Bacterial shape can significantly vary among different species and is employed in identification of certain bacterial strains. Two major shape classes are **cocci**, which are spherical, and **bacilli**, which are rod-like, though there are many variations on these themes. According to the question stem, the bacteria on hand are strepto*coccus*, which implies them to be spherical. The correct answer choice is A.

937. B is correct. As per the passage, the sperm tail is full of actin among other contractile proteins. For the purpose of achieving contraction, the highest concentration of actin would be expected in muscle tissue, where actin/myosin myofilaments shorten the sarcomeres. Most cells have a small concentration of actin as a component of the cytoskeleton, while muscle cells are practically all actin. The sperm head region is not expected to be full of actin.

Independent Questions (Questions 938-947)

938. C is correct. Generation time is the average amount of time between the appearances of 2 successive generations, for example parents and offspring. To have both great-grandparents and offspring on the same media plate requires the appearance of 4 successive generations, which requires 3 generation times to pass:

great-grandparents → grandparents → parents → offspring. 3 × 12 hours = 36 hours or 1 → days. The correct answer choice is C.

939. B is correct. All bacteria require carbon for growth and reproduction. **Autotrophs** are self-feeders who get their carbon from CO_2. Most bacteria, however, are **heterotrophs** and derive carbon from organic nutrients such as sugar. Some heterotrophic bacteria survive as parasites, growing within another living cell and using the nutrients and cell machinery of their host. Some autotrophic bacteria, such as **cyanobacteria**, use sunlight to produce sugars from CO_2. Others depend instead on energy from the breakdown of inorganic chemical compounds, such as nitrates and forms of sulfur.

940. B is correct. An **ecosystem** is a system whose members benefit from each other's participation via symbiotic relationships (positive sum relationships). It is a term that originated from biology and refers to self-sustaining systems. A **niche** is the potential array of conditions under which an organism can survive, the array of resources that it can possibly use, and the maximum potential array of interactions it can participate in with other organisms.

941. C is correct. The Linnaeus System works by placing each organism into a layered hierarchy of taxonomy groups: Kingdom, Phylum, Class, Order, Family, Genus, and Species. **Mneumonic: K**ing **P**hillip **c**ame **o**ver **f**or **g**reat **s**paghetti. Simply knowing the two-part scientific name makes it possible to determine the other six groups.

In biology, the **genus** is a grouping having one or more related or morphologically similar species. The name of an organism is composed of its genus (capitalized) and a species identifier, for example *Homo sapiens*.

942. A is correct. The **genotype** is the genetic makeup of an individual, in the form of DNA. It codes for the phenotype of that individual. The **phenotype** is the specific manifestation of a trait (i.e., hair color) as physical appearance. Phenotype is determined by the genotype.

943. D is correct. Two eukaryotic organelles, namely mitochondria and chloroplasts, are generally considered to be derived from endosymbiotic bacteria.

944. B is correct. Genetics is a union of biochemistry and molecular biology. Genetic engineering is used to modify DNA for some kind of practical end. Population genetics is aimed at understanding and explaining the effect of genes on phenotypes and the role of genes on a population. Epigenetics is the study of inherited features not strictly associated with changes in the DNA sequence.

945. B is correct. Horizontal gene transfer can occur through the following three of the most common mechanisms:

Transformation is the random uptake and insertion of novel DNA into a bacterial cell. **Transduction** occurs when a virus randomly inserts its genetic material into a cell. **Conjugation** is the transfer of genetic material between bacterial cells via a pilli bridge.

946. B is correct. Mature sperm cells develop in the testes from the diploid **spermatogonium** progenitor cell, which divides by the process of mitosis until it begins to undergo meiosis by changing into a **primary spermatocyte**, the first step in the process of sperm cell formation, or **spermatogenesis.** **The primary spermatocyte** gives rise to a **secondary spermatocyte**, which becomes a **spermatid** and later on turns into a mature sperm cell.

947. D is correct. The **founder effect** occurs when a particular allele is represented in many descendants in a population that began with only a few individuals. **Genetic drift** is simply a change in the frequency of an allele in a population over time. The drift may be toward higher or lower values. A **population bottleneck** is an evolutionary event in which a significant percentage of a population is killed or otherwise prevented from reproducing, and the population is reduced by several orders of magnitude. (A graph of this change resembles the neck of a bottle, from wide to narrow; hence the name.) **Natural selection** is an essential mechanism of evolution proposed by Charles Darwin and generally accepted as the best explanation of speciation as evidenced by the fossil record. The basic concept is that environmental conditions (or "nature") determine (or "select") how well a particular trait can serve the survival and reproduction of an organism; an organism lacking this trait might die before reproducing, or might be less fecund.

Passage 907 (Questions 948-957)

948. B is correct. According to the passage, missense, nonsense, frameshift, and some mRNA regulation mutations have all been identified in individuals with a BRCA1 problem. There are 4 mutation types tested on the MCAT:

Severity of damage: nonsense > missense > silent

A **missense mutation** is a single base pair *substitution* that causes an error in 1 codon, coding for 1 incorrect amino acid.

A **nonsense mutation** is a change in the codon sequence that causes a premature stop codon, coding for a truncated protein.

A **silent mutation** is a single base substitution that causes an error in 1 codon but still codes for the correct amino acid.

A **frameshift mutation** is a shift in the reading frame during protein synthesis, caused by an insertion or deletion of a number of nucleotides that is NOT divisible by 3: three nucleotides code for an amino acid.

949. A is correct. There are 4 different nucleotides that make up all genetic material and are divided into **purines** and **pyrimidines** on the basis of their nitrogen rings. Purines have two-member nitrogen base rings, while pyrimidines carry one-member rings.

Mnemonic:

Purines: "Pure As Gold"

Adenine and **G**uanine are found in both DNA and RNA.

Pyrimidines:

Uracil is found only in RNA; **thymine** is found only in DNA; **cytosine** is found in both DNA and RNA.

950. B is correct. According to the passage, the protein truncation test (PTT) identifies mutated RNA extracted from **lymphocytes** (immune system cells). Lymphocytes, otherwise known as white blood cells, are produced by the bone marrow to combat infectious agents and are subdivided into **T-cells** (part of cell-mediated immunity) and **B-cells** (part of the humoral immunity). **Plasma cells** are antibody-producing B-cells. **Stem cells** give rise to all blood cell types (i.e., red blood cells, platelets, white blood cells) and are also found in the bone marrow. However, they are progenitor cells, not lymphocytes.

951. C is correct. According to the question stem, reversion is a back mutation. A **point mutation**, like a base pair substitution, for example, causes an error in just 1 codon. For this reason, point mutations have the highest possibility of reversion. Mutations that add or delete nucleotides show the lowest frequency of reversion.

952. C is correct. According to the passage, protein truncation test (PTT) is used to identify mutations that result in truncation or protein shortening. This is a major limitation; cancers that fail to produce shortened peptides will not be picked up by the PTT. PTT is not time consuming because it enables a rapid analysis of large DNA fragments. However, it is a multi-step process that requires a direct sequence analysis to be performed once a truncated protein has been identified. Multi-step testing leads to errors and higher cost.

953. D is correct. Homologous chromosomes, each one obtained from each parent, carry alleles for the same genes: not identical genes, homologous genes that code for a similar product. For example, the paternal and maternal chloride channel gene would always be found on chromosome 7. By examining a karyotype, it becomes apparent that homologs often differ in size and shape.

954. C is correct. All RNA, mRNA, tRNA, and rRNA are present in the **nucleus** before being released into the cytoplasm to guide protein synthesis. However, rRNA specifically is produced in the area of the nucleus called the **nucleolus**. **This is a High Yield MCAT fact.** Ribosomes bind with rRNA before initiating protein synthesis.

Passage 908 (Questions 948-955)

955. B is correct. Protein "targeting," which guides each peptide to a specific intracellular compartment, is carried out by the **Golgi apparatus**, which is also the main cellular site for post-translational protein modification.

956. B is correct. According to the passage, fragile X syndrome is caused by the expansion of the CGG triplet repeat sequence that prevents the expression of the FMR1 gene, which leads to the absence of FMR1P protein. FMR1P is a RNA-binding protein that shuttles between the nucleus and cytoplasm. The correct answer choice is B.

In normal individuals the FMR1 gene normally has 6-50 CGG repeats. A premutation is an intermediate number of CGG repeats between 51 and 230 CGG triple repeats. Clinically normal males can carry the premutation without being mentally retarded.

957. C is correct. There are 4 different nucleotides that make up all genetic material and are divided into **purines** and **pyrimidines** on the basis of their nitrogen rings. Purines have two-member nitrogen base rings, while pyrimidines carry one-member rings. As per the passage, fragile X syndrome is caused by a large expansion of the CGG triplet repeat.

Mnemonic:

Purines: "Pure As Gold"

Adenine (A) and **G**uanine (G) are found in both DNA and RNA.

Pyrimidines:

Uracil (U) is found only in RNA. **Thymine** (T) is found only in DNA. **Cytosine** (C) is found in both DNA and RNA.

958. B is correct. Because Mark is male (males are represented by a square), the only possible answer choices are A or B. Individuals 3 and 4 are both female, represented by a circle. Individual 3 is Nancy, Mark's sister. According to the passage, fragile X is caused by a CGG triplet repeat expansion beyond 230 bases. Only individual 2 fits that description based on the cytogenetics results. Mark's brother, individual 1, is suffering from a different, non CGG triplet repeat, disease.

959. C is correct. As per the passage, silencing the FMR1 gene prevents the **translation** of new proteins. **Translation** is the conversion of RNA into protein. **Transcription** is the conversion of DNA into RNA. **Replication** is the conversion of DNA into "new" DNA.

960. B is correct. All individuals with more than 50 CGG triple repeats are expected to have "fragile sites".

According to the passage, Fragile X displays the following pattern of inheritance:

6-50 copies of CGG triple repeat is considered normal, without any associated fragile sites;

51-230 copies of CGG triple repeat is considered a premutation. These individuals are unaffected but according to the question stem display a few fragile sites;

231-4,000 copies of CGG triple repeat is considered to be a full-blown mutation, with numerous fragile sites. According to the cytogenetics diagram, three persons in Mark's family have more than 50 copies of CGG. Thus, the correct answer choice is B.

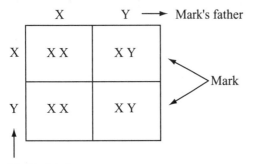

961. C is correct. According to the cytogenetics diagram, Mark's sister has 2 male siblings (each represented by a square) and 1 female sibling (represented by a circle).

962. C is correct. According to the passage, fragile X is an X-linked disorder. Because Mark is male, he had to receive the Y chromosome from his father; as a result, he did not get the disease from him. Answer choices B and D can be eliminated. Fragile X is NOT a spontaneous mutation. Rather, it is triple repeat expansion disease, making C the correct answer choice. When females with the premutation transmit the gene to their offspring, there is often an expansion of the premutation to the full mutation of 231-4,000 CGG repeats. Both male and female children are at risk for receiving the full-blown mutation.

Passage 909 (Questions 963-968)

963. B is correct. As per the passage, *B. burgdorferi* must produce and secrete a unique protein that could be detected in the blood of an infected individual by western blot, which uses an antibody to recognize the protein of interest. Antibodies are produced by **B-cells**, not T-cells, of the humoral immune system. Antibodies are obtained by immunizing animals, usually rabbits or goats, with the Lyme disease protein and collecting the antibodies (the animal produces against that protein). Also, the western blot does not detect proteins that are rapidly degraded.

964. C is correct. A population without any migration and in which the birth rate equals the death rate is considered to be stable.

965. D is correct. As per the passage, *Borrelia burgdorferi* stain a weak gram-negative color by default, as **safranin**

is the last dye used. The difference between gram-positive and gram-negative bacteria lies in the ability of the **cell wall** of the organism to retain the crystal violet dye.

During a **gram stain**, cells are heat fixed and then stained with several dyes. **Crystal violet dye** is taken up in similar amounts by all Gram positive and negative bacteria. The slides are then treated with an I_2 to fix the stain, washed briefly with 95% alcohol, and finally counterstained with a paler dye called **safranin**. Gram-positive organisms retain the initial crystal violet stain (appear blue), while gram-negative organisms are decolorized by the organic solvent and show the pink safranin counterstain.

966. D is correct. The **rough endoplasmic reticulum** is lined with ribosomes, which carry out high rate protein synthesis. As per the passage, the rate of protein synthesis is best assayed using the radioimmune precipitation (RIP) assay. The western blot analysis can detect different protein in a mixture but has several limitations, which depend on the protein half-life.

967. D is correct. Most bacteria come in one of three shapes: rod, sphere, or spiral. Rod-shaped bacteria are called **bacilli**. Spherical bacteria are called **cocci**, and spiral or corkscrew-shaped bacteria are called **spirilla**. Some bacteria come in more complex shapes. An "S" shaped hair-like form of spiral bacteria is called **spirochete**. As per the passage, Lyme disease is caused by a spirochete.

968. D is correct. As per the passage, the white-footed mouse, the natural reservoir for *Borrelia burgdorferi*, spreads Lyme disease to white-tailed deer, humans, and other warm-blooded animals via a tick vector. Based on this information, the most effective way to eradicate Lyme disease is by the administration of antibiotics to the entire population of white-footed mice. A tick is not a mammal, so answer choice C could be eliminated.

Independent Questions (Questions 969-977)

969. A is correct. Convergent evolution is an evolutionary process in which organisms not closely related independently acquire some characteristics in common. This usually reflects similar responses to similar environmental conditions. Structures that are the result of convergent evolution are called **analogous;** they should be contrasted with homologous structures, which have a common origin.

970. B is correct. The nucleus is the largest organelle in the cell. It is surrounded by a nuclear envelope, which is similar to the cell membrane that encloses the entire cell. The nuclear envelope is riddled with nuclear pores, which allow specific materials to pass in and out of the nucleus. All RNA is transcribed in the nucleus and is expelled into the cytoplasm to guide protein synthesis.

Where do nuclear proteins (DNA polymerase and histones) come from? The nucleus cannot carry out protein synthesis. Thus, protein synthesis takes place in the cytoplasm on free ribosomes or in the rough ER. Once the Golgi completes all necessary post-translational modifications, these nuclear proteins are transported from the cytoplasm into the nucleus.

971. D is correct. The body regulates the rate of cellular division via **tumor suppressor genes** that code for tumor suppressor proteins (i.e., p53, Rb protein). For example, when p53 senses DNA damage, it halts the synthesis of DNA until needed repairs are made. Each person carries 2 sets of chromosomes, on from each parent, and therefore carries 2 sets of tumor suppressor genes. Both sets of genes must be damaged for cancer to result; this concept is called the "second hit hypothesis." According to the question stem, smoking is a carcinogen. **Carcinogens** are agents that cause cancer by inducing "second hit" mutations, which deactivate tumor suppressor genes.

Smoking does not cause premature menopause or make women resistant to chemotherapy.

972. C is correct. According to the question stem, the most common cystic fibrosis mutation is an inframe (a deletion of 3 codons: 3 is divisible by 3) base deletion. The correct answer choice is C.

There are four mutation types tested on the MCAT:

Missense mutation—a single base pair substitution that results in **1 abnormal codon** and one incorrect amino acid.

Nonsense mutation—a change in a base sequence that results in a **premature stop codon**. The synthesized protein is usually truncated and nonfunctional.

Silent mutation—a single base substitution that results in a new codon that still codes for the proper amino acid, the most benign mutation.

Frameshift mutation—three codons code for an amino acid. A deletion or addition of codons by a number not divisible by 3 causes a shift in the ribosome reading frame during translation (protein synthesis). This is a severe mutation.

973. B is correct. Disease is the best example of a density-dependent factor. If a population is dense, with individuals living close together, then each individual will have a higher probability of catching the disease than if the population were less dense, with people living farther apart. In general, density-dependent factors are biological factors, such as diseases, parasites, competition, and predation.

Extreme fluctuation in temperature or drought conditions would affect a population independently of density.

974. D is correct. Spermatozoa are produced in the **seminiferous tubules** but leave the testis neither motile nor able to fertilize an egg. To acquire these abilities, spermatozoa must undergo maturation in the **epididymis**, which takes anywhere from 1 to 14 days. Mature spermatozoa leave the epididymis, are carried by a long, muscular tube, **the vas deferens**, toward the **ejaculatory duct**, and then more through the urethra.

975. A is correct. A diploid **homozygous dominant** trait has 2 identical dominant alleles at a specific locus (position) on 2 homologous chromosomes. A diploid **heterozygous** trait has 2 different alleles (1 dominant and 1 recessive) at a locus on 2 homologous chromosomes.

With simple dominance, the dominant allele is the only one expressed. A heterozygous individual is a carrier of the recessive allele but the recessive allele is not expressed at all. As a result, it is impossible to differentiate a homozygous dominant individual from a heterozygous individual without looking at the genotype. (Homozygous dominant and heterozygous individuals have identical phenotypes.)

In humans:

Dominant	Recessive
Brown eyes	Blue eyes
Tongue roll	No tongue roll
Widow's peak	No widow's peak

976. A is correct. DNA and RNA are nucleic acid polymers, made up of monomers called mononucleotide units or nucleic acids. Each nucleic acid contains a phosphate unit, a 5-sided ribose sugar unit (not a 6-sided hexose sugar unit), and a nitrogen base.

977. C is correct. As per the question stem, selective atmospheric scattering is inversely proportional to the wavelength of radiation and, therefore, decreases in the following order of magnitude: far UV light (lowest wavelength) > near UV light > violet light > blue light > green light > yellow light > orange light > red light > infrared light (highest wavelength). Accordingly, the most severely scattered radiation is that which falls in the ultraviolet, violet, and blue bands of the spectrum. The scattering effect on radiation in these three bands is roughly ten times as great as on the red rays of sunlight.

Passage 911 (Questions 978-984)

978. B is correct. A **frameshift mutation** results following an insertion or deletion of one or more nucleotides in a gene, when the number of base pairs inserted or deleted is not a multiple of 3. If the addition or deletion occurs in multiples of three, the unaffected nucleotides in the genome remain in the proper order ("frame") to be correctly translated into protein; in such cases of insertions or deletions *not* causing a frameshift, a functional protein may still be produced by the cell. Frameshift mutations are severe and cause profound changes in the synthesized protein. **FYI:** Three codons code for one amino acid.

979. **C is correct. Platelets** are colorless particles present in the blood. When bleeding occurs, platelets gather at the wound site in an attempt to prevent blood loss. The mineral calcium, vitamin K, and a protein called fibrinogen help the platelets form a clot. A platelet dysfunction manifests with easily bruised skin, nosebleeds, and extended bleeding times. Chronic infections, poor immune response, and frequent hospitalizations would be symptomatic for a **white blood cell** disorder. Fatigue, anemia, and poor tissue oxygenation is seen in people deficient in **red blood cells**.

980. **A is correct.** As per the passage, secondary complications associated with albinism include visual defects, light sensitivity, crossed eyes, etc. The eyes are part of the nervous system. The correct answer choice is A.

981. **D is correct.** Inflammatory bowel disease occurs in the distal digestive track. The small and large intestines usually fall under the "bowel" subheading. **FYI:** The large intestine is otherwise known as the colon. The colon concentrates fecal matter by reabsorbing water.

982. **A is correct.** As per the passage, Hermansky-Pudlak syndrome (HPS) is an autosomal recessive disease. For an autosomal recessive disease, two healthy parents have a 25% risk of having a child with Hermansky-Pudlak syndrome only if they are both carriers of the disease. *One parent* should be tested for the diseased gene. If the test is negative, the parents have a 0% chance of having a child with an autosomal recessive disease. Both parents must be silent carriers in order to pass an autosomal recessive disease to their child.

983. **B is correct.** As per the passage, *tyrosinase-negative oculocutaneous albinism* is caused by the inactivity of the enzyme *tyrosinase*, which prevents the cell from using amino acid tyrosine in the formation of the pigment melanin; there would be an accumulation of tyrosine in individuals with tyrosinase-negative oculocutaneous albinism, unless high levels of protein were eliminated from the diet. In *tyrosinase-positive oculocutaneous albinism*, *tyrosinase* activity is normal and would not be associated with the accumulation of amino acid tyrosine. The correct answer choice is B.

984. **D is correct.** As per the passage, an increase in the level of urinary dolichol excretion indicates pathology of the kidney, which belongs to the renal system. However, no pathology is present in a person with a normal concentration of urine dolichol.

Passage 911 (Questions 985-992)

985. **C is correct.** As per the passage, classic galactosemia is caused by enzyme defects in both galactose-1-phosphate uridyl transferase and galactokinase. By looking at diagram 1, affected patients are expected to accumulate galactose and galactose-1-phosphate in the blood. Neonates also fail to thrive, vomit, and have liver disease.

986. **B is correct.** As per the passage, blindness is caused by galacitol that is produced by the NADPH-dependent *galactose reductase*, which is found in *neural tissue* (nervous system tissue), for example the lens cells of the eye. All the other answer choices do not belong to the nervous system.

987. **C is correct.** As per the first paragraph, galactose is derived from a disaccharide milk sugar called **lactose,** which is found in dairy products such as milk, cheese, and butter: lactose is a disaccharide of a glucose and a galactose. Human diet contains mostly **sucrose**, a disaccharide of glucose and fructose. **Fructose** is five-member ring (furanose) monosaccharide.

988. **C is correct.** According to Figure 1, galactose is the reactant utilized by the *galactose reductase* to produce galacitol.

989. **C is correct.** As per the passage, galactosemia is an autosomal recessive disease (not X-linked), meaning it requires a newborn to inherit 2 recessive genes to be fully affected. A heterozygous newborn would most likely present with milder symptoms in comparison to kids who are fully homozygous recessive. There is no such thing as heterozygous recessive.

990. **C is correct. Erythrocytes**, or red blood cells, carry out the exchange of oxygen and carbon dioxide between the lungs and body tissues. As they mature in the bone marrow, erythrocytes lose their nuclei and all other organelles (i.e., mitochondria, Golgi apparatus, smooth ER, etc.). All metabolic processes to supply erythrocytes with ATP are carried out in the cytoplasm and across the cell membrane. This question has nothing to do with metabolism of galactose but rather is asking whether red blood cells have intracellular organelles.

991. **D is correct.** In the passage, it states that the presence of galactose in urine is known as *hyper-galactose-uria*. It is safe to assume that the *-uria* suffix can be used to describe anything present in the urine: *hyper-aminoacid-uria* must describe the discovery of amino acids, the building blocks for protein, in the urine.

992. **B is correct.** As per the passage, classical galactosemia is tested for by determining the amount of galactose-1-phosphate that is prevented from binding to the *galactose 1-phosphate uridyl transferase* by introducing the radioactive C^{14}-galactose-1-phosphate into the solution. Therefore, C^{14}-galactose-1-phosphate is a competitive

inhibitor for the active site used by the galactose-1-phosphate.

Independent Questions (Questions 993-1001)

993. C is correct. Carrying capacity defines the maximum density of organisms that a particular environment can sustain in perpetuity. It therefore describes the equilibrium population density as determined by the resources available in the region bounding the population in question.

994. C is correct. A **population** is a group of interbreeding individuals of the same species that is isolated from similar groups of the same species. A population lives in the same area, uses the same resources, and is exposed to the same environmental conditions. A **fundamental niche** is the potential array of conditions under which an organism can survive, resources it can possibly use, and the maximum potential of interactions it can participate in with other organisms. A **realized niche** describes the array of conditions/resources/roles within that area that individuals are *actually* observed to tolerate/use/or play.

995. B is correct. The question stem provides a clue to answer this question. A female (XX) with two X chromosomes can have one of the following genotypes for an X-linked disease: 1) homozygous unaffected, 2) heterozygous, or 3) homozygous affected. Males (XY) possess a single X chromosome and can have one of two possible genotypes: 1) unaffected or 2) affected. Remember, males are **hemizygous** with respect to X-linked genes because they have only one X chromosome.

996. A is correct. MEIOSIS I: During *prophase I*, homologous chromosomes pair up to form **synapses**, which allows **chiasmata** to develop at sites where genetic crossing over took place: this DOES NOT happen in mitosis. During *prometaphase I*, the nuclear membrane disappears and kinetochores form, one per chromosome. *Metaphase I* is marked by chromosomal alignment along the **metaphase plate**. During *anaphase I*, chromosomes separate and move to opposite poles.

At this stage, each daughter cell is haploid, with 2 identical sets of 23 chromosomes. *Telophase I* is the 4th and final phase of meiosis 1, during which the nuclear envelope reforms.

MEIOSIS II is very similar to **mitosis**. However, there is no interphase "S" phase between meiosis I and II. Meiosis II separates the 2 identical chromatids, producing two daughter cells each with 1 set of 23 chromosomes, with each chromosome having only 1 chromatid.

997. B is correct. Analogous structures are NOT evolutionarily related, such as the legs of vertebrates and the legs of insects. **Homologous structures** share some aspect of evolutionary ancestry, meaning that the structures evolved from some structure in a common ancestor; for example the wings of bats and the arms of humans are homologous.

998. A is correct. Metabolism is a set of enzyme-catalyzed reactions that convert foods into either ATP or other useful products. A **catabolic pathway** produces energy by breaking down large compounds (i.e., glucose) into waste products. An **anabolic pathway** or synthetic pathway (i.e., protein synthesis) builds large compounds by consuming the body's energy stores.

999. B is correct. A person with **type-A blood** (I^AI^A, I^AI^o) has red blood cells with type-A surface antigens and antibodies directed against type-B antigens. A person with **type-B blood** (I^BI^B, I^BI^o) has red blood cells with type-B surface antigens and antibodies directed against type-A antigens. **Type-O blood** (I^oI^o) has NO surface antigens and serves as a **universal donor**. **Type-AB** (I^AI^B) people have both A and B surface antigens on their red blood cells, make NO antibodies, and are known as universal recipients.

1000. D is correct. The lungs are part of the respiratory system, which is derived from the embryonic mesoderm. The pancreas is an accessory organ of the digestive tract, which secretes enzymes into the small intestine. The pancreas and the other 2 accessory organs of the digestive tract, the liver and the gall bladder, are derived from the embryonic endoderm.

1001. C is correct. A **population bottleneck** is an evolutionary event in which a significant percentage of a population is killed or otherwise prevented from reproducing, and the population is reduced by several orders of magnitude. (A graph of this change resembles the neck of a bottle, from wide to narrow; hence the name.) When a population rebounds from a bottleneck, it usually remains homozygous at most gene loci. A classic MCAT example for a population bottleneck is the current **cheetah population**, which seems to have passed through a period of small population size with its accompanying genetic drift. According to research, these animals remain homozygous at all 52 loci. The lack of genetic variability is so profound that cheetahs can accept skin grafts from each other just as identical twins can. Whether a population with such little genetic diversity can continue to adapt to a changing environment remains to be seen.

Phenotypic plasticity describes the degree to which an organism's phenotype is determined by its genotype. A high level of plasticity means that environmental factors have a strong influence on the particular phenotype that develops.

———————————

299

About the Author

Alex Merkulov is an aspiring surgeon and third-year medical student at UMDNJ-New Jersey Medical School. He has taught for the MCAT with ExamKrackers for the past three years and sat for the actual MCAT numerous times as both a pre-med student and MCAT instructor. In what little free time that medical school affords (and when he's not writing MCAT books), he is a self-professed eBay junkie and runs his own children's toy store on-line.